Library of
Davidson College

On the Nature of Music

Composed in Century Expanded typeface by Ms. Prints Type and Design of Oneonta, New York, and in Helios typeface by The Village Printer of Laurens and Barton-Butler Graphics of Cooperstown, New York. Layout by John Davey/Stonewood Graphics of Delhi, New York, and Hewitt Pantaleoni, Joanne S. Shultis, Jean Manley and Su Hartley of Oneonta, New York. Printed and bound by Hamilton Printing Company of Rensselaer, New York. Jacket design by Timothy G. Pantaleoni. Illustrations by Hewitt Pantaleoni except where otherwise credited.

To Patricia
my dear wife and best friend

On the Nature of Music

by
Hewitt Pantaleoni

Welkin Books

Hewitt Pantaleoni, Publisher
Oneonta, New York

COPYRIGHTS

Copyright ©1985 by Hewitt Pantaleoni

All rights reserved. No part of this book may be reproduced by any means without written permission from the publisher, except for the inclusion of brief passages in articles and reviews that refer to both author and publisher.

Library of Congress Catalog Card Number 85-50599
ISBN 0-9614873-0-5

Published by:  Welkin Books
28 Watkins Avenue
Oneonta, N.Y. 13820, U. S. A.

Copyright Acknowledgements: Text

Permissions for the use of copyrighted material appearing in the main text of this book are listed below by the page on which the material appears. Sources referred to in parentheses are given in full in the Bibliography/Discography. An extended effort has been made to identify all protected material and obtain the right to use it. Any omissions are unintentional and will be corrected in future editions if brought to my attention.

2	"those things most basic..." (Nettl 1983) quoted with permission of the publisher, the University of Illinois Press; copyright © 1983 by the Board of Trustees of the University of Illinois.
6n	"the inexpensive opportunity..." (Engel 1968) quoted with permission of the publisher, Macmillan and The Free Press; copyright © 1968, Crowell Collier and Macmillan, Inc.
10	"Let us give..." (Partch 1974) quoted with permission of the publisher, Da Capo Press, Inc.; copyright © 1949, 1974 by Harry Partch.
10	"[Musical] investigators..." (Partch 1974) quoted with permission of the publisher, Da Capo Press, Inc.; copyright © 1949, 1974 by Harry Partch.
19	"a point-mass..." (Read 1976) quoted with permission of the author.
26	"Recently an expert..." (Bergeijk, Pierce, and David 1960) quoted with permission of the publisher, Doubleday and Company, Inc.; copyright © 1960 by Educational Services Incorporated.
27	"The main function..." (Roederer 1974) quoted with permission of the author and the Music Educators National Conference; copyright © 1974 by Music Educators National Conference.
31	"A chain..." (Watzlawick, Beavin, and Jackson 1967) quoted with permission of the publisher, W. W. Norton & Company, Inc.; copyright © 1967 by W. W. Norton & Company, Inc.
33	"Sensory..." (Watzlawick, Beavin, and Jackson 1967) quoted with permission of the publisher, W. W. Norton & Company, Inc.; copyright © 1967 by W. W. Norton & Company, Inc.
34	"The alternation..." (Roederer 1974) quoted with permission of the author and the Music Educators National Conference; copyright © 1974 by Music Educators National Conference.

COPYRIGHTS

34	"that willing suspension..." (Coleridge 1965) quoted with permission of the publisher, Oxford University Press.
34	"the pleasures..." (Bronson 1969) quoted with permission of the publisher, University of California Press; copyright © 1969 by The Regents of the University of California.
37	"Yesterday..." (John Lomax 1947) quoted with permission of the holder of the copyright, Alan Lomax; copyright © 1947 by The Macmillan Company.
37	"Since..." (Willis James 1955) quoted with permission of the publisher, Atlanta University; copyright © 1955 by Atlanta University.
38	"calls and cries..." (Courlander 1963) quoted with permission of the publisher, Columbia University Press; copyright © 1963 by Columbia University Press.
39	"I cannot give you..." (Epstein 1963) quoted with permission of the publisher, The Music Library Association; copyright © 1963 by The Music Library Association.
39	"have a peculiar..." (Leigh 1921) quoted with permission of the holder of copyright, Ernest Benn Ltd.; no copyright indicated.
40	"each sound..." (Strunk 1965) quoted with permission of the publisher, W. W. Norton & Company, Inc.; copyright © 1965 by W. W. Norton & Company, Inc.
52	"a completely free..." (Courlander 1963) quoted with permission of the publisher, Columbia University Press; copyright © 1963 by Columbia University Press.
60	"That's a holler..." (Folkways FA 2941) quoted with permission of the publisher, Folkways Records and Service Corporation; copyright © 1953 by Folkways Records and Service Corporation.
60n	"Well, I practiced..." (Folkways FH 5458) quoted with permission of the publisher, Folkways Records and Service Corporation; copyright © 1965 by Folkways Records and Service Corporation.
60f	"Yes, I ain'..." (Folkways FA 2941) quoted with permission of the publisher, Folkways Records and Service Corporation; copyright © 1953 by Folkways Records and Service Corporation.
66n	"both Jewish..." (Mc Kinnon 1979-1980) quoted with permission of the publisher, The Royal Musical Association; copyright © 1980 by The Royal Musical Association.
70n	"It would not be..." (Treitler 1982) quoted with permission of the publisher, The American Musicological Society, Inc.; copyright © 1982 by the American Musicological Society, Inc.
72	"little or no..." (Werner 1959) quoted with permission of the publisher, Columbia University Press; no copyright indicated.
81n	"in Charlemagne's time..." (Sachs 1960) quoted with permission of the publisher, The American Musicological Society, Inc.; copyright © 1960 by The American Musicological Society, Inc.
94	"often seem..." (Raynor 1972) quoted with permission of the publisher, Schocken Books, Inc.; copyright © 1972 by Henry Raynor.
119	"When I can read..." (Cohen 1963) derived from the sound track of the film *The High Lonesome Sound* with permission of the film's producer, John Cohen.
123n	"In our church tradition..." (Ritchie 1981) quoted from a personal letter with permission of the author, Jean Ritchie.
126	"in the bosom..." (Bronson 1969) quoted with permission of the publisher, University of California Press; copyright © 1969 by The Regents of the University of California.
128n	"the glory..." (Barrand 1983) quoted with permission of the author.
130f	"Dark/Was the..." (Folkways FA 2656) derived from the recording with permission of the publisher, Folkways Records and Service Corporation; copyright © 1956 by Folkways Records and Service Corporation.
136	"I heard..." (Folkways FA 2952) derived from the recording with permission of the publisher, Folkways Records and Service Corporation; copyright © 1952 by Folkways Records and Service Corporation.
137	"congregations..." (Bailey 1978) quoted with permission of the publisher, Black Perspectives in Music; copyright © 1978 by the Foundation for Research in the Afro-American Creative Arts, Inc.
137	"usually reserved..." (Bailey 1978) quoted with permission of the publisher, Black Perspectives in Music; copyright © 1978 by the Foundation for Research in the Afro-American Creative Arts, Inc.
138n	"It was no uncommon..." (Patrick 1949) quoted with permission of the publisher, Oxford University Press; copyright © 1949 by Oxford University Press.
141	"rings..." (Katzarova-Koukoudova 1954) quoted with permission of the publisher, Macmillan Accounts & Administration, Ltd.; copyright © 1954 by St. Martin's Press, Inc.
142	"marriage celebrations..." (Kremenliev 1952) quoted with permission of the publisher, University of California Press; copyright © 1952 by The Regents of the University of California.

COPYRIGHTS

142 "Farewell, family..." (Kremenliev 1957) quoted with permission of the publisher, the American Folklore Society; copyright © 1957 by the American Folklore Society.

146n "carries the values..." (Raim 1975) quoted with permission of the publisher, Sing Out! Magazine; copyright © 1957 by Sing Out! Magazine.

147 "lingual articulation..." (Baines 1960) quoted with permission of the Pitt Rivers Museum and Department of Ethnology and Prehistory, University of Oxford; copyright © 1960 by the Pitt Rivers Museum.

154 "the chief purpose..." (Kremenliev 1957) quoted with permission of the publisher, the American Folklore Society; copyright © 1957 by the American Folklore Society.

158 "Amateur folklore..." (Katzarova-Koukoudova 1954) quoted with permission of the publisher, Macmillan Accounts & Administration, Ltd.; copyright © 1954 by St. Martin's Press, Inc.

159 "seek out..." (Katzarova-Koukoudova 1954) quoted with permission of the publisher, Macmillan Accounts & Administration, Ltd.; copyright © 1954 by St. Martin's Press.

162 "Such arrangements..." (Markoff 1976) quoted with permission of the author.

162 "To the large..." (Gronow 1975) quoted with permission of the editor of *Ethnomusicology*; copyright © 1975 by The Society for Ethnomusicology, Inc.

178 "some eighty..." (Temko 1955) quoted with permission of the author; copyright © 1952, 1955 by Allan Temko.

178 "thousands of serfs..." (Temko 1955) quoted with permission of the author; copyright © 1952, 1955 by Allan Temko.

178 "One night..." (Temko 1955) quoted with permission of the author; copyright © 1952, 1955 by Allan Temko.

180 "Singulis canonicis..." (Hanschin 1932) quoted with permission of Dr. Häusler, General Secretary of the International Musicological Society; copyright © 1932 by the International Musicological Society.

185f "To the Easter victim..." based in part on (Ruhland 1968) with permission of Dr. Konrad Ruhland.

190 "Our manner..." (Ruhland 1968) quoted with permission of Dr. Konrad Ruhland; no copyright indicated.

194 "Let me speake..." (Davey 1921) quoted with permission of G. Schirmer, Inc., U. S. Agent for holder of copyright; copyright © 1921 by J. Curwen & Sons.

195 "Si begunde..." (Hickmann 1936) quoted with permission of the publisher, Bärenreiter-Verlag; copyright © 1936 by Bärenreiter-Verlag.

198 "Like thunder..." (Sumner 1962) quoted with permission of the publisher, Macdonald Futura; copyright © 1952 by Macdonald and Company.

199 "two very large..." (Sumner 1962) quoted with permission of the publisher, Macdonald Futura; copyright © 1952 by Macdonald and Company.

200 "the congregation..." (Bittermann 1929) quoted with permission of the publisher, The Medieval Academy of America; copyright © 1929 by The Medieval Academy of America.

200f "composed..." (Salmen 1957) quoted in translation with permission of the publisher, the Société Belge de Musicologie; copyright © 1957 by the Société Belge de Musicologie.

209 "I was told..." (Arbatsky 1953) quoted with permission of the publisher, The Newberry Library, Chicago; copyright © 1953 by The Newberry Library.

209f "a sense..." (M. Hood 1971) quoted with permission of the publisher, McGraw-Hill Book Company; copyright © 1971 by McGraw-Hill, Inc.

211f "The experience..." (Langer 1953) quoted with permission of the publisher, Charles Scribner's Sons; copyright © 1953 by Charles Scribner's Sons.

213 "What I want..." (Watanabe 1972) quoted with permission of Springer-Verlag New York, Inc.; copyright © 1972 by Springer-Verlag, Berlin-Heidelberg.

215n "between 15 and 20 msec..." (Hirsh 1959) quoted with permission of the author and the American Institute of Physics; copyright © 1959 by the Acoustical Society of America.

234 "We have..." (Thalbitzer 1921) quoted with permission of the publisher, I Kommissionen for Videnskabelige Undersøgelser i Grønland (The Commission for Scientific Research in Greenland), Copenhagen; copyright © 1921 by The Commission for Scientific Research in Greenland.

237n "Indigenous scholars..." (McAllester 1975) quoted with permission of the author.

238 "I come..." (Southall 1975) quoted with permission of the author; copyright © 1975 by the African Studies Association.

239 "Their temporal..." (Pilbeam 1972) quoted with permission of the publisher, Macmillan Publishing Company, Inc.; copyright © 1972 by David R. Pilbeam.

241 "One hears..." (Johanson and Edey 1981) quoted with permission of the publisher, Simon and Schuster; copyright © 1981 by Donald C. Johanson and Maitland A. Edey.

COPYRIGHTS

243   "If The Indians' Book..." (Curtis 1923) quoted with permission of Barbara B. Wedell; copyright © 1923 by Harper and Brothers.

246   "To the unsentimental..." (New York Times 1980) quoted with permission of the publisher, The New York Times Company; copyright © 1980 by The New York Times Company.

250   "land of sweeping..." (Brandon 1961) quoted with permission of the publisher, American Heritage Publishing Company, from *The American Heritage Book of Indians*; copyright © 1961 by American Heritage Publishing Company, Inc.

251   "elite soldier..." (Brandon 1961) quoted with permission of the publisher, American Heritage Publishing Company, from *The American Heritage Book of Indians*; copyright © 1961 by American Heritage Publishing Company, Inc.

251   "riding up..." (Fire/Lame Deer and Erdoes 1972) quoted with permission of the publisher, Simon & Schuster, a Division of Gulf & Western Corporation; copyright © 1972 by John Fire/Lame Deer and Richard Erdoes.

252   "If we offer..." (Fire/Lame Deer and Erdoes 1972) quoted with permission of the publisher, Simon & Schuster, a Division of Gulf & Western Corporation; copyright © 1972 by John Fire/Lame Deer and Richard Erdoes.

261   "are still known..." (Merriam 1967) quoted with permission of the holder of copyright, the Wenner-Gren Foundation for Anthropological Research, New York; copyright © 1967 by Wenner-Gren Foundation for Anthropological Research, Inc.

264   "that coincidence..." (Merriam 1967) quoted with permission of the holder of copyright, the Wenner-Gren Foundation for Anthropological Research, New York; copyright © 1967 by Wenner-Gren Foundation for Anthropological Research, Inc.

264f   "does not require..." (Densmore 1920) quoted with permission of the publisher, the Archaeological Institute of America; no copyright indicated.

269   "who rowed women..." (Nayo 1964) quoted with permission of the author.

270   "Other headmen..." (Ladzekpo 1971) quoted with permission of the publisher, the African Music Society (South Africa); "all rights reserved."

278   "deliberate opposition..." (Jones 1934) quoted with permission of the publisher, Witwatersrand University Press; copyright © 1934 by Witwatersrand University Press.

291   "the endeavor..." (Symonds 1911) quoted with permission of Encyclopaedia Britannica (Chicago); copyright © in the United States 1911 by The Encylopaedia Britannica Company.

291   "made young men..." (Symonds 1911) quoted with permission of Encyclopaedia Britannica (Chicago); copyright © in the United States 1911 by The Encyclopaedia Britannica Company.

295   "Respected Sir..." (D'Accone 1961) quoted with permission of the publisher, the American Musicological Society, Inc.; copyright © 1961 by the American Musicological Society.

314   "that the music..." (Palisca 1963) quoted with permission of The Musical Quarterly; copyright © 1963 by G. Schirmer, Inc.

332   "[G]iven that they..." (Harrison 1973) quoted with permission of the translator, Dr. Frank Ll. Harrison; copyright © 1973 by F. Ll. Harrison.

334n   "the only way,..." (Kirby 1968) quoted with permission of the publisher, Witwatersrand University Press; no copyright claimed.

335   "Most of my..." (Lester 1967) quoted with permission of the publisher, The New York Times Company; copyright © 1967 by The New York Times Company.

335   "two young men..." (Higgins 1972) quoted with permission of the publisher, The Society for Asian Music; copyright © 1972 by The Society for Asian Music, Inc.

336   "only the musician..." (Ries 1969) quoted with permission of the publisher, The Society for Asian Music; copyright © 1969 by The Society for Asian Music, Inc.

339   "twenty years..." (Higgins 1976) quoted with permission of the publisher, The Society for Asian Music; copyright © 1976 by The Society for Asian Music, Inc.

339   "In a room,..." (Menon 1957) quoted with permission of the publisher, the Institute of Traditional Cultures, Madras.

340   "The *gurukula*..." (Viswanathan 1977) quoted with permission of the publisher, The Indian Fine Arts Society, Madras.

341   "continuously..." (Johnson 1972) quoted with permission of the publisher, Oxford University Press; copyright © 1972 by Oxford University Press.

342   "Composers..." (Titon 1977) quoted with permission of the author and *Essays in Arts and Sciences*; copyright © 1977 by the University of New Haven.

342   "the number known..." (Boatwright 1960) quoted with permission of the author, Howard Boatwright; copyright © 1960 by Howard Boatwright.

COPYRIGHTS

343f "[s]ystematic training...' (Viswanathan 1977) quoted with permission of the publisher, The Society for Asian Music; copyright © 1977 by The Society for Asian Music.

349n "a popular song..." (Wade 1979) quoted with permission of the publisher, Prentice-Hall, Inc.; copyright © 1979 by Prentice-Hall, Inc.

354 "by the time..." (Wasserman 1980) quoted with permission of *American Way*, inflight magazine of American Airways; copyright © 1980 by American Airlines.

355 "My job..." (Schwartz 1979) quoted with permission of the publisher, The New York Times Company; copyright © 1979 by The New York Times Company.

357 "An object..." (Meyer 1956) quoted with permission of the publisher, The University of Chicago Press; copyright © 1956 by The University of Chicago.

358 "when an organism..." (Meyer 1956) quoted with permission of the publisher, The University of Chicago Press; copyright © 1956 by The University of Chicago.

359 "we cannot say..." (Blacking 1973) quoted with permission of the publisher, the University of Washington Press; copyright © 1973 by the University of Washington Press.

365 "By the desire..." (Winslow 1972) quoted with permission of the locator of this source, David J. Winslow; his version used.

366 "Dec. 31,..." (Buechner 1964) quoted with permission of the publisher of this version of the source, Folkways Records and Service Corporation; copyright © 1964 by Folkways Records and Service Corporation.

366f "Jan. 21,..." (Buechner 1964) quoted with permission of the publisher of this version of the source, Folkways Records and Service Corporation; copyright © 1964 by Folkways Records and Service Corporation.

373 "we are not sent..." (Schafer 1963) quoted with permission of the publisher of this version of the source, Duke University Press; copyright © 1963 by Duke University Press.

373f "Every natural man..." (Schafer 1963) quoted with permission of the publisher of this version of the source, Duke University Press; copyright © 1963 by Duke University Press.

374 "reason..." (Schafer 1963) quoted with permission of the publisher of this version of the source, Duke University Press; copyright © 1963 by Duke University Press.

374n "Away from whites..." (Maultsby 1979) quoted with permission of the author; copyright © 1979 by Portia K. Maultsby.

384n "Here the world..." (Downey 1969) quoted with permission of the author; copyright © 1968 by James C. Downey.

399n "Twenty years..." (Kupferberg 1978) quoted with permission of the publisher, Parade Publications, Inc.; copyright © 1978 by Parade Publications, Inc.

399n "can be distinguished.../ a society where..." (Johnson 1972) quoted with permission of the publisher, Oxford University Press; copyright © 1972 by Oxford University Press.

402 "when we move..." (Hutchinson 1976) quoted with permission of European American Music Distributors Corporation, sole U.S. agents for B. Schott's Soehne; copyright © 1976 B. Schott's Soehne, Mainz, all rights reserved.

406 "[T]he masterpieces..." (Hart 1973) quoted with permission of the publisher, W. W. Norton and Company, Inc.; copyright © 1973 by W. W. Norton & Company, Inc.

406f "according to..." (Brustein 1977) quoted with permission of The New York Times Company; copyright © 1977 by The New York Times Company.

407n "with industry's financial..." (Howe 1974) quoted with permission of the Exxon Corporation; no copyright claimed.

Copyright Acknowledgements: Figures

Permissions for the use of copyrighted material appearing in the figures illustrating this book and in the captions to these figures are listed below by the number of the figure in which the material appears. Sources referred to in parentheses are given in full in the Bibliography/Discography. An extended effort has been made to identify all protected material and obtain the right to use it. Any omissions are unintentional and will be corrected in future editions of this work if brought to my attention.

Fig. 2	adapted from (Brödel 1946) with permission of the publisher, W. B. Saunders Company; copyright © 1946 by the W. B. Saunders Company.
Fig. 3	adapted from (Saunders 1948) with permission of the publisher, W. H. Freeman and Company Publishers; copyright © 1948 by Scientific American, Inc.
Fig. 8	drawn from the singing of Huddie Ledbetter (Folkways FA 2941) with permission of the publisher, Folkways Records and Service Corporation; copyright © 1953 by Folkways Records and Service Corporation.
Fig. 11	"la-me-nas-se-ah..." (Idelsohn 1914) quoted with permission of the publisher, Breitkopf & Härtel Musikverlag; copyright © 1914 by Breitkopf & Härtel, Leipzig.
Fig. 11	"for the director..." (Bible 1966) quoted with some alteration with permission of the publisher, Doubleday & Company, Inc.; copyright © 1966 by Doubleday & Company, Inc.
Fig. 12	drawn from the singing of Jakob Goldstein (RCA Victor LM 6057) with permission of the holder of copyright, EMI Music, Ltd.; copyright © 1957 EMI Records, Ltd.
Fig. 14	drawn from the singing of the monks of St. Beuron (Deutsche Grammophon ARC 3102) with permission of the publisher, Polydor International GMBH; copyright © 1957 Deutsche Grammophon Gesellschaft.
Fig. 15	drawn from the singing of the monks of St. Beuron (Deutsche Grammophon ARC 3102) with permission of the publisher, Polydor International GMBH; copyright © 1957 Deutsche Grammophon Gesellschaft.
Fig. 16	adapted in part from (Catholic Church 1959) wherever the heading "[LU]" appears, with permission of the publisher, Desclée Company; copyright © 1956 by Desclée & Cie.
Fig. 18	drawn from the singing of the monks of St. Peter at Solesmes-sur-Sarthe (London A 4501) with permission of Polygram Record Operations; no date of copyright indicated.
Fig. 21	"No English verse..." (Smith 1946) quoted with permission of the publisher, The Huntington Library, Art Gallery, and Botanical Gardens; copyright © 1946 by the Henry E. Huntington Library and Art Gallery.
Fig. 22	drawn from the singing of members of the Regular Baptist Church of Jeff, Kentucky (Cohen 1963) with permission of the publisher, John Cohen.
Fig. 23	drawn from the singing of Jean Ritchie (Tradition TLP 1011) with permission of The Everest Record Group, 2020 Avenue of the Stars, Concourse Level, Los Angeles, California 90067, from whom the record can be purchased directly; no copyright indicated.
Fig. 24	drawn from the singing of Mary Price (Folkways FA 2656) with permission of the publisher, Folkways Records and Service Corporation; copyright © 1956 by Folkways Records and Service Corporation.
Fig. 26	drawn from the singing of Magda Mavrokova, Magda Beluthova, Penka Chukarinova, and Vesa Zinkova as recorded in the field by Martin Koenig and Ethel Raim in 1968, with permission of Martin Koenig and Ethel Raim.
Fig. 27	player drawn from plate in (Katzarova-Kukudova and Djenev 1976) with permission of the Bulgarian Copyright Protection Agency, Jus Autor; copyright © 1958, 1976 by R. Katzarova-Kukudova and K. Djenev.
Fig. 27	views of chanter drawn from drawings in (Maheu 1976) and used with permission of the author.
Fig. 28	drawn from the singing of Vasilka Andonova and Kremena Stancheva as recorded in the field by Martin Koenig and Ethel Raim in 1968, with permission of Martin Koenig and Ethel Raim.
Fig. 29	"A tya mu se..." (Raim 1977), romanization of Cyrillic text quoted with permission of the source, Ethel Raim.

COPYRIGHTS

Fig. 29	drawn from a private recording of the singing of The Pennywhistler in 1964, based on an arrangement sung by the Bulgarian State Ensemble for Folksongs and Folk Dances, with permission of The Pennywhistlers.
Fig. 30	drawn from (Harrison 1958) with permission of the United States publisher, Dover Publications, Inc.; copyright © 1958 by Frank Ll. Harrison.
Fig. 31	reproduced from (Dittmer 1969) with permission of the Institute of Mediaeval Music, Ltd.
Fig. 33	drawn from the photograph by Inge Morath (Jacobs 1968) with permission of the publisher, American Heritage Publishing Company, Inc., and the licensor, Magnum Photos, Inc., photograph copyright © 1968 by Inge Morath.
Fig. 34	drawn from the singing of Otto Johnson and the Danish State Radio Chorus (Haydn Society HSE 9100) with permission of Ralph Colucci of Esoteric Records.
Fig. 35	drawn from the singing of the Capella Antiqua München (Telefunken-Decca SAWT 9530-B/9531-B) with permission of the publisher, TELDEC (Telefunken-Decca Schallplatten Gesellschaft); no copyright indicated.
Fig. 36	instrumental ensemble drawn from Additional Manuscript 27695, f. 13, with permission of The British Library.
Fig. 40A	drawn from photograph (Sachs 1943) with permission of the publisher, W. W. Norton & Company, Inc.; copyright © 1943 by W. W. Norton & Company, Inc.
Fig. 40B	drawn from photograph (Stapelberg 1958) with permission of the publisher, Bärenreiter-Verlag (Kassel); copyright © 1958 by Bärenreiter-Verlag.
Fig. 43	drawings adapted from (Jennings 1978) with permission of the publisher, W. H. Freeman and Company; copyright © 1978 by W. H. Freeman and Company.
Fig. 45	drawn from the sound of (Folkways FE 4445) with permission of the publisher, Folkways Records and Service Corporation; copyright © 1953 by Folkways Records and Service Corp.
Fig. 52	"deliberate opposition..." (Jones 1934) quoted with permission of the publisher, Witwatersrand University Press; copyright © 1934 by University of the Witwatersrand.
Fig. 55	drawn from the sound of (Musical Heritage MHS 617) with permission of the holder of copyright, Éditions Costallat, 60 rue de la Chaussée d'Antin 75009, Paris; no date of copyright indicated.
Fig. 56	drawn from the sound of (Westminster XWN 18809) with permission of the holder of copyright, Éditions Costallat, 60 rue de la Chaussée d'Antin 75009, Paris; no date of copyright indicated.
Fig. 60	derived from the standard notation in (Pirrotta 1968) with permission of the publisher, Cornell University Press; copyright © 1968 by Cornell University Press.
Fig. 61A	reproduced from (Groth *et al.* 1977) with permission of Dr. Groth; copyright © 1977 by W. H. Freeman and Company.
Fig. 61B	reproduced from (Julesz 1971) with permission of the holder of copyright, Bell Telephone Laboratories; copyright © 1971 by Bell Telephone Laboratories.
Fig. 66	"Where Have All the Flowers Gone?" by Pete Seeger, copyright © 1961 by Fall River Music, Inc. All rights reserved. Used by permission.
Fig. 69	drawn from the cover of (Folkways FR 8903) with permission of the publisher, Folkways Records and Service Corporation; copyright © 1964 by Folkways Records and Service Corporation.
Fig. 71	rhythms derived from (World-Pacific 1437) with permission of the holder of printed-music copyright, Har-bock Music (c/o United Artists Music Company); no date of copyright indicated.
Fig. 72	chart adapted from (Wade 1979) with permission of the publisher, Prentice-Hall, Inc., Englewood Cliffs, N.J.; copyright © by Prentice-Hall, Inc.
Fig. 78	text derived from (Atlantic 1351) with permission of The Pentecostal Temple and Church of God in Christ, Memphis, Tennessee, Bishop J. W. Patterson, pastor.

Contents

Copyright acknowledgements: text	iv
figures	ix
List of figures	xiv
Preface	xvii

Introduction

1. The making of musical traditions   3
   A plural art—The audience rules—Timbre as identity—Innovation from within—Our need for music

2. Hearing music   14
   The mechanical means—The electrical means—Imagination

Part One: Melody

3. The nature of melody   31
   Passage and predictability—Anticipation—Stability

4. The black American holler   36
   The holler as melodic passage—The Western octave series—The tune formula

5. Gregorian chant   64
   Jewish roots—The Roman Catholic tradition—Melodic modes

Part Two: Harmony

6. The nature of harmony — 99
   The harmony of partials—The harmony of articulation—The harmony of the environment—The harmony of musical notes—Patterns of harmony

7. The heterophony of lining out — 108
   A brief history—Performance styles—Modern white lining out—Modern black lining out

8. Bulgarian harmony that "rings like a bell" — 139
   The harmony of village song—The influence of the bagpipe—Medieval sound in the modern village—The new national style

9. Early Western harmony at Notre Dame — 164
   The singers—The cathedral—Organum—Discant—Discant versus organum—Instrumental harmony

Part Three: Rhythm

10. The nature of rhythm — 207
    The flow of time—Rhythm versus form—The sources of musical rhythm—Measured music and gait—Meter—Imprecision

11. Native American rhythm — 234
    Cross-cultural perception—The concept of primitive—The Dakota Sun Dance—The Salish Gift Dance

12. West African rhythm — 266
    The Anlo of Anyako—The musical club—Non-equidistant governing accents—Diverging, simultaneous rhythms—The function of layers of sound—The compatibility of Western and West African rhythms

13. The rhythm of Renaissance harmony 290
    The Renaissance—The sound of the new humanism—From solo to choral harmony—Enlarging the range of a harmony—The polyphony of Josquin des Pres—Triads and harmonic destinations—Metrical harmony and opera

Part Four: Form

14. The nature of form 319
    The cohesiveness of the parts—The extension of the whole—The strophic relationship—The serial relationship—The rondo relationship—The developmental relationship

15. Developmental form in the art music of India 332
    "High" cultures—Music as religion—The forces of change—Raga alapana—Tala

16. Emotion and form in American spiritual singing 354
    "Real feeling"—The emotional content of music—Of ecstasy and constraint—Constrained congregational song—The singing school—"Fuging" tunes—The camp-meeting chorus—The ecstatic force of call and response

Coda

17. The meaning of music 393
    Meaning—Levels of musical meaning—Music as ritual—The social meaning of music—Folk music versus popular music—The meaning of art music

Bibliography/Discography 411
Index 431

List of Figures

1. Pitch and space, 17
2. The parts of the ear, 20
3. Multiple vibrations, 22
4. *My Country 'Tis of Thee*, 42
5. *Arwhoolie*, 44
6. The Western octave series, 48
7. The piano keyboard, 50
8. *I Don' Know You*, 55f
9. The Jewish/Catholic prayer hour, 67
10. The Roman Catholic hours, 68
11. The phrasing of *Psalm 8* (Yemenite tradition), 73
12. A Yemenite tune formula, 74
13. The melodic content of vocal expression, 78
14. A Gregorian tune formula, 80
15. *Alma Redemptoris Mater*, 83f
16. A Gregorian mode, 88
17. A scale, 90
18. *Inclina Domine*, 92f
19. A note for a bass player, 103
20. Flats and sharps on the piano keyboard, 104
21. *Psalm 23*, part A, 110
    parts B and C, 115
22. *When I Can Read My Title Clear*, 120
23. *Wondrous Love*, 124f
24. *Dark Was the Night*, 132f
25. *I Heard the Voice of Jesus*, 135f

LIST OF FIGURES

26. *Ne Treperi*, 144
27. The kaba gaida, 153
28. *Vetar Vee*, 156
29. *Todoro* (Westernization of harmony), 160
30. The placement of the choir, 166
31. Soloists harmonizing, 170
32. The plan of Durham Cathedral, 172
33. The flying butresses of Notre Dame, 176
34. *Viderunt Omnes*, 182
35. *Victimae Paschali Laudes*, 189f
36. Small organs, 196
37. *The Battle Hymn of the Republic*, 216
38. *Todoro* (melodic rhythm), 221
39. Equidistant and asymmetrical meters, 225
40. Mental music, 226
41. Classic Roman poetic meter, 228
42. English poetic meter, 231
43. An age of ice, 249
44. *A Dakota Sun-Dance Song*, 255
45. *A Salish Gift-Dance Song*, 263
46. The Anlo homeland, 267
47. A governing Anlo meter, 273
48. Mapping time, 275f
49. Other rattle duets, 277
50. Anlo ensemble relationships, 279
51. Rhythms that talk, 281
52. Opposing rhythms, 282
53. The role of pitch ranges, 284f
54. Composite rhythm, 288
55. *Et Incarnatus Est*, 298f
56. *Ecce Maria*, 302f
57. Triads, 304f

58. Metrical harmony, 308f
59. A shift in poetic taste, 310f
60. Thoroughbass style, 312f
61. Natural cohesiveness, 321
62. The cohesive effect of patterns, 322f
63. The expansive effect of patterns, 324
64. The expansive effect of repetition, 325
65. Development, 328
66. Simultaneous musical forms, 330
67. A simplified map of India, 337
68. Development in rāgā ālāpana, 344f
69. The Sarasvatī vīnā, 346f
70. The buzzing bridge, 348f
71. Tāla versus rhythm, 350f
72. Rhythmic development, 352
73. A hard-shell Baptist hymn, 361
74. A "fuging" tune, 371f
75. Camp-meeting song forms, 379f
76. African call-and-response song forms, 385f
77. The center of slaving in West Africa, 387
78. Call and response as a cycling engine, 388f

Preface

This book was written for the curious nonspecialist—the reader as interested as I am in finding something out about the basic nature of that fragile yet indestructible human force we call music. To pursue this goal certain sacrifices had to be made. For example, there is no discussion of the most familiar figures of Western "art music," that elite European heritage represented by composers from Bach to Berio, performers like Caruso and Rostropovitch, conductors like Toscanini and Caldwell. Instead, I examine the foundations of their tradition —its melody, harmony, and rhythm—as they were shaped and set in place in some of our earliest music. And because most people in this world shape their own musical foundations differently than we, many chapters in this book concern traditions different from that of our Western art music. In this diversity of music an underlying unity can be seen which, I believe, would escape us in the study of just one of its traditions. Indeed, from the materials gathered here there emerge a common purpose and a common set of principles that add to our understanding and enjoyment of the particular music we know best.

This book owes its beginning eleven years ago to a jazz violinist and scat singer, my daughter Mary, who suggested I quit complaining about the lack of a non-Western music text and write one myself. But nothing can be taught in terms of itself alone, and I found it impossible to discuss the "non" of non-Western music without also discussing the "Western."

Alan F. Turner, then an editor at Harper and Rowe, lent the support of a contract and a sincere personal interest in the early stages of this broadly based project, which could never have moved forward without the unfailing help and cooperation of Norma Lamb and her staff at the Gulfport Public Library in St. Petersburg, Florida, backed by the interstate library loan system as administered by Jenny Henning at the Florida State Library in Tallahassee with the assistance of Judy J. Atwood. The staff at Milne Library, State University of New York at Oneonta, gave me the same high quality of help and cooperation in the later stages of the project, and for many small but critical attentions I am in debt to Carey S. Bliss, curator of rare books at the Huntington Library in San Marino, California; Rosemary L. Cullen, special collections librarian at Brown University, and associate specialist Elizabeth C. Coogan; Barbara McDaniel, secretary of The Southern Baptist Theological Seminary in Louisville; and Joseph C. Hickerson, head of the Archive of Folk Song in Washington.

The chapters that follow contain my personal opinions and point of view, of course, and some of my own primary research. Most of the writing relies heavily on the work of other people. Some have been credited in the text. Others I would like to thank here for tips, good conversation, or the more extended effort of reading and commenting on portions of the text. I do so with the reservation that full credit for the errors and misunderstandings I have injected into their contributions remains with me: Anthony G. Barrand of Boston University; Paul Berliner of Northwestern University; Stephen Bonta of Hamilton College, who read through the manuscript in both its early and final stages; Leo Brennan, sutler of The Company of Fifers and Drummers, Madison, Connecticut; Ann Briegleb of the Ethnomusicology Archive at U.C.L.A.; Ralf E. Carriuolo of the University of New Haven, who gave early support; my colleague Margaret E. Cawley, who read much of the manuscript; Francis Collinson of the School of Scottish Studies in Edinburgh; Stefan Eleverov of the Department of Bulgarian Literature in

Sofia University; John Eliot of the University of Maryland College Park, who read the entire manuscript in an early version; my former colleague Elinore Gilroy; Steve Gorn of New York City, who read an early version of the manuscript; the late Jon B. Higgins of Wesleyan University; Jackson Hill of Bucknell University, who read the manuscript in both its early and final stages; my former colleague Margaret Honour; Pandora Hopkins of Rutgers University; Mantle Hood of the University of Maryland Baltimore County; Cynthia Irwin-Williams of the University of Nevada, Reno; Jesse D. Jennings of the University of Utah; Thomas F. Johnston of the University of Alaska, who read an early version of my chapter on Native American song; my former colleague Savak Katrak, who read the chapter on the classic music of India; Kate Van Winkle Keller of Radnor, Pennsylvania, and the National Tune Index; Kobla Ladzekpo of the California Institute of the Arts, who read the chapter on drumming; Alan Lomax of New York City; Richard F. Maheu of Los Angeles, who read my discussion of the Bulgarian kaba gaida; Irene Markoff of York University in Toronto, who read my early Bulgarian chapter and provided text translations; Portia K. Maultsby of Indiana University; David P. McAllester of Wesleyan University, Connecticut, who read the chapter on Native American song; Terry Miller of Kent State University; my colleague William Morgan; Lawrence E. Older of Lake Hamilton, Florida, who read a now-abandoned chapter of folk fiddling; my daughters Mary and Maud Pantaleoni, who read portions of the manuscript, and my son Timothy Pantaleoni, who helped revise some of the illustrations; Robert Perrin of Brooklyn, New York, who read an early chapter on troubadour music; Jean Ritchie Pickow of Port Washington, Long Island, who read an early version of the chapter on lining out; William K. Powers of Rutgers University at New Brunswick, New Jersey; Ethel Raim of the Ethnic Folk Arts Center in New York City, who read the chapter on Bulgarian singing; my colleague Albert J. Read, who read my chapter on hearing; Willard Rhodes of Sun City, Arizona; my colleague Paul Scheele; Anne Dhu Shapiro of Harvard University; Joel and Kathy Shimberg of Mt. Vision, New York, who read an early chapter on folk fiddling; Datus C. Smith, Jr., of Princeton, New Jersey; Johanna Spector of The Jewish Theological Seminary of America in New York City; William H. Tallmadge of Berea College; Nicholas Temperley of the University of Illinois at Urbana; Jeff Todd Titon of Tufts University, who read the chapter on American spiritual singing; Gen'ichi Tsuge of the Kutinachi College of Music in Japan; Richard Wallis, formerly of the State University of New York at Binghamton; John M. Ward of Harvard University; Don Yoder of the University of Pennsylvania; and Charles D. Zimmer of the University of Maryland College Park, who read an early version of the manuscript.

To my friend and editor, Evelyn Duncan of Oneonta, New York, I owe a special debt for guiding my text through what she has cheerfully told me is sometimes called "the swamp of the English language." Her professed ignorance of musical matters was particularly helpful to me in my efforts to communicate clearly with nonspecialists. My thanks also go to Gwen Laing for her typing of the early version of this book and to Hilda S. Mercun for her typing of the final version. I am grateful to Mrs. Jocelyn Hillgarth of Toronto for giving me the benefit of her considerable experience by preparing the index, and to Merrilee R. Gomillion and Joan U. Dorr for their skill as proofreaders.

Hewitt Pantaleoni

Oneonta, N.Y., January 17, 1985

Introduction

... those things most basic to a society are frequently the ones hardest to define simply and clearly, constituting, as it were, the axiomatic part of the culture.

—Bruno Nettl, *The Study of Ethnomusicology,* p. 16

1
The Making of Musical Traditions

A Plural Art

Music is a play of sound. Like a play of firelight on our surroundings, music creates motion. Like a play we see at the theater, it projects more intensely and with stricter form than everyday happenings. And like the play of a game, it has rules.

The rules differ from one musical culture to another just as the general attitudes, values, and circumstances in those cultures differ. The cracked singing voice of an old person makes music that is beautiful in Japan but comical or embarrassing in America—an obvious reflection of the differing ways old age is viewed in these two countries. In West Africa the Ewe living in the southeastern corner of Ghana favor low-pitched, relaxed singing, while the Ewe living some fifty miles further north favor high-pitched, tense singing. The right way to end a piece for symphony orchestra, jazz band, or concert choir is to have the players stop at exactly the same time; the right way to end a piece for *gamelan*, the traditional orchestra of Java, is with a slight scattering of final notes among the players.

Within the bounds of a single country we usually find more than one musical culture. Americans don't sing blues the way they sing opera, nor fiddle the way they play their violins. They don't even gather in the same way to hear different kinds of music: the cabaret musician works a noisy crowd that would demoralize a concert choir.

Cultures change. Indeed, the culture that does not change probably does not last very long. Ways of making music are therefore not only diverse but in flux, the speed of the change varying with circumstances.

Music performed for a changing public changes rapidly and in obvious ways. Among the Hausa people of northern Nigeria, for example, the *mai-kalangu* drummer does not feature the same dance rhythms from one year to the next because he plays at the changing pleasure of young people of marriageable age. In America the same pressure forces continual change upon rock music.

A musical tradition with stable support is itself stable. In the same area where the *mai-kalangu* drummer entertains, musicians attached to the court of the Emir of Zaria sing the songs of praise their grandfathers sang. Due to a similar institutional stability today's officially approved way of singing the chants of the Roman Catholic Church in Latin is unchanged from the Solesmes method developed by our great-grandfathers in the second half of the 19th century and accepted by Rome in 1903 (Berry 1979: 201).

But even the most stable institutions change, however slowly and however much the change is presented as a continuation of past traditions. Our own Supreme Court is an example. In the early 1970's it changed its stance noticeably as the result of several new appointments. Each new ruling was backed by precedent, but observers saw enough change to start calling the justices "the Burger court," after the new Chief Justice, and to contrast their work with that of the earlier "Warren court." The music of the Roman Catholic Church no less than the decisions of the Supreme Court must eventually change to reflect changes in the society it serves.

*   *   *

The Audience Rules

An old saying tells us that the one who calls the tune must pay the piper. The converse is equally true: the one who pays the piper calls the tune. A society has its way in all matters that depend on society for support, whether matters of law, religion, music, or anything else.

The way society asserts control is sometimes obvious. Every day, for instance, some educational issue is raised, contested, or resolved in our newspapers. The audience for music, however, asserts itself more indirectly: it quietly grants or withholds financial support. The professional musician and the composer depend entirely on this support, which they receive either directly through the box office and the recording companies or indirectly as salaried employees of an institution not immediately influenced by popular taste. Thus the audience, whether it be the buying public, an institutional employer, an individual patron, or an art council distributing grants, is in a general sense the real composer of the music.

When I turned in my review of a local symphony concert, I was shocked by my editor's comments. He didn't want my artistic opinions.

"Don't give me so much about the music," he said. "How large was the crowd? How did *they* like it?"

My interest was the music, not the applause, and I remained shocked at his attitude for a long time. But he was right: the opinion of the audience is of fundamental importance in music. I had reviewed a symphony concert, and symphonic music was losing its audience at that time. In the 1960's it no longer dominated American concert life or the music of America's schools.* The majority of younger listeners was

---

*At the end of the 1960's about 2% of the people in this country were attending symphony concerts, counting both children and adults and both free and paid admissions. Moreover, the paying part of that audience was older than the general audience for the elite arts and was not growing as fast as the population in general (Hart 1973: 387-89).

Perhaps the presence of the upper classes at symphony concerts intimidated

turning to other sounds. The most important news about that concert was, indeed, the size of the symphony audience and its reaction to the music.

Two things should be made clear about the audience that controls music. First, it includes the performer, who listens and criticizes in addition to producing the sound. Second, the audience exerts control through small pressures extended over a long time, much the way society enforces proper dress or proper speech.

The process of enforcement is hard to document. Often the application of pressure is far from overt. Dissatisfied listeners rarely rise up in anger at a concert (although it does happen once in a while); usually they simply avoid repeating the experience. Nor can the observer be sure that a particular instance of control is in fact an effective instance; that a result apparently due to some specific corrective action is not really due to a chain of other corrective actions in the past, or to the added force of some nonmusical factor.

An audience exerts control even when it does not share the musical tradition of a performance. Indeed, changes occur more rapidly and obviously in performances serving such an audience than they do in performances serving listeners within the tradition.

An example of this occurred in the late 1960's and early 1970's when West African dancing and drumming was exported to this country. Americans watched the Africans and listened to them, but the subtle shifts of pattern and the many dialogues between the drums were mostly missed. Nor could Americans appreciate what to the West Africans was the most important aspect of a performance of dance drumming: the words of the songs.

In the face of our restlessness the West Africans learned to

---

the general public; but Hans Engel, a sociologist, found that "the inexpensive opportunity of listening to music and the elimination of social shyness" offered by radio broadcasts and record sales had not broadened the market at all for symphonic music (Engel 1968: 573).

reduce to five or ten minutes a musical expression that often might have lasted half an hour or more back home. They began to splice together styles of drum music usually performed separately. Dancers began to modify their motions to get a better audience response. The songs become a minor element.

In brief, beneath the surface of the different-sounding musical traditions lies a universal principle: the audience rules.

Timbre as Identity

A second universal of music is that every musical tradition —that is, every established audience—demands above all a particular quality of sound. By "quality of sound" I mean *timbre*, the aspect of a sound which tells us that the source is a trumpet, say, and not a flute.

The *sitar* of North India, Rāvi Shankar's instrument, is deliberately built to produce a buzzing timbre; the European guitar is deliberately built not to do so. The two instruments share basic features of structure and technique but speak for entirely different audiences. Similarly, a flute is a flute the world around, a cylinder in which a column of air vibrates from the turbulence created by an airstream directed against an edge of the cylinder. Yet the flute playing of a villager from northern Bolivia cannot be enjoyed by the average American. Its extremely breathy timbre renders the sound unacceptable and even meaningless.

At one of the "Pops" concerts given a few years ago in my town by the local symphony orchestra I heard a single electric bass guitar substitute successfully for the entire bass-fiddle section of the orchestra. Because the music was an arrangement from the rock-music tradition, the change of timbre was acceptable. But I notice that the financial managers of our traditional symphony orchestras do not press for this obvious economy. The change involved is apparently not trivial.

Timbre is identity. Your mother's voice on the phone is

your mother's voice primarily because of its timbre; your favorite kind of music is basically your favorite kind of sound. A recording of country western songs arranged for symphony orchestra or string quartet would never capture the Nashville-buying public.

To change the timbre of an aspect of our culture is to provoke an identity crisis. After all, we know who we are only by feedback: by the way others react to us, by the visual stability of our surroundings, by the sonic stability of our everyday contacts. Parents of the 1960's who resisted rock music were protecting not so much their children's morals as their own sense of themselves.

Our preference for one timbre over another has nothing to do with its ultimate worth but everything to do with where we grew up. For example, we may think that if a piano buzzes when it's played, it sounds terrible; the sound is undeniably interesting, but we just aren't used to it.

My grandfather once tuned our upright piano for me. He was by training a chemist and an engineer, by inclination an inventor and musician. When he found me working on the sitting-room piano with a tuning hammer, he promptly took over to show me how it should be done.

Now the central range of the piano is sounded by three strings to each key on the keyboard. Because each key is meant to produce just one note, those three strings must have the same sound. The characteristic timbre of a well-tuned piano derives in large part from the unity of these strings. Well, of course! you say. No, it's not a matter of course at all, but of peculiar preference. Strings slightly distuned would throb, an effect abhorred by the pianist but actually preferred in many cultures to the "dead" sound of exact unisons.*

---

*A good piano tuner actually does allow a minute amount of distuning: not enough to create a throb but just enough to promote the duration of the tone by getting the adjacent strings of a note sounded by three strings to vibrate in opposite directions. This fact has only recently been recognized and understood (Weinreich 1979: 123-27).

When my grandfather took the tuning hammer from me, I had just put the strings of one note into exact agreement with each other. To my great surprise he promptly put them out of tune again—not badly out of tune, just a bit more than needed to produce a throb. Then he did the same to the strings of several other notes.

The result was strangely familiar: a sound we call today "honky-tonk" and associate with the barroom scenes in Westerns. My grandfather did not grow up in a bar, nor was he ever allowed to spend time in them. He grew up in the second half of the 19th century, however, when houses did not have central heating. The parlor piano was an important feature in middle-class homes of that era and was probably more or less out of tune all the time as a result of fluctuations in temperature and humidity. "Honky-tonk" was the timbre he knew and preferred.

The voices of Pete Seeger, John Denver, and Gordon Lightfoot fit the tradition of a lyric tenor sound, a timbre that goes back through the musicals and filmed musicals of the 1940's and 1930's to the operettas so popular with the middle class at the turn of the century. Most of our leading popular singers owe their success as much to conformity as to individuality: they win our acceptance by preserving, or, at the most, modifying the timbres we have known and prefer.

The importance of timbre forces some artists to perform silently on television. Take for example a rock group that has a best-selling record. If the electronic effects on this record cannot be duplicated in live performance before the television cameras, then the group will go through the motions of performing while a machine reproduces the sounds of the recording.

Innovation from Within

The audience dictates, timbres are honored, but in any live musical tradition there is always room for innovation. Timbres are modified; musical effects are borrowed from other traditions;

novel effects are introduced. In some cases the changes go practically unnoticed and in others are too drastic to be immediately accepted. Aaron Copland's *Appalachian Spring* (1944) was an instant success, though its lovely melodies and orchestral colors cover a surprising amount of very modern dissonance. Arnold Schoenberg's twelve-tone music, lacking singable melodies and familiar harmonies, has yet to be accepted by the general public, though a dedicated minority has kept it alive for almost sixty years through concerts and recordings.

Successful innovation is made with a feeling *for* the tradition rather than against it, with a sense of how to expand our musical resources without violating our expectations. At the cutting edge of innovation are those who cannot hold this middle ground but must work a new vein at any cost. As the late Harry Partch put it:

> Let us give to nuts and bolts the standardization of thread that we have come to expect, but let us give to music—magic, to man—magic.
> *(Partch 1974: xii)*

Partch found his magic in working with pitches better adjusted to each other than those of our standard well-tempered tuning; to sound those pitches he had to invent a new set of instruments and train his own set of musicians to play them. It was too much: a complete substitution of these resources rather than an expansion of them. His music is not often performed.

Though Partch never found the middle ground, he knew where it was:

> [Musical] investigators and experimenters are at least as reverent toward our European heritage as the average music lover—probably more so, because they are acolytes of the creative spirit that has produced such phenomena as the last three hundred years of Western music. But . . . [theirs] is a *dynamic* reverence.
> *(Partch 1974; xvii, italics added)*

The Need for Music

What is there about music, about this insubstantial art of vibrations, that gives to sounds of the past the power to control sounds of the future? that lets people with no special musical qualifications rule the careers of trained musicians? that demands reverence as if music were a thing of substance?

Each of us lives in a particular culture and cannot help absorbing its sounds and their associations. We are all carriers of a musical tradition, whether or not we perform music or even enjoy it. We are, in fact, experts compared with those who stand outside the tradition. Years of listening to music, by accident or intention, years of listening to its cues, associations, and acceptable levels of performance constitute a technical training of a high order even among those of us who do not command the skill or specialized vocabulary of musical analysis.

I said earlier that music, like the games we play, is defined by rules. But these rules are themselves an expression of general attitudes, values, and circumstances within a particular society, as has been pointed out by John Blacking, the English musician, social anthropologist, and student of musical systems (Blacking 1972-73: 58). By conforming to a society's set of sonic rules, music in its own special way presents the essence of that society, conveying a sense of the particular social web people have interacted with all their lives in learning their repertoire of acceptable physical and emotional behavior. That particular social web, Blacking argues, must be the deciding element controlling the surface design of the music so that it communicates feeling successfully (Blacking 1973: 73).

Our musical past commands reverence and controls the musical present because it makes direct, supportive reference to our social past and our social present. In plain language, we associate our music with how we were and how we want to be. The timbre, forms, and styles of past, approved performances represent to us our best selves both as individuals and as a group.

If, as I think, the insubstantial vibrations of music take on substance and power because they reinforce and reaffirm our sense of ourselves, it is hardly surprising that every culture in the world has music. It must fill a need more fundamental than the needs filled by many other things.

Consider the most trivial case first: a game like baseball is not universal, though the basic materials for the game are universally available; obviously the "need" for baseball does not run deep in the human heart. To a lesser degree the same can be said for the pursuit of superior wealth: it is not a game played in every culture, though every human is driven to survive. Even the "need" to relate one's daily life to a single, all-governing deity is not universal, though every culture practices some kind of religion.

The need to make music lies on a deeper level, one as fundamental as the very need to play, to nourish oneself, and to worship; for the fact is that sound sources are everywhere, and everywhere they are sounded.

We serve ourselves badly, then, to trivialize music. I'm not referring to our popular-music industry. It gives us pieces to accompany our talking, our dancing, our courtship, and such accompaniment is trivial only to a minority of people trained to give music their undivided attention. Nor do I refer to Muzak, a corporation which dispenses sounds calculated to lull our minds in the supermarket or fire them up as they tire towards the end of a hard day at the office. The Muzak product certainly seems trivial to the attentive listener, and I myself hang up the phone and dial again rather than endure being put on hold and having to listen to that kind of music; but to those who make it and those who buy it, that kind of music is serious business worth a great deal of effort and money.

I refer instead to an upward trivialization practiced by a sincere group of people who would remove music from its fundamental place in the lives of everyone and put it on a pedestal beyond the reach of all but the specially talented. We need the specially talented, of course; we must encourage them and honor their achievements. In every society the leadership of such people keeps musical traditions at their liveliest. But if music is the fundamental human activity I think it is, we do our society no service when we promote the art music of the elite over other musical traditions or when we emphasize the training of talented persons and fail to make sure that everyone has the opportunity to participate. Our concern should be that people have access to music as they do to physical play, nourishment, and worship.

2
Hearing Music

In its quality at any given moment unmusical sound differs in no measurable way from musical sound. What one culture considers inappropriate may be highly regarded by another, and the variety of effects offered by the music of the world is overwhelming. Musical sound is simply sound accepted as musical.

This broad definition is forced upon us because sound is subjective, an impression triggered by—but not necessarily the same as—impulses the ear receives from the surrounding air. The impression of sound arises only after the brain has interpreted these impulses by considering other incoming data and the memory of past experience.

The impulses travel by mechanical means from their source to the threshold of the brain. Beyond the threshold of the brain they travel electrically. The final stages, the processes of interpretation, are at present not understood. The best we have for them is the vague word "imagination."

The Mechanical Means

The impulses received by the ear in the first stage of the process of hearing are formed by rapid variations in the pressure of the surrounding air. In music these variations come from the regular vibration of one or more material objects

—a taut string, a partially enclosed body of air, the curved metal plate of a gong, the cardboard cone of a loudspeaker. In an amount of air the size of the head of a pin there are at any one moment well over two million billion molecules (Backus 1977: 38). With each vibration the surface of the object thrusts outward against these molecules and then withdraws, causing among them momentary compression followed by momentary rarification.

If a vibrating object were in a vacuum with only a single layer of air molecules clinging to its thrusting surface, these molecules would be propelled from that surface like Ping-Pong balls struck with a paddle. Because the object is not in a vacuum, the molecules lying against its vibrating surface strike outward against the next layer of molecules and bounce back. These neighboring molecules in turn strike outward against *their* neighbors and bounce back, and so on. Thus the vibrating object sends outward through the air an expanding shell of compression followed closely by a shell of rarification, then another shell of compression, another shell of rarification, and so on, the moment between shells being a time when the pressure of the air is in transition from one extreme to the other.

Actually, of course, each individual molecule of air does not lurch back and forth, as I've described, but pursues its own erratic path at a speed determined by the prevailing temperature and in a direction determined from moment to moment by its collisions with other molecules. (The distance it travels between one collision and the next is never more than a few molecular diameters.) The shells of compression and rarification generated by the vibrating object nevertheless move through this turbulent scene *as if* the molecules of air were specks trapped in clear Jello, jiggling back and forth but not shifting their basic positions.

Shells reaching the ear less frequently than forty every second—that is, twenty compressions in alternation with twenty rarifications—are inaudible; they simply feel like what they are: variations in the pressure of the air surrounding the ear. Shells reaching the ear more frequently than 30,000 every second—that is, 15,000 compressions in alternation with 15,000 rarifications—make no impression at all, at least upon the average ear. Between these limits the brain interprets a repeating variation in the pressure of the air as sound (Roederer 1974: 25).

Shells of compression and rarification travel at a uniform speed determined by the atmospheric conditions of the moment. Shells leaving an object that vibrates in a repeating pattern therefore maintain a repeating pattern of spaces among themselves as they move away. Slow vibrations of the object generate shells widely spaced; rapid vibrations, shells narrowly spaced.

Any object vibrating naturally will vibrate at several rates of speed at the same time. If the shells of compression and rarification produced are predominantly widely spaced, the low frequency of their arrival at the ear causes the brain to hear what we call a sound of "low pitch"—for example, the voice of a man compared with that of a child. If narrowly spaced shells predominate, the high frequency of their arrival causes the brain to hear what we call a sound of "high pitch"—for example, the voice of a child compared with that of a man. "Pitch" is the musician's term for that particular quality of a sound which is determined by the spacing of the dominant shells. (Figure 1 illustrates the difference in spacing of the dominant shells when a bass singer duets with a boy soprano.)

Fig. 1

Like the link between the air and the original vibrating object, the link between the air and the ear is mechanical. Approximately one inch in from the opening of the ear a membrane seals off the inner mechanism of hearing. Changes in the pressure of the outside air cause changes in the shape of this membrane, which is called the "eardrum."

Three tiny levers of bone transfer the motions of the eardrum to the "inner ear," a small chamber filled with fluid within the bone of the skull itself. The levers, attached to the walls of their own small chamber between the eardrum and the inner ear, are linked in series. The outer end of the outermost

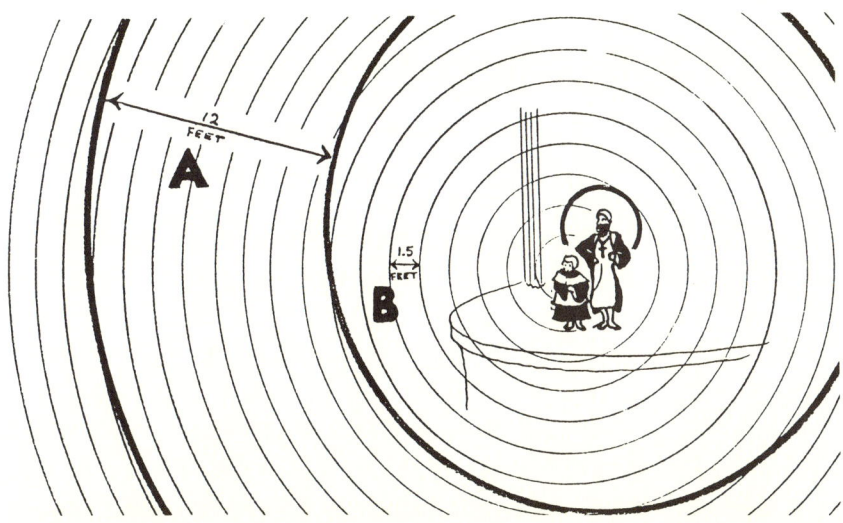

FIGURE 1: PITCH AND SPACE. *At a temperature of 68° Fahrenheit and an atmospheric pressure normal to sea-level areas, shells of compression and rarification travel outward from a vibrating object at the uniform speed of 1,130 feet every second (Backus 1977: 43). A different set of atmospheric conditions will impose a different uniform speed. Changes in the speed or violence with which an object vibrates have no effect on the speed of transmission of the vibration.*

(A) The vibrating vocal chords of an adult male singer may send out shells of greatest compression (shown here as thick, curved lines) as infrequently as 87.5 times a second. These shells will be spaced twelve feet apart in an opera house at sea level where the temperature is 68° Fahrenheit (1,130 feet divided by 87.5 shells). The listening brain responds to dominant pressure changes of such relatively low frequency by hearing a sound we call "low in pitch," pitch being the musical term for the brain's perception of any steadily repeating change in air pressure with a frequency between twenty and 15,000 times a second.

(B) The vibrating vocal chords of a singing child may send out shells of greatest compression (shown here as thin curved lines) as frequently as 753.33 times a second. These shells will be spaced one and a half feet apart in the same opera house (1,130 feet divided by 753.33 shells). The listening brain responds to dominant pressure changes of such relatively high frequency by hearing a sound we call "high in pitch."

lever rests against the inner surface of the eardrum. The inner end of the innermost lever forms part of the wall enclosing the fluid of the inner ear. Vibrations passing through these levers from the eardrum to the inner ear are intensified tenfold. Muscles that modify the angle of the levers keep the inner ear from receiving traumatic shocks.

The chamber containing the levers is called the "middle ear." It is filled with air supplied from the mouth cavity through a narrow tube. The air insulates the bony levers from vibrations caused by bodily functions because the transfer of motion from air to bone is far weaker than the transfer of motion from bone to bone. (Figure 2, on p. 20, illustrates the general arrangement of parts within the ear.)

The inner ear has two functions, balance and hearing. Balance is handled at one end of the chamber by three loops, each in a different plane. The inertia of gelatinous material within these loops registers on special nerves whenever the head is moved. Hearing is handled at the other end of the chamber by a spiralled cone called the "cochlea." Motions conveyed from the eardrum to the fluid of the inner ear register on special nerves set within the cochlea. The next few paragraphs describe this process.

Two membranes run the length of the cochlea, forming a double-walled partition that divides it into smaller, parallel cones. At the base of the cochlea, where the cones are widest, one of them opens directly into the fluid-filled main chamber of the inner ear while the other ends at a membranous window set into the bony wall separating the inner ear from the middle ear. At the tip of the cochlea, where the cones are narrowest, they connect with each other. Motions in the fluid of the inner ear travel up one cone and down the other, ending at the membranous window. The air of the middle ear insulates the levers of bone from the vibrations of this window, so that each motion of the air outside the eardrum travels through the cochlea only once.

The motion of almost every naturally vibrating object is

not a simple back and forth but a composite of several simultaneous motions in various directions, some of them more vigorous than others. For example, a metal bar suspended by a string and swung against a hard surface vibrates along its length, across its width, and from front to back, and in each of these directions not only as a whole bar but in segments as well. The strengths of these motions are never equal; that is, the bar moves a greater distance in one direction than another depending on its shape, how it is suspended, where on its surface the strike takes place, and how compressible the striker is.

These many vibrations generate a complex pattern among the shells moving outward from the object. There is, however, a simple way to deal with the complexity: one imagines an ideal gas molecule jiggling back and forth in response to these shells but not leaving its basic position; motion away from the vibrating object creates compression; motion toward it, rarification. As a friend and colleague, the physicist Albert Read, once explained to me:

> a point-mass like the ideal musical gas molecule can have only one speed [and direction] at a particular instant. But its back-and-forth vibration can have irregularities in it as if it were following a combination of different simple oscillations all superimposed on the same hapless particle.
> *(Read 1976)*

The path of a line showing the rapid changes in air pressure caused from one moment to the next by a vibrating object can be thought of as a line tracing the back-and-forth motion of the ideal musical gas molecule. This line is not hard to produce: a microphone near the vibrating object translates changes of air pressure into changes in the flow of an electrical current, and these electrical changes are used either to project the line on a television screen or to move a pen from side to side as it passes over a sheet of paper. The multiple vibration of different objects produces strikingly different irregular repeat-

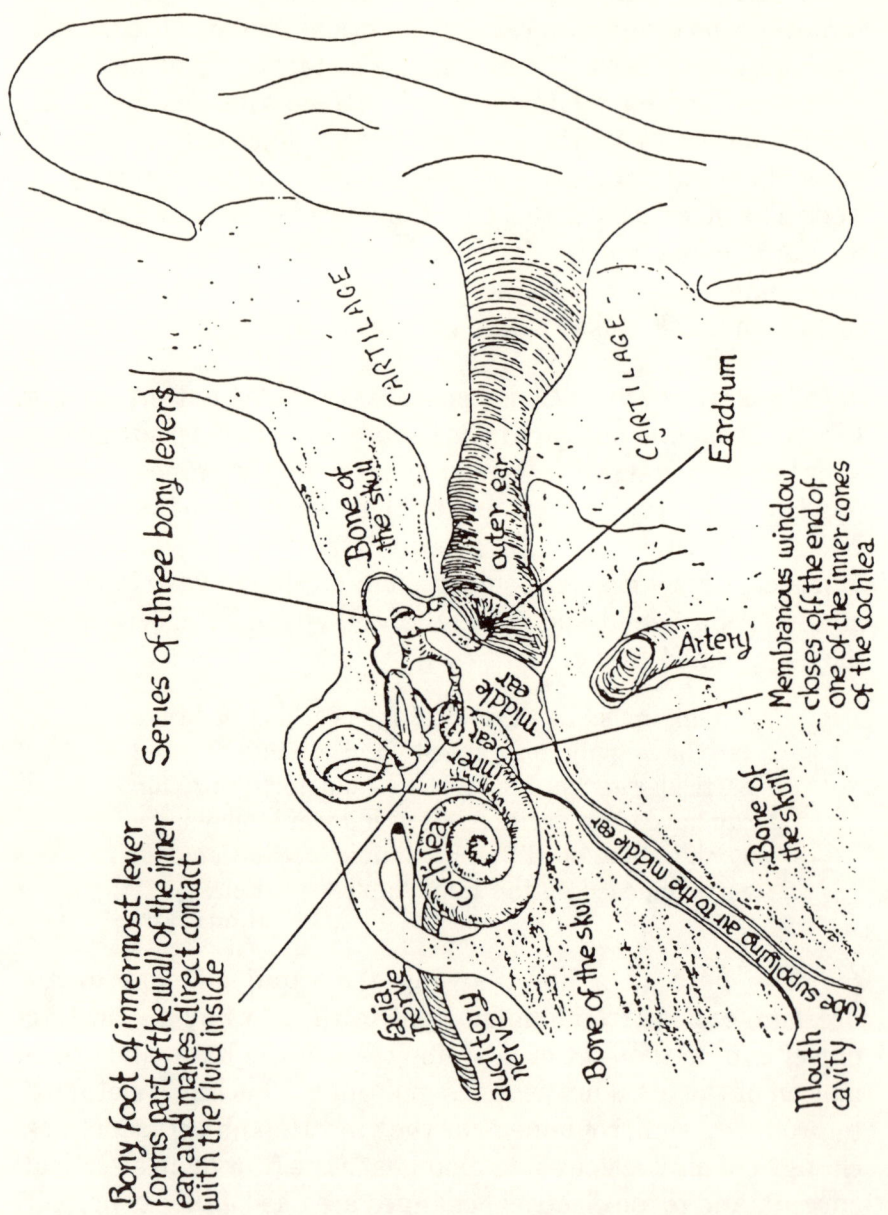

FIGURE 2: THE PARTS OF THE EAR. *This shows a person's left ear viewed from the front. Bone and cartilage surrounding the system are shown as flat surfaces while the system itself is shown three-dimensionally (adapted from Brödel 1946: fig. 1).*

Rapid changes in air pressure, channeled into the opening of the outer ear, move the eardrum, which is a membranous seal between the outer ear and the middle ear. Three levers of bone attached to the walls of the middle ear are linked in series and transmit this motion to the inner ear, intensifying it tenfold as they do so.

Three loops at one end of the inner ear give a sense of balance and direction. Embedded in the bone of the skull, they move as one with the head. The fluid inside them lags behind this motion, and the lag is noted.

A spiralled cone at the other end of the inner ear, the "cochlea," is where the motions generated by a sounding object finally meet the brain, and "hearing" begins. Inside the cochlea are two conical channels joined at the tip of the spiral. The base of one channel opens into the inner ear. The fluid of the inner ear fills both channels, and motion transmitted to the fluid by the three bony levers travels through this open base, then on to the tip of the spiral, over into the other channel, and down to its base, where it is dissipated in the movements of a membranous window that faces the middle ear.

One of the membranes separating the two conical channels is an elastic organ of graduated stiffness in which thousands of nerve endings are embedded. The stiffer end of the membrane responds best to the more rapid vibrations in the cochlear fluid; the more flabby end responds best to the slower vibrations. Thus at various points along its length the membrane responds to the various rates of vibration which the original sounding object created. The movement of the membrane as it responds causes the nerve endings at each responding point to fire signals to the inner parts of the brain. The location of the firing nerves corresponds to the rate of vibration being recorded; the number of nerve endings excited at each location corresponds to the vigor of the vibration.

The nerves send electrical signals through what seems to be a single system of complex circuits. No objective basis has been found for considering the electrical part of the cochlea separate in any way from the brain itself.

ing patterns. (See Figure 3.)

A body that returns to its initial position after being moved by an outside force is called "elastic." The more rigid the elastic body, the more rapidly it returns; the less rigid, the more slowly. A vibrating body is one that is continually moving from its initial position and returning to it. A more rigid body therefore has a faster natural rate of vibration than a less rigid body.

FIGURE 3: MULTIPLE VIBRATIONS. *An object usually vibrates in different directions and at several rates of speed simultaneously. The changes in air pressure it produces around itself can be translated by a microphone into changes in an electrical current. A pen that leaves a track on moving paper can be designed to respond to these changes by moving from side to side, one direction representing rising pressure, the other, falling pressure. This back-and-forth motion of the pen records the way we imagine an ideal molecule of air would move alongside a vibrating object, were the molecule somehow forced to remain in one basic position.*

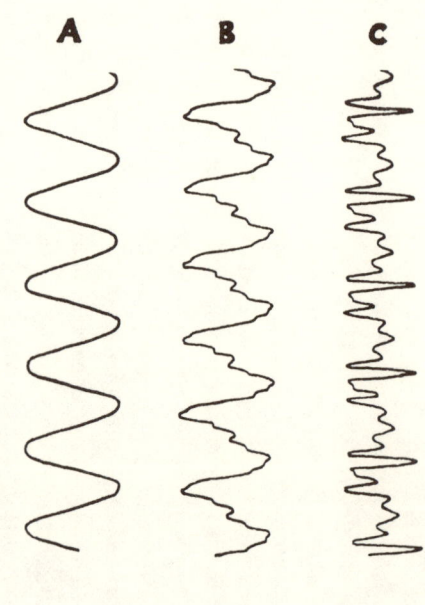

In the figure shown here the vibrating object is somewhere off to the left, the listener off to the right. Rising air pressure moves the pen to the right, falling pressure moves it to the left, and the lines drawn by the pen run from the top of the page downward. In response to three different sounding objects the pen has left three different tracks (from Saunders 1948: 38).

(A): the simple vibration of a tuning fork, for comparison with the other tracks. A very plain curve is recorded. The distance from one repetition of the pattern to the next reflects the spacing of the shells of

One of the two membranes dividing the cochlear cone into narrower, parallel cones is both elastic and of graduated thickness. The thicker end, being more rigid, responds best to rapid vibrations in the cochlear fluid; the thinner end, being more flexible, responds best to slow vibrations. The membrane as a whole is thus a kind of analyzer capable of responding at various points along its length to vibrations in the cochlear fluid which have speeds matching the natural rate of vibration of the membrane at these points.

Since the ear transmits the vibrations of the outer air to the fluid of the inner ear, the repeating, irregular motion of the ideal gas molecule discussed above can be thought of as occurring again in the cochlea as the repeating, irregular motion of an ideal liquid molecule. The elastic membrane responds at appropriate points along its length to each of the various original vibrations of the object, all of which are present in the repeating, irregular motion of the ideal liquid molecule.

---

compression and rarification as they travel through the air. This distance does not change here or in the other two tracks, and so in each case we hear a sound of unchanging pitch. Note, however, that in this track the repetitions are spaced just a little further apart than they are in track B and therefore represent a slightly "lower" pitch.

(B): the multiple vibration of a sounding violin. The string, the surfaces of the wooden instrument, and the air inside create vibrations that reinforce and interfere with one another in a repeating manner to produce a repeating, irregular pattern of pressure changes in the air. The fixed spacing of the repetitions of this pattern gives the listener the impression of a sound of fixed pitch. The fixed irregularities of the pattern give the listener the impression of a particular timbre.

(C): the multiple vibration of a sounding oboe. The timbre of this instrument differs from that of a tuning fork or a violin, and so does the pattern of pressure changes it creates. The pattern is not as wide as those shown in tracks A and B because the amount of compression and rarification is not as great; in other words, the oboe is making a softer sound. Note that the repetitions of the oboe's irregular pattern occur slightly further apart than those of the violin and therefore represent a slightly "lower" pitch.

The Electrical Means

The link between the elastic membrane and the mind is electrical. In fact, it is not really possible to separate this electrical link from the electrical activity of the mind. In other words, the brain begins here at the elastic membrane.

Embedded in the elastic membrane of the cochlea are thousands of nerve endings. When a certain part of the membrane vibrates, the endings at that location discharge small amounts of electricity which travel back along the nerves to the main center of hearing in the brain. The location of the discharging nerves identifies the rate of vibration; the number of discharges per second identifies the vigor of the stimulation. The brain centers receive this information and "hear" the appropriate pitch at the indicated level of loudness.

The nerve endings in the elastic membrane are not the brain's only source of information. The nerve lines from the cochlea to the brain centers are themselves primary sources for sound effects; they form, as it were, a second ear. In other words, stimulation of the elastic membrane fails to account for all that we hear: some information is generated only later in the chain of communication.

One day when I returned from classes and opened my apartment door, I heard the middle of a glorious, high tenor note such as Enrico Caruso used to put on heavy shellac records back in the early 1900's. Radio stations occasionally play these records, and I thought my radio was turned on.

Not at all. The "note" finally dissolved into a liquid gurgling and sputtering, and I realized that it came from our steam radiator. The difference between the sound of an old recording of Caruso's voice and the sound of an old steam radiator lies not so much in the quality of the sound as in the way that sound begins.

When an object starts to vibrate it generates certain patterns of pressure lasting only a tenth of a second or so and giving way immediately to the more sustained effects associated with the object. During their brief life these beginning patterns are in continual flux, first building up and then decaying. Only along the nerve lines to the centers of hearing can this flux be monitored and recognized. There are at least five main lines, all interconnected. They pass through at least eight different units in the brain which in effect generate new raw data by responding selectively to transmissions from the elastic membrane and from each other. They are, in this sense, a second ear, listening not to patterns of pressure but to patterns of electrical relationships.

Imagination

In sorting and comparing electrical signals the brain can create for itself sensations of pitch that correspond to none of the incoming information. That is how we manage to hear the complicated vibration of a plucked guitar string as a single pitch instead of many pitches: it's not that one of the string's many vibration patterns happens to be so strong it masks the others; it's just that a taut string naturally vibrates in multiples of a single value, and when the brain recognizes two neighboring multiples it automatically "hears" the original value *whether or not that value exists* in the vibrations of the cochlear fluid.

For example, the lowest string of a guitar in standard tuning vibrates at many different speeds, the slowest among them being the rates of 80, 160, 240, 320, 400, and 480 times a second. These six rates are the most prominent and the most important. Now, as you can see, all six values are simple multiples of 80. The brain recognizes the multiple relationship between neighboring pairs in this series and is stimulated by each recognition to hear a pitch corresponding, in every case, to 80 vibrations a second. The power of the brain's imagination "drowns out," so to speak, the "sound" of these upper values and they are not recognized as separate pitches.*

---

*Since the difference between each neighboring pair of values in the series is 80, their vibrations reinforce each other 80 times a second and defeat each other midway between those reinforcements, thus creating on their own a secondary cycle

Let's go further into the brain's creative role. We can imagine a musical sound when there is no external stimulation at all. Most of us, for example, can imagine the sound of a harmonica, a flute, a baby's cry, a passing motorcycle. Composers develop this skill to a high degree. Ludwig van Beethoven began to lose his hearing at the age of thirty, began to use an ear trumpet when he was forty-six, and was almost completely deaf by the age of fifty. Yet he continued to create new pieces with great success throughout this period and beyond.

People can hear at will what they are used to hearing—the sound of a friend's voice, the air brakes of a truck, the instruments of an orchestra. Indeed, when I've had occasion to transcribe speech from a tape recorder I've found it all too easy to "hear" words not uttered, just by imagining that they *were* uttered. There have been some fascinating experiments in this area:

> Recently an expert in psychoacoustics familiarized a group of subjects with a certain piece of choral music by playing it to them repeatedly until they knew it very well. He then played the music to each of the subjects in the presence of a loud white noise [sound consisting of all vibration rates in equal strength] and gradually lowered the volume of the music to zero. He asked each subject to indicate at what point the music disappeared. The subjects all heard the music for a considerable time after it had been turned off.
> *(Bergeijk, Pierce, and David 1960: 69)*

Now, if you can imagine a sound, you can anticipate it. Listening to music, in fact, is not just a matter of receiving

---

of compression and rarification in the air at that speed of 80 cycles a second. But researchers have discovered that if they feed one of the upper values into one ear and a neighboring value into the other ear, the brain still puts the two together and hears a vibration rate of 80 times a second. In other words, the effect arises in the circuitry of the brain without a corresponding mechanical effect in the air.

pressure signals or imagining them, but of expecting them. Juan G. Roederer makes this point in summarizing his work on the psycho-physics of musical perception. He finds in our expectant attitude an explanation for some of the power music has to affect us.

> The main function of the [cerebral cortical] system is to determine and remember the causal relationships in the surrounding physical world, to determine the most likely behavior of those other species in the animal world with which the individual interacts, and to provide short-term predictions that are used to determine the individual's own response (behavior). Thinking is nothing more than exercising by internal stimulation this ultracomplex prediction mechanism. But listening to music *also* implies an exercising of this prediction mechanism. When we listen to a piece of music, our prediction mechanism activates our auditory cortex—our internal "musical TV screen"—even *before* the signals from the ear arrive there. Whenever this prediction mechanism fails during the perception of music—because of an unexpected passage, for example, or a mistake in the performance—the extra work required for re-identification gives a particular sensation of "musical tension."
>
> *(Roederer 1974: 29-30)*

Of what does music consist, then? Of sound and silence, of time and expectation. It's entirely in your head: a wealth of stored experience reacting imaginatively to patterns of pressure in the air; a learned activity as much as an automatic one. To put it another way, the music you enjoy has taught you to enjoy the music you enjoy.

The process need not form a closed circle, however. To enjoy new music you only have to allow time for it to teach you —time, as Roederer might say, for an appropriate prediction mechanism to develop. There's a lot of strange but lovely music in the world; making its acquaintance can nourish your mind as much as new ideas do, even if you can never bring to your listening the stored experience of native carriers of the various traditions.

Earlier I argued that music satisfies a level of our nature as deep as that which makes us seek play, nourishment, or worship. Strangely enough, becoming acquainted with the music of another culture intensifies this satisfaction: in gaining a new fund of stored experience we seem also to gain understanding of the fund we already have; we seem to hear the music we have always known as if we know it well yet have never heard it before. The experience is, in a word, refreshing.

Part One: Melody

3

The Nature of Melody

Passage and Predictability

The essence of melody is passage—a purposeful linking of one moment to the next.

The brain naturally finds any sensory experience more or less continuous which occurs at a single place in a single span of time. Within this basic continuity, however, the musical experience demands more. One sound cannot simply replace another, it must pass into it; the brain must be persuaded to impose continuity upon change. The musician's art is to persuade, but even the finest musician cannot succeed when the sound lacks one basic ingredient: predictability.

The basic condition of predictability is restricted choice.

> A chain of events in which every element has at all times an equal chance of occurrence is said to show randomness. No conclusions can be drawn from it and no predictions can be made about its future sequence.
>
> *(Watzlawick, Beavin, and Jackson 1967: 34)*

Any one composer or musical tradition makes use of only certain sounds and uses them in only certain ways. We may praise the fertile imagination of Beethoven or The Beatles, but clearly they did not compose a great many different kinds of music. The name for the predictability of a composer's work or a musical tradition is "style," and the name refers to the sameness of the items constituting that work or tradition. Modern composers have raised a furor by introducing random choice into their music, but with few exceptions they have never been able—or perhaps willing—to allow randomness to outweigh the predictability of their sound.

In the early 1960's the American composer John Cage gave a concert at my college in which he combined simultaneously a live lecture with three taped lectures, all read by him and all composed of short anecdotes and reflections written by himself (he writes extremely well). There were long pauses between items in each lecture, and from time to time he would walk over to one of the tape machines and turn it off or turn it on again.

"I have no idea how it will come out each time," he told a group of us afterwards. "What you hear and how you put it together depend on chance and on where you are sitting. I time myself and the machines with a watch in this piece. For my next piece I'm going to throw away the watch."

Of course it was impossible for the audience to follow any one lecture due to competition from the other lectures. One had to piece together the "concert" for oneself. An angry student of mine, a married woman with a young family to care for, stalked out of the concert muttering, "I can hear *that* any night at the supper table."

Indeed, if one were trying to understand words and sentences, there was only the babble of several voices speaking at once. But if one were listening to the lectures as a flow of sound, the effect was musical: a weaving together of melodies, always interesting and often beautiful. At times there were even effects a musician would call fugal. That is, during a chance moment of silence a single voice would resume its discourse and be followed shortly afterward by a second voice, then a third, each entering with different words but the same general rising and falling of loudness and pitch.

When I had drawn back from the sound as language, I

found listening to it a moving experience. Despite elements of randomness, the piece held together: a melodic flow pulled me along. The basic condition of predictability had been amply met, for every voice was the voice of John Cage: timbres were uniform, and the rhythms and intonations were in a single style.

Anticipation

The essence of melody is the linking of one sound to another, as I've said, not the mere juxtaposition of sounds in time. To put it another way, the important thing about a change of sound in music is the relationship established. What we understand about the nature of perception seems to explain why this should be so.

> Sensory and brain research have proved conclusively that only relationships and patterns of relationships can be perceived, and these are the essence of experience. Thus when, by an ingenious device, eye movement is made impossible so that the same image continues to be perceived by the same areas of the retina, clear visual perception is no longer possible. Likewise, a steady, unchanging sound is difficult to perceive and may even become unnoticeable.... [A] process of change, motion, or scanning is involved in all perception.
> (Watzlawick, Beavin, and Jackson 1967: 27-28)

Life itself is a continual transition—an undefinable now, sandwiched between an immediate past and future. The present is anticipation standing on the shoulders of memory.

Continual anticipation of change is another important aspect of the melodic experience. As any tune unfolds, it cultivates certain sound-relationships and ignores others. The total range of possibilities perceived by the brain on the basis of past experience quickly narrows to the few that characterize the tune and its style group. The listener begins to anticipate as well as hear.

The twists and turns of melody are not always what one expects. The more familiar a tune and its tradition, the more enjoyable its mixture of divergence and conformity. One researcher explains our enjoyment as exercise:

> The alternation of regular, ordered patterns with surprise and uncertainty—a characteristic common to *all* sensorial input that is thought of as "aesthetic" —may ultimately be a manifestation of man's inherent desire to exercise his super-redundant neural network by engaging in biologically non-essential information-processing operations of changing or alternating complexity, just for the fun of it!
> *(Roederer 1974: 24)*

How can a tune produce "surprise and uncertainty" when it is familiar? The American ballad scholar Bertram H. Bronson finds the explanation in what the early 19th century poet Samuel Taylor Coleridge called "that willing suspension of disbelief for the moment, which constitutes poetic faith" (Coleridge 1965: II, 6). Bronson argues that for the traditional singer of ballads and for the singer's traditional audience

> the pleasures of suspense are just as vivid whether or not the outcome is known, and surprise is re-experienced at every fresh telling. . . . Under the spell of the art experience, the listener imaginatively resumes the condition of ignorance even while he knows the issue. He knows but he doesn't know.
> *(Bronson 1969: 6)*

Repetition is more than repetition: it is re-enactment, and we participate the more fully the more often we have the chance. Surprises become better surprises; divergencies from the norm become more entertaining.

* * *

Stability

Counterbalancing such delights are the elements of melody not subject to capricious change: timbre, of course, and the pitch frame. Tunes of every culture create, as they unfold, a stable framework of levels of pitch which gives direction to the motion of the melody. "Up" or "down" becomes "to" or "from" certain emphasized levels. Motion becomes passage. To feel the kind of musical direction I'm talking about, just chant this sentence on a single level of pitch, pausing for the commas but not changing pitch until the final syllable, when you go *up*. That "up" drew its force from its importance as a step away from the prevailing pitch level.

Tunes of every culture, as they unfold, create recurring patterns. These become stable elements as important as a pitch frame, for they tie what you are hearing to what you have already heard. Sometimes the tie involves just rhythm, sometimes both rhythm and pitch, and sometimes pitch alone. Whatever the case, the recurrence strongly encourages predictability.

Melody, as you can see, is a work of the mind, which connects one sound to another, one pattern to an earlier one, one pitch to a stable framework of pitches, and the whole experience to past experiences of a similar kind. Our culture, however, is awash in words: words, not sounds, control our lives. And so it may seem to us that a play of sound, just sound, cannot be important unless it accompanies words or stands for something we can put into words. By itself it cannot be anything weightier than recreation, like hiking or playing cards—fun for some people, but basically of no import.

Yet melody is everywhere, in every culture. Like breathing or social intercourse it is an essential part of living, though we don't yet understand why. It is therefore not a frill but an activity deserving serious attention and support, both in adult life and in our preparation for adult life; for making melody is not just something we do, it is apparently something we have to do.

4

The Black American Holler

The holler may be a black American invention.* One voice alone sings a winding melody of slow notes, slides, and fast turns, a line smooth and continually shifting like the press of the wind on tall grass.

A single syllable may carry the line, which is why people often call this music a holler or "hallo," a musical shout, a yell, a cry, wailing, yodeling, whooping, or just "eeohing." The motion is free and easy, with some sounds straight and strong, some in flux. Scholars consider the holler to be the ancestor of today's instrumentally accompanied blues (Nettl 1973: 229–230).

---

*Alan Lomax, who has been in close contact with the music of black Americans throughout his life, disagrees vigorously with this opinion. A singer of folk songs himself, a folk collector of immense energy and wide reputation, the author of many books on folk music, and the driving force behind a pioneering and controversial attempt to relate musical behavior of different kinds to cultures of different kinds (Alan Lomax 1968), he feels that I have brought together here under one label two different kinds of black American song and that both of them derive from Africa: (1) a bluesy holler that developed in the levee camps of the Mississippi Delta, and (2) a song for signalling at a distance, which is cousin to the yodel.

The interested reader can hear an example of a bluesy holler and a highly similar song from Africa brought together by Lomax for comparison on New World recording NW 252, side 1, band 1; the pygmies of the rain forest of northeastern Zaire sing in the yodeling style cited by Lomax and can be heard on Lyrichord LLST 7157. I fail to hear in these or other black African examples the melodic traits I discuss in this chapter as characteristics of the holler: sliding pitch and a widely spaced pitch frame.

The same kind of melody can be heard in black American hymn singing. Hollers as such are not part of worship, but their style suits an emotional approach to religion. Thus back in 1850 in Macon, Georgia, Fredrika Bremer noticed one black participant in a religious camp meeting

> walking about by himself and breathing hard; he was hoarse, and sighing, he exclaimed to himself, "Oh! I wish I could hollo!"
> *(Southern 1971: 106)*

The holler can be a signal. John Lomax was moved by such a song, which he heard outside Wiergate, Texas, in 1933.

> Yesterday I heard for the first time the wail of the Negro woodsman as a fine tree that he is cutting sways and then falls to the earth with a shuddering crash. Shrill, swift, wavering, the shout swings to a sudden and dramatic conclusion, just as does the tree when the cry ends and the tree surrenders.... It is a dirge of the dying pine and at the same time a warning signal to other woodsmen.
> There is music in that cry, and mystery, and wistful sadness.
> *(John Lomax 1947: 119)*

It was the custom among black farmers to use the holler as a general nighttime signal when out walking.

> Since it takes time to visit and return, the man will give out his night cry as he journeys along. He will also do the same thing when returning to his home. This avoids the visitor's being entirely separated from other human beings.... For sheer charm and mystic potency, no musical utterance can be more arresting than the cry of a gifted Negro moving in the night unseen, unknown.
> *(Willis James 1955: 20)*

Characteristically the holler is solo music, but not always.

For example, when John Lomax set up his recording apparatus to make a permanent record of the Texas woodsman's signalling cry, a *group* of black Americans sang it for him. And before the Civil War, in 1855, a northern newspaper reporter described what seems to have been a group holler at a railhead near the Pedee River in eastern South Carolina.

> ... the loading gang of negroes had made a fire and were enjoying a right merry repast. Suddenly one raised such a sound as I never heard before; a long, loud, musical shout, rising, and falling, and breaking into falsetto, his voice ringing through the woods in the clear, frosty night air, like a bugle call. As he finished the melody was caught up by another, and then, another, and then, by several in chorus.
> *(Olmsted 1968: 394)*

Several former slaves have recalled for interviewers that hollering and singing went along with corn shucking, which was an intense but festive group activity. Joseph Holmes, remembering old times as a Virginia slave, told Ila B. Prine:

> One man would git on dat pile. Hit usually was one who was kinda niggah fo'man dat could sing an' get de wuck out of de odder niggera. Dis fo'man would sing a verse somethin' lack dis:
>   Polk an' Clay went to war
>   An' Polk come back wid a broken jar
> Den all de niggers would sing back to him, an' hallo, a kiner shoutin' soun'.
> *(Federal 1941: I, 199)*

The slaves sang mostly in the fields, and many of their field songs were solo hollers. Singers in Livingston County, Alabama, told Harold Courlander that

> calls and cries were used in the old days in the corn and cotton fields, in the woods, and on the rivers, wherever men and women worked. There were calls to communicate messages of all kinds—to

bring people in from the fields, to summon them to work, to attract the attention of a girl in the distance, to signal hunting dogs, or simply to make one's presence known.

(Courlander 1963: 81)

The Holler as Melodic Passage

Wherever found and however sung, whether signal or recreational song, the holler was to white ears not only moving but strange. Early observers would often write, in effect, "I cannot give you the least idea of it" (Epstein 1963: 206). Both timing and pitch were more flexible than what these observers were used to. As one put it, black American voices "have a peculiar quality, and their intonations and delicate variations cannot be reproduced on paper" (Leigh 1921: 156). These difficulties make the holler an excellent music with which to begin the study of melody; the motionless black dots of our regular notation cannot be used, and we are free to focus on what I've called the essence of the melodic experience: passage.

For over nine hundred years Western Europe has written its music as if melody were a series of fixed pitches, which just isn't so. The system works because the series is a kind of shorthand providing information to a performer who already has a feeling for the proper style; what we write is only half of a double system, the visual cues for behavior learned by ear. Within the tradition this system is highly efficient. Outside the tradition, where there's no learned behavior to cue—or rather, where the learned behavior is different—these visual cues are apt to be misleading. In short, our notes don't sound the way they look.

Our system derives from the work of a teacher of music from Paris who spent some of his professional career in Arezzo, Italy, and is known as Guido d'Arezzo. Schools in his time, the first half of the 11th century, were run by the Catholic Church to train young boys to sing the music of the services. Other subjects were a secondary consideration; reading Latin was emphasized, of course, for that was the language of the songs they sang, but understanding Latin was not.

The boys traditionally learned their songs by rote. Though classes were small (usually under ten), this method was slow. Guido found a way for them to sight-read music, a system of both verbal and visual cues by means of which he could start them out on a new piece of music and they could finish singing it on their own the first time through.*

The verbal cues—different syllables assigned one to each note of the scale—are known today as solfège and can be heard in the "shape-note" singing of our rural south and southwest (see Chapter 16). In our art-music tradition new verbal cues have replaced the old ones, but the system itself remains the same: syllables are assigned to the various pitches used in the musical tradition; the melodic relationships between these pitched syllables are learned through drills; and at the same time, a correspondence is established between these pitched syllables and a written system of notation.

As Guido described the written part of his system, which has also survived,

> each sound, however often it may be repeated in a melody, is found always in its own row [in the form of a *punctum*, a large, square dot]. And in order that you may better distinguish these rows, lines are drawn close together, and some rows of sounds occur on the lines themselves, others in the intervening spaces.
>
> *(Translated in Strunk 1965: 118-119; my insert)*

His *puncta* are with us today as the large, oval dots forming the heads of many of our musical notes. Though he did not invent this symbol, he promoted its use over the use of straight and curved lines for showing the flow of a melody. Today we notate

---

*Pope John XIX (1024-1033) heard of Guido's work and brought him to Rome for a demonstration (in 1028, according to tradition). As Guido tells it, the Pope tried the system himself, studying Guido's rules and then successfully singing from Guido's notation without first hearing the tune (Strunk 1965: 122).

a melodic sound of changing pitch in his way, as a series of *puncta*. His other written symbols, the lines "drawn close together," have come down to us as the familiar five-line musical staff.

If carriers of the black American holler tradition were to write their songs in Guido's system—or any other way, for that matter—they would still sing the music in their sliding style. The art of the holler, like every musical art, is unwritten knowledge. No written system can transmit it to people outside the tradition. Every musical notation ever invented has this limitation. A notation that has lasted several centuries, as ours has, must suffer the added limitation of not being able to convey even music it once served, whenever the unwritten tradition of that music no longer survives.

The pictorial notation of Figures 4 and 5 belongs to no particular musical tradition. I designed it to convey the outline of a melody accurately enough to support discussion and directly enough to communicate with readers lacking technical musical training. It relies on two conventions already well established among Westerners: time moves, as in reading words, from left to right across the page and line by line from the top of the page to the bottom; and within each line higher pitch is shown by higher placement on the page—that is, placement closer to its upper edge.

In the school-music style shown in Figure 4 on p. 42, (1) the melodic line characteristically shifts abruptly from one level of sound to another; (2) each level receives about as much emphasis as any other; and (3) the levels emphasized are close together in pitch. In the holler style shown on p. 44 as Figure 5, (1) the melodic line characteristically slides from pitch to pitch instead of shifting abruptly, and instead of levels of pitch one often hears the melody bending back and forth within a narrow pitch range; (2) only a few levels of pitch (typically not more than three, as here) receive emphasis; and (3) the emphasized levels are far apart. In this particular holler the melodic line seems to hang on its three emphasized levels of

Fig. 4

Fig. 5

pitch like Christmas trimmings on the branches of a fir tree.

White American school music serves a melodic preference developed among the several educated classes of 19th-century

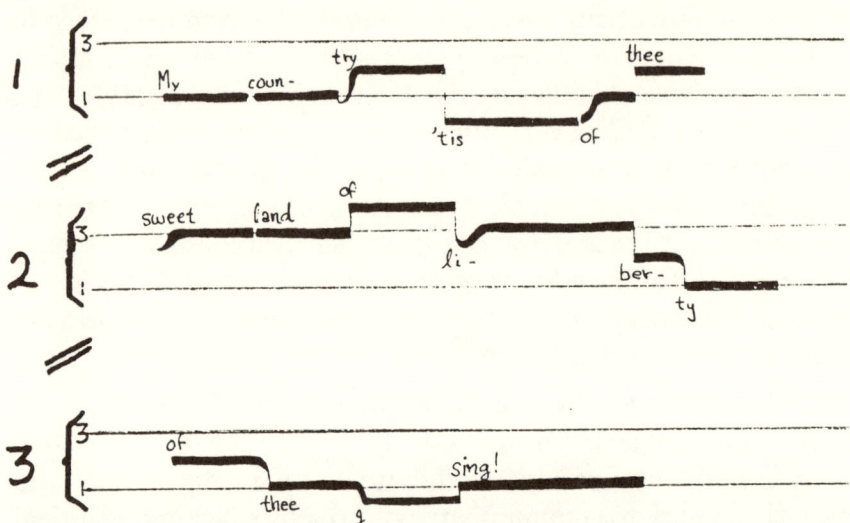

FIGURE 4. *MY COUNTRY 'TIS OF THEE.* This figure represents my own singing of the first part of this song in a style learned in white schools of northeastern America.

Read the lines of melody from left to right and one after another from top to bottom. Heavy horizontal parts of the melodic line represent unchanging pitch; heavy curving parts, changing pitch. The higher the visual level within each line, the higher the pitch. The thin parts of the melodic line do not represent sound but provide visual connections where there is a feeling of melodic connection.

The lightly drawn horizontal lines accompanying each line of melody are for reference, providing each line with the same pitch frame. The number at the left end of each of these lightly drawn horizontals gives the pitch level of the line according to the Western octave series, as explained on pp. 45-46.

Melodies in school-music style characteristically move abruptly from one level of pitch to another, as in this example; the levels are close together, as here, and each of them is emphasized to approximately the same degree; sliding pitch is rare. Compare these characteristics with those of the holler in Figure 5.

Western Europe. It was people from those classes, and American carriers of their traditions, who reported on the field holler in the 19th century. Trained in a melodic style of fixed pitch levels, they found the very different style of black American melody hard to describe and impossible to notate.*

It's not hard to play a holler on the piano, it's impossible. Sliding and bending of the line occur often and at the most important places. In the holler they are not auxiliary effects—as, for example, the slide is in Western opera—but main notes. In both the holler and the blues moving pitches carry the heart of the melody. Now a term frequently heard in reference to melodic moments in black American melody which seem strange to white American ears is "blue note." Sometimes the melodic moment is an unchanging sound pitched at a level not used in music of the Western European tradition. More often, however, the term refers to a sound of changing pitch, a brief effect most easily grasped—or at least verbalized—by carriers of the Western European tradition as a strange but unchanging note.

Despite the sliding and bending so basic to its nature, each holler considered as a whole does not slide around: it creates a stable framework of pitch levels to which it ties itself firmly. This is what one would expect given the basic fact, discussed in Chapter 3, that a melody reaches its audience (among whom we must include the performers themselves) by moving in a somewhat predictable manner. Above and beyond obvious predictables like timbre and a general division into phrases,

---

*They also found it hard to accept on an equal footing with white concert music. It moved them, yes, but it remained the music of slaves, of lesser people. Thus a small choir from an all-black university in Tennessee, the Fisk Jubilee Singers, met coolness and indifference when they first introduced the Negro spiritual to Northern concert audiences in 1871. Ticket sales and donations provided barely enough to keep the group going. They did keep going and eventually won international fame because white missionaries and missionary church organizations gave them continual support, and because George L. White, a white school teacher from Cadiz, New York, had worked with them for years to suppress dialect and to make their harmonies and timbre conform to the expectations of the white concert stage (Marsh 1880: 8-32; Work 1940: 14-15).

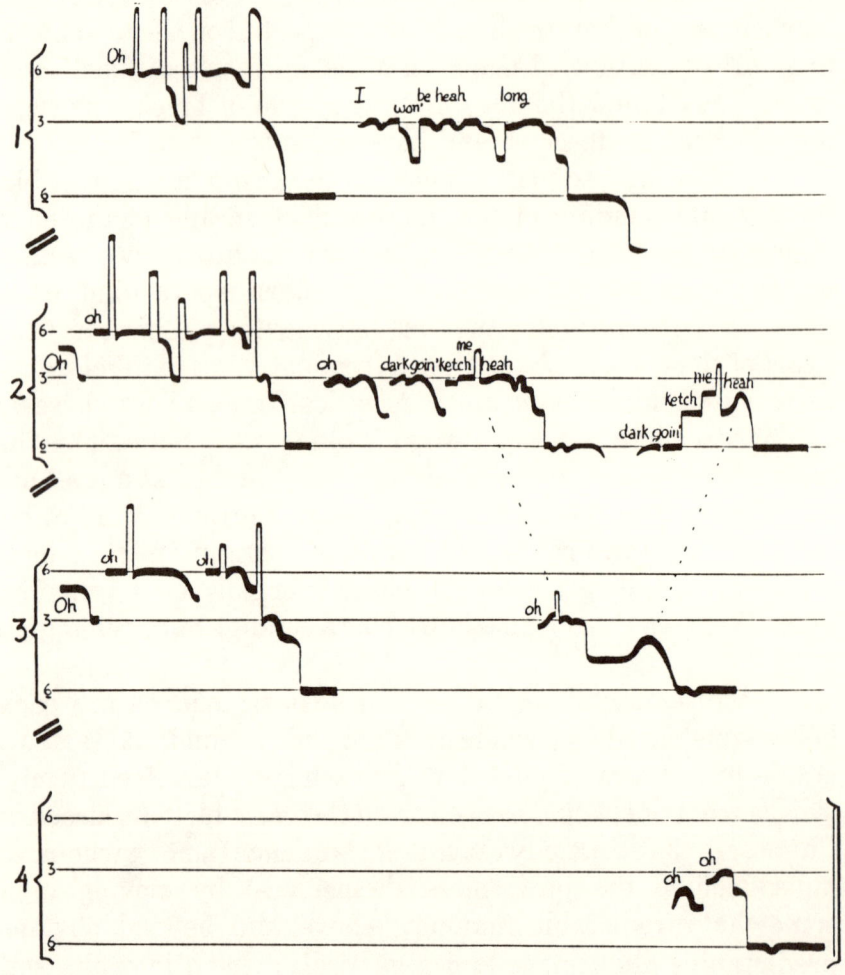

FIGURE 5: *ARWHOOLIE.* This figure represents a complete performance of the holler Arwhoolie *by Thomas J. Marshall at Edwards, Mississippi, as recorded by John Lomax in 1939 at the Southern Christian Institute of Mount Beulah College, where Marshall was a student (Library of Congress AAFS-L8: side 1, band 6).*

For a general explanation of the notation see the caption for Figure 4. Since parts of Marshall's melody seem to be variations of other parts, I have spaced the phrases so that variants appear together in vertical alignment. (The last phrase of line 3 is aligned midway

melody captures our minds by moving *in a direction;* pitch makes sense from moment to moment because it is moving away from, or returning to, an established level.

The Western Octave Series

The established pitch levels in the examples drawn in Figures 4 and 5 are marked by thin horizontal lines. The number standing at the left of each line identifies the pitch of the line according to a simple system used by Western musicians. I shall explain this system in the next few paragraphs because I plan to use it in the rest of this book.

All the pitch levels we need for a discussion of any music in the Western tradition are contained in the first musical phrase of *Joy to the World,* a tune so convenient that I will use it despite the specific religious content of the words. A tune more neutral in connotation would be welcome were it also as handy and as well known.

The first phrase of *Joy to the World* contains eight words, each on a different level of pitch. Here is the series with the levels numbered in descending order:

"Joy to the world, the Lord is come."
  8 7 6   5   4   3 2   1

---

between the last two phrases of line 2 because it seems to combine both of them.) This piece uses the tune-formula technique explained on pp. 51-53.

Holler melodies characteristically slide from one level of pitch to another, as in this example, rather than shift abruptly as in Figure 4. (The several abrupt and brief upward leaps are yodeling effects that do not oppose this sliding quality in performance as they seem to do in the drawing.) Only three widely spaced levels of pitch are emphasized, which is typical of the holler. Moments of changing pitch are plentiful, which is also typical, and include not only slides but also passages in which the voice bends the melodic line back and forth within a narrow range. Compare these characteristics with those of white American school music shown in Figure 4.

Strangely enough, note 8 and note 1 are not completely different: one is higher than the other in pitch, to be sure, yet somehow they are the same. If you sing the first phrase of *Joy to the World* starting on a rather high note, you will find that when you reach the word "come" you can substitute the word "joy" for it and begin the phrase over again right there, starting at that level of pitch and going on down.

In other words, the series of notes we use for traditional Western song, when arranged by level of pitch from highest to lowest, is a repeating series: after seven notes we seem to arrive at the note on which we started even though we are on a much lower level of pitch; the eighth note seems identical with the first. This apparent identity makes it possible for people to sing a tune together even though some sing high and some sing low.

Because the series repeats at every eighth note, I have decided to call it the "Western octave series," "octave" being an English noun derived from the Latin adjective *octavus*, which means "eighth." The noun "octave" names both the note that is eighth in the series, starting from any point, and the distance from any level of pitch to the pitch next above or below which sounds identical. Figure 6 on p. 48 shows twenty-two levels of pitch constituting three consecutive statements of the series and representing the total range of pitch used by the average Western church choir. Only the sopranos would feel comfortable on the highest notes, only the basses on the lowest ones.

Fig. 6

Note a most important fact: the levels of pitch are not evenly spaced apart; the distance from 8 to 7 and from 4 to 3 is half as great as that between any other two neighboring levels.* It may not be easy to hear the difference when you sing the first phrase of *Joy to the World*, but the following simple experiment proves that it's there: (1) sing the first phrase of *Joy to the World* several times out loud so that the pitch levels become temporarily established in your memory; (2) im-

*There are other, more subtle differences in the spacing of the series, but they need not be discussed here to make the point that concerns us.

mediately sing the phrase once again starting one level lower *in the same series*—on 7, that is, instead of on 8. The tune sounds really strange; in fact you may not be able to perform the experiment. If you find it hard to keep your bearings, use the piano: the white keys are tuned to the Western octave series, and the first phrase of *Joy to the World* is played by going from right to left striking every white key you come to until you have struck eight. You will notice that you have to start in the right place (one of the keys marked by an arrow in Figure 7 on p. 50) or the tune won't sound right.

Fig. 7

This exercise demonstrates the irregular spacing of the sound since, were every level of pitch in the Western octave series equally spaced apart, one could start the tune at any point in the series and it would sound fine. The levels are not equidistant, and so it matters very much just where in the series one starts a tune.

It's as if you were standing on a ladder. Were the rungs equidistant, your hand would find a rung at the same distance above your head no matter on which rung you stood. Were the rungs not equidistant, your hand would find the rung above your head at different distances when you stood on different rungs. Substitute levels of pitch for rungs, and singing for reaching up with your hand, and the metaphor of the ladder describes how a melody fits the Western octave series. Each tune has its own characteristic set of "reaches" and must be placed on the right rung for the set to fit the ladder.

The horizontal lines that frame the melodies of Figures 4 and 5 carry identifying numbers to their left. These numbers stand for levels of pitch in the Western octave series. *My Country 'Tis of Thee* moves around and between levels 1 and 3; *Arwhoolie* moves around and between levels 6̲, 3, and 6. The numbers are different not only because the melodies have a different amount of distance from their highest to their lowest points, but also because the arrangement of the spacing between these points is different: that is, each tune emphasizes a different part of the Western octave series.

$\overline{8}$ - Joy ⬅ [treble clef, sharp, high note]
$\overline{7}$ - to

$\overline{6}$ - the

$\overline{5}$ - world,

$\overline{4}$ - the
$\overline{3}$ - Lord

$\overline{2}$ - is

$\overline{1}$ - come! = 8 - Joy ⬅ [treble clef, sharp, note]
                   7 - to

                   6 - the

                   5 - world,

                   4 - the
                   3 - Lord

                   2 - is

[bass clef, sharp, note] ➡ 1 - come! = $\underline{8}$ - Joy
                                    $\underline{7}$ - to

                                    $\underline{6}$ - the

                                    $\underline{5}$ - world,

                                    $\underline{4}$ - the
                                    $\underline{3}$ - Lord

                                    $\underline{2}$ - is

                  [bass clef, sharp, low note] ➡ $\underline{1}$ - come!

One further point about the Western octave series: it can be moved around. Pitch level 1 of the series can be any pitch that feels comfortable; once it is chosen, however, the pitches to either side must take their proper spacing or it will not sound like pitch level 1. A singer who knew both the holler style and the school-music style, in other words, could start *Arwhoolie* and *My Country 'Tis of Thee* on the same pitch level; the spacing of the neighboring pitch levels would be different in each case, reflecting the fact that the starting pitch was in each case a different member of the Western octave series. This is exactly what happens when an accompanist who plays piano by ear fits

FIGURE 6: THE WESTERN OCTAVE SERIES. *The first phrase of* Joy to the World *contains all seven levels of pitch used in our older traditional Western songs, the eighth level being recognized by Western ears as a repetition of the first even though it surely is not the same pitch. The Latin word for "eighth,"* octavus, *provides the name for this special distance at which two levels of pitch sound identical. We call it the "octave." By extension I call the sequence of pitch levels making up the octave used in our traditional song "the Western octave series."*

The three octaves of Figure 6 span the full range of pitch levels sung by the average church choir, from the highest "joy," which only sopranos can reach comfortably, to the lowest "come," which is strictly for basses. The numeral notation distinguishes octaves above and below the central one by the placement of a horizontal stroke above or below the numbers. For those who read music I have suggested in staff notation a specific pitch range for this example. One may, of course, place the central octave at any level of pitch.

The members of the Western octave series are not spaced equally apart. The average person singing the first phrase of Joy to the World *is probably not aware of making leaps of different sizes from note to note, but that is what happens. The irregular musical spacing offers a wealth of melodic possibilities we would not have if every note had the same relationship to its neighbors. I've shown this irregular musical spacing visually: the distance between levels 8 and 7 and levels 4 and 3 is half as great as the distance between every other adjacent pair of levels in the series. Actually there are many more subtle differences in the spacing of the series, but these two suffice to make the point.*

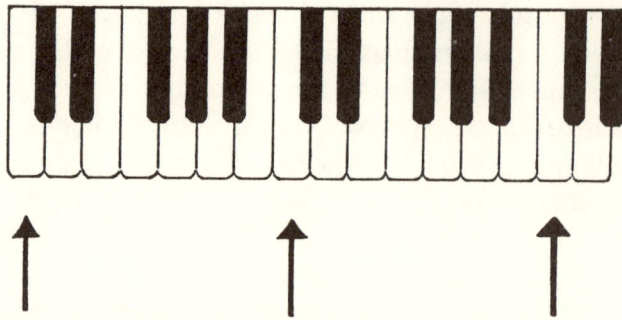

FIGURE 7: THE PIANO KEYBOARD. *The earliest of our keyboards contained only the levers we know today as the white keys of the piano (plus one extra lever I will discuss later). The high-sounding end of the keyboard was on the right, as it is today. Then, as now, these levers produced the pitch levels of a single Western octave series.*

If you start at the right place among the white keys of the piano you can play any of the older traditional Western songs, because the Western octave series sounded by the white keys embodies all the pitch relationships these songs require. (Arrows mark three places an octave apart from each other where the tune Joy to the World *begins; because the Western octave series is a repeating series, the full piano keyboard offers more than one place on which to start a tune.)*

If you start at the wrong place among the white keys of the piano, the tune you are trying to play will sound wrong. The pitch relationships of the Western octave series are irregular, as you saw in Figure 6: every level of pitch is not the same musical distance from its neighbor. Therefore to move a melody a little bit left or right on the keyboard not only raises or lowers its general pitch but also changes the kind of pattern one hears.

People have different kinds of voices; their best notes are not the same. A keyboard player needs to be able to pitch a tune differently for different singers, and this is not possible when the keyboard offers only one Western octave series. The player needs a keyboard with enough choices on it to allow the correct musical distances to be found starting from any level of pitch. The black keys of the piano solve this problem. They are the levers added one by one over the years to provide more and more choices. (Even the earliest keyboards had one additional

the song a singer wants to sing to the best notes the singer has: the pitch levels of the best notes cannot be changed, so the accompanist moves the Western octave series up or down on the piano until the melody lies on those best notes. (Moving the series is called "changing the key.")

Having described *Arwhoolie* in terms of the Western octave series, I must point out that it really doesn't fit that series: the melodic activity of the song does not observe the distribution of large and small spaces shown in Figure 6; it differs from that distribution in a small but consistent way. The Western octave series is in fact only one of many possible series, and some of these other possibilities may be encountered in "Western" music. The musical culture of America, like that of every other nation in the world, is plural.

The Tune Formula

Music reproduced in performance is said to have been composed. Music invented during performance is said to have been improvised. Live music is always a mixture of the two. That is to say, a composition is never reproduced without some invention, and an improvisation is never invented without some reproduction. For example, the "serious" or "classical" music of Western Europe is almost entirely a tradition of pieces reproduced in performance—of compositions, in a word; yet our classical performers improvise to some extent in matters of speed, timbre, loudness, and decoration. Jazz, on the other hand, is an improvised tradition; yet an underlying arch of precomposed material—successions of harmony, rhythmic figures, melody—guide every performance. And every jazz soloist relies heavily on familiar melodic fragments for material

---

lever allowing the player to play in a second Western octave series pitched three "white" keys higher than the main series. This lever survives as the key furthest to the right in the group of three black keys you see on the modern keyboard.)

with which to build an apparently "free" improvisation. In short, the difference between composition and improvisation is one of degree.

Harold Courlander, who collected folk songs from southern black Americans, felt that the holler was an improvisation,

> a completely free music in which every sound, line, and phrase is exploited for itself in any fashion that appeals to the crier.
> *(Courlander 1963: 82)*

Obviously I consider that somewhat overstated. Most of us are only moderately gifted; we are not able to invent everything we perform, but must rely on material established earlier. The "fashion that appeals to the crier" will almost always be an established one.

Mary Shelley, famous as the inventor of the scientist Frankenstein and his monster, learned from personal experience that complete originality does not exist. In a preface to her famous horror story she made the point particularly well:

> The Hindus give the world an elephant to support it, but they make the elephant stand upon a tortoise. Invention, it must be humbly admitted, does not consist in creating out of void, but out of chaos. . . . It can give form to dark, shapeless substances, but it cannot bring into being the substance itself.
> *(Shelley 1957: 7)*

The substance of the holler comes from the tradition in which the singer grew up, from earlier hollers by that singer and by others, and from borrowings outside the tradition. A little substance goes a long way in this kind of music. The artistry lies more in decoration and in rearrangements of the sequence of phrases than in the major invention of new material.

Sometimes the rearrangements follow a grammatical plan known as a "tune formula," not only in the holler but in many other kinds of music.

Formulas abound in storytelling. A Muganda from East Africa typically ends his tale with, "And that is what I saw." An American Ballad singer often starts his song with "Come all ye." Fairy tales begin, "Once upon a time." Everyday conversation is full of formulas. They serve to introduce, to conclude, to signal the nature of the encounter, and so forth. The Hungarian composer Béla Bartók spent his last years in America and could never get used to the fact that when we say, "How are you?" we often don't really want to know.

In a tune formula, one bit of melody is for beginnings — perhaps only beginnings of a major sort—while another bit of melody is for lesser beginnings; other bits of melody stand for various degrees of pausing; still other bits, for endings. From piece to piece and from one tradition to the next the bits differ but the principle stays the same: to shape a complete melody with a given set of materials but without reproducing a given composition. (Variation, by way of contrast, accepts a given composition and decorates it.)

I call the tune formula a grammatical plan because musicians use it the way a writer uses grammatical structure: to give the thing being created a recognizable shape. The device is common in the chanting of people all over the world, and we will meet it in the music of the Roman Catholic Church discussed in the next chapter; but it survives to some extent in all music because in all music the arrival of a major pause is signalled by one or more effects that carriers of the tradition recognize as standard endings. (Indeed, I think the universal presence of ending formulas is a fair argument for the hypothesis that the tune formula is older than the fixed tune; but this, of course, can never be more than speculation.)

In some hollers we find the tune formula in its full form, as in *I Don' Know You* (Figure 8 on pp. 55–59), shown as the black American folk singer and concert artist Huddie Ledbetter sang it for Frederick Ramsey, Jr., in New York City in 1948. This

Fig. 8

FIGURE 8: *I DON' KNOW YOU*. *This represents a complete performance of the holler of this title by Huddie Ledbetter, as recorded by Frederick Ramsey, Jr., in 1948 in Ledbetter's New York City apartment (Folkways FA 2941: side 2, band 2).*

For a general explanation of the notation see the caption for Figure 4. An interesting feature of this particular example is that Ledbetter alters the pitch frame halfway through the piece: in stanza 4 he lowers the lowest level of the frame, tentatively at first (end of line 10) and then clearly and decisively (line 14). Most of the world's melody gives us a feeling of forward motion by establishing fixed levels of pitch as reference points; but these reference points can be changed from time to time within a piece (how often depends upon the tradition). Such changes are called "modulations."

Ledbetter uses the tune-formula technique explained on page 53. The fragments of the formula and their significance are shown at the bottom of the music, and melodic phrases corresponding to each fragment are in vertical alignment with it. One reads the music as in the previous examples, from left to right and line by line from the top to the bottom, ignoring the occasionally wide gaps imposed by the process of alignment.

Two main characteristics of the black American holler set it apart from all examples of black African melody I know and are abundantly evident in this classic example: the wide spacing of the emphasized levels of pitch, and the sliding, both from one level of pitch to another and back and forth within a very narrow pitch range (as at the end of line 12). Clearly a concept of melody broad enough to cover more than the style of Western European art music cannot be tied exclusively to patterns created by fixed pitches.

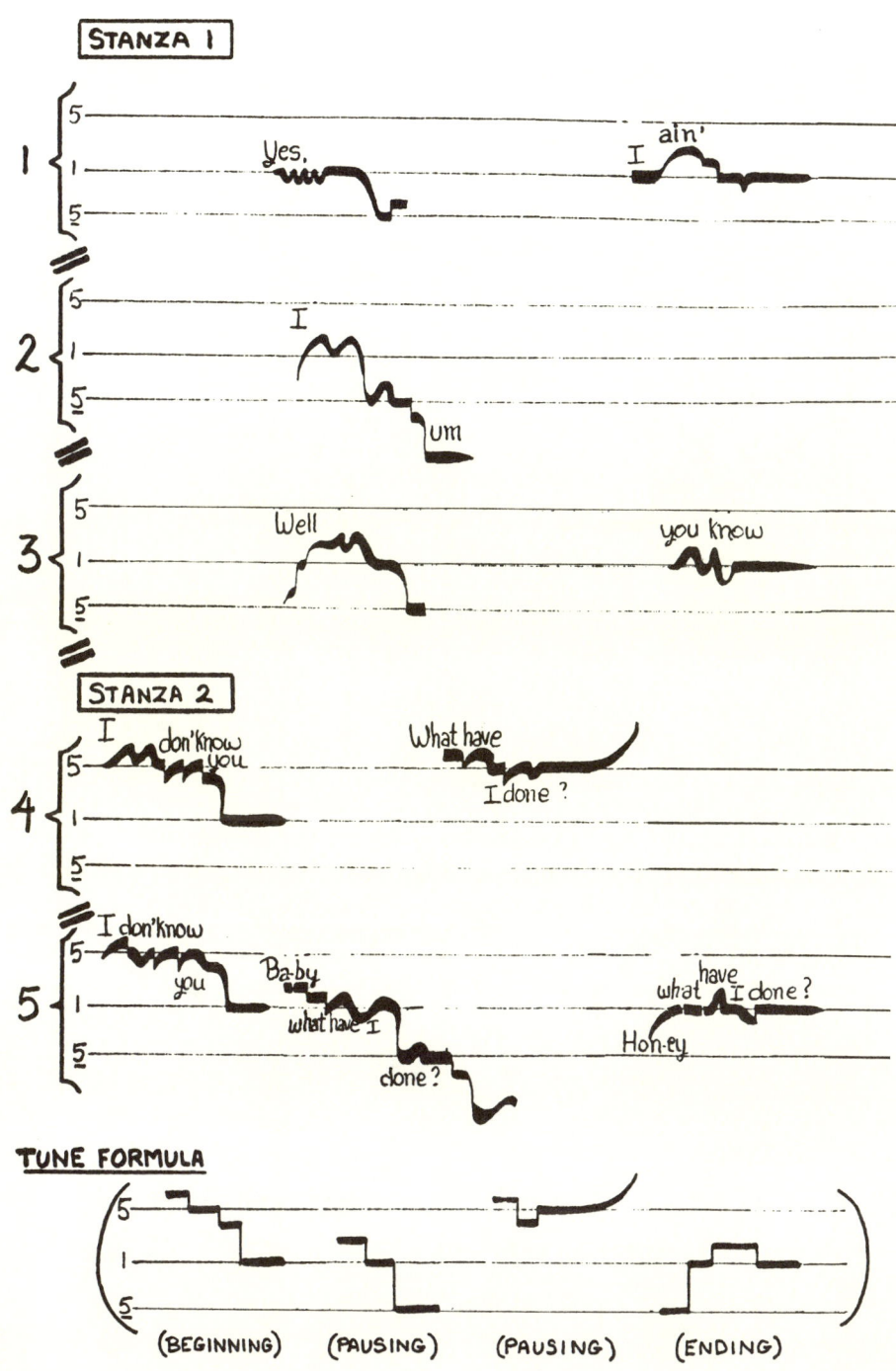

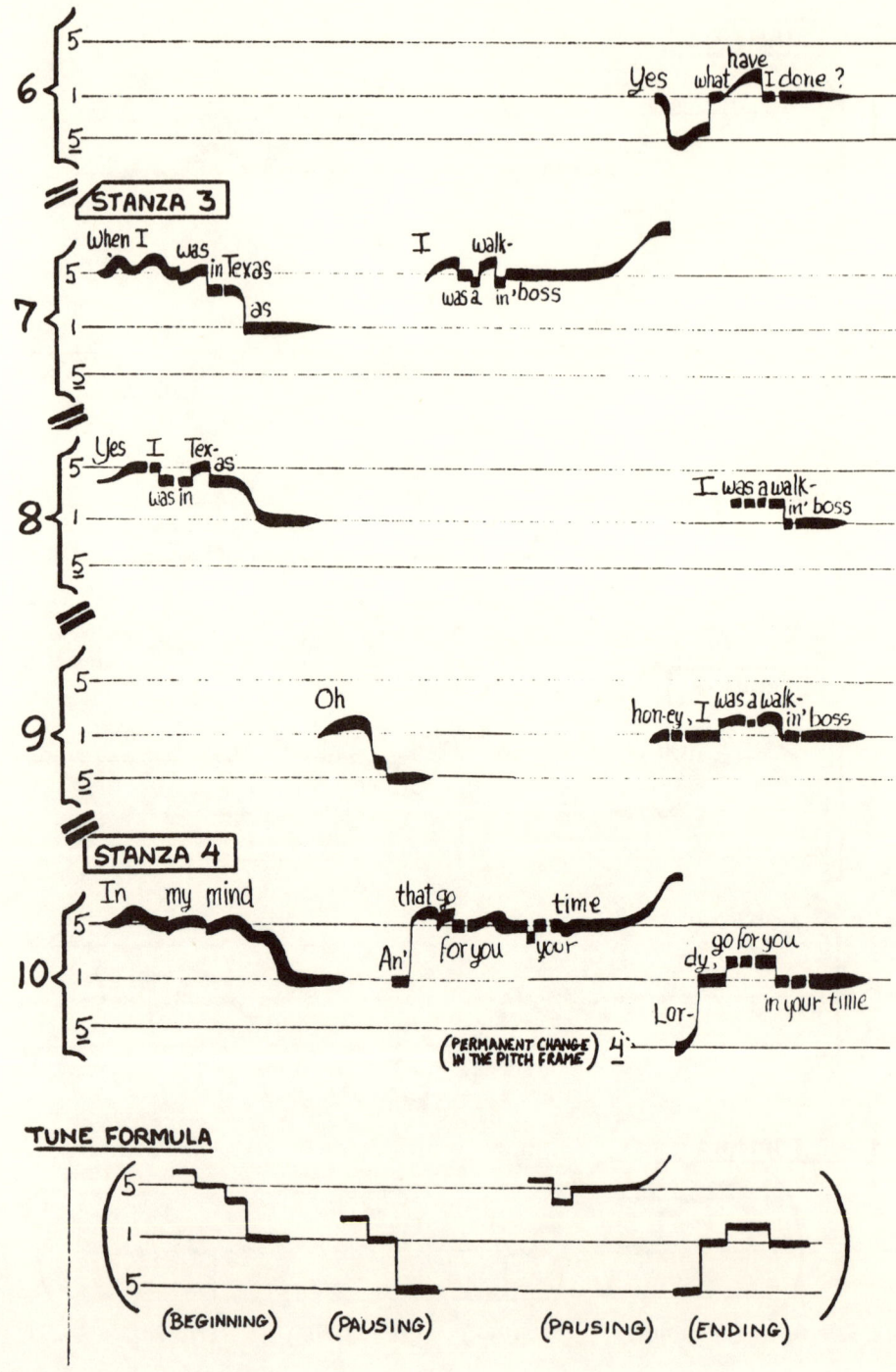

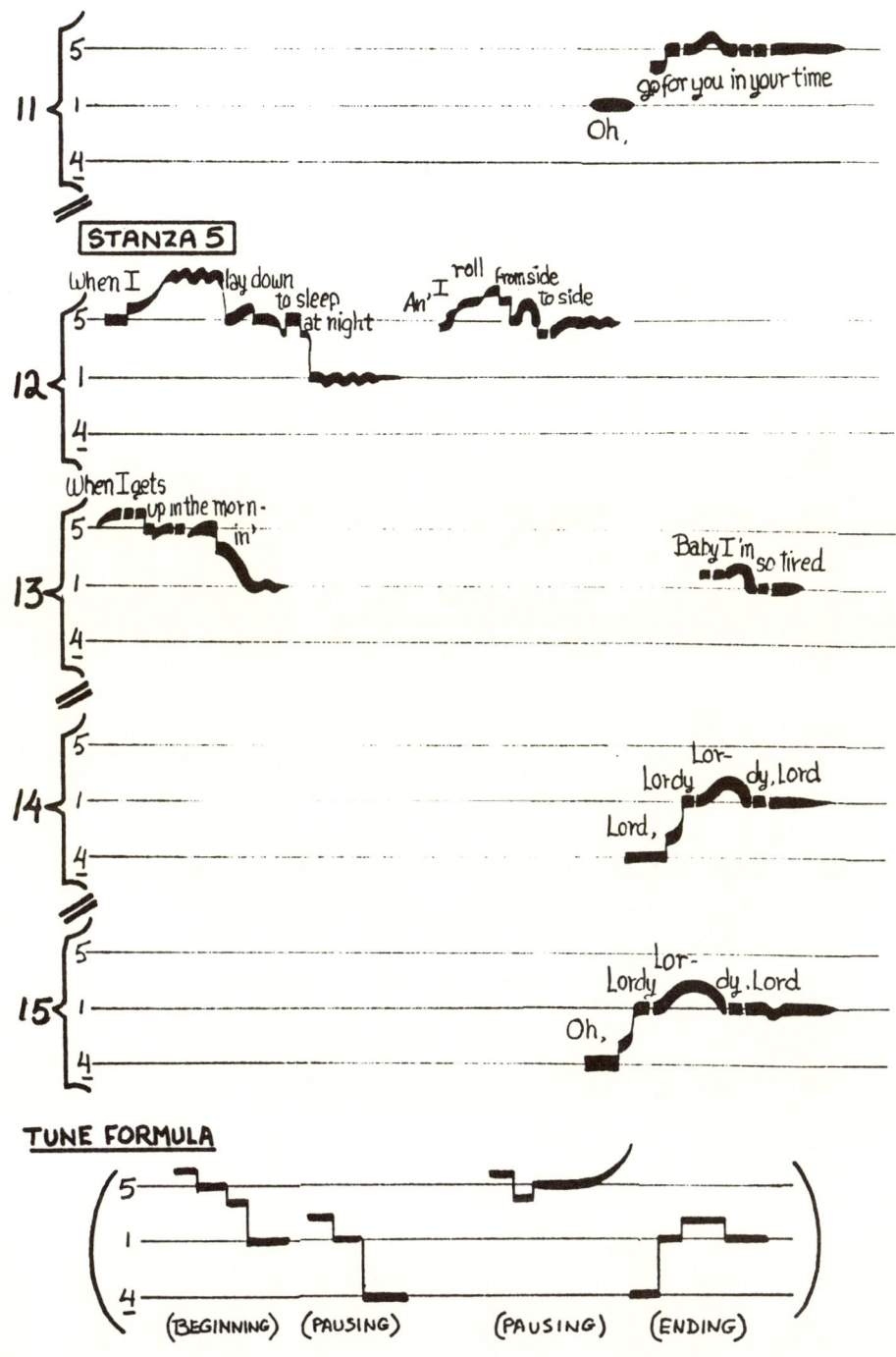

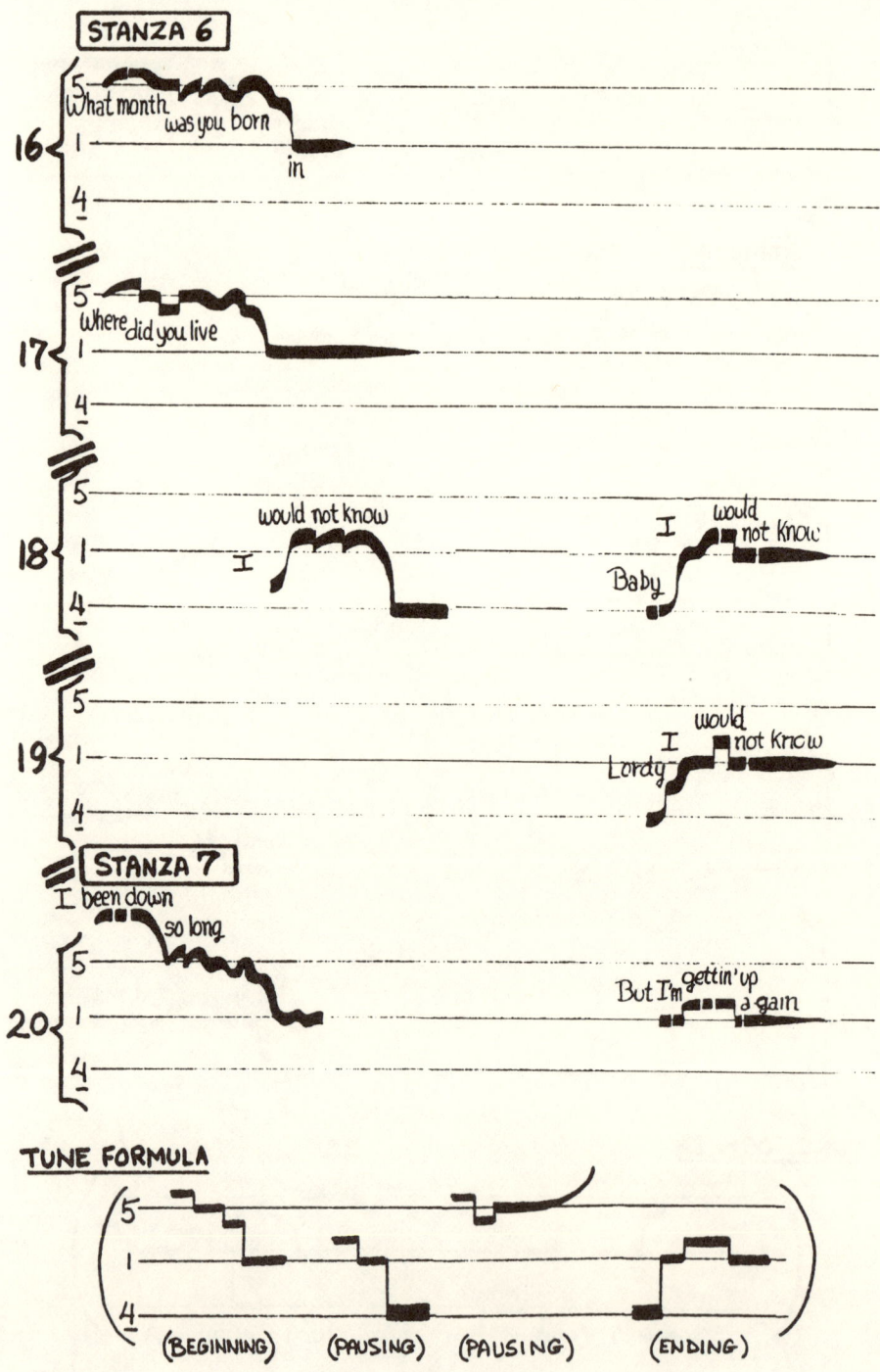

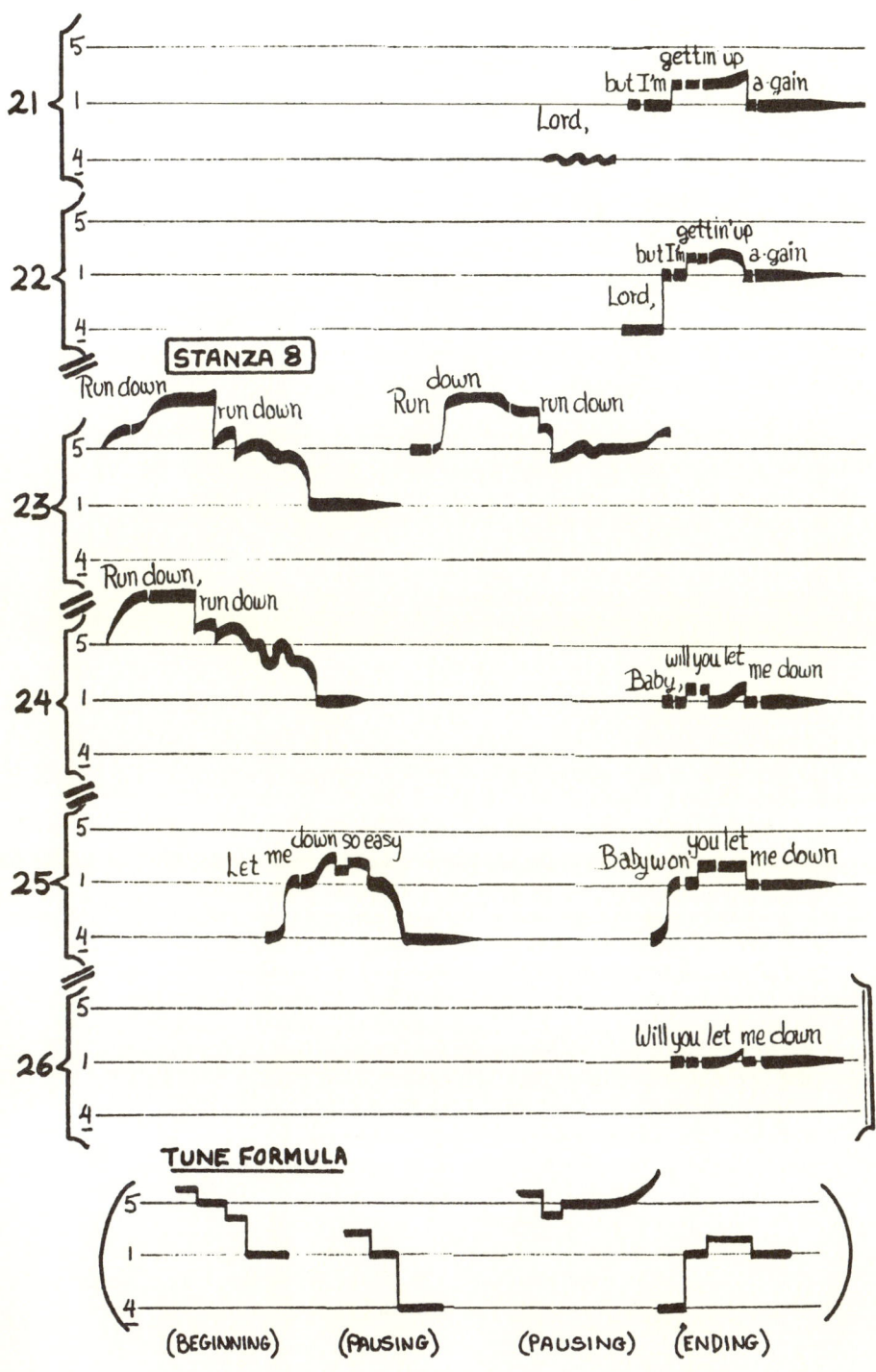

recording session was the first time Ledbetter had ever sung for a reel-to-reel machine, and thus the first time he had ever been free of the three-minute time limit imposed by the earlier system of cutting an aluminum disc. The freedom had a creative effect, as had the earlier limitation.* Ledbetter sang songs he had never recorded before, among them *I Don' Know You*. He said to Ramsey after singing it, "That's a holler. You ain' never heard that" (Folkways FA 2941: side 2, band 2). He may have meant it wasn't available on any of his recordings,† or simply that he had never sung it for Ramsey. I tend to think he meant he had never sung that holler that way before.

The looseness of the text itself conveys the looseness of the musical construction. The words are evocative, their meaning not always clear—vehicles for sad, private thoughts:

> 1.
> Yes, I ain'.
> I–um.
> Well, you know.

---

*The Appalachian banjo player Dock Boggs recently told Mike Seeger how it was to record within such limits back in 1927. He makes it clear that on a creative musician the restriction had a creative effect:

> Well, I practiced an awful lot, and I even took a watch and timed myself, 2 minutes and 40 seconds, and if my song wasn't hardly long enough for to go the 2 minutes and 40 seconds, why I'd alternate a verse. Just pick it open and not sing. . . . pick over a piece if I didn't have hardly enough to make a record, 'till I'd make it come out to a 2 minute and 40 second record.
> *(Folkways FH 5458: side 1, band 6)*

† In 1935, when Huddie Ledbetter came out of the Angola State Prison Farm in Louisiana and began his concert tours with John Lomax, folk music was a field for scholars and archivists, and for performers who simply played locally. Ledbetter became one of the first nationally known folk artists. He was an electrifying performer who offered many kinds of folk song, but the public was not yet ready for his brand of popular entertainment. Born sometime around 1888, he died in 1949 without ever having had a large following.

Like many folk singers Ledbetter, widely known as "Leadbelly," was a composer. His song *Irene, Goodnight* is still widely sung. Some of his pieces, like the present example, were as much improvisations as compositions.

2.
I don' know you.
What have I done?
I don't know you.
Baby, what have I done?
Honey, what have I done?
Yes, what have I done?

3.
When I was in Texas
I was a walkin' boss.
Yes, I was in Texas;
I was a walkin' boss.
Oh, honey, I was a walkin' boss.

4.
In my mind—
An' that go for you in your time,
Lordy, go for you in your time;
Oh, go for you in your time.

5.
When I lay down to sleep at night
An' I roll from side to side,
When I gets up in the mornin',
Baby, I'm so tired!
Lordy, lordy, lordy, lord,
Oh, lordy, lordy, lord!

6.
What month was you born in?
Where did you live?
I would not know,
Baby, I would not know,
Lordy, I would not know.

7.
I been down so long,
But I'm gettin' up again,
Lord, but I'm gettin' up again,
Lord, but I'm gettin' up again.

8.
Run down, run down!
Run down, run down!
Run down, run down!
Baby, will you let me down?
Let me down so easy!
Baby, won' you let me down?
Will you let me down?

In a general way the music is strophic; that is, the melody repeats, roughly speaking, for each stanza of the text. It is a flexible repetition. A musical phrase repeated in one stanza may not even appear in another, or be stated there only once; and even the repetitions of phrases are masked by variation. The strophic effect comes through because every stanza follows the same tune formula.

Figure 8 on the preceding pages gives the melody in pictorial notation following principles discussed earlier (pp. 41, 45). The melodic bit Ledbetter uses for beginning is always placed at the left end of the pitch frame. The two melodic bits he uses for pausing are always placed in the middle of the pitch frame. The ending bit is always at the right. The variation he gives to each melodic bit can be easily seen by comparing all the beginnings, or pauses, or endings; for each kind of material lies in its own column. At the bottom of each column is a skeletal outline of the melodic bit in generalized form.

The similarity of this vocal style to that of Figure 5 is clear: in both we find a widely spaced pitch frame and a melodic line as often curved as straight. The curves, moreover, come as often as not at moments of emphasis; they are main "notes," whether or not our standard musical notation system can recognize them as such. *Arwhoolie* and *I Don' Know You* are typical hollers warning us that the essence of melody is not pitch, or a series of pitches, but *passage*: motion in a direction. To define that direction a melody establishes as it flows fixed levels of pitch to and from which it seems to move. And to enhance that motion a melody presents recognizable repetitions of material—whole phrases, fragments of a tune formula, certain sustained tones—which intrigue the listening mind with suggestions of predictability.

The next chapter discovers these principles and others in a music not related at all to the holler: Gregorian Chant, the ancient song of the Roman Catholic Church and the earliest recorded layer of our Western European melodic tradition.

5
Gregorian Chant

Gregorian Chant is the commonly accepted name for the official song of the medieval Roman Catholic Church, an institution that dominated Western Europe from Poland to Spain and from England to the southern tip of Italy. Indeed, the term "Western Europe" signifies the lands so dominated, just as the term "Eastern Europe" signifies the lands dominated since the Middle Ages by the Eastern Orthodox Catholic Church. We might with all good reason call the subject of this chapter "Western Catholic Chant," but tradition has attached to it the name of Pope Gregory I (590-604), who concerned himself deeply with the sung ritual of Roman Catholics.*

The repertoire of Gregorian Chant is immense. In a month of continuous singing one could never perform all the music preserved in manuscripts, not to mention all the thousands of ritual words never written down with music because they were chanted to a few easily remembered melodic patterns. This chapter will not deal with such a vast amount of material but will make just three points: first, the roots of Gregorian Chant lie in the synagogue of the Jews; second, the music of Gregorian Chant incorporates many of the techniques we have already examined in the black American field holler; and third, Gregorian melody runs in families—that is, certain tunes share

---

*The earliest manuscript source for this tradition identifies the Pope simply as "Gregory," and it remains uncertain to this day among scholars whether Gregory I (590-604) or Gregory II (715-731) was meant (Hucke 1980: 444).

one limited set of behavior patterns, other tunes share another limited set of behavior patterns, and so forth. We call each limited set a "mode," and to say that more than one mode exists in most of the world's music is probably no exaggeration. Modes are pools of restricted material from which the song makers draw what they need to make their songs—pools of what Mary Shelley called "substance," to which the inventiveness of the creative person gives form (see p. 52).

Jewish Roots

Christ grew up in the Jewish faith, and his first followers were Jews. To them he was the Redeemer prophesied in Jewish tradition; taking his message to the Temple and the synagogues they sought to convince other Jews. When Simon Peter began to convert Gentiles, he shocked the other Apostles (Bible [1611]: Acts 10, 11). If early Christians thought of themselves as Jews, they must have worshipped with Jewish music.

There were two kinds of Jewish music. The older tradition was in the Temple at Jerusalem, where trained instrumentalists and singers performed.* Then in 586 B.C. Nebuchadnezzar

*The following Biblical account describes a cleansing ceremony in the Temple in 724 B.C. Note the minimal role of the congregation:

> And he set the Levites in the house of the Lord with cymbals, with psalteries, and with harps, according to the commandment of David, and of Gad the king's seer, and Nathan the prophet: for so was the commandment of the Lord by his prophets.
> And the Levites stood with the instruments of David, and the priests with the trumpets.
> And Hezekiah commanded to offer the burnt offering upon the altar. And when the burnt offering began, the song of the Lord began also with the trumpets, and with the instruments ordained by David king of Israel.
> And all the congregation worshipped, and the singers sang, and the trumpeters sounded: and all this continued until the burnt offering was finished. (Bible [1611]: II Chronicles 29; 25-28)

sacked Jerusalem and destroyed the Temple. The Jews who survived, captive in Babylon five hundred miles to the east, invented an alternative.

They could not build the Temple in Babylon, for the Temple belonged to that one spot of holy ground in the city of Jerusalem which had been the physical center of the Jewish faith since the days of King Solomon. The music of professionals which accompanied the priestly sacrifice of the Jews was Temple music. It, too, had no place outside Jerusalem. As a substitute for Temple services and Temple music, the Jews of Babylon began to gather regularly for prayers, discussion, scripture reading, and the singing of Psalms. This was the beginning of what we call the synagogue. Fifty years later the Babylonian captivity ended and the Temple was rebuilt, but the synagogue was not abandoned. Six hundred years later, when Jesus began to collect his disciples, it was flourishing among the Jews.

The earliest Christians gathered, like the Babylonian Jews, for prayer, discussion, scripture reading, and Psalm singing. In the opinion of most scholars they sang the communal music of the synagogue, not the music of the specialists of the Temple. As Roman Catholic ritual developed out of these early gatherings, all but a few of the services focused on prayer and the singing of Psalms, with discussion gradually replaced by special readings.* Figure 9 demonstrates with a specific comparison the fact that even today there is not much difference in format and general content between the prayer meetings of Jews and Catholics.

Fig. 9

The prayer meetings of the Roman Catholic Church are known collectively as the "Hours." Only two at first, a morning and an evening gathering (Weakland 1967: 105), their number grew eventually to eight, distributed across the twenty-four

---

*You should know that this traditional view is now seriously challenged by fresh research suggesting that "both Jewish and Christian psalmody were comparatively late developments which took place without benefit of mutual influence. They had in common [only] that each stemmed in some fashion from scriptural cantillation [i.e., sung recitation]." (Mc Kinnon 1979-1980: 85)

SHAHARIT, the dawn prayer specified for the Sabbath of the Jews (Saturday). (Roth, Wigoder 1970:1726)	COMPLINE,* the last service specified for the Sabbath of Roman Catholics (Sunday). (Catholic Church 1934:32-35)
BLESSING	BLESSING
READING Old Testament Rabbinical writings	READING New Testament
	CONFESSION
SONGS Blessing Psalms	SONGS Prayer Psalms Hymn Reading from the Prophets
Canticle Blessing	Canticle Prayer
PRAISES	
COVENANT	
PRAYER 18 Blessings	PRAYER Kyrie Lord's Prayer Apostles' Creed 4 Blessings 4 Petitions
	PRAYER TO MARY Prayer Blessing Hymn Lord's Prayer Hail Mary
READING OF THE LAW	
CONCLUSION Blessings Psalm Reading of Law and Prophets Creed Consecration of the dead	Apostles' Creed

*Prior to changes decreed by Rome in 1955.

FIGURE 9: THE JEWISH/CATHOLIC PRAYER HOUR. *The Roman Catholic prayer hour grew out of the prayer hour of the Jewish synagogue, and retains an order of service strikingly similar to that of its model. The chart above compares the two in juxtaposed columns. The dawn prayer for the Jewish Sabbath is on the left (Roth and Wigoder 1970: 1726); the evening prayer for the Roman Catholic Sabbath is on the right (Catholic Church 1934: 32-35, 78-80).*

68 MELODY

Fig. 10 hours of the day as shown in Figure 10 below. (Number 3, Prime, has recently been suppressed, so now there are only seven Hours.)

In the worship services of both Jews and Catholics much of the material is sung. One might ask why a congregation intent on reciting or listening to holy words would tolerate the

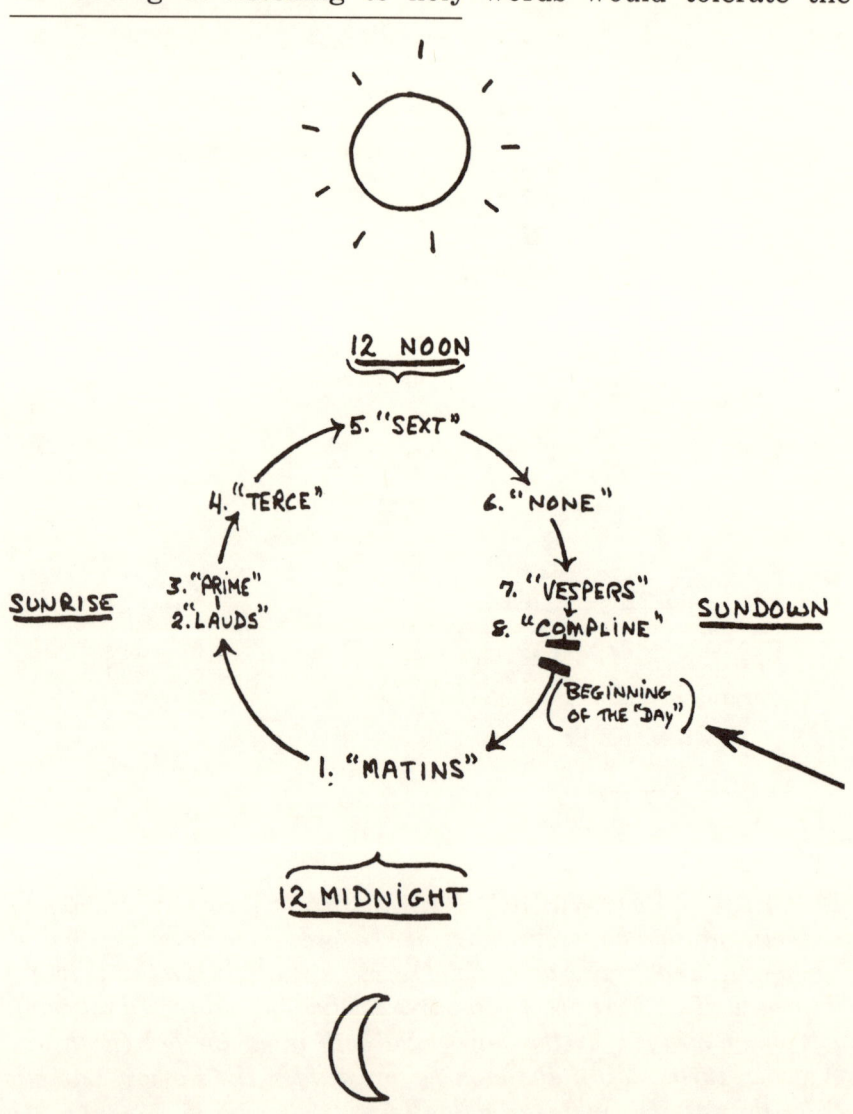

addition of melody. The answer seems to be that melody is not really an addition to speech but an inseparable part of it.

> Even when the listeners do not exceed the small circle that can be reached by the ordinary speaking voice [in other words, disregarding the case in which one must project to a large gathering], the delicate shade of meaning to be conveyed by the structure adopted for the sentence will not be appreciated by them unless certain conventionalities of pitch are introduced in utterance. These conventionalities of pitch result in an elementary form of song ...
>
> (F.L. Cohen [1964]: 537)

This elementary song becomes more developed when personal conversation becomes public address. Singsong appears: beginnings, pauses, endings become distinct musical shapes; the musical content may even become more pronounced than the verbal content.

FIGURE 10: THE ROMAN CATHOLIC HOURS. *The eight prayer services of the Roman Catholic day in the Middle Ages have been placed in this diagram in a clockwise order. The Christian ritual day, like the Jewish ritual day, began at sundown of what we normally think of as the previous day. Many Protestant sects have broken with this practice, but it survives in the Anglican and American Episcopal churches as well as among Eastern and Western Catholics.*

The names of the Hours are Latin or Latin-derived. Matins ("morning") has three parts and has always been observed before dawn, often in the middle of the night. Lauds ("praises") and Prime ("first hour of daylight") were run together as one service at dawn. (Prime has recently been suppressed.) Terce ("third hour of daylight") takes place around 9 a.m., Sext ("sixth hour of daylight") around noon. The service known as Mass, which is independent of the Hours, usually takes place between Terce and Sext. None ("ninth hour of daylight") occurs around 3 p.m. Vespers ("dusk") and Compline ("ending") were run together and mark the end of daylight and of the ritual day.

In such tones the phone company tells you you have not reached a working number, please hang up and dial again. In such tones the airline hostess reads her passengers Federal scripture about seat belts and oxygen masks. One hears reason replaced by ritual and sober instructions turned to lyrics. Store clerks do this to put certain customers at a distance. Speaking in singsong is a way of treating people impersonally.

Preachers, newscasters, game-show hosts, and other professional speakers address a more or less distant audience and therefore speak to some extent impersonally. As a result, they use singsong—certain "conventionalities of pitch," as Rabbi Cohen described it in the remarks just quoted, not to mention certain conventionalities of rhythm. The conventions seem to be limited within any one profession. Listening in quick succession to the voices speaking on the stations available on a radio, one can usually identify the singsong before it becomes clear just what the speaker is saying.

In ritual speech the conventionalities of pitch and rhythm become even more standardized; the individuality of the speaker is submerged beneath orthodox inflections. Public rituals require a heightening of these inflections because the speaker, though duly submerged, must project and impress: orthodox inflections therefore become melodic fragments, and the speaker becomes a singer.* These melodic fragments shape a sung sentence grammatically, as inflections shape a spoken one: a certain fragment signifies the beginning, another signifies a minor pause, another a major pause, etc. We call a set of these fragments a "tune formula."

We met the tune formula in the previous chapter as a device for melodic improvisation. Now we find it in a religious context as a device for achieving the very opposite kind of performance: the reproduction of an established ritual. My first example

*Evidence of this transition appears in the earliest musical notation of Roman Catholic ritual and has led one eminent scholar to conclude: "It would not be overstating the case to say that [Gregorian] melody was conceived of and functioned as an extension of the prosody of language" (Treitler 1982: 244).

comes from Jewish practice, my second from Roman Catholic.

An early example of Jewish chanting in the synagogue would be particularly interesting because it would give us some idea of how tune formulas worked when Christians first began using them in their own services. There are no ancient musical notations of Jewish chant to look at, however, for the people of those days did not write down their music; nor can we transport a tape recorder back in time and make field recordings. We can, however, observe the chanting of an ultraconservative group of Jews effectively isolated from the outside world since the beginning of the Christian era. The tune formulas they use are probably not very different from those of the early Christians.

Sana is the capital and major city of the Yemen Arab Republic, an isolated up-country area in the southwestern corner of the Arabian Peninsula, between the Red Sea and the Indian Ocean. The Jews of Sana say that their ancestors settled there before the destruction of the first Temple by Nebuchadnezzar—as long ago, in fact, as 628 B.C.—and that the prophet Jeremiah led 75,000 Jews to join this settlement when that disaster occurred. Scholars, finding no written proof of this tradition and being themselves conservatives committed to written records, concede only that a temporary settlement of merchants and agents may have developed into a permanent community at some time after Nebuchadnezzar's victory.

Whatever its origin, the Yemenite Jewish community is certainly older than the Christian era. Always on uneasy terms with the Arabs surrounding them, these Jews responded to persecutions in the 19th century with a mass migration to Jerusalem which began in 1882.

Observers in Jerusalem were astonished. The speech and dress, the art, the dances of these Yemenites seemed not of the 19th century but of ancient times. Just before the first World War a German named Abraham Zebi Idelsohn went to Jerusalem to study their music. He wrote down their tunes and even recorded some singing on wax cylinders. An Austrian scholar, Eric Werner, later compared this material with 20th-century singing among Roman Catholics and found "little or no difference" (Werner 1959: xix). If the religious singing of the Jews in Yemen developed mainly from the music of the land they fled so long ago, the ancient Jewish kingdom in Palestine, then Catholic singing evidently derives from the same source (see also Avenary 1971: 571-572).

Christians chanted all the holy texts of the Jews. We call these texts as a group the Old Testament of the Bible. Most often chanted were the Psalms of the Old Testament. A Yemenite text for Psalm 8 which Idelsohn wrote down at the beginning of this century appears in Figure 11. These words were sung for Idelsohn to a tune formula, and as the lower part of Figure 11 shows, the tune formula clarified the meaning of the words by gathering the lines into grammatical groups.

Fig. 11

FIGURE 11: THE PHRASING OF *PSALM 8* (YEMENITE TRADITION). *Hebrew syllables on the left are as Idelsohn transcribed them from the performance of a Yemenite Jew in Jerusalem (Idelsohn 1914: I, 64-65). The English translation on the right is line by line (Bible 1966: XVI, 48-51, adapted).*

(A): the phrasing of Psalm 8 by pauses in the singing of Cantor Jakob Goldstein, supposedly according to the Yemenite tradition (RCA Victor LM 6057: side 4, band 1, opening). The pauses are shown by line endings. Each line contains a complete phrase of text, except for lines 9, 10, 13, and 14. The grammatical force of the phrases is not always clear, however: line 4 is surely the beginning of a sentence, but does line 5 or line 6 end it? Does the phrase that is spread across lines 9 and 10 go with the verb in line 7 or the verb in line 11? It is the function of a tune formula to clarify these points.

(B): the phrasing of Psalm 8 by the tune formula Cantor Goldstein uses. I have rearranged the Hebrew text to show the distinctions imposed by the music: separate stanzas are separate sentences, and each line is a complete clause or pair of clauses. In the English translation I have placed commas at phrase endings of lesser force, colons or semi-colons at phrase endings of greater force, and a virgule (/) wherever a pause made by the singer does not coincide with the end of a line.

A

(1)	lä-mĕ-näṣ-ṣê-aḥ	for the director
(2)	ʿal häǧ-ǧi-ṯiṯ	upon the gittith
(3)	mi-z-môr lĕ-ḏo-wiḏ	a Psalm of David
(4)	ă-ḏô-noj ă-ḏô-nê-nu	lord, our lord
(5)	moh äd-dir-ši-mĕ-ḥo	how glorious your name
(6)	bĕ-ḥol ho-o-räṣ	through all the earth
(7)	ă-šår tĕ-noh hô-ḏĕ-ḥo	I will adore your majesty
(8)	ʿal häš-šo-mo-jim	above the heavens
(9)	mip-pij ʿô-lĕ-lim	with the mouths of babes
(10)	wĕ-jô-nĕ-gim	and sucklings
(11)	jis-säḏ-to ʿôz	you built a fortress
(12)	lĕ-må-ʿan ṣô-rå-rä-ḥo	for your habitation
(13)	lĕ-häš-biṯ	having silenced
(14)	ô-jêḇ	your adversaries
(15)	u-miṯ-nag-gêm	the foe and the avenger

B

lämĕnäṣṣéaḥ   For the director
ʿal häǧǧiṯiṯ   upon the gittith:
mizmôr lĕḏowiḏ   a Psalm of David.

ăḏônoj ăḏônênu   Lord, our Lord,
moh äddiršimĕḥo bĕḥol hooräṣ how glorious your name/
                        through all the earth;
ăšår tĕnoh hôḏĕḥo   I will adore your majesty;
ʿal häššomojim   above the heavens [will I
                        adore your majesty].

mippij ʿôlĕlim wĕjônĕgim   With the mouths of babes
                        and sucklings [will I
                        adore your majesty].

jissäḏto ʿôz   You built a fortress
lĕmåʿan ṣôråräḥo   for your habitation;
lĕhäšbiṯ ôjêḇ umiṯnaggêm   [you] having silenced/your
                        adversaries,/the foe
                        and the avenger.

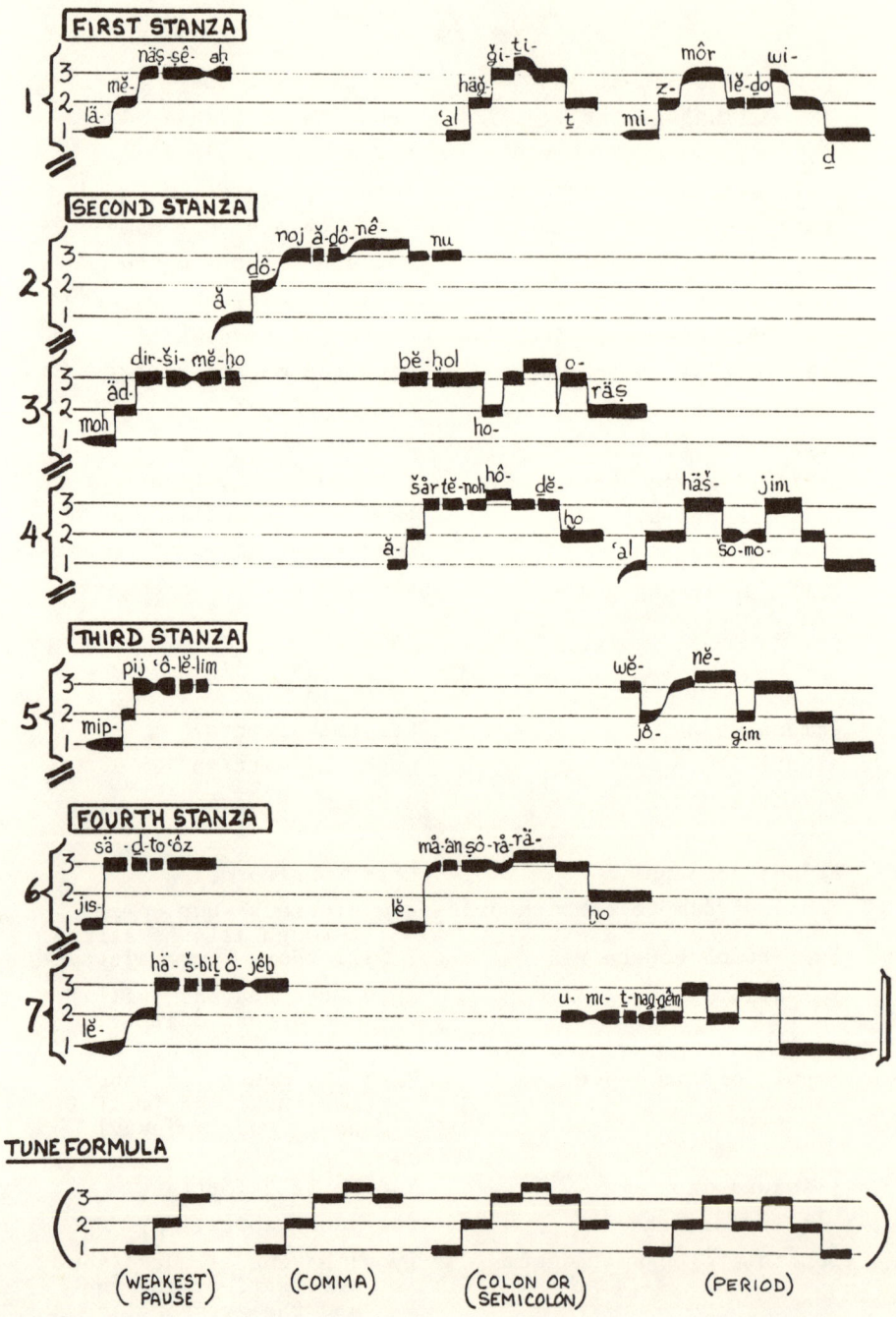

The music responsible for this grouping is shown opposite in Figure 12. Note that the technique is the same as that found in the hollers of the previous chapter. Rather than seek an historical connection between Yemenite Jews and black African slaves, however, it seems more reasonable to suppose that the tune formula exists in different cultures because it grew out of speech, which is grammatical (or, conversely and more interestingly, that speech patterns grew out of melody in which grammatical organization was a basic feature).

Fig. 12

I've used the word "chant" up to now without defining it. There are musical characteristics for what we commonly call chant, however, just as there are for the holler and the white tradition of school music. The first characteristic is a narrow pitch frame. The second is the presence of one level of pitch emphasized much more than any other. And the third, a general wordiness because most of the words are crowded together on one pitch level (we call this pitch level a "recitation tone"). Figure 12 shows these features and offers a striking contrast to the wide-ranging lines of the holler, in which, as you recall, a single syllable often extended over many changes of pitch.

FIGURE 12: A YEMENITE TUNE FORMULA. *This is a drawing of the melody that Cantor Jakob Goldstein sang in the 1950's in London (RCA Victor LM 6057: side 4, band 1, opening) as an approximation of the Yemenite melody for Psalm 8 notated by Idelsohn in Jerusalem prior to World War I (Idelsohn 1914: I, 64-65). See the caption of Figure 4 for an explanation of the general principles of the notation I have used.*

The stanzas of music correspond to the stanzas of text in Figure 11-B on p. 73, where words have been grouped and punctuated according to the grammatical sense imposed upon them by this melody.

A set of melodic fragments which signals grammatical punctuation is called a tune formula. The tune formula for this example appears in schematic form at the bottom of the page, each schematic fragment vertically aligned with the corresponding performance fragment above. Figure 5 (p. 44) and Figure 8 (Figure pp. 55-59) show how tune formulas are used in black American hollers.

The Yemenite tradition is oral rather than written. Because European scholarship is based on written evidence, it is understandably hard for a European scholar to accept mere patterns of sound on a modern Yemenite's lips as an historical document. There have thus been skeptics who doubt that Yemenite chanting actually goes back in time very far. They ask for proof that there have not been outside influences on Yemenite practice. No one can provide such proof, of course. There probably *have* been outside influences—though the likelihood is roughly the same as that of forgery or distorting bias in a medieval manuscript.* With such reservations, I accept the testimony of Yemenite tradition.

Song combines two different channels of communication in the brain. One channel processes the language of the song, which is sound as a code for ideas. Decoding seems to be the work of the left side of the brain in most people, according to experiments. The other channel processes the music, which is sound that simply refers to remembered sound. Such direct reference seems to take place in the right side of the brain in most people. A single, thick cable of nerves connects the two sides, and the extent of their interaction and interdependence is not clear (Pines 1973).

This interesting advance in our understanding of the brain seems to me to point once again to the importance of music in human life. The speechless tune, whether an instrumental melody or a vocalization, involves only the right side of the

---

*Jan Vansina (1965) and Ruth Finnegan (1970) have attacked in a constructive way, and I think successfully, the idea that to be valid, history and literature must be written. As recently as the 1920's the distinguished British historian A. P. Newton declared that Africa, where almost all records are oral, had no history before the white man began to write about it (Fage 1970: 1). This view is being rapidly discredited.

As to outside influence on Jewish practice, it is significant that scripture melodies of the European Jews published by the Catholic scholar Johannes Reuchlin in 1518 are "in all essential points" the same as those used today by European Jews (Werner 1960: 1295) though subject to daily outside influence from a vigorous Gentile culture for more than four hundred years.

brain; and in theory tuneless speech involves only the left side of the brain. But tuneless speech seems to be nonexistent. Music pervades to some degree the entire range of vocal expression from song to dry commentary, as suggested in Figure 13 on the next page. The conclusion seems inescapable that melody, so widespread and so heavily used, must be an ancient presence no less fundamental to human relations than the use of vowels and consonants. If so, music is far more than skillful recreation: it is basic to our lives.

Fig. 13

A final point about this Yemenite chant concerns the limit imposed upon musical illustration by the nature of time and entertainment. With the best of intentions, our scholarship and musical instincts cannot recreate the sounds of former ages. We cannot go back in time, physically or esthetically. Our present traditions of performance flow from earlier ones, to be sure, but for the most part irreversibly. Points of view change. More specifically, the audience for music changes and demands a difference in its entertainment.

The musicians who play concerts and make recordings today qualify for their jobs through years of immersion in the styles demanded by today's audiences. Art musicians perform, with rare exceptions, in a style developed in the 19th century and still favored by the art-music audience, whether the pieces themselves were composed in the 19th century or not. Music is performed today in today's styles, a point worth remembering when you listen to any recordings of "early" music (including those I have drawn upon for this chapter).*

---

*The Yemenite example is an intriguing case in point. The recording uses a singer with a Western European Jewish name, Jakob Goldstein; the voice production sounds Western, and in certain details the tune is not what Idelsohn wrote down (Idelsohn 1914: No. 16); and we know that Idelsohn made no recording of this particular example. In short, we seem to have a re-creation of Idelsohn's material by a Western Jew locked into his own traditions of timbre, phrasing, speed, and decoration. The differences between this re-creation and the sound heard by Idelsohn can only be imagined. They do not impair the usefulness of the example in this chapter, however, since a tune formula remains a tune formula regardless of these particular aspects of sound.

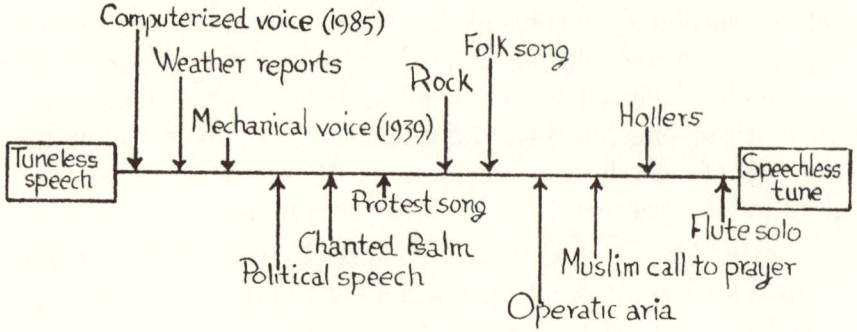

FIGURE 13: THE MELODIC CONTENT OF VOCAL EXPRESSION.
The relative amount of wordiness in some familiar kinds of American sound is shown here by the relative position of that sound on a line running from speechless tune on the right to tuneless speech on the left.

While some might disagree with the placement of specific items here, no item can be moved all the way to the left. That is, all sound with which we communicate is tuneful to some degree. (It is interesting to note that the nonhuman voice generated today for the robots we see in movies and televison is far less melodious than the mechanical voice demonstrated at the 1939 World's Fair in New York City. We are no longer inclined to minimize the difference between what is human and what is not.)

The right and left sides of the diagram represent in a rough way the degree of involvement of the right and left sides of the human brain. Recent experiments (Pines 1973) seem to indicate that to a great extent each side of the brain processes a different kind of information. A right-handed person decodes the meaning of word sounds in the left side of the brain and comprehends music or visual relationships in the right side. The case is not clear for left-handed persons.

Song involves both sides to varying degrees, but even speech requires melody and presumably also involves both sides. The implication is that musical sensitivity is far more fundamental in human affairs than generally acknowledged.

The Roman Catholic Tradition

Today's officially approved style of performing Gregorian Chant was successfully promoted at the end of the 19th century by a young monk, André Mocquereau, trained in the National Conservatory of Music in Paris as a cellist.* This official Catholic style, like the style of performing our art music, has not changed since then. Manuscript sources for Catholic ritual song give no directions for performance. Presumably singers have always tried to make the sound of the Church conform to the taste of their particular time and place. At the end of the 19th century, elite taste in rhythm and timbre favored smoothness and sweetness, as it still does; and Mocquereau found a ready acceptance in the church when he applied these values in a systematic way to Gregorian Chant.

There is no reason to suggest that Western elite taste has always been the same, and there is good reason to suggest that it has not. Among the poor of Europe one finds patterns of behavior preserved for a surprisingly long time—lyres being bowed in this century the way artists pictured them in the late Middle Ages, for example, and a medieval play on the ascension of the Virgin Mary into Heaven still being given yearly in the village of Elche in southeastern Spain (Preece 1981: 40f). The poor often copy the rich, moreover, and it might just be that the focused, agile, clear, hard-edged singing now heard among the rural poor all over Europe was once the style for music of the

---

*Mocquereau quit his studies in 1875 to join the Benedictine abbey of St. Peter at Solesmes-sur-Sarthe, not far from Paris. By 1889 he was musical director there. He published facsimile editions of early Church manuscripts and made modern editions of the same material with special signs to indicate his rhythmic interpretations. His smooth-flowing, sweet, elastic style has much in common with the style of late 19th-century symphonic music. Papal approval came in 1904.

Mocquereau's work was part of a reform movement sparked by Dom Prosper Guéranger, who in 1833 founded a community at Solesmes-sur-Sarthe devoted to restoring to the Church the rich and unified ritual of earlier ages. Diverse rituals had developed in the 18th century, and the French Revolution (1779-1789) created greater chaos by attempting to wipe out all organized religion in France. When Guéranger began his work, French Catholics could choose from among ten different ways to conduct their services.

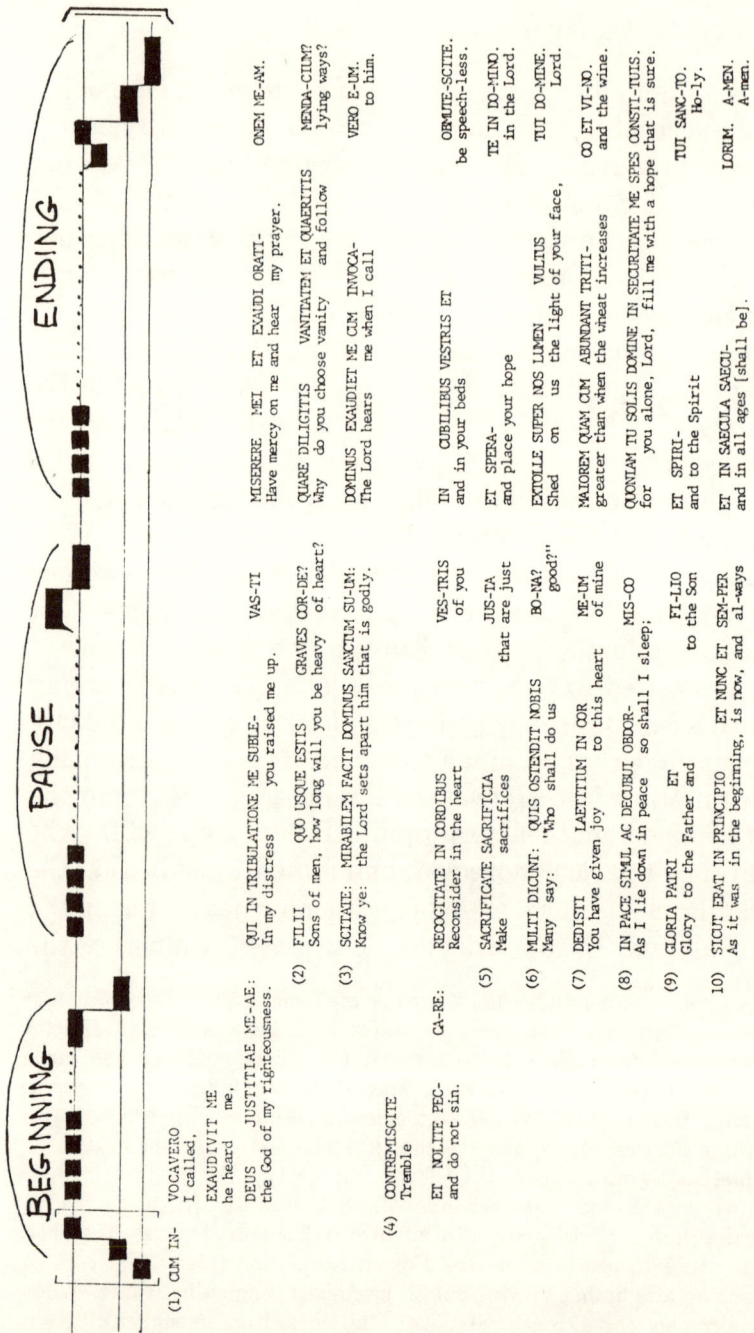

FIGURE 14: A GREGORIAN TUNE FORMULA. *Known as the "eighth tone," this example was transcribed from the singing of the monks of St. Martin in Beuron, West Germany (Deutsche Grammophon ARC 3102: side 1). Note the resemblance between these melodic fragments and those of the Yemenite formula (Figure 12 on p. 74).*

educated classes.*

Conjecture, of course, but worthwhile conjecture. It reminds us once again that in music there is no universal right or wrong: every cultural tradition has its own rules and its own rate of change. The hard, ringing sound that produced the examples in Chapter 8, present-day Bulgarian singing, may once have been the sound of cathedral and monastery choirs. In that case the smooth-flowing sweetness of the sound you would hear if you played the recordings I've used for the remaining examples of this chapter misrepresents medieval Roman Catholic performances.

A large and ancient portion of Gregorian Chant consists of tune formulas. One does not find them written out with the thousands of texts they serve, however, because they are relatively simple patterns easily applied to whatever sentence structure comes along; performers need only be given the name of the formula they are to use. (The text is often set out with signs to help the singer fit the words to the formula.) Figure 14 opposite gives the structure of a Gregorian tune formula as sung by Benedictine monks observing evening prayer on Christmas Day.

Fig. 14

Despite its name, much of Gregorian Chant does not have the chanting effect of the example just presented. In many pieces the pitch frame is not particularly narrow, as it is here, and more than one level of pitch is emphasized; moreover, such pieces do not have the wordy effect of this example. In short, during much of a Roman Catholic service the listener hears a tuneful singing rather than chanting. Yet even in their tuneful songs the composers of Gregorian Chant relied upon tune-formula technique to some extent.

*At least in northwestern Europe; for, as the late Curt Sachs reminded us, "in Charlemagne's time Italian church singers protested against the 'bestial' song of the Franconians who with an artless, barbaric voice crushed the melodies in their throats" (Sachs 1960: 44).

Fig. 15

Figure 15 (opposite and overleaf) shows a hymn to the Virgin Mary, *Alma Redemptoris Mater*, in which two basic (and beautiful) phrases supply all the melodic material of the song and some grammatical force as well, the first phrase implying a beginning, the second a continuation and ending. The Latin text eulogizes the Virgin in a series of brief descriptive and vocative phrases; the music expands these phrases into expressions that have the force of full sentences, thus increasing the devotional fervor of the song (see Figure 15-B on p. 85).

As I suggested in discussing the holler, something of the tune formula survives in most melody, if only in the use of a recognizable ending pattern. A comparison of the present example with Figures 5 and 8 (pp. 44 and 55-59) shows that in this hymn the tune-formula technique is just as extensive.

Many so-called Marian texts entered Catholic ritual during the late Middle Ages (1000-1450 A.D.) when there was a general upsurge of devotion to the Virgin Mary. Just as the sculpture, painting, and literature of the time were strongly affected, so was the music. Songs like *Alma Redemptoris Mater* were added to the Hours, while in the Mass—that special

FIGURE 15: *ALMA REDEMPTORIS MATER. This hymn by Hermannus Contractus (first half of the 11th century) is transcribed from the same source as the tune formula shown in Figure 14. For a general explanation of the notation, see the caption for Figure 4.*

(A): the entire melody, which is drawn from the first two phrases. The first phrase has the force of the beginning of a sentence and the second provides the continuation and ending of a sentence. By vertical alignment I have shown to which of these phrases the remaining portions of the melody belong, taking for a "portion" all the music sung between adjacent pauses. As you will see by a comparison with pp. 44 and 55–59, there is little difference between the structure of this hymn and that of a holler: in either case a tune formula governs the progress of the melody. I have drawn the tune formula of this example in schematic form below the pictorial notation of the performance. (Figure 15–B with its caption is on p. 85.)

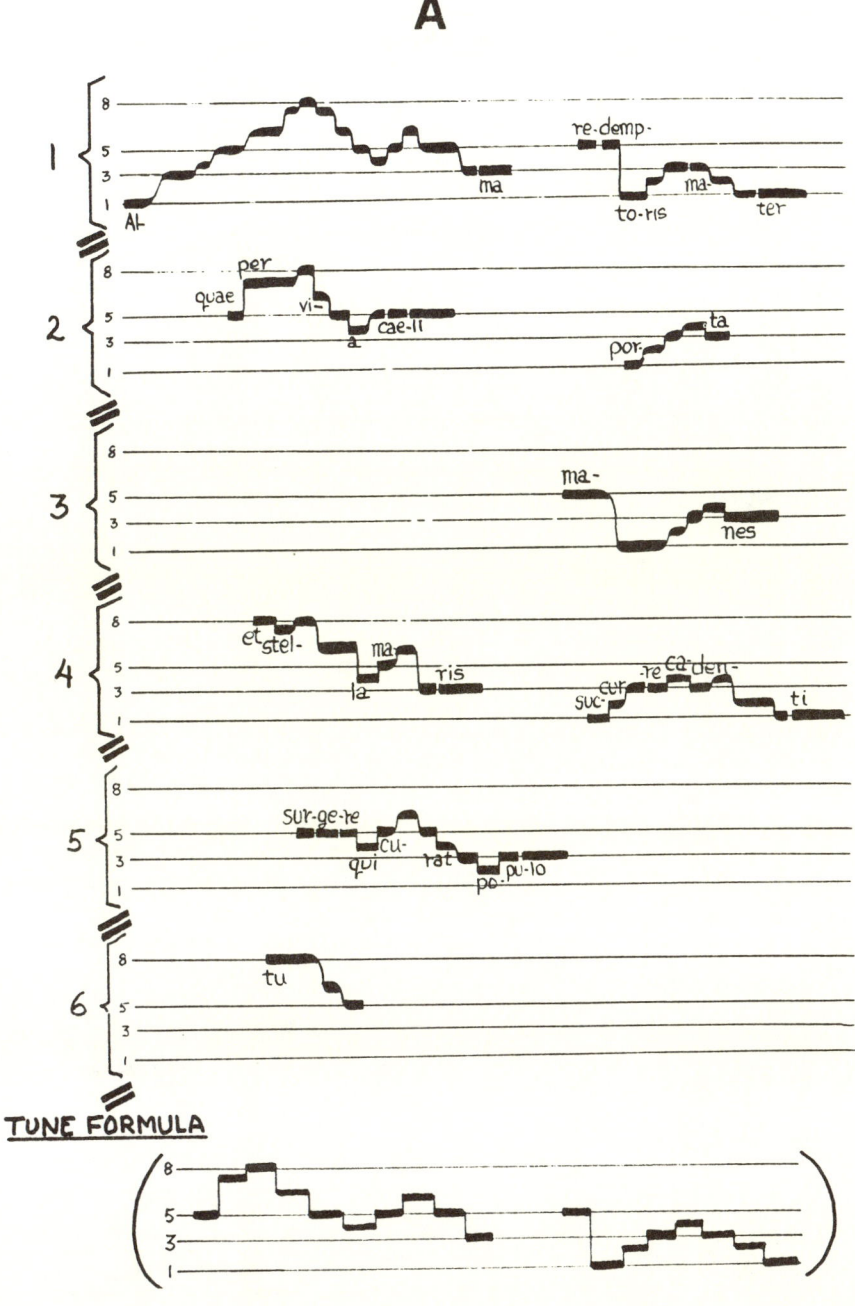

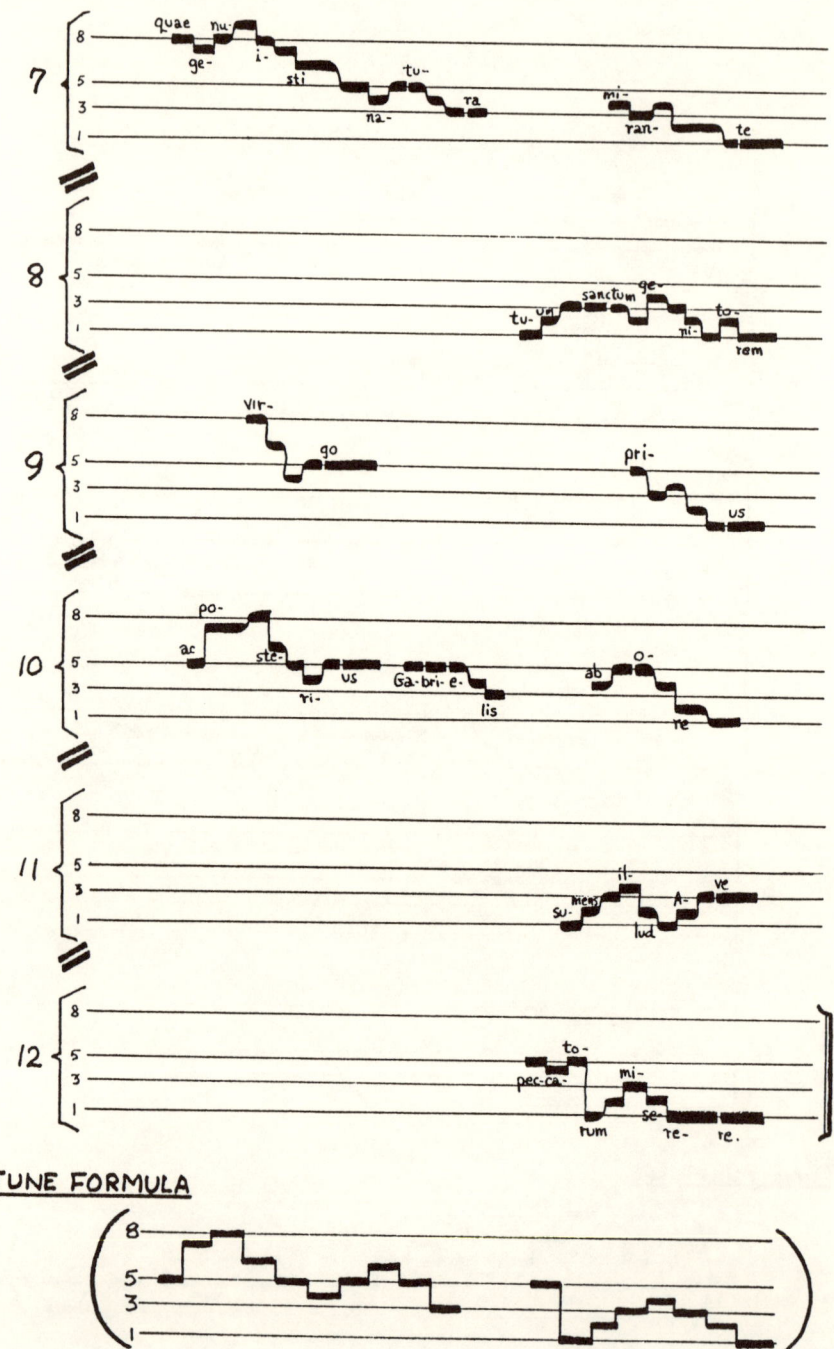

TUNE FORMULA

Catholic service of sacrifice which Jesus himself invented for his disciples on the eve of his crucifixion—new devotional material appeared.

The core of the Marian movement was in the monasteries. A Benedictine monk at the monastery of Reichenau, on the western end of Lake Constance in southwestern Germany, composed *Alma Redemptoris Mater* in the first half of the 11th

---

B

1	ALMA/ REDEMPTORIS MATER/
	[Oh] maiden, mother of the Redeemer!
2-3	QUAE PER VIA CAELI/ PORTA/ MANES/
	[Oh you] that stands by the gates of heaven!
4	ET STELLA MARIS/ SUCCURRE CADENTI/
	[Oh you] star of the sea, help the faltering!
5	SURGERE QUI CURAT POPULO/
	[Help] the people who seek to rise.
6	TU/
	You!
7-8	QUAE GENUISTI NATURA/ MIRANTE/ TUUM SANCTUM GENITOREM/
	[Oh you] who gave birth, as Nature marveled, to your holy Father!
9	VIRGO/ PRIUS/
	[Oh you who were] a virgin at first!
10-12	AC POSTERIUS/ GABRIELIS/ AB ORE/
	[You, left still virgin] afterwards by Gabriel's words,
	SUMENS ILLUD AVE/ PECCATORUM MISERERE/
	[who] received that "Hail Mary!," have pity on sinners.

(B): the lines of text, set out according to their melodic treatment. A virgule (/) represents a pause made by the singers; the end of a line represents the end of a sentence. The bracketed portions of the English translation are expansions of the literal meaning of the Latin into the full sentences implied by the tune formula.

As you can see, expanding vocative or descriptive phrases into full sentences intensifies the message of the hymn: a mere listing of the Virgin's attributes becomes a series of invocations.

century. We even know his name, Hermann The Crippled ("Hermannus Contractus"), because the popularity of his work won it mention in several manuscript sources, some of which name him as the composer.

We don't know how the monks of Reichenau sang *Alma Redemptoris Mater* in the 11th century. The aural tradition governing their voice quality has very probably been lost during the nine hundred years this piece has been sung. Timbre was never written down, nor were other aspects of vocal style, such as sliding the pitch, singing rapid decorations around the main notes of the tune, or making changes in loudness and speed. All we have for sure besides the text are the basic changes of pitch, for Hermann wrote down his melodies not by recording levels of pitch, as his contemporary Guido d'Arezzo advocated (see p. 40), but by naming the intervals between successive notes. These intervals give us the melodic structure, which is all I am concerned with here.*

Melodic Modes

The third and final point of this chapter concerns melodic "modes." The Gregorian melodies we have inherited run in families; that is, many of them behave in a particular manner, many others in another particular manner, and so forth, each manner quite clearly distinguished from the others. We call each manner a "mode."

The principle features of a melodic mode are its pitch frame, its characteristic fragments, the pitches it emphasizes, and its decorative style. The last of these, the decorative style,

---

*The rich, sweet, flexible melodic line promoted by André Mocquereau at Solesmes-sur-Sarthe is the model for the singing of the monks of Beuron who provided the example shown in Figure 15. The style seems well designed for the stone-walled chapel in which it was recorded, and perhaps, after all, there has not been much change over the centuries. We know that medieval men were well aware of how sound reverberates, for they set hollow clay pots in the vaulted stone roofs of late medieval churches, the mouths of the pots facing outward to catch and amplify the sound. For Hermann's notation see Rougnon 1925, p. 366.

has been lost in the writing down of Gregorian Chant in almost every case, for only the main notes or intervals were recorded. (An exception seems to be the solo songs called "Tracts," which appear in the service of the Mass during the season of mourning called "Lent"; these are extremely elaborate in a way that suggests that the actual decorations were written down.)

Note that a melodic mode is not a tune. The characteristic fragments of a mode can appear in any order, and the melody in which they appear may contain other fragments as well. The successive ideas of a tune, on the other hand, have only one order, and all the fragments that occur are part of the tune.

Nor is a mode a tune formula. The characteristic fragments of a mode do not have grammatical functions; they flow one into another in any order and imply nothing about the sentence structure of the accompanying text. Tune formulas are each constructed within a certain mode, of course, and in such cases the fragments of the mode naturally take on grammatical functions. Perhaps in the beginning of the Gregorian tradition a tune formula was the source for each mode; but the modes as they appear in the written record are no longer tied to this source, if indeed they ever were.

Figure 16 (overleaf) shows a Gregorian mode in its essentials: first the pitch frame and overall melodic curve characteristic of the melodies of the mode, then typical extensions of the curve upward and downward, and finally a more elaborate melodic line summarizing the behavior patterns of tunes in the mode. This summary is a convenient way of showing all the typical melodic movements of the mode in typical juxtaposition. The sequence of the whole need not be preserved, nor does any part of it have grammatical force.

Fig. 16

*   *   *

From the Middle Ages to the present, theorists have tended to define a melodic mode as a "scale"—that is, as a list of pitch levels arranged in ascending or descending order. Figure

88

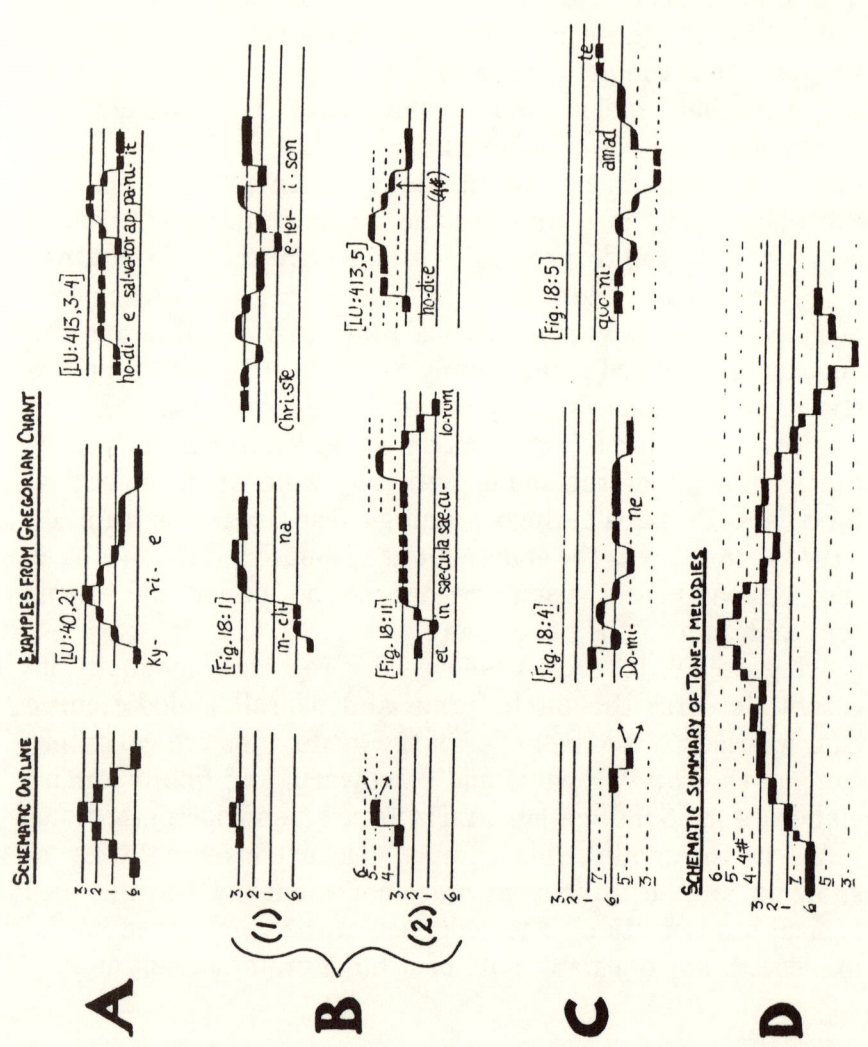

FIGURE 16: A GREGORIAN MODE. *A melodic mode is a pattern of pitch behavior characterized by a certain pitch frame, pitch emphasis, decorative style, and melodic movement. Illustrated here is the melodic mode known to medieval theorists as "Primus Tonus" (Tone 1). Decorative style is omitted as well as features not bearing on melodic mode such as rhythm, timbre, loudness, and the specific pitch of performance.*

Each row of examples begins with a schematic outline, followed in all but row D by two illustrations from Gregorian Chant. The printed source for each illustration appears in brackets above it. "Fig. 18" refers to Figure 18 on pp. 92–3; the following number is the pitch frame. "LU" refers to **The Liber Usualis** *(Catholic Church 1959), an anthology of the major chants of the Catholic Church year; the following number is the page, and the number after that the pitch frame.*

(A): *the arch characteristic of Tone-1 melodies.*

(B): *two successively greater upward extensions of the Tone-1 arch. In Extension 1 the peak always returns to pitch level 3 before the melody moves on. Extension 2 has no such restriction, but a pitch level foreign to the octave series of the mode sometimes precedes or follows pitch level 5 (an arrow marks such a place in the second Gregorian illustration). This foreign level is pitch 4 of the octave series, sharped (4♯).*

(C): *downward extensions of the Tone-1 arch.*

(D): *a schematic summary of Tone-1 melodic behavior. Emphasized pitches are longer than most; pitches only occasionally used are shorter than most. Juxtaposed portions of the outline typically occur together in melodies using this mode, but by no means always. Compare this summary with Figure 17 on p. 90, which presents the pitches of Tone 1 as a scale, an ascending series devoid of relationships.*

Fig. 17 17 below is the scale one can derive from Tone 1. As you can see, this scale fails to present typical melodic movements, nor does it define the basic pitch frame or emphasis of the mode. In short, it says nothing about the music. I will take a moment longer on this point, because in my opinion the concept of a scale holds an unjustified position of importance today in theoretical discussions of music.

A musical scale is just a list. It has no role in making music (except, of course, when a tune happens to *be* a scale). Indeed, it seems almost anti musical in the way it denies melodic shape. If we imagine for a moment that performing a piece of music is like moving between and around various counters in a store, we can see that the scale used by the music has no more to do with the flow of sound than a shopping list has to do with the to-and-fro of shopping: the shopping list itself is not among the items being sought, nor is the musical scale itself the object of the musical activity; the sequence of items on the shopping list does not determine the shopper's route, nor does the sequence of

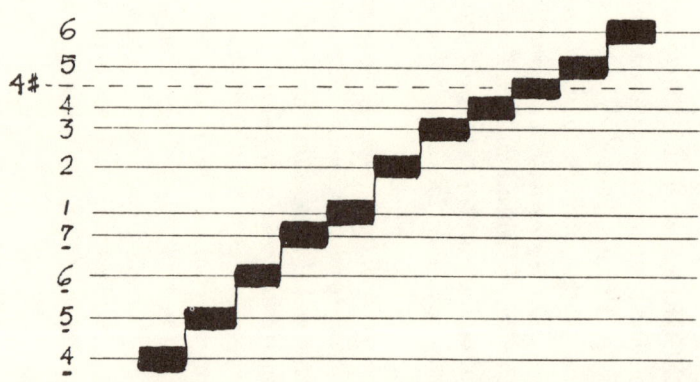

FIGURE 17: A SCALE. *The pitch levels characteristic of the mode Tone 1 shown in Figure 16 have been listed in ascending order. Although theorists have continually preferred to define a mode as a scale, clearly to do so eliminates almost all the aspects of a mode which make it that particular mode. Compare the scale shown here with Figure 16(D), the summary of melodic motions typical of Tone 1.*

pitch levels in the scale determine the music's melody; finally, a shopping list does not usually distinguish between trivial and important items, just as the musical scale gives very few clues about which levels of pitch a particular piece will treat as critical. The essence of melody is not a collection of pitch levels but the process of passing among them.

A word about decoration. Were you to hear the smooth, simple melodies of the Catholic songs I've used so far, you would never imagine that trills, slides, yodeling, and rapid runs and turns might once have been an essential part of the music of the Catholic Church. To judge from the record of such things in manuscripts of the 13th and 14th centuries, however, there was a time when decoration was applied to church song—not just in solo performance but in group singing. And judging from melodic modes current in India and Greece today, this decoration was probably applied differently to different modes by the medieval Western singer.*

Echoes of medieval vocal decoration perhaps survive in the notation of those Gregorian melodies passed down to us in a particularly elaborate form such as the Tracts I mentioned earlier. What was originally an improvised effect may have pleased enough to become a permanent part of the tradition in one cathedral or monastic community, to be written out from then on as part of the basic tune and adopted eventually by the Church as a whole.

The entrance music for the Roman Catholic Mass on the twenty-second Sunday after Easter seems to be a melody with such fixed decoration. I show it in Figure 18 (overleaf) and call your attention to line 4 and the last part of line 2, where a basically descending line is embellished by the rapid alternation of neighboring pitches. The monks of Solesmes-sur-Sarthe sing these passages today in careful unison, but perhaps in a much earlier day one of the group improvised the embellishment while the others sang a simpler line.

Fig. 18

*A brief discussion of melodic decoration as modal material occurs in the caption for Figure 23 on p. 125, which concerns Appalachian solo singing.

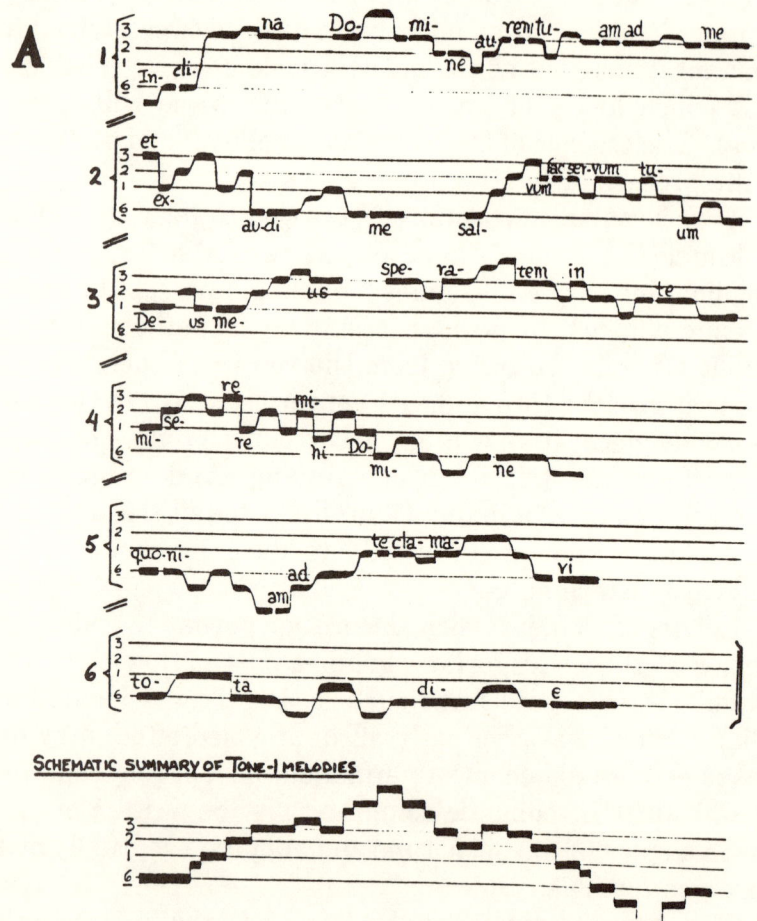

FIGURE 18: *INCLINA DOMINE.* This is a drawing of the entrance music ("Introit") for the Roman Catholic Mass on the twenty-second Sunday after Easter as sung by the monks of St. Peter at Solesmes-sur-Sarthe outside of Paris (London A 4501: side 5, band 1). The mode is Tone 1 (see pp. 88–89), a summary of which appears below the music. The piece is in three sections, the first and third of which are the same.

(A): the first section, which also closes the piece, called an "antiphon" because, in the early days of Christian worship, such a section was a brief refrain sung between verses of a Psalm to give

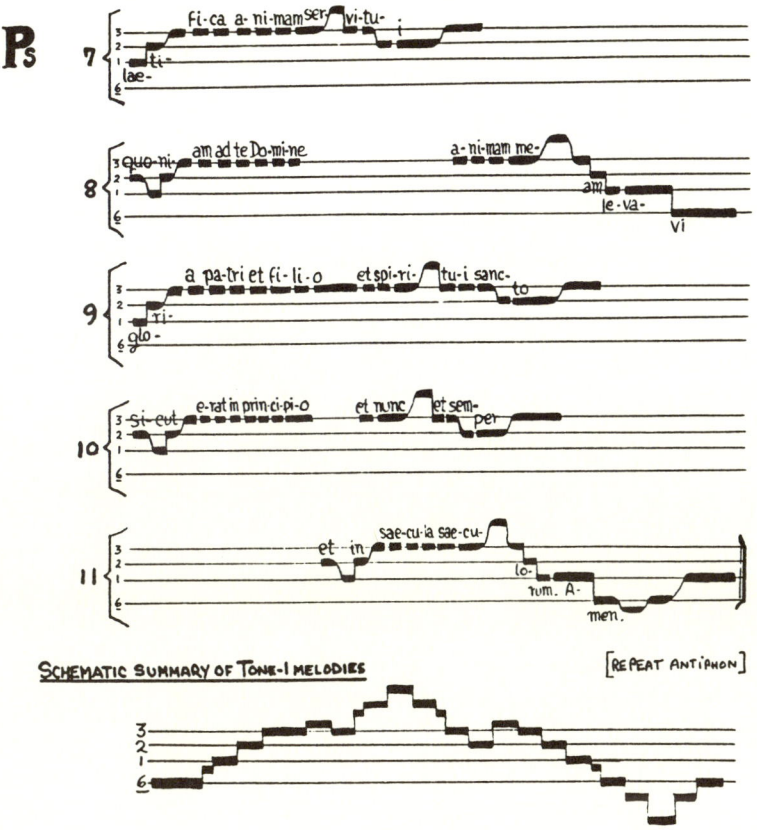

increased opportunity for the practice of antiphony, the alternation of sections of a piece between two performing groups. The relatively wide range of every phrase, and the presence of several equally emphasized levels of pitch, create a more tuneful effect than the middle section does.

(Ps): the middle section, all that remains of what was once the many verses of a complete Psalm. The more chanting effect of this section results from the extreme emphasis upon one level of pitch and the resulting rather narrow range of most of the music.

The point of this example is that many different melodies can belong to the same mode. Here, the same mode rules the Psalm as the antiphon, even though the melodic effect of these two sections is strikingly different.

Figure 18 makes an important point about mode. You see a chanted Psalm (the middle section, labelled "Ps.") introduced and concluded by a separate, more tuneful song called an "antiphon" (first and third sections, labelled "A."). Despite their different styles, both Psalm and antiphon are Tone-1 tunes, as you can tell by comparing their melodic outlines with the summary of Tone 1 taken from p. 88 and here placed at the bottom of each section. The example illustrates the fact that mode does not dictate style. Mode merely commits a melody to using certain pitches in certain small groupings ordered in any way and with or without repetition. The free selection and arrangement of a limited number of melodic moves can produce a wide variety of subtly related songs.

We do not know how the modes were developed. As I suggested earlier, they may have evolved from tune formulas. Each mode is simply a group of melodic ideas unified by history, as far as we can tell—a pool of ideas that have always travelled together. In 1323 when the exiled Pope John XXII held court in Avignon, in southern France, he cautioned his composers to stay within the pool of material proper to a mode. He complained that they

> often seem to be losing sight of the fundamental sources of our melodies...the modest rise and temperate descents of plainsong [that is, of Gregorian Chant], by which the modes themselves are recognized, are entirely obscured.
> *(Raynor 1972: 36-37)*

The restrictions of a melodic mode enhance the pleasure of a tune because they increase the predictability, and hence the anticipation, of the melodic flow.

Undoubtedly the present example was once mostly chanting. When early Christians gathered to sing Psalms, after every verse or two they would sing a short refrain. The chanting of the Psalm must have dominated the musical effect at first. During the first four centuries of Christian worship, however, trained choirs came to assume the duty of singing, and the refrains became more numerous and more elaborate as these trained singers sought opportunities for greater musical expression. Because musical matters have never been regulated in the Roman Catholic Church as strictly as matters of dogma, this development of refrains went on for a long time. More than a thousand have come down to us,* preserving in their own more tuneful way the same modes preserved in the chanting of the Psalms.

The next chapter begins a discussion of harmony. Before I leave the subject of melody, let me summarize the basic ideas developed so far.

Not only music but all spoken communication employs melody, the essence of which is passage. The key ingredient for making melodic passage meaningful to those who hear it is predictability. And the basic elements of melodic predictability are those I've introduced in this section: the restricted set of pitch levels a melody establishes as the frame within which it will move, and the restricted set of movements it makes. Regulation of melodic movement can be severe enough to have the force of a grammar, or loose enough to create only a vague impression that the melody belongs to a certain type. The progress of a known text chanted to a known tune formula, for example, is fairly predictable, but the progress of a known text sung in a known mode is predictable only in a most general way (which narrows from time to time to a specific expectation when the beginning of a familiar melodic fragment is recognized).

These principles will be found, I expect, to apply to the melody of every culture. In the two kinds of melody I've discussed, the black American holler and white European Gregorian Chant, one finds them equally in force.

---

*They are called antiphons because originally they created or increased the opportunity for a call-and-response effect (called "antiphony") in Psalm performance. As we know them today, some are short, others long enough to stand by themselves as complete songs. Some occur after every verse or two of the Psalm, as all antiphons did originally, whereas others now appear only at the Psalm's beginning and end. Some have become permanently fixed to a single Psalm verse, as in the present case. Others have lost their Psalm entirely.

Part Two: Harmony

6

The Nature of Harmony

Harmony is the coincidence of sounds—a mesh existing in the present musical moment rather than the moment's passage from the past into the future. Both art and accident contribute to the mesh: a barbershop quartet carefully harmonizes the songs it sings; a concert audience harmonizes the music it hears with unplanned coughing and the rustling of programs. The coughing, the rustling, and the quartet create harmony, but only the quartet is commonly thought to do so. This chapter treats the combination of both pitched and unpitched sounds as harmony and examines partials, articulation, and environmental sound before considering harmony in the traditional sense of different musical notes combined.

I've called harmony a "mesh" of sound to suggest, which is true, that it affects our hearing not as several sounds in juxtaposition but as a single sound of a certain character. The components of a harmony are subordinate to its total effect. When this ceases to be true—when, for example, an audience hears unplanned coughing as a sound separate from the sound of the musicians on stage, then the experience is, strictly speaking, not of harmony but of counterpoint. That is, we perceive not the blend but the juxtaposition ("counterpoint" comes directly from the old Latin term for the technique of composition in which one sound, or written note, is set against another: *punctum contra punctum*).

The Harmony of Partials

A single musical tone has harmony in it because every natural sound producer vibrates in a complex way and therefore jostles the surrounding air with several different but simultaneous rates of shaking. Each of these rates registers at a specific spot along the elastic membrane inside the cochlea, as I explained earlier (p. 24). Thus a single musical tone presents the brain with several pitches simultaneously.

Rates of vibration in a complex numerical relationship cause the brain to hear a harmony of indefinite pitch. A whisper and a clash of cymbals are examples of this kind of harmony. Numerical relationships more closely approaching that of simple whole numbers produce sounds of more definite pitch. When the six slowest rates of vibration are multiples of one another—that is, when all six can be derived from any one of the six, through multiplying it or dividing it by 1, 2, 3, 4, 5, and 6—then the brain blends all six into a single tone having the pitch of the slowest of the six rates of vibration (see discussion on p. 25).

We call the component vibrations of the sound emitted from a single source "partials." With training, one can pick out some of the partials in a sound of definite pitch. They are particularly clear in the ringing of a bell, but one can learn to hear them in the sustained note of a flute or violin. Timbre, the quality of sound that distinguishes a flute from a violin, is largely determined by the particular harmony of partials the instrument generates with every note it sounds. Both the rates of vibration and their strengths are critical factors.

Using this principle, various electronic instruments provide a variety of timbres with a small amount of circuitry: they offer a basic set of vibrations in variable strength; the performer produces the desired timbre by selecting certain partials and adjusting their strengths. The same principle works in much of the harmony a composer creates among the various instruments of a symphony orchestra: to modify the sound of a melody played by the violins, for example, the flutes may be added at the unison or octave and play the same melody with such a blending of sound that one does not hear them as separate instruments. In effect the composer has created a new harmony of partials for the violin.

The Harmony of Articulation

In addition to the harmony of partials there is in music what we might call the "harmony of articulation," the harmony of extra sounds that give the beginning of a note its definition. Thus the organ builder adjusts the flute pipes of the instrument so that they will speak with an initial noise called "chiffing," a sound like that of the "ch" in "church"; the singer adds throaty effects for their dramatic value; and the country fiddler traditionally gives a lot of noisy "bite" to each stroke to create a rhythm that will propel the dancers' feet. We hear these effects not as additional sounds but as changes in a continuing sound. One might call them momentary alterations in the harmony of partials.

The Harmony of the Environment

Another kind of harmony is extremely important in music: the harmony of the environment. A symphony proceeds in a context of silence, or it should; mainstream jazz proceeds amid the sounds of a crowd. Bluegrass is "up front" music meant to dominate whatever other sounds might occur at the same time; Muzak is designed as a background filler.

The environment can control even musical content. The stone of a cathedral creates a reverberation that enhances the performance of medieval music but makes the singing of modern hymns with their quickly changing harmonies quite unpleasant. The medieval style was born in the cathedral; the hymn style is an importation.

In short, the sound of music includes the sound of its environment. As might be expected, the two influence each other. Some composers even depend on this relationship. They give the ending of a song in opera or rock an extra amount of musical force in order to generate the true final harmony of the event: a roar of applause. (But rock for dancing typically fades out; no applause is expected.) Similarly, we hear comic routines at the theatre and on television punctuated by bursts of music or mechanical laughter which harmonize and encourage bursts of laughter from the audience. Cocktail music harmonizes the murmur of patrons and is therefore unobtrusive. On the other hand, the bars in my town which cater to college students raise the loudness of their taped music to deafening levels over the course of an evening in order to match, if not induce, a mood of "wiping out" in the crowd. Similarly, brass bands in southern German beer halls play loudly and disjointedly to create a forcefully chaotic context as well as to fit in with it.

The Harmony of Musical Notes

The harmony that theorists study—the sound of separate musical notes combining—is but one kind of harmony in music. The notes that are studied are imagined to be the way Guido d'Arezzo pictured them in the 11th century: clear, unwavering sounds occupying a few fixed levels of pitch in the octave (see pp. 40-41 for discussion of this notation).

The truth is otherwise, as you know: musical sounds are often of changing pitch, and often unclear. And as you may not know, even the sounds of fixed pitch occupy many more positions in the octave than suggested by Guido's visual system. In fact they occupy more positions than can be sounded by the keyboard of the piano or distinguished by our standard notational signs.

I once heard the American composer Walter Piston tell how he had illustrated the limitations of the keyboard. A bass player from the Boston Symphony Orchestra was in front of his students demonstrating the range and techniques of this very large stringed instrument, the lowest-sounding member of the violin family. Mr. Piston asked his guest to sound the written note shown in Figure 19.

The symbol ♭ which appears in Figure 19 is called a "flat" and has the effect of lowering the pitch level of the note immediately following that symbol. On the piano keyboard this lowering is accomplished by playing the next key to the left, whether white or black. The unflatted form of the note Mr. Piston requested is a white key on the piano keyboard, as you can see in Figure 20, where it is marked with an upward-pointing arrow. The flatted form of the note is therefore the next key to the left, which is black.

Fig. 19

Fig. 20

The symbol # , called a "sharp," has the effect of *raising* the pitch of the note immediately following that symbol. The pianist responds to a sharp by playing the next higher key—that is, the next key to the right, whether white or black.

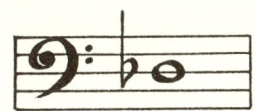

FIGURE 19: A NOTE FOR A BASS PLAYER. *The late composer Walter Piston wrote this note on the blackboard and asked a professional musician whose instrument was the string bass—the largest member of the violin family—to play it. (Note for those who read musical notation: music for string bass is written an octave higher than it sounds.)*

The strings of this instrument are so long that even a slight change of pitch requires a noticeable change in the position of the finger pressing the string against the fretboard. By accompanying the string player on the piano and changing from one supporting harmony to another Mr. Piston caused him to make a clearly visible change in finger position, thereby demonstrating that the precise pitch of a written musical note is not determined by that note but by the musical situation in which it is used.

The player himself insisted he had made no change, so deep was his commitment to the idea that a written note has only one pitch. Actually, it has several different pitches, a fact he obviously "knew" as a performer responding to the sound of music.

A glance at Figure 20 shows that flatting the white key marked by an arrow must be the same on the piano as sharping the next white key to the left, since both actions lead to the same

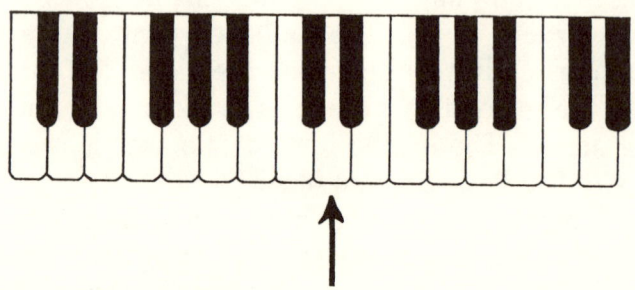

FIGURE 20: FLATS AND SHARPS ON THE PIANO KEYBOARD. *Excessive exposure to the piano has led many people to imagine that the variety of Western pitch levels is far less than it actually is. The piano does not have enough levers to sound all the different pitches we use. It hasn't enough even to make some of the distinctions we make in our standard musical notation.*

As you may know, the white keys of the piano sound levels of pitch corresponding to the levels represented by the lines and spaces of the five-line musical staff. To notate a level that has been raised or lowered a little, we draw a special symbol on the corresponding line or space: a "sharp" (#) to raise it, a "flat" (♭) to lower it.

The pianist attempts a corresponding change of pitch on the piano keyboard by substituting for the original white key the key right beside it, whether white or black: the key on the right gives a raised ("sharped") pitch; the key on the left gives a lowered ("flatted") pitch. As you can see in the figure provided, flatting the pitch of the white key marked with an arrow is, for the pianist, identical with sharping the pitch of the next white key to the left, since both changes lead to the same black key between them.

This identity is a gross approximation. In Western music performed on more flexible instruments—violin, voice, flute, etc.—this flatted pitch and this sharped pitch do not coincide but lie next to each other, the sharped lower note a little lower than the flatted higher note.

black key. People familiar with this fact about the piano keyboard are apt to assume that it reflects a fact about Western music, namely that flats and sharps are different names for the same pitch. They are not. On the bass fiddle, as Mr. Piston was about to prove, and on any other instrument that allows the player to adjust the pitch while playing, flatting one note in the Western octave series produces a different pitch level than sharping the next lower note in the series.

One makes slight adjustments in the pitch of a wind instrument by changing the angle or shape of one's mouth and tongue. On a stringed instrument one can make them by changing the length of the vibrating part of the string. To change the length, one changes the point at which the finger stops the string's vibration. A long vibrating string requires a greater change in length than a short one to produce the same amount of change in pitch.

The strings of the bass fiddle are long. Even a slight pitch change requires a marked change in finger position on the sounding string. Mr. Piston wrote on the blackboard the note he wanted the bass player to play (shown on p. 103). He then accompanied the man on the piano and, after a little while, changed the harmony so that the bass player could stay in tune only by playing not this flatted note but the sharped version of the white note just below.* The bass player instantly moved his press point up the neck of his instrument to create a slightly longer vibrating string and a slightly lower-sounding pitch. The sharp was clearly not the same note as the flat (even though the bass player himself, who was still looking at the note Mr. Piston had written for him, insisted he had made no change). The bass player's ear had led him to lower his pitch and give an unchanged written note its proper fit in a new harmony. On the piano the same pitch serves both harmonies (and fits neither

*In technical language, he established D flat as the root of a D-flat major chord, then shifted to an A major chord with its third, C sharp, omitted so that the bass player was free to find for himself a satisfactory C sharp. Had C sharp been included in the piano chord, the bass player would have tuned his own C sharp to that of the piano, where it is identical in pitch with D flat.

one well).

The piano does not have enough keys to sound all the fixed pitches used by a Western musician playing a more flexible instrument. Even our standard notation, which at least distinguishes sharps from flats, cannot distinguish the various degrees of sharping and flatting called for by different melodic and harmonic situations that occur in Western music. Thus what theorists call harmony—the combining of fixed sounds of definite pitch—is actually taught today only in part because it is taught by means of our standard notation and, almost always, with the help of the piano.

Patterns of Harmony

The function of harmony, like the function of every other aspect of music, is to communicate. Therefore harmony, like melody, rhythm, timbre, etc., follows accepted models in order to be meaningful to the audience as well as to the performer. Kinds of harmony and patterns of harmonic change differ from culture to culture, of course, since a culture is by definition a distinguishing set of behavioral patterns.

An important aspect of harmonic behavior is the interplay of consonance and dissonance. Consonant harmony is harmony that can be prolonged with pleasure. Dissonant harmony is harmony that cannot be prolonged with pleasure. A harmony is consonant or dissonant not according to any natural law* but according to cultural habit, the usage to which carriers of a certain musical tradition have become accustomed. According to its particular usage a culture will find some harmonies unbearable or unsettling, others neutral or relaxing, and still

---

*Ll. S. Lloyd expressed quite neatly the view generally accepted today that "natural laws"—that is, the laws of physics—do not govern our taste in music. In a letter to the musicologist Klaus Wachsmann written around 1948, he passed on his response to a colleague's learned paper on the subject of "natural" harmony:

> Sir, I grant you the chord of nature if you will delete the words chord and nature.
>
> *(Wachsmann 1962: I, 139)*

others extremely attractive. Musicians within the tradition manipulate these values to construct pieces that satisfy their audiences.

Chapter 7 introduces you to a kind of harmony not tolerated today in American school music, concert music, or almost all kinds of commercial recordings: heterophony. The chapter after that considers a kind of harmony we *do* tolerate, or at least understand better than heterophony, but one in which the behavior of consonance and dissonance is a little different from what we expect.

Our own harmonic values are rooted in the music of the Middle Ages, and Chapter 9 is devoted to medieval harmony. Out of medieval harmony there later developed, in the 16th century, the kind of harmony still used in our hymn books, folk-song accompaniments, and simple popular music. I will delay discussion of this later development until Chapter 13, where the rhythm of harmonic patterns can be considered. For the present I will simply point out one striking fact about Western harmony.

Throughout the one thousand years for which we possess documentary evidence, the harmonic tolerance of Western European ears has been steadily increasing. That is, harmonies treated as dissonant in the earliest records later became consonant while harmonies once unthinkable, or at least unprintable, later appeared as dissonances and then, in their turn, became consonant. The process seems to be continuing, and what people find harmonically shocking in modern music will no doubt be the sounds of repose at some time in the future.

7

The Heterophony of Lining Out

Lining out began as a performance technique allowing a group to sing unfamiliar words to a familiar tune. The leader gives out a line of text and the group sings it; the leader gives out another line of text and the group sings that, and so on. The technique is probably as old as the need for group singing.

The leader can line some songs without interrupting the forward motion of the music. *On Top of Old Smokey*, for example, leaves plenty of time for the leader's part at the end of every phrase. *My Country 'Tis of Thee*, on the other hand, gives the leader no time; the music must come to a halt again and again if it is to be lined.

Lining out has developed considerable grace and power among certain Protestant congregations despite—or perhaps because of—this problem of fitting the leader's lining of the text into the flow of the music. The style has a distinctive timing, decoration, and harmony, and the leader's part has become a solo chant carrying the congregation from one full-sounding line of text to the next.

The characteristics of the style place it outside the accepted norms of school music: its timing is so slow as to appear nonexistent, its decoration so individualistic as to appear chaotic, and its harmony, far from being one composer's blend of different melodic lines, is the disagreement of many "composers" singing one line in different ways at the same time. We call this kind of harmony "heterophony": the simultaneous variation of a single melody. The purpose of this chapter is to make you familiar with heterophony, because most of the world's harmony is heterophonic. Our Western tradition of precise unisons and carefully planned counterpoint is, in the broad view, peculiar.

A Brief History

Lining out appeared in the historical record of English-speaking people over three hundred years ago, during that brief period in the middle of the 17th century when the British monarchy collapsed and Parliament ruled.

The country was predominantly Protestant at the time, having cut all official ties to Roman Catholicism back in the 1530's. Protestant religious views ranged from conservative to radical. For the sake of simplicity, the following summary describes only the extremes of this diversity.

Conservatives retained the structure and rituals of the Roman Catholic Church while rejecting the authority of the Pope. Radicals rejected everything Catholic—the hierarchy of bishops, the rituals, the religious symbols, and the music of priests and paid musicians. Conservatives belonged to the Church of England, the head of which was the reigning monarch; authority flowed downward from the ruler to the Archbishop of Canterbury, from the Archbishop to lesser bishops, from each of these to the priests of his* diocese, and from each priest to laymen appointed to serve under him. Among radicals, authority flowed upward from the individual to the congregation, from the congregation to its elected leader, and from the elected leaders to those, if any, whom they might choose to place above themselves.

The music of conservative Protestants, like the regulation of their worship, came from above. That is, paid choristers and

---

*Women were not allowed to hold positions of authority in either religious or secular affairs at this time. Society was a patriarchy.

instrumentalists were trained by a music master and performed for the congregation music that he selected; and the ritual chants sung for the congregation by the priest and the choir were ordained by tradition and church regulations. Among radical Protestants the ultimate authority lay with the individual worshipper and his view of what the Bible said; if this view allowed singing in public worship, it was the individual and others of like mind who sang, and what they sang was up to them.

The radicals helped bring down the British monarchy in the middle of the 17th century. They joined together in what might be called a republic of congregations, sent delegates to a convention at Westminster, and with their combined voices strongly influenced the only effectively governing body left in the country, the House of Commons. As a result the Church of England was outlawed in all its aspects, from its vestments and rituals to its bishops, priests, and minor officials. Even the crucifix was banned from the meeting houses in which the radicals gathered to worship.

By these actions the radicals sought to "purify" worship and return to the ways of the earliest Christians. In England they called themselves "Puritans," and in both England and Scotland they used only biblical texts in their public services. Congregational singing, the musical style that radicals preferred, became the officially approved style throughout the country; and when radical congregations sang, they sang only biblical words.

Most of the songs in the Bible are found in the Book of Psalms. The conservative Church of England adopted a lyric English prose translation from the Hebrew and Greek originals in the 1540's, soon after the break with Rome. Figure 21-A opposite is a sample from the beginning of Psalm 23. During the following hundred years conservative congregations heard priests and professional singers chant this lyric prose to Roman Catholic tune formulas (the Church of England had no quarrel with Catholic music; the break with Rome was motivated by

Fig. 21-A

politics, economics, and philosophy, not by aesthetics).

Radical Protestants wanted nothing to do with this chanting. When they gained the upper hand in the 1640's, the Psalms their congregations sang were in a different style, one already long established in public worship in Scotland, in the parish churches of England, and in the private devotions of both radicals and conservatives.* The style was a tuneful

FIGURE 21: *PSALM 23. Radicals among the English breaking with the Roman Catholic Church in the first half of the 16th century went on to break with the religious substitute formed by King Henry VIII, the Church of England. The radicals protested, among other things, having the priests and paid musicians of the Church of England doing their musical worship for them.*

(A): the beginning of Miles Coverdale's lyric English prose translation of Psalm 23 made for the Great Bible of the Church of England, 1539-1541. The Church's priests and trained singers chanted these words to the tune formulas used by the Roman Catholics (see Figure 14). Coverdale's translation (given here in modern spelling) is still used in both the Church of England and the Protestant Episcopal Church in America. (Figure 21(B,C) and caption are on pp. 114-115.)

A

```
    1  The Lord is my shepherd:
therefore can I lack nothing.
    2  He shall feed me in a
green pasture:  and lead me
forth beside the waters of
comfort.
    3  He shall convert my soul:
and bring me forth in the paths
of righteousness, for his
Name's sake.
            (Clapton 1934: 49)
```

*Scotland was an independent nation before 1603. The break with Rome had not come there officially until 1560, but even before it came congregational Psalm singing had become an established custom.

singing instead of chanting (the difference is discussed on page 81). The tunes, invented or borrowed from the stock of melodies commonly known, made use of a very small number of musical forms. So that the Psalms would fit these forms, poets translated them into rhymed and measured English verses. The best known collection of these verses was begun in the 1530's by Thomas Sternhold, a gentleman at the court of Henry VIII. More Psalms were added by John Hopkins, a student at Oxford, and still more by other Protestant poets. The complete collection, containing verse translations of all one hundred fifty Psalms of the Old Testament, appeared in 1562 and has been known ever since as "Sternhold and Hopkins."

Radical Protestants wished to sing only biblical words in their public worship, if they sang at all. In the Hebrew and Greek sources of the Old Testament, however, the Psalms were not in rhymed and measured verse. Changes in the biblical text had to be made. Here is how the radicals of the Massachusetts Bay Colony argued the matter in the preface to their own collection of measured Psalms published at Harvard College in 1640:

> [Now] no protestant doubteth but that all the bookes of the scripture should by Gods ordinance be extant in the mother tongue of each nation, that they may be understood of all, hence the psalmes are to be translated into our english tongue; and if in our english tongue wee are to sing them, then as all our english songs (according to the course of our english poetry) do run in metre, soe ought Davids psalmes to be translated into meeter, that soe we may sing the Lords songs, as in our english tongue soe in such verses as are familiar to an english eare.
> *(Bible 1912: original preface [8]-[9])*

Fig. 21-B Figure 21-B on p. 115 shows how the "english eare" of Thomas Sternhold cast the beginning of Psalm 23. In 1640 the Protestants of the Massachusetts Bay Colony used the same basic, four-
Fig. 21-C line pattern for their own translation of this Psalm (see Figure 21-C

on p. 115) because most of the tunes they knew fitted it.*

Measured Psalms were known in several translations when the Puritans of England came to power in the middle of the 17th century. They set about selecting one translation for use by all their congregations. In 1644 they passed an ordinance explaining how the people were to learn to perform the official words:

> That the whole congregation may join herein, everyone that can read is to have a psalm-book, and all others, not disabled by age or otherwise, are to be exhorted to learn to read. But for the present, where many in the congregation cannot read, it is convenient that the minister, or some fit person appointed by him and the other ruling officers, do read the psalm line by line before the singing thereof.
>
> *(Scholes 1962: 265)*

This seems to be the earliest known reference in English to the practice of lining out.

Performance Styles

Measured Psalms must have been performed in a spritely manner in the early days, for when the Reverend John Cotton of

---

*Close structural bonds between tune and text raise the basic question, Which came first? The American scholar Bertrand Bronson feels that the form of the melody determines the form of the text in American ballads (Bronson 1959-1972: I, ix-x), and the Danish musicologist Hjalmar Thuren recognized this control in the Inuit singing of East Greenland (Thuren 1914: 7).

To appreciate the force a melody exerts on a song text, imagine trying to sing *On Top of Old Smokey* to words like the following:

> On top of Old Smokey
> All covered with pale
> White snow, it was there that
> We met, I and Dale.

When text and tune combine, the tune forces "pale" to be a noun instead of an adjective and insists that the phrase "I and Dale" is the object of the verb "met" rather than an expansion of its subject, "we."

Boston published some remarks on Psalm singing in 1647 he made the following specific reference to the "Sternhold and Hopkins" collection:

> There be Cathedrall Priests [that is, priests of the Church of England] of an Antichristian spirit, that have scoffed at Puritan Ministers, as calling the

FIGURE 21 (B,C): *the 1st stanza of Psalm 23 as rhymed and metered by Thomas Sternhold (d. 1549), Groom of the Robes to King Henry VIII. He owed his appointment at court to his Psalm verses and enjoyed the strong support of Henry's son, Prince Edward. Almost all his Psalms are cast, like this one, in quatrains alternating four stresses with three stresses and rhyming every seventh stress. In the 1612 edition consulted, one stanza usually comprised, as here, two quatrains. Sternhold's language (given here in modern spelling) is plain in all his Psalms; his syllabic rhythm is always iambic (short long, short long, etc.); and his words always form phrases corresponding in length to the lengths of the lines. The strongest break between phrases always occurs at the break between quatrains. A modern tune in this pattern is* America the Beautiful *("O beautiful for spacious skies..."); another is* Auld Lang Syne *("Should old acquaintance be forgot...").*

Though scorned in literary circles, this unpretentious poetry had an immense impact. As Hallett Smith has observed (1946: 251), "No English verse whatever was so familiar to English ears in the second half of the sixteenth century." Sternhold's verses retained their dominant position throughout the next century as well: by 1640 at least 280 editions had appeared, and by 1700 there had been over 150 more.

Scholars call the type of quatrain that Sternhold used "ballad stanza" because the majority of British traditional ballads use this form. Another term is "fourteeners," referring to the number of syllables from one rhyme to the next. In hymnals the form is known as "common meter" and abbreviated C.M. In the 16th century, however, it was known as "Sternhold's meter." Almost no British ballad texts can be dated as early as Sternhold's verse; therefore traditional British balladry probably owes its frequent use of ballad stanza to the fact that Sternhold popularized the form.

(C): the first two stanzas of Psalm 23 translated into Sternhold's meter by Puritan ministers of the Massachusetts Bay Colony and

people to sing one of Hopkins Jigs, and so hop into
the pulpit.
(Chase 1966: 16; my insert)

It is unlikely that in this spritely style the words were lined out, since lining would have interrupted the musical flow (and provided a further object for conservative Protestant ridicule).

---

published by them at Cambridge, Massachusetts, in 1640 as part of a complete book of Psalms versified for congregational singing (and generally considered to be the first book printed in the colonies). Each stanza, given here in modern spelling, has but one quatrain. An example of a tune current today for which these stanzas could have been written is Amazing Grace *("Amazing grace, how sweet the sound, . . . "); another is* Row, Row, Row Your Boat.

B

```
My shepherd is the living Lord
   nothing therefore I need.
In pastures fair with waters calm,
   he sets me for to feed:
He did convert and glad my soul,
   and brought my mind in frame:
To walk in paths of righteousness,
   for his most holy name.
```
                    (Bible 1612: 14)

C

```
The Lord to me a shepherd is,
   want therefore shall not I.
He in the folds of tender grass
   doth cause me down to lie:

To waters calm me gently leads
   Restore my soul doth he:
he doth in paths of righteousness:
   for his name's sake lead me.
```
                    (Bible 1912: Ps. 23)

If the Puritans normally sang their verse Psalms vigorously enough to be made fun of, how did they sing them when it became necessary to line out the words? The procedure they followed has been clearly summarized by Morag Macleod in her notes to a recent Scottish recording of Gaelic Psalm singing:

> The standard procedure for singing a Gaelic Psalm in the traditional manner is actually quite simple . . . : the minister, or head of the household as the case may be, will read the Psalm, or a portion of it if it is a long one. He will then say how many verses are to be sung—this varies between two and four—and will read the first two lines of the first verse. The precentor will sing those two lines to the tune that he [the precentor] has chosen (the name of the tune is not announced except in special circumstances such as during a BBC or other recording session); members of the congregation will gradually join in with him when they have ascertained what the tune is, and precentor and congregation will complete the singing of the first two lines together. It is not necessary for the precentor to precede those lines with a chant, as the congregation remembers the text from the reading. For the third and subsequent lines, right through to the end of the portion to be sung, the precentor intones the words before the congregation joins with him in singing them to the proper melody.
> *(Tangent TNGM 120: notes, p. 3, col. A)*

Macleod's description fits current American practice* among

---

*Three points excepted: American congregations that line out (1) sing hymns rather than Psalms, (2) do not have the text read through before lining out begins, and (3) line out the words one line at a time. In the service I attended in April of 1979 at the Left Beaver Old Regular Baptist Church in Floyd County, southeastern Kentucky, Elder Russell Jacobs, Moderator, simply called on a member to start a hymn after each preacher had finished (there were three preachers that day). The member called upon would not announce his choice (only men led the hymns) but simply start singing the first phrase of the melody, without lining the words. As others recognized the hymn they would join in.

the descendants of English and Scottish pioneers living today in the Appalachian uplands. It also fits earlier accounts of lining out in England and lowland Scotland.

Modern lining out is slow. It became that way by the 1660's, to judge from a contemporary account.* By the turn of the century English reformers had launched a campaign to speed it up (and to make other changes as well). By 1710 the reform had spread to the American colonies.† In 1721, for example, the young Reverend Thomas Walter contributed to the effort in Boston with a textbook entitled *The Grounds and Rules of Musick Explained*, in which he proposed that

> by the just and equal timing of the notes, our singing will be reduced to an exact length, so as not to fatigue the singer with a tedious protraction of the notes beyond the compass of a man's breath, and the power of his spirit;—a fault very frequent in the country, where I myself have twice in one note paused to take breath.
>
> (G. Hood 1970: 149)

The "tedious protraction" of the melody began, I'm sure, soon after Puritan congregations adopted lining out in the mid-17th century.†† Lining breaks up the musical flow of a song, as I've pointed out, but this effect can be minimized by reducing speed until the ending of a span no longer seems to come too abruptly. It seems hard to imagine a congregation practicing

---

*The diary of Samuel Pepys, entries for January 6, 1661 and January 5, 1662 (evaluated in Temperley 1979: I, 92).

† Entries for the winter of 1710-1711 in the diary of a wealthy planter from tidewater Virginia, William Byrd, establish this point (Byrd 1941: 272, 276, 292). The first sign of the reform in New England is the advertisement of private instruction in "Singing Psalm Tunes" which appeared in *The Boston News-Letter* for April 12–19, 1714 (Seybolt 1970: 13).

††Nicholas Temperley (1979: I, 64, 99) finds some evidence that people were already singing Psalms slowly by the end of the 16th century. He suggests that the ordinance of 1644 imposed lining out on this practice in order to reassert the primacy of the text in what had become a beloved musical ritual.

lining out and at the same time insisting on singing the disconnected phrases of the tune rapidly enough to emphasize their fragmentary nature. What Rev. Walter called a "fault" was, on the contrary, a triumph of musical instinct.

A second change may have taken place at an equally early date: the lining of the text was turned from reading into chanting, so that the ending of a span of the tune became merely the point at which one kind of musical flow changed into another. The chanting was not borrowed from the Catholic or conservative Protestant traditions, of course; it must have simply evolved, as they did, from the "conventionalities of pitch" inherent in our language (see the discussion on pp. 69-70). The American historian George Hood appreciated the musical continuity this chanting created. In 1846 he observed:

> It is but a year or two, since the writer frequently attended church, in one of the western states, where the clerk, a lawyer of some note, used to dole out the hymn two lines at a time—... always having the good fortune, to be able to run out of the tune into the words, and from the words into the tune, without stopping or changing either the pitch or time.
>
> *(G. Hood 1970: 201)*

Modern White Lining Out

As the dates of the observations I've quoted indicate, the reform movements of the early 18th century did not stop lining out either here or abroad. A modern example of white American lining out can be heard on the sound track of "High Lonesome Sound," a documentary film John Cohen made in 1962 (Cohen 1963). The singers are attending a service of the white Regular Baptist Church at Jeff, near the town of Hazard in southeastern Kentucky. Song leader and congregation are in regular alternation, as you can see in the text given below, where the congregation's part is underlined.

1.

When I can read my title clear
To mansions in the skies,
To mansions in the skies,
I'll bid farewell to ev'ry fear,
I'll bid farewell to ev'ry fear
And wipe my weeping eyes,
And wipe my weeping eyes.

2.

Should earth against my soul engage,
Should earth against my soul engage,
And fiery darts be hurled,
And fiery darts be hurled,
Then I can smile at Satan's rage,
Then I can smile at Satan's rage . . . [fade out]

(Cohen 1963: near beginning)

Disagreements in the details of the singers' lines give the music a rough, unrehearsed sound but also a warm, communal character. The notation in Figure 22 on p. 120 shows some of these disagreements. In performance the effect is not pronounced.

An observer from the Western concert-hall tradition might think at first hearing that these singers lack training and haven't rehearsed. They have been training all their lives, of course. The disagreements of their heterophony are deliberate, rooted in the philosophy that persuaded many Protestants in the 16th and 17th centuries to shun the pyramidal structure of the Church of England: the philosophy that God deals with every human being directly, not through a priest, and that each individual Christian must seek God's will by attention to conscience and the Bible. Like the Puritan congregations of the 1640's, a Baptist congregation of today is a voluntary association; its leader directs by consent. No one has the right to impose conformity on others. Among Regular Baptists even the pre-

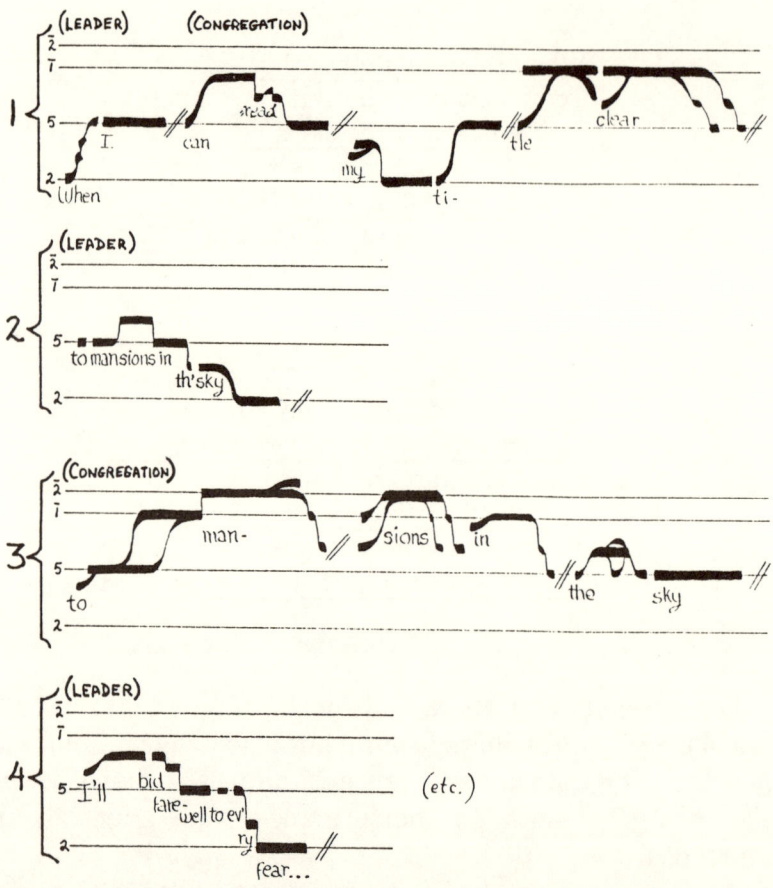

FIGURE 22: *WHEN I CAN READ MY TITLE CLEAR.* *The 17th-century practice of lining out survives in our rural South. This pictorial notation records the beginning of a performance of Isaac Watts' hymn,* When I Can Read My Title Clear, *in the Regular Baptist Church at Jeff, Kentucky, as John Cohen filmed it for his documentary of southeastern Kentucky music,* High Lonesome Sound *(Cohen 1963: near the beginning). For a general explanation of the notation, see the caption for Figure 4.*

Different members of the congregation sing the tune different ways. The resulting disagreement is only partial and occasional, producing what we call heterophony: the harmony of simultaneous variation. For visual simplicity the less prominent sound of the women's voices an octave higher has been omitted.

paring of a sermon—the rehearsing of one's thoughts, so to speak—is frowned on. They agree upon a program of worship for their meetings, but within that program the individual hopes to act as the hand of God will direct. In such a setting heterophony is the most natural kind of harmony.

Our example does not have the vocal quality of the concert hall: the singers' tone is "straight," like the tone you would use to call across the street to someone; they sing loudly; and they stress the beginning of every syllable. Our concert halls promote a smoother, more gentle style borrowed at the beginning of the 19th century from the musical entertainments of the European upper classes. These entertainments were greatly admired for their "refinement."

The American composer Samuel Holyoke was an early champion of the European style. In 1802 he published twenty-eight "necessary rules" designed to correct the kind of singing he heard around him. I quote four of them to show how close his message was to that of the modern music teacher, and how close the singing style of the Regular Baptists of Jeff is to the singing style Holyoke opposed, a style so generally accepted in his time that he had to publish rules against it.

> 2. Form the voice in as pleasing a tone as possible . . .
> 4. Practice the swell and diminish frequently [that is, often make your notes grow louder and softer].
> 5. Never force the voice beyond its natural compass or strength. Many singers suppose that they perform well when they exert the full strength of the voice; but this precludes all delicacy of taste and expression, . . .
> 19. Take breath between the proper passages and in proper time, and never catch the breath in the middle of a word [see "title in Frame 1 and "mansions" in Frame 3 of Figure 22] . . .
>
> *(Macdougall 1940: 109; my inserts)*

Heterophony is absent from present-day performances of Western European art music, except where it has been created deliberately in compositions of the last few decades. It is not taught in our conservatories, and it is vigorously opposed in our schools. The "educated" ears among us are therefore not used to it, which is too bad: much of the world's music is heterophonic, as I've mentioned, and our own art music *was* heterophonic prior to the 19th century. John Milton, for example, obviously took heterophony as the normal practice when he described in 1644 what he would have schoolboys listen to for the purpose of "recreating and composing their travailed spirits":

> The interim of unsweating themselves regularly, and [of] convenient rest before meat may both with profit and delight be taken up ... with the solemn and divine harmonies of musick heard, or learnt; either while the skilfull *Organist* plies his grave and fancied descant [that is, improvisation], in lofty fugues, or the whole Symphony with artful and unimaginable touches adorn and grace the well studied cords of some choise composer; ...
> *(Milton 1959: 409-410)*

Nowadays the "whole Symphony," the people playing the orchestral music of the elite tradition, play only what they find written down and do not presume to add "unimaginable touches" of their own, which would create heterophony wherever two players had the same part but different ideas.

If one listens to the music of Figure 22 *for the words*, the effect is plodding. The author himself, the Congregational minister Isaac Watts of London (1647-1748), knew the lining-out way of singing and "disliked the heavy motion, tedious syllables, the tiresome extent and the no-meaning style" (Macdougall 1940: 137). He was a poet, in fact the most influential hymn writer of the 18th century, and I think his attention was on the words rather than the musical flow of what he listened to. Lining out indeed offers a heavy, tediously drawn-out verbal experience.

But if one listens as a musician rather than as a poet, one hears phrases flowing with powerful effect one into another. And if one joins in the singing of a lined-out hymn, the experience requires neither explanation nor apology: the loudness of the voices, the clashing sound of the heterophony, the monumental wave created with each slow-moving phrase, all express perfectly the basic message of the singer, which is the isolation of the human animal and the need of that isolated being to communicate with God.

Let us turn for a moment from the heterophony of lining out to the embellishments that produce much of the heterophony. You can hear them in the solo singing of Jean Ritchie shown in the music of Figure 23* on pp. 124-5. Her ancestor James Ritchie came to Virginia from England around 1768, whence her people moved into the southeastern corner of Kentucky. She was born there, in the small community of Viper, where lining out is a strong tradition. The hymn *Wondrous Love* recorded in Figure 23 is sung the way she learned it from her family. It was a favorite of her mother's father, John Hall.

Fig. 23

Wondrous Love is not a verse translation of a Psalm. It is a hymn: a religious song text of nonbiblical origin. Radical Protestants of the 16th and 17th centuries did not sing hymns in their public services, where the only guides for worship were the words of the Bible and one's private conscience. Some radical congregations would not even sing Psalms together in

---

*Sung in lining-out style but without the lining of the text you find in lines 2 and 4 of Figure 22 on p. 120. As Miss Ritchie explained to me:

> In our church tradition, the "lining out" is done only when there are others (congregation or family group, etc.) to join in the singing. My mother often sang her religious songs about the house, when she was working, but she'd never think of "lining them out" just for herself. Sometimes now, during a performance on stage, I will "line out" a hymn in order to give the audience a feeling for the sound of it, but usually it *is* a functional thing and not a permanent part of the song.
>
> (Ritchie 1981: 1)

For some of her anecdotes about lining out see Ritchie 1980: 82-83, 93.

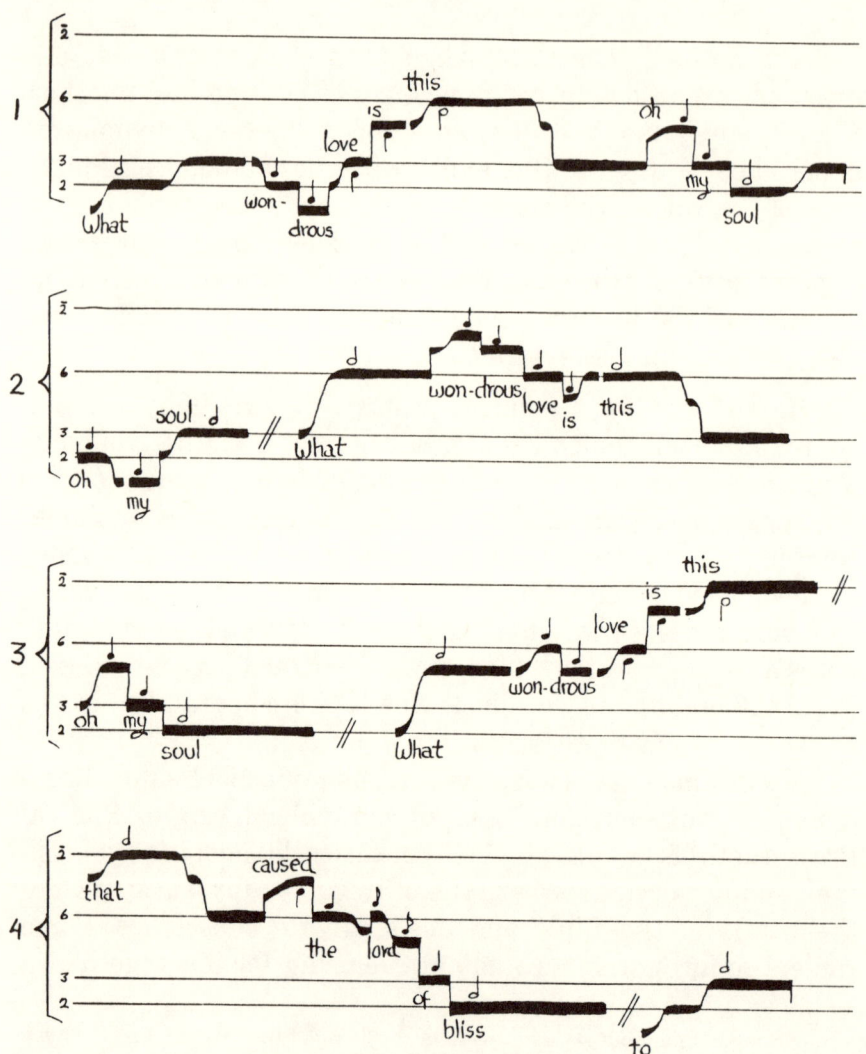

FIGURE 23: *WONDROUS LOVE. This first verse of an anonymous early 19th-century hymn is sung by Jean Ritchie of southeastern Kentucky in the decorated style her people use when singing a lined-out hymn (Tradition TLP 1011: side 2, band 1). For a general explanation of the notation see the caption for Figure 4.*

Standard musical notes have been added to mark levels of pitch which appear in the hymn books carrying the music for these words. Jean Ritchie sings many other pitch levels, some of them extended enough to be considered main notes in the tune. Her style was

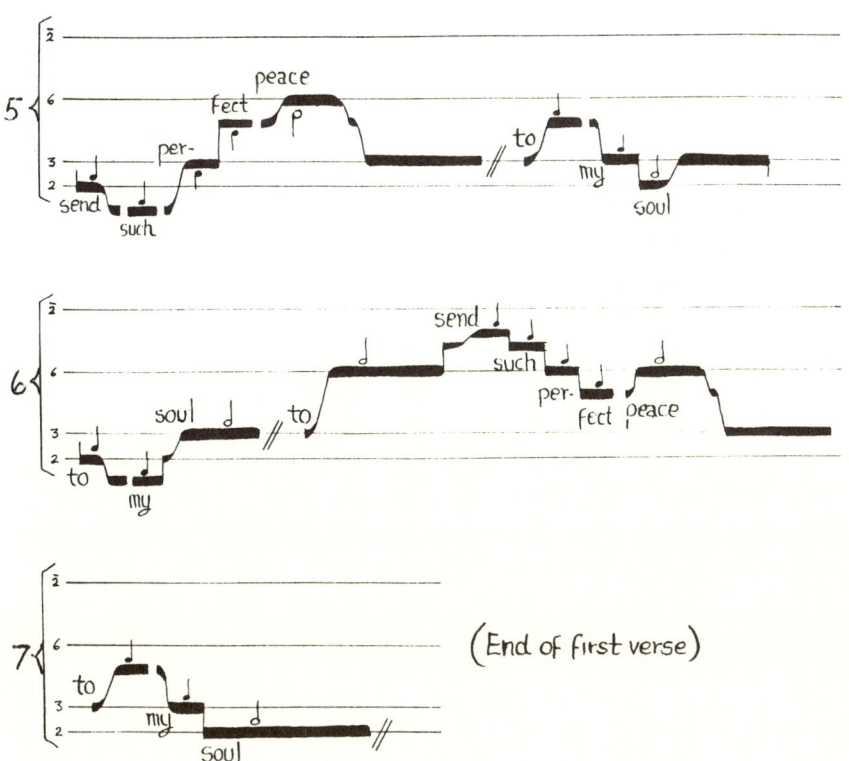

apparently well known in the 18th century, and the heterophony it created in group singing was a familiar sound.

The music analyst typically thinks of Jean Ritchie's melodic line as the personal decoration of a "basic" melody, which is the simpler version printed in hymn books. It seems likely, however, that much of her "personal decoration" is in fact the material of a melodic mode and represents a group of basic ideas that have travelled together for a long time. Notice that the "decoration" consists of but a few melodic turns often used (the prominent "decorative" shape given the word "this" in Frames 1 and 2 appears again with the singing of "peace" in Frames 5 and 6, and "that" in Frame 4; compare also the singing of "soul" in Frames 1, 2, 5, and 6 with "to" in Frame 4). This restricted group of melodic turns may not be used by everyone who sings Wondrous Love, but they may well be used by Ritchie and others who share her tradition whenever they sing tunes of a certain kind. By dismissing these turns as mere decoration we may miss the presence of a "basic" set of melodic behaviors that constitute the mode of the music.

public services, fearing that unbelievers might endanger them all by hypocritically joining in.

These attitudes did not change until the 18th century. An exception occurred in a Baptist congregation at Southwark, the commercial-dock section of London, under the leadership of Benjamin Keach. Hymns were sung there as early as 1670, and in Philadelphia, under the influence of Benjamin's son Elias, probably by the end of the century. The views of father and son supporting the practice were included in a Confession of Faith adopted by Baptists in New Jersey beginning as early as 1712 and by the one formal alliance of Baptist churches in the colonies, the Baptist Association, in 1742 (McGlothlin 1911: 294-295). Settlers moving through the Appalachians during the 18th century were accompanied by Baptist ministers connected with this association. Hymn singing got an early start on the American frontier.

We know practically nothing about the origin of the hymn *Wondrous Love*, shown on pp. 124-125. Some sources credit the words to "Christopher" or "F. Christopher," while others give no author. The striking meter of the poem links it to secular songs of the past four hundred years, from today's raucous singing of "My name is Samuel Hall,/ Samuel Hall, Samuel Hall" back to a song beginning "My lufe is lyand seik, / Send hym ioy, send hym ioy," mentioned in *The Complaynt of Scotlande*, a book published around 1549. Religious songs in the same meter are equally old, and one experienced scholar suggests that the parent mold for all these songs was cast "in the bosom of the [Catholic] Church, in England, at some time in the later Middle Ages" (Bronson 1969: 36). Here is the first stanza of *Wondrous Love* as Jean Ritchie sings it.

> What wondrous love is this,
>   Oh my soul, oh my soul?
> What wondrous love is this,
>   Oh my soul?
> What wondrous love is this
> That caused the Lord of bliss

> To send such perfect peace
> To my soul, to my soul,
> To send such perfect peace
> To my soul?

Ritchie's tune appeared with these words in rural hymn books as early as the 1840's (Reynolds 1976: 239). The song is but one drop in a flood of religious expression that poured from the educated and uneducated alike once the barriers to hymn writing were down. Where the tune came from is presently no better known than the source of the words.

To the pictorial notation on pp. 124-125 I've added symbols from standard musical notation wherever a pitch that Ritchie sings corresponds to a note in the common printed version of this hymn. As you can see, much of what she sings is not to be found in a hymn book. She has added—or, to put it the other way around, the printed version has omitted—many clear and sustained pitches, as well as short slurs and fixed pitches only briefly touched in passing. Prominent sliding, a feature of the holler, is rare in this style (but see "oh" in Frame 1 and "caused" in Frame 4).

Jean Ritchie's way of singing was well known to American composers of the late 18th century. They expected to hear a tune sung differently from the way it was printed. Andrew Law (1749–1821) spoke of

> these little notes that are sprinkled here and there among the common notes of the tune and add nothing to the [notated] time of the bar in which they are sung, but are to be sung in connection with the notes to which they belong.... If rightly sung they give to the sounds a turn that is exquisitely nice and delicate.... Sometimes they are merely notes of "transition" from a preceding to a succeeding sound, but more frequently they are considered principal notes, dwelt upon somewhat longer than the notes with which they are connected.
> *(Macdougall 1940: 107)*

Some of the pitches peculiar to Ritchie's version sound, as Andrew Law put it, like principal notes rather than transitions between principal notes; and her transitions themselves seem in no way less responsible for the melody than those more emphasized moments. Indeed, if one learns to sing a verse of this hymn in Ritchie's style, imitating her exactly, and then sings the same verse using only the printed notes, each version will seem powerful in its own way, neither one the shadow of the other.*

Modern Black Lining Out

Black Americans also practice lining out. They learned to do so in former centuries as slaves observing their white masters. In the development of slave song, as the pioneer black educator and political leader William E. B. Du Bois observed,

> the first [step] is African music, the second Afro-American, while the third is a blending of Negro music with the music heard in the foster land. The result is still distinctively Negro and the method of blending original, but the elements are both Negro and Caucasian.
>
> *(Du Bois 1903: 256)*

The first slaves were brought to America in 1619, a year before the Pilgrims landed in New England, but not until the end of the 18th century did Christian missionary work among this captive population become more than occasional. An early effort was that of the Presbyterian minister Samuel Davis of Hanover, Virginia, who in 1751 sent away for copies of the

---

*The music theorist is wont to assume that the essence of a melody lies in its main points of emphasis and overall direction. A performer would disagree, claiming that the detailed sequence of sounds is as important as any more general aspects. Tony Barrand, himself a fine singer of folksongs, calls the small differences in performances of the same song "the glory of... seemingly infinite variety," adding that "it is not the same basic forms which drive the artist in any field but the expressive possibilities of slight but significant nuance" (Barrand 1983: 2).

hymns of Isaac Watts because, as he wrote,

> I cannot but observe, that the *Negroes*, above all the Human Species that I ever new, have an Ear for Musick, and a kind of extatic Delight in Psalmody; and there are no books they learn so soon, or take so much Pleasure in . . .
>
> *(Epstein 1963: 199)**

They responded with enthusiasm when the material arrived, as he later reported:

> Sundry of them lodged all night in my kitchen; and sometimes when I have awakened at two or three in the morning, a torrent of sacred psalmody has poured into my chamber. In this exercise some of them spend the whole night.
>
> *(Chase 1966: 80)*

Until the first half of the 19th century it was *not* usual to segregate black worshippers from white, and even then the practice was not universal. Sidney Bonner, a former slave in Pickens County, Alabama, recalled in an interview that

> de quality white folks belonged at Big Creek [Baptist Church] and when dere slaves got sho'nuff 'ligion, day have 'em jine at Big Creek and be baptized at de swimmin' hole. Some of de niggers want to have dere own meetin's, but Lawd chile, dem niggers git happy and get to shoutin' all over de meadow where dey built a bresh arbor. Massa John quick put a stop to dat.
>
> *(Federal 1941: I, 40)*

Ruby Pickins Tartt collected specific evidence of white songs in the slave repertoire from Amy Chapman, born a slave to Governor Reuben Chapman of Alabama:

---

*Watts had some of his hymns published as "Psalms of David imitated," and Davis and many others have ever since referred to them as Psalms, although these poems were never mere verse translations and usually not even strict paraphrases of the biblical Psalms.

> Us didn't go to no nigger church, caze dere warn't none. ... de song I lacked bes' was a white folks song. Twarn't no nigger song. It was lack dey sing it now, 'cep' mo' lovely, Miss, mo' lovely.
>
> > Dark was de night,
> > Col' was de groun'
> > On which my Savior lay.
> > Blood in drops of sweat run down,
> > In agony he pray:
> >
> > Lawd 'move this bitter cup,
> > If sich dy sacred will;
> > If not content, I'll drink it up,
> > Whose pleasure I'll fulfill.
> > *(Federal 1941: I, 59)*

This is indeed a "white folks song." The words were composed by Thomas Haweis, a white priest of the Church of England, who published it first in 1792 under the title *Gethsemane*.

We don't know what tune Ms. Chapman sang, since her interviewer did not note it down; but Mary Price, a black American from Louisiana, recorded the same words and perhaps the same tune in 1954. As you may be able to guess from the text transcribed below from her singing, she performed in lining-out style: substantial pauses, shown here as line endings, divide the text into single words and very small word groups; they also occur in the middle of words, between lines three and four and between lines seven and eight; and in the underlined part of line five the characteristic lining of the text takes place, a rapid chanting of words yet to come in the slow singing of the tune. (Unlike Jean Ritchie, Mary Price lines out the words even though she is singing by herself.)

> Dark
> Was the night
> And cold the
> [Th]e ground
> <u>On which the Lord was laid.</u> On which

The
Lord wa[s]
[W]as laid.
(Folkways FA 2656: side 2, band 2)

The vocal style of Mary Price is much more elaborate than that of Jean Ritchie. Figure 24 on the next two pages shows the melody, which can be compared with *Wondrous Love* on pp. 124-125. Note that a good deal more music is given to each word by Mary Price and that she sings many pitches with *vibrato,* a rapid but slight fluctuation of pitch often used as a conscious vocal technique by black Americans but rarely by white American folk singers.

The effect of a congregation singing heterophonically in the style of Mary Price is quite different, as you can imagine, from what one hears when a congregation sings hetero-

Fig. 24

FIGURE 24: *DARK WAS THE NIGHT. The opening of a late 18th-century English hymn,* Gethsemane, *is drawn on pp. 132-3 as performed in lining-out style by the black American singer Mary Price (Folkways FA 2656: side 2, band 2). For a general explanation of the notation see the caption for Figure 4.*

This is a much more ornate melodic line than that of Jean Ritchie shown on pp. 124-125, and to show the rapid passages of decoration more clearly I have spread them out so that they appear slower than they are. Vibrato, a rapid fluctuation between extremely close pitch levels, has been shown as a generalized wavering of the vocal line which does not portray that fluctuation in specific detail. As the notation at the beginning of Frame 2 and midway in Frame 4 indicates, vibrato is a conscious technique applied or withheld by the singer. A double virgule (//) marks the temporary end of forward motion. Other breaks in the melodic line do not seem to be pauses so much as gulps of silence—tense moments in which the forward motion is sustained.

Though singing alone, Mary Price lines out her words (Frame 4). This may have been done for the benefit of Frederick Ramsey, Jr., who made the recording, but I think not; rather, I expect she simply sang as a whole what she learned by ear as a whole: what began as a technique for teaching new words to an old tune has become part of the song among carriers of the tradition.

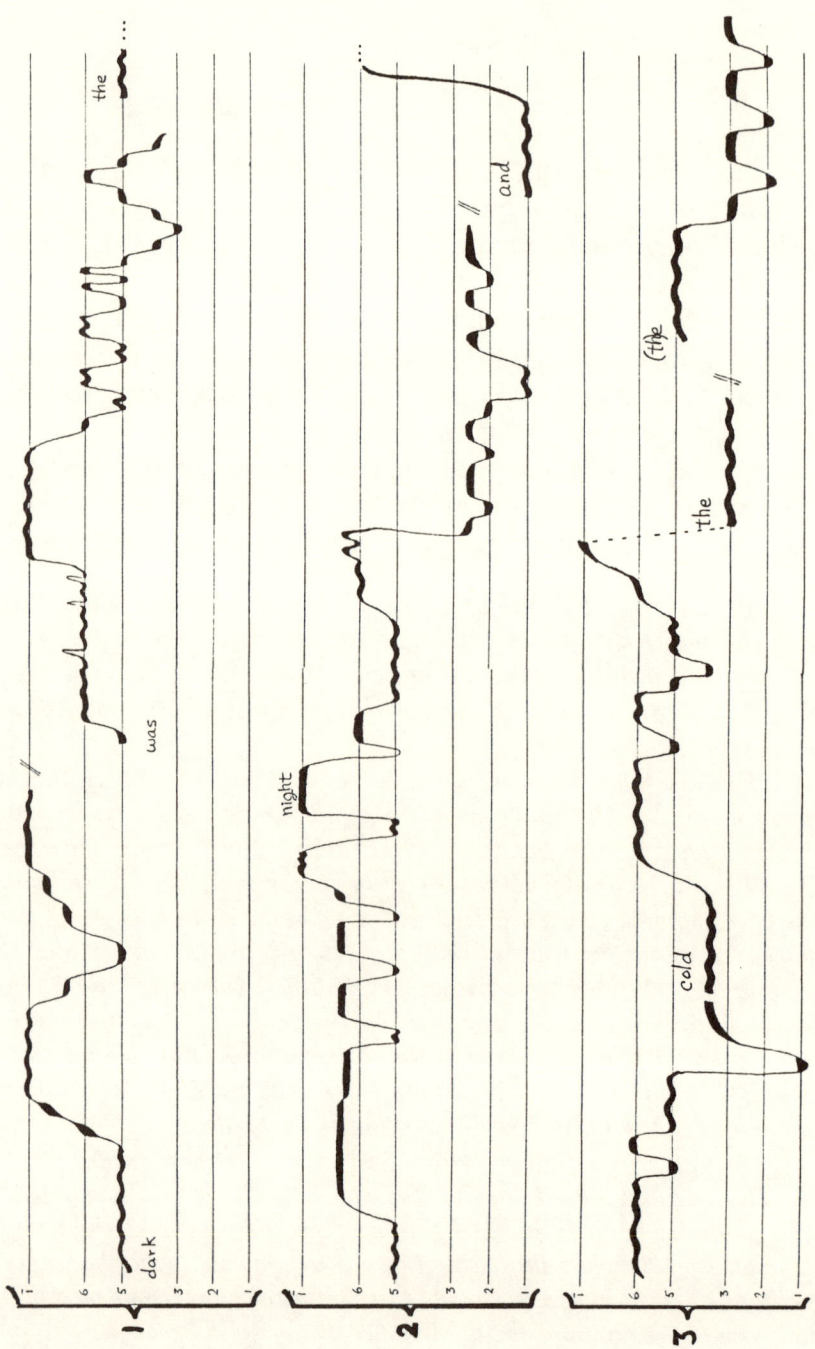

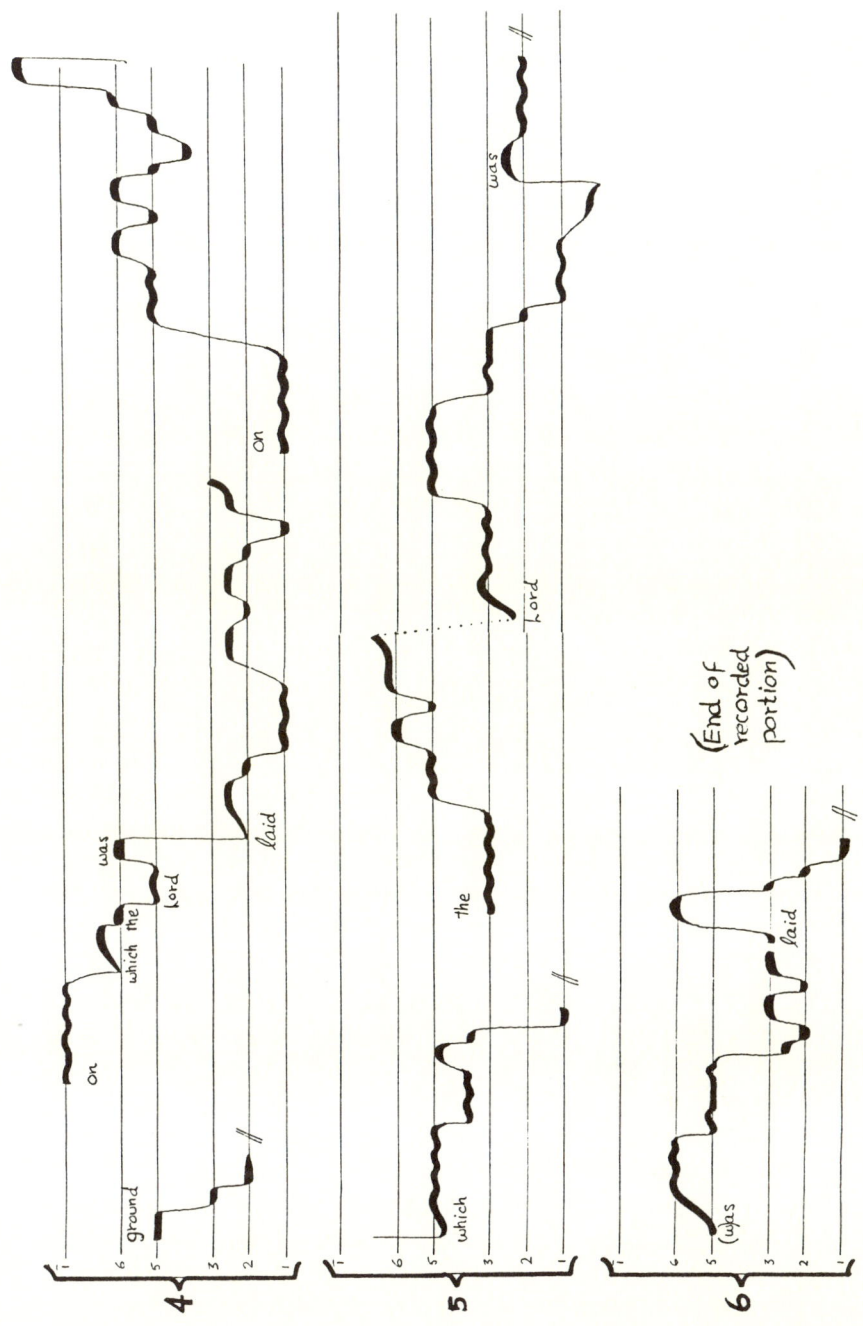

phonically in the style of Jean Ritchie: the simultaneous versions of the tune differ more from each other, even to the extent of becoming at times separate, juxtaposed melodic lines, as in the example that follows.

Fig. 25

In early September of 1926 a black American preacher from Atlanta, Georgia, the Reverend J. M. Gates, travelled with some of his congregation to Camden, New Jersey, where they recorded "sermons with singing" for Victor and four other companies (Dixon and Godrich 1970: 38-40). The singing included lined-out hymns, among them *I Heard the Voice of Jesus*, which is transcribed from their performance in Figure 25 opposite and overleaf. Compare this complexity with that of the singing of the white Regular Baptists shown on page 120.

FIGURE 25: *I HEARD THE VOICE OF JESUS. The opening of a mid-19th-century Scottish hymn,* The Voice from Galilee, *is drawn here as it was lined out in a recording studio by a black American preacher, the Reverend J. M. Gates of Atlanta, Georgia, assisted by three of his congregation, two women and one man (Folkways FA 2952: side 3, band 2). For a general explanation of the notation see the caption for Figure 4.*

Solid black lines represent the congregation's parts, a hatched line the part of Rev. Gates. For clarity, all voices have been drawn as if equally loud, although in fact two congregational voices, one male and one female, were barely audible. The text extracted on page 136 follows the phrasing of Rev. Gates, who sang the loudest. Vibrato has not been shown because it does not seem to vary significantly.

The ensemble generates three main vocal lines, each a different version of the same tune. Rev. Gates sings the tune at its proper place in the Western octave series and creates the most elaborate version (compare the first word they sing together in Frame 1). Only slightly less elaborate is the line sung softly by the male member of the congregation a fourth or fifth (and occasionally an octave) below him. The decorative style of this line recalls the singing of Mary Price on the preceding page. A fourth or fifth above Rev. Gates two women sing the plainest line of all with occasional heterophony between themselves.

When simultaneous variations diverge (continued at top of p. 137)

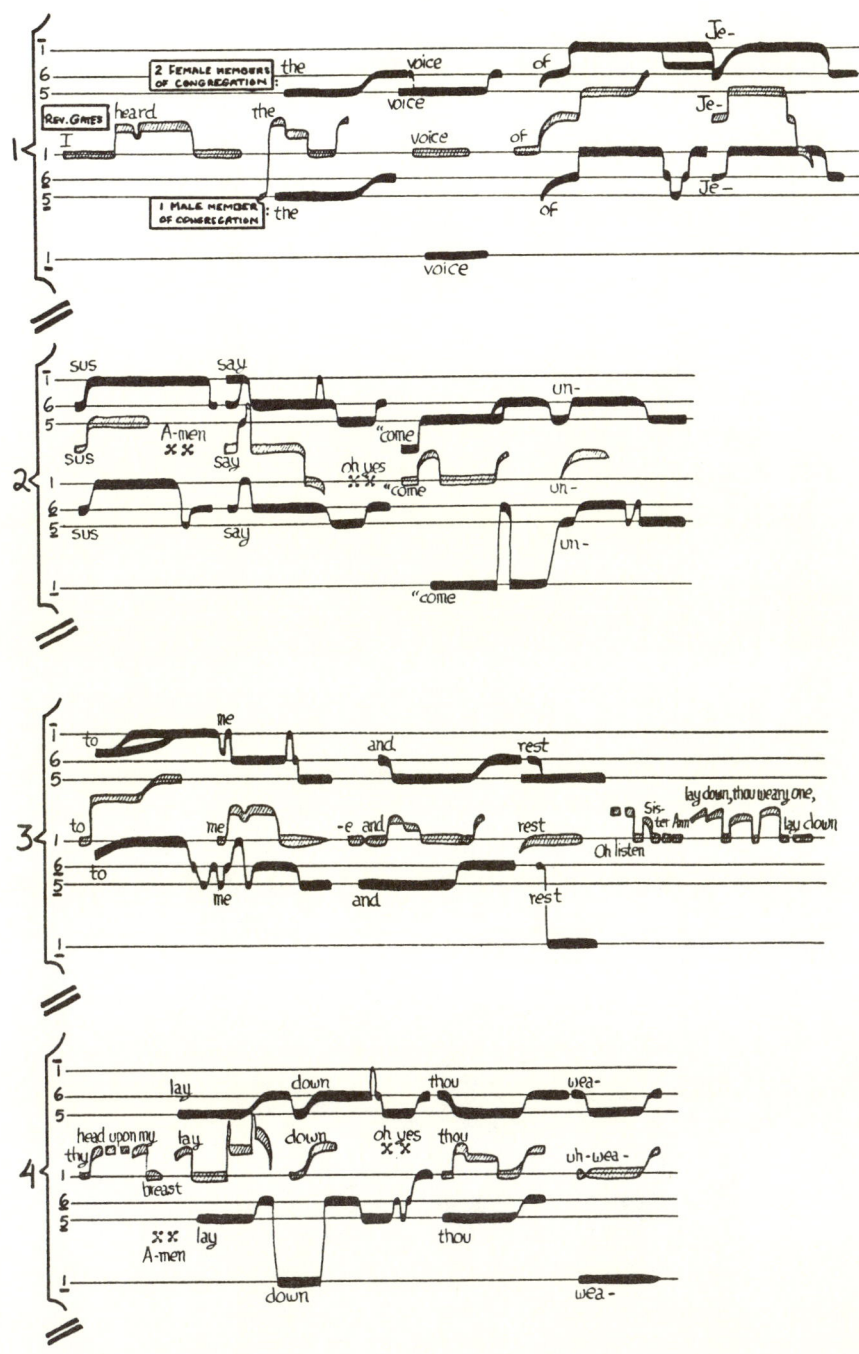

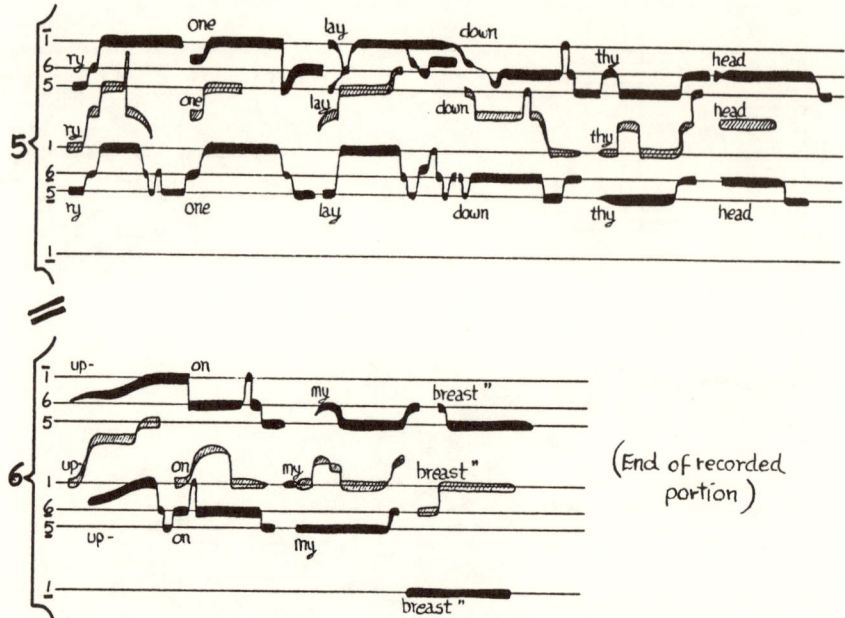

In the text transcribed below you can see the characteristic effects of lining out: the dividing of the words into small groups, the frequent breaking apart of individual words, and the uninterrupted lining of verses to come. Words sung or spoken alone by Rev. Gates are not underlined; those sung or spoken by members of his congregation are. Syllables separated in performance by a pause are here separated by a virgule (/). Words not part of the original hymn text appear in brackets.

I heard / the / voice / of / Je- / sus [Amen!] / say: / [oh, yes!] / "Come / un- / to / me- / e and / rest. /
[Oh listen (?)Sister (?)Ann]
Lay down, thou weary one, lay down
Thy head upon my breast. [Amen!] /
Lay / down, [oh, yes!] / thou wea- / ry / one, / lay / down / Thy / head / u- / pon / my / breast."

(Folkways FA 2952: side 3, band 2)

enough they become different melodies. Each of us has a separate idea of how much is too much, and when that point is reached, heterophony becomes counterpoint. In the present example, I hear that happen when the lowest voice drops down to pitch level 1 in Frames 3, 4, and 6 and when the congregation first joins Rev. Gates in Frames 1 and 4. Others might not share my perception and they would be equally correct, for music is a subjective experience.

This is, once again, a "white folks' song." The words were composed by the white Presbyterian minister Horatius Bonar at Kelso, Scotland, and published in 1846 under the title *The Voice from Galilee* for the use of the Free Church of Scotland.

Ben Bailey has found the practice of lining hymns still flourishing today in black congregations in central Mississippi. Unlike the white practice, the black practice is predominantly urban. Two of the churches Bailey surveyed, moreover, have "congregations made up largely of highly educated, professional classes" (Bailey 1978: 9). Though sometimes used to climax a sermon as in white congregations, the lined hymn was found by Bailey to be

> usually reserved for performance in the devotional or "prayer service" which precedes the worship service proper. The elders of the church seat themselves before the congregation and take turns in "raising" (that is, choosing and leading) the hymns and praying.... [The] worshippers will stand to sing the last stanza and then, after sitting down, continue to hum at least one more stanza as the elder or deacon prays. . . . Once the prayer is finished, another elder raises another hymn and the entire procedure is repeated until it is time for the worship service to start, generally signalled by the arrival of the minister in the pulpit, the sound of the piano or organ, and the procession of the choir. Used in this way, the lined hymn helps to set an emotional tone for the service which is to follow.
>
> *(Bailey 1978: 4)*

In the nineteen congregations Bailey surveyed, a total of only eight lined hymns were in use. This one by Bonar was among them. A small repertoire has always been typical of congregations that line out their hymns. It was one of the defects of Protestant worship in both England and America, according to reformers of the early 18th century.* They tried to improve the situation by teaching congregations to sightread their songs from printed music. In America their efforts established two civic choral traditions, one followed regularly in our concert halls, the other hidden until recently in the rural uplands of our southern states. This second, lesser-known tradition will be discussed in Chapter 16.

*Millar Patrick, writing of the song leader ("precentor") in British congregations of the 18th and 19th centuries where lining out was the custom, tells us:

> It was no uncommon thing for him to know only three or four tunes. At one church a visiting minister was told by the precentor before the service, "I can sing only twa [two] tunes, sir, so ye maunna gi'e oot [musn't give out] three psalms."
> *(Patrick 1949: 130-131)*

8

Bulgarian Harmony That "Rings Like A Bell"

Bulgaria lies just north of Greece. A mountain range forms their common border, and in its narrow valleys and thickly forested slopes many villages have practiced traditional music in almost complete isolation for centuries.

The area suffered Turkish occupation for five hundred years, beginning in the 14th century. During that time there was no chance for influence from the West to penetrate. The occupying Turks made no attempt to impose their ways upon the villages; they quartered themselves in the larger towns and controlled the surrounding peasant communities from there. Experts find today no trace of Turkish musical style in the songs of this mountainous border country, not even among the *pomaks*, the descendants of Bulgarians forcibly converted by the Turks from Christianity to the Muslim faith.

The Christianity of Bulgaria is Eastern Orthodox, a branch of the Catholic faith administered from Istanbul rather than Rome. King Boris I of Bulgaria opened his country to missionaries from this church when they converted him to Christianity in the 9th century. Since then all major events in the lives of Bulgarian peasants have been sanctified by Eastern Orthodox rituals and ritual music. Over the past thousand years this ritual music has undoubtedly influenced village music.

A second influence in recent times has been the radio,

which broadcasts urban songs, folk performances from other areas of the country, and music in Western style. Since the Second World War (1939-1945), the number of radio sets in the villages has greatly increased, and it is hard to imagine that radio programs have not affected the music of even the most remote communities.

A third influence may be school music. In America, public and private schools and summer camps use both folk and popular musical traditions but alter them by discarding their indigenous styles of performance, especially their timbres, in favor of the style proper to Western European art music. This process creates a separate musical tradition renewed year after year within these institutions and passed down outside them from one generation to the next by those who remember their institutional experience with pleasure. This derivative tradition has had little effect upon the original traditions it draws on. It celebrates a separate set of social relationships and therefore lacks any connections with those traditions through which it might influence them. Furthermore, the original traditions themselves are under no pressure to adopt the performance style of schools and camps.

In Bulgaria the situation is much the same but with one important difference. Like us, the national government promotes musical performances based on folk traditions, and regional styles have been modified in favor of a national style. The difference is that in Bulgaria army groups, civic organizations, factory employees, and the people in schools and universities are encouraged to compete on a local, regional, and national level. Adult villagers with musical ability can gain wide recognition by participating. Thus the program pressures the carriers of folk traditions to fit into a national style and may have considerable influence on village tradition.

This chapter presents three examples of Bulgarian vocal harmony, the first two in a village style apparently not influenced by the government's program or the radio, the third in the newly developed national style.

The Harmony of Village Song

Bulgarian villagers sing together both heterophonically and with a blending of independent melodic lines no different, in principle, from the blending in our own vocal music. Village ears, however, enjoy sustained clashes of sound our own ears do not tolerate more than a moment. The Bulgarians themselves say this clashing sound "rings like a bell" (Katzarova-Koukoudova 1954: 209b). They hear as consonant, in other words, what we hear as dissonant. Harmonic values are not universal; like every other aspect of musical communication, they vary from culture to culture.

Our first example comes from the village of Obidim, which lies at the end of a road about thirty miles north of the Greek border, on the eastern slope of Pirin Mountain. It is a song sung by women as they sew the red and white silk banner carried in a wedding procession. Three stanzas of the strophic text are given below.

1

NE TREPERI,   BELA KOPRI
Don't tremble, white silk,

BELA, BELA KOPRINO,   I!
White, white silk,   ee!

2

TEPURVA   KE ZATREPE,
Time will come for you to tremble,

KE ZATREPE(RISH),   I!
For you to tremble,   ee!

3

JE KOGA NA   DEVER DARI,
When   to the *dever*   gifts,

JE NA   DEVER DARI DA(DESH), I!
When to the *dever*   gifts you give,   ee!

(Koenig and Raim 1984)

"White silk" in the first stanza clearly refers both to the banner and to the bride in her white veil. The *dever* is the best man, usually the groom's brother, and he joins with the couple and their godparents in the Eastern Orthodox marriage ritual. An important part of the folk ceremony surrounding this ritual is the gift of clothing from the bride to the *dever* and others. Girls begin preparing their gifts when they are eight or nine years old, and by the time they marry in their early twenties they may have made well over a hundred articles by hand.

Boris Kremenliev, a composer and musicologist who is himself from a small village in Bulgaria, has made clear the highly traditional nature of wedding songs, noting that

> marriage celebrations always last for several days, in the course of which a whole group of traditional songs will be sung. Often there are as many as thirty to forty songs in such a cycle. . . . For each step in the preparation of the wedding and for every day during the week which precedes the ceremony there are special songs . . . . Many [of them] . . . reveal a strong sentiment that for the two newly married young people the carefree days are over, that the new life may prove to be as difficult as it will be different.
>
> *(Kremenliev 1952: 115, 120)*

The bride suffers the most. She must leave her family forever, exchanging her relatively pleasant girlhood for the hard physical labor of managing her husband's home and helping in the fields. Kremenliev has translated a wedding song that says this well:

> Farewell, family and relatives,
> Farewell my own mother;
> Do not forget to water my flowers
> With fresh water in the morning,
> With tears at noon.
>
> *(Kremenliev 1957: 313)*

Ne Treperi, the song on p. 141, was performed for Ethel Raim and Martin Koenig by four older women of Obidim. One sang the highly ornamented part drawn in Figure 26, overleaf, as a narrow black line. The others sang the simple sustained lower part drawn as a broad, hatched line in the same figure.

Fig. 26

The two parts are sometimes different and sometimes the same, as you can see. Those who interpret the interaction as a unison with many disagreements hear the harmony as heterophony; those who interpret it as the combining of different pitches, but with many unisons, hear the harmony as counterpoint. The distinction between heterophony and counterpoint is one of degree and, like all musical perception, subjective. It is possible to hear the example either way, or sometimes one way and sometimes the other, and different people will not necessarily hear it the same way at the same time. (The same is true of the hymn lined out by Rev. Gates and his congregation which was discussed on pp. 134-137.)

Take a closer look at the harmonies of this example: the main tones are either in unison or on adjacent levels of the Western octave series. Westerners hear the harmony of adjacent pitch levels as dissonant, especially the harmony levels lying particularly close together (such as 3 and 4 in this example). We enjoy such dissonance when it briefly spices the more pleasant harmony of pitches further apart, and in the present century the spice has become more sustained in both elite compositions and arrangements used by dance bands (though not in our traditional harmonies for hymns, country dances, and folk songs). In this example, however, the traditional singers of Obidim use almost no other harmony but that of unison and adjacent pitch levels. For them it is clearly a consonance.

The Influence of the Bagpipe

The clashing sound of the harmonies of the singers of Obidim is emphasized by a piercing vocal timbre remarkably

144

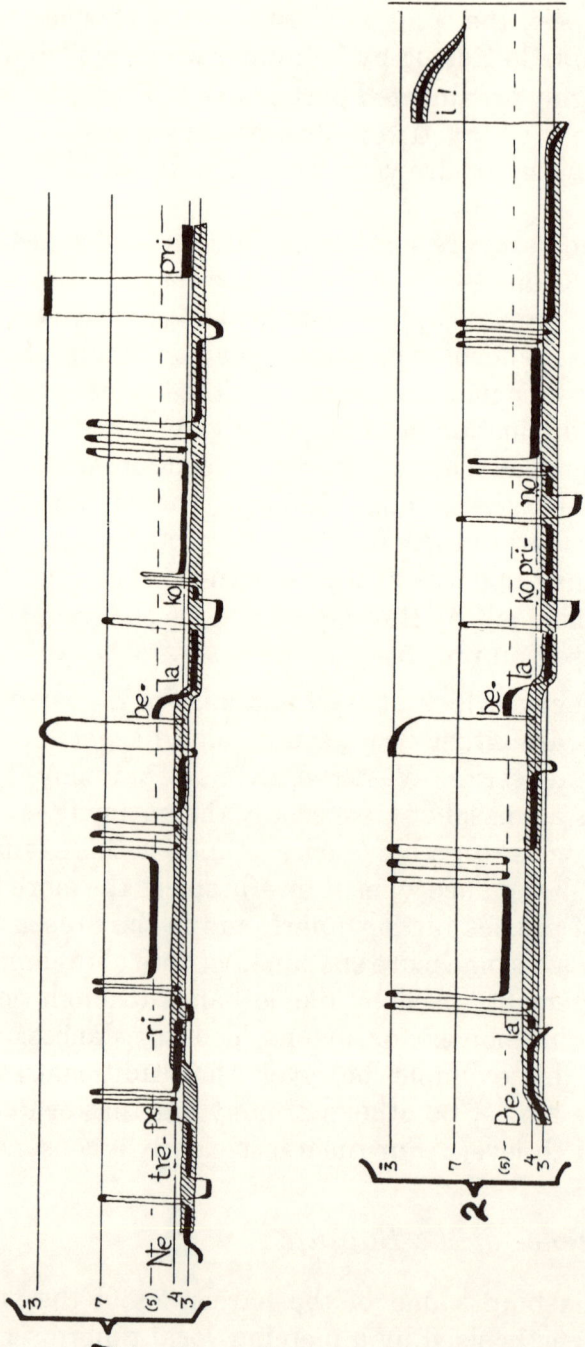

FIGURE 26: NE TREPERI. This is the first stanza of a traditional wedding song sung as a vocal duet for female soloist and female unison chorus as recorded in the late 1960's by Martin Koenig and Ethel Raim in the mountain village of Obidim in southwestern Bulgaria (from field tape in Koenig and Raim 1984; approximately the same sound on Nonesuch H 72038: side 1, band 3). The caption for Figure 4 explains the notation.

Soloist Magda Georgieva Mavrikova sings the highly decorated line drawn in solid black. Her rapid single, double, and triple oscillations are yodeling effects derived from the decoration used by players of the local bagpipe, the **kaba gaida** (shown on p. 153). The brief downward drop of her voice before a change of syllable is her equivalent of the effect created by the bagpiper's "closed fingering," a style of playing in which the piper neatly separates the notes of his melody by closing all the holes of his pipe after fingering one note and before fingering the next, thereby inserting between them the sound of the pipe's lowest note.

Magda Borisova Beluthova, Penka Nikolova Chukarinova, and Vesa Atanasova Zinkova sing the simple, slow moving line drawn with slanted hatching. Because each pitch is sustained long enough to have the effect of a drone, the combination of these pitches with those of the soloist is called "drone harmony." The two parts are usually at the unison or on adjacent levels of pitch. To Western ears the harmony of adjacent pitch levels is dissonant—that is, it cannot be sustained with pleasure; to Bulgarian ears, however, it is evidently consonant—Bulgarians sustain it with pleasure, saying that it "rings like a bell."

Frame 2 has been offset to the right so that its melodic content aligns vertically with almost identical content in Frame 1. The stanza is essentially a single phrase and its repetition.

like that of the bagpipe played by men of the region, the *kaba gaida* (Figure 27 on p. 153). After briefly discussing this vocal timbre, I will point out other connections with the *gaida* to be found in the vocal decoration and, perhaps, the drone harmony of *Ne Treperi*.

In the concert hall we shun the plain, harsh sound of these women's voices, but outside the hall it is widespread because it is natural. Rural folk singers like Almeda Riddle of Arkansas, Roscoe Holcomb of Kentucky, and Marie Hare of Maine use it, and it is common among everyday country folk like the Regular Baptist congregation of Jeff, Kentucky (see p. 121). Children in both city and country use it, and if you don't hear it at school assemblies you certainly do on the playground.

For singing Western art music we use a sweeter sound apparently adopted in the early 19th century from the singing patronized by the elite classes of Western Europe.* Some evidence of this adoption comes from the American singing-school movement and will be discussed in Chapter 16. For the present I wish to emphasize that one kind of singing is not "better" than any other but simply different. Judgements we make about foreign musical traditions can not be based on their content, obviously, because we are not competent to evaluate that content; we can only judge it as if it occurred within our own musical tradition and call it, accordingly, "fine," "awful," "rough," "nasal," "boring," etc. The conclusions we draw from judging this way have no application to the music itself.

The soloist in our example uses two kinds of decoration apparently derived from *gaida* playing. The first is the prefacing of new syllables or major changes of pitch with a sudden downward turn of the voice (see "tre-" at the beginning of Frame 1 in Figure 26, for example). The *gaida* makes this downward turn because the player, like most European pipers, uses "closed" fingering: that is, after almost every note of his

---

*A persuasive teacher and advocate of the Obidim timbre, Ethel Raim, has pointed out that Western art music "carries the values of 'sophisticated' and 'refined,'" and that our schools therefore promote the art-music timbre regardless of what a child's vocal personality is really like (Raim 1975: 8).

tune he closes all the finger holes on his melody pipe, or "chanter," before opening those required for the next note. With all holes closed, the chanter sounds its lowest pitch; thus closed fingering inserts a low note before almost every melody note.

Why does the *gaida* player double his work by using closed fingering? One would think it easier to go from the fingering for one note directly to the fingering for the next. The answer lies in the player's desire for clearly defined notes. His mouth is not on the chanter. Instead, he blows into a goatskin bag, which then delivers the air to the chanter under steady pressure and without interruption.* Therefore

> lingual articulation—the "tonguing" of the reed by which a woodwind player obtains clarity of attack, many degrees of staccato [that is, detachment of one note from another], and neat reiteration of the same note—is denied to the bagpiper. His reeds, save in exceptional species, sound continuously. Yet music demands articulation, and so the piper has to find it in another way. This is by deft finger-work, separating and accentuating notes by grace notes executed with great speed...
> *(Baines 1960: 22)*

---

*The air enters a tubular reed projecting into the bag from the end of the chanter. The end of the reed projecting into the bag is closed; the end fixed in the chanter is open. Air enters the chanter through a tongue cut in the side of the tubular reed in the direction of the chanter.

The tongue is carefully shaped to stand slightly away from the main body of the reed. Sometimes a thread is wedged under the tongue to help it stand away. (In Western clarinets and saxophones the tongue is a separate piece, usually of cane, clamped over a hole in the flattened underside of a tubular mouthpiece; the mechanics of sound production in these instruments are the same as described below for the *gaida*.)

Under sufficient pressure, air entering the reed from the bag will suck the tongue down, just as air passing over the wings of an airplane will suck the wings upward. When the tongue closes down against the main body of the tubular reed, air ceases to enter the chanter, and the pressure of the air inside the reed suddenly drops.

As the last of the pressure is transmitted away from the reed and down the

The *gaida* player uses these grace notes as well as closed fingering to separate and accent the notes of his melody, though of course a bagpiper playing with open fingering uses grace notes more. These grace notes constitute the second kind of decoration our vocal soloist apparently derives from bagpipe technique. They can be seen in Figure 26 (p. 144) as brief spans of yodeling.

The song of the women of Obidim contains drone harmony as well as the harmonies of heterophony and counterpoint. A drone is a sound sustained much longer than any of the sounds it accompanies (or a sound repeated so frequently that it has the effect of such a sustained sound). The simpler melodic part in Figure 26 moves so slowly it sounds like a series of drones.

The *gaida* drone is sounded by a pipe some three feet long attached separately to the same bag of air that supplies the chanter. A tubular reed with a tongue cut in its side is fixed in the end of the drone pipe as it is in the end of the chanter, but the larger mass of air inside the main bore of the drone pipe causes the tongue in the reed of the drone to cycle more slowly than the tongue in the reed of the chanter. The pitch of the drone therefore lies well below the pitch of the chanter, which is little more than a foot long.

The drone is jointed with mortise and tenon to allow it to be

---

length of the chanter from one air molecule to another, it is followed by a rarification, just as the crest of a ripple is followed across the surface of a pond by a trough. (Statistically speaking, the air molecules transmit the pressure by lurching slightly out of their positions, creating pressure as they hit the next molecules, which in turn lurch slightly out of position and pass the pressure on; by lurching out of position, each molecule creates rarification in the spot it left.)

Just as the trough on the surface of the pond is followed in its turn by a compensating crest, so the rarification travelling down the chanter is followed by a compensating increase in air pressure. (Statistically speaking, each air molecule that lurched out of position regains its place, and the rarification at that place ceases.)

The return of pressure within the tubular reed is enough to let the tongue spring back to the open position. Air from the bag rushes into the opening and the cycle repeats. A cycle recurring twenty or more times a second creates an alternation in the pressure of the air rapid enough to be heard as sound.

tuned to the chanter. Sliding the parts together makes a shorter pipe with less air in it and allows the tongue to work faster, producing a higher pitch; sliding the parts away from each other makes a longer pipe with more air in it and forces the tongue to work more slowly, producing a lower pitch. Bagpipers tune their drones with great care.

Europe's professional pipers were apparently able to sound a continuous drone long before they added the bag to their instruments at the end of the 12th century. They used "circular breathing," inflating the cheeks with air while blowing into the reed, then expelling that air to cover the necessary interruption as they inhaled fresh air through the nose. (The technique is still practiced from the lands of the Mediterranean basin eastward to India and Indonesia.)*

Probably the piper adopted the bag because, by squeezing it under his arm, he could sustain a greater pressure of air against his reeds than he could with simple lung power. Greater air pressure means louder sound on a reed instrument, and louder sound would have been an advantage in playing outdoors, as the medieval itinerant musician often had to do. The bag also freed him from incessant blowing. Thus when he gave up lingual articulation he gained not only louder sound but also intermittent rest and the chance to shout or sing to his own playing. To an itinerant piper the economic advantage of being one's own singer was probably reason enough for him to add the bag to his pipes.

Medieval Sound in a Modern Village

Traditional Bulgarian vocal technique and timbre have been little modified by recent outside influence, as I pointed out at the beginning of the chapter. But if this singing descends

*The technique was supposedly known in the art music of Western Europe as late as the 17th and 18th centuries. I remember seeing the late Josef Marx of New York City demonstrate it on an oboe using music from that time. Some American jazz musicians have used it. Anthony Baines has suggested persuasively that medieval pipers probably did the same (Baines 1960: 35, 66).

from a style flourishing before the Turks seized the country—and that assumption seems logical—then it may represent to some extent the way people sang in both Eastern and Western Europe in medieval times. We shall never know for sure, because no part of Western Europe has enjoyed such isolation, nor did Western medieval writers evaluate the singing of their times with our ears or use terms in the same sense we use them. Some support for the medieval connection of Eastern and Western musical practice, however, comes from the drone harmony Bulgarian singers use today and from one of their decorations not yet discussed, the *tremolo*.

Drone harmony is not unusual in the West but it is not pervasive. The fiddle, three-string dulcimer, and five-string banjo use it, as well as guitars fingered in open tuning. It also occurs in elite entertainment, but as an occasional effect rather than a continuous one. To some extent a drone is in itself a harmony, of course, since almost every kind of sound is made up of partials (see p. 100).* What we usually mean by drone harmony, however, is the combination of a drone with some other sound. Like heterophony, this drone harmony can be perceived as either a blend of sounds or a juxtaposition of sounds, depending on the background and focus of the observer (see p. 99).

In the Middle Ages drone harmony pervaded music at all levels of society. Many bowed instruments were so broad-bellied they could hardly have avoided sounding a drone (Bachmann 1969), and the distribution of finger holes on the many bagless double pipes of the period strongly suggests drone accompaniment (Sachs 1940: 281-282). The music played on these instruments has not survived, if indeed it was ever written down.

Important feast days of the medieval Roman Catholic Church were at times occasions for drone harmony, and some of

*The South Indian violinist V. V. Subramanian once remarked to me after a concert at Colgate University that in the sound of the South Indian drone instrument, the four-string *tanbura*, he heard "every note of the *rāga*"—that is, all the pitch levels available to him in whatever melodic mode he wanted to use.

this harmony has survived. (I will discuss it in the next chapter). To produce it a soloist would stretch out a few notes of Gregorian Chant into a series of drones, while a second soloist—sometimes a second and a third in duet—would decorate the series with a faster melodic motion. This kind of harmonizing can be heard today in the Eastern Orthodox Church and no doubt represents a survival from medieval practice. The music of the Eastern Church has been heard in Bulgaria since the 9th century, and may well be the source for the kind of drone harmony in *Ne Treperi*, where the simpler melody is composed of a few notes drawn out into drones. Solid evidence for the connection is lacking, of course.

A second indication of a medieval presence in modern village singing in Bulgaria is the use of the *tremolo*. On first acquaintance it would seem to derive, like other vocal decoration, from the technique of the *kaba gaida*.

Near the top of the chanter in Figure 27-B (p. 153) is a "flea hole," a small hole containing a short tube of metal, cane, or quill which extends into the bore of the pipe. When the player uncovers this hole he raises the pitch of the pipe slightly; thus by tapping the hole rapidly he causes a rapid fluctuation in the pitch of whatever note he is sounding. This fluctuation is sometimes called the "bagpiper's vibrato."

Fig. 27

The modern Bulgarian singer creates the same effect by letting the glottis at the back of the throat oscillate freely, producing what sounds like the percussive throbbing of a single pitch. This throbbing is actually an alternation between two pitches and two levels of loudness, the second pitch being too soft to be noticed distinctly. Western singers no longer use this decoration, though singing it does not seem to be difficult for some of them. It survives in orchestral string music, where the players produce it by moving the bow back and forth rapidly through a very small distance without altering the pitch of the string.

In the early 17th century the *tremolo* (then called *trillo*) was well known to singers of Western art music, as we know

FIGURE 27: THE *KABA GAIDA*. *This bagpipe is played by men in southwestern Bulgaria, alone, accompanied by the piper's own singing, or in ensemble with another* gaida, *voices, or other instruments. Its drone harmony, decorative style, and technique of inserting a low note between main melody notes seem to be the models for a traditional singing in the area.*

(A): a player in the Bulgarian State Folk Song and Dance company (Katzarova-Kukudova [=Koukoudova] and Djenev 1976: photo 7). The bag is the whole skin of a goat with pipes inserted in the neck and forelegs. Where the blow pipe joins the bag, a one-way valve keeps the air from rushing back into the player's mouth. The melody pipe, or "chanter," is fingered with the thumb (not visible), three fingers of the right hand, and four fingers of the left hand. The right index finger covers the "flea hole" (see detail in B). The long drone pipe can be lengthened or shortened at the adjustable joints to put it in tune with the chanter.

(B): side view of the chanter (Maheu 1976). The tubular reed is usually made of cane or, more often, elderberry. The end of the tubular reed is closed; air enters the pipe from the bag through a tongue cut downward in the side of the reed. When the air pressure is strong enough the tongue snaps shut and springs open in rapid succession, sending bursts of pressure into the pipe fast enough to be sensed by the brain as sound. A similar tongue in the end of the drone pipe works the same way, but the greater mass of air in the longer pipe forces the tongue to move more slowly, producing a lower pitch.

(C): cross section of the chanter (Maheu 1976), showing the round bore, hexagonal exterior, and the placement of the finger holes along one of the hexagonal edges.

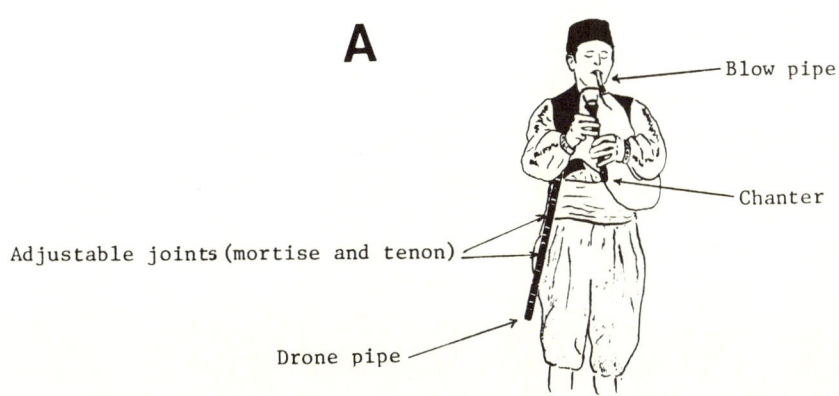

A
- Blow pipe
- Chanter
- Adjustable joints (mortise and tenon)
- Drone pipe

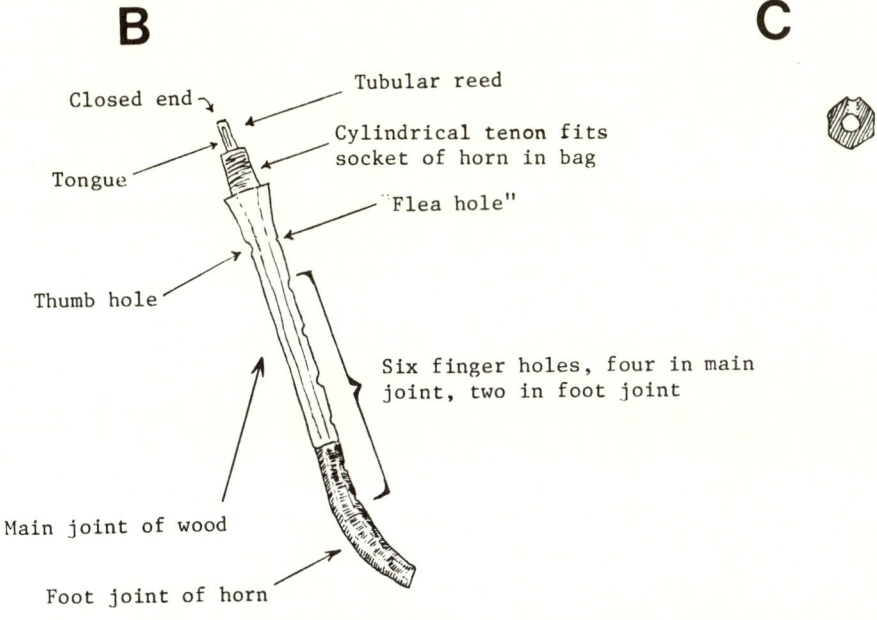

B
- Closed end
- Tubular reed
- Cylindrical tenon fits socket of horn in bag
- Tongue
- "Flea hole"
- Thumb hole
- Six finger holes, four in main joint, two in foot joint
- Main joint of wood
- Foot joint of horn

C

because they left us examples of it written out in standard musical notation. It goes back much further than that, however. In his 9th-century training manual, *Musica Disciplina*, the French Benedictine monk Aurelian de Réôme wrote that the *tristropha*, an ornamentation written as three successive single notes of identical pitch, should be sung "as a rapid beat, like a vibrating hand" (Apel 1969: 862b).

Fig. 28   Figure 28 (p. 156) shows this rapid beating, the "bagpiper's vibrato," in the duet *Vetar Vee* sung by two women from the Shope region of Bulgaria, the broad plain and gentle slopes surrounding the capital city of Sofia some eighty miles north of Obidim. The text is one stanza of a haying song. All able-bodied members of a Shope family reap and gather the hay in early July, and men and women usually sing songs like this one together. Here are the words and their translation.

> VETAR VEE   HJE!   I GORA   SE LALÉ, HE!
> The wind blows, hey!   and the forest sways, lalé, hey!
>
> HE!   I GORA   SE LALÉ, JE! I!
> Hey! and the forest sways, lalé, yey! Eee!
>
> *(Koenig and Raim 1984)*

Reapers swing their scythes in a slow and steady rhythm, but you don't hear that rhythm in this example: the music moves even slower than a reaper's swing, and without any rhythmic regularity. As Boris Kremenliev points out,

> the chief purpose of the work song in Bulgarian folk music is to create a more pleasant environment and not, as has been shown to be the case in some countries and for certain occupations, to set a tempo calculated to improve speed and efficiency. If there were a direct relationship between tempo and task, a Bulgarian harvest would never have been completed, since the traditional songs for harvest time are among the slowest Bulgarian folksongs.
>
> *(Kremenliev 1957: 311)*

These slow songs, he adds, are sung at different times of day. Songs about nature, as in this example, tend to be sung in the morning on the way to work in the fields. Songs actually used for accompanying work have the same slow, free motion.

In many ways the music of the Obidim and Shope Bulgarian traditions are similar, as you can see by comparing the pictorial notation found on pp. 144 and 156. In both cases the music is a duet between a slower and a faster part. The faster part includes changes of syllable prefaced with a brief downward shift in pitch, decoration by yodeling, and a sudden high note to signal the end of the stanza. The slower part creates a series of drones. The two parts frequently form together the harmonies of identical and adjacent pitch levels. And in each song the stanza is essentially a single phrase and its repetition.

In Bulgaria, vocal duets are sometimes more than vocal duets. Martin Koenig, who recorded our examples along with Ethel Raim, noted that in the Obidim region one often encounters close friendships expressed in this form. Two girls will develop a special bond while very young and from then on sing duets only with each other. They may be sisters, but are often not even related (Koenig 1970: note to band 4 of side 2).

In the midst of musical analysis we should recall that music is not an object but an act. Music is personal, like a handshake, and the hearing of it is a personal experience like feeling that handshake. Performers share this act and this experience. Their association is intimate, even when brief and, judged by other criteria, impersonal. To sing with only one particular person is the logical expression of an awareness of this intimacy. One may not go to this extreme in making music, but one can recognize the basis for doing so.

The New National Style

Oddly enough, an incursion of Western-style harmony characterizes the new national style of vocal music promoted by the Communist government of Bulgaria.

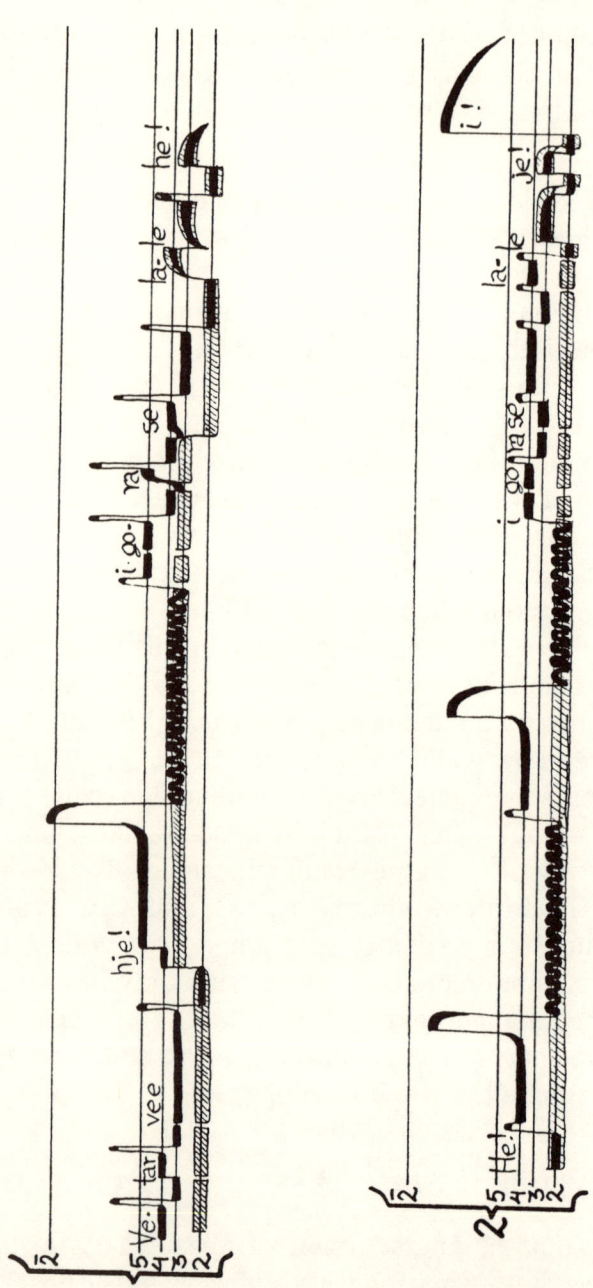

FIGURE 28: *VETAR VEE.* Words and melodies for the first stanza of a traditional haying song from the Shope region just south of the capital city of Bulgaria, Sofia, are shown here as sung by Vasilka Andonova and Kremena Stancheva from the villages of Leva Reka and Kovachevtsi. Martin Koenig and Ethel Raim recorded the two women in the late 1960's (field tape in Koenig and Raim 1984; approximately the same sound can be heard on Nonesuch H 72034: side 1, band 1). Both have since become professional singers. See the caption for Figure 4 for an explanation of the notation.

Here the decorating voice makes far less use of the yodel and of the low note prefacing a change of syllable than in the example from Obidim on p. 144. The women singing Vetar Vee are a generation or more younger than those singing Ne Treperi, and using plainer decoration is part of the modern way of singing traditional songs. In both pieces the voices create drone harmony. The harmony of adjacent pitch levels appears less often in Vetar Vee, but this is a regional difference rather than a modernization of traditional practice.

At three places in the stanza the decorating voice executes a tremolo, an alternation between two levels of pitch so close together and so rapidly interchanged that the effect is of a single pitch being rapidly repeated. As early as the 9th century a Western European monk instructed singers of Gregorian Chant to sing repeated pitches "as a rapid beat, like a vibrating hand" (Apel 1969: 862b). In view of Bulgaria's long isolation from Western music (from the beginning of the 14th century to the beginning of the 20th), it seems possible that Bulgaria's traditional folk singing may preserve aspects of European vocal technique, like the tremolo, which predate the 14th century.

The drone melody in Frame 2 is not the same as Frame 1. Nevertheless Frame 2 seems in its details to be a variation of Frame 1, and the stanza is therefore made up, like a stanza of Ne Treperi, essentially of a single phrase and its repetition.

After the Second World War Bulgaria, which had sided with Germany against Russia, was occupied by the Russians and its political system was changed. Communist ideology emphasizes the importance of the proletariat, the laboring class, which in Bulgaria is the peasantry. It became the official policy of the new government to encourage peasant traditions.

A decade after the end of the war an official in the government's folk program reported success:

> Amateur folklore activities have rapidly found their place among youth and workers' organizations, they have penetrated into the factories and the schools, into the co-operative farms, into the army, etc. Numerous folklore groups have been formed, who cultivate and disseminate folksongs and dances; they study the living folklore and on this foundation build up their own activities, . . .
> *(Katzarova-Koukoudova 1954: 211)*

The new tradition emphasizes concerts. Groups tour the country, compete in festivals, and contribute performers to a national troupe that travels abroad. This means that audiences carrying various musical traditions must be won over to what is presented on stage. Special effects, careful timing, refreshing contrasts, and a polished presentation become important. Aspects of village style that seem to mar the enjoyment of the crowd tend to disappear under the pressure for a successful repertoire. Long spans of unvaried music are shortened, and what one might call "dialects" are abandoned in favor of a national voice. (American audiences forced comparable changes upon West African dancing and drumming in the 1960's, as I mentioned on pp. 6-7.)

The recognized musical authorities appointed by the Bulgarian government to promote peasant musical traditions were qualified by their university training as well as their musical gifts. Eastern European universities model themselves on the Western universities of Germany, where Western European art music is the approved tradition. Thus the most prestigious judges of Bulgarian folk music were considerably biased in favor of the sound of Western art music. They naturally followed this bias in encouraging the newly formed folklore groups* to

> seek out, lead and raise up talented singers and dancers, directing them along the road to perfection.
> *(Katzarova-Koukoudova 1954: 211)*

The Bulgarian State Ensemble for Folksongs and Folk Dances gave its first concert before Western audiences in Paris in 1955 under the direction of Philip Koutev, who has been called "the master of arrangements for folk choir" by an American scholar of Bulgarian music (Markoff 1976). Figure 29 on p. 160 shows a part of his arrangement of the folk song *Todoro*, drawn from a private recording of a concert by The Pennywhistlers, an American group, in 1964. The lowest-sounding part creates a series of contrasting Western chords—that is, a succession of complete changes of harmony rather than the partial changes one hears when voices harmonize above a drone. The drone of the original folk song has apparently been retained in the second-to-lowest voice; it has been reduced to a barely audible level, however, and fails to modify the Western effect of the harmony.

Other aspects of the performance are also Western: variations in loudness, both gradual and abrupt; a slowing down at the end; and modifications of timbre used to support these effects. The "clashing" harmony of adjacent pitch levels occurs rarely, but the infrequent use of this harmony is

---

*The same kind of imposition is represented by the annual prize competition begun in 1968 by the African Studies Center of the University of California at Los Angeles. Open only to African artists in Africa, the first winning entry in the plastic-arts/graphic-arts division was, not surprisingly, an acceptably Western cubist sculpture by Amir I. M. Nour of the Republic of Sudan (Rubin 1969: 9-11). (In all fairness I should point out that the prize for music awarded the following year went to the Chopi musician and song composer Vinancio Mbande for his latest contribution to the repertoire of the traditional xylophone orchestras of southern Mozambique, a music not influenced by the West. Of course, like the sculpture by Amir Nour, Vinancio's music had to have Western appeal to win.)

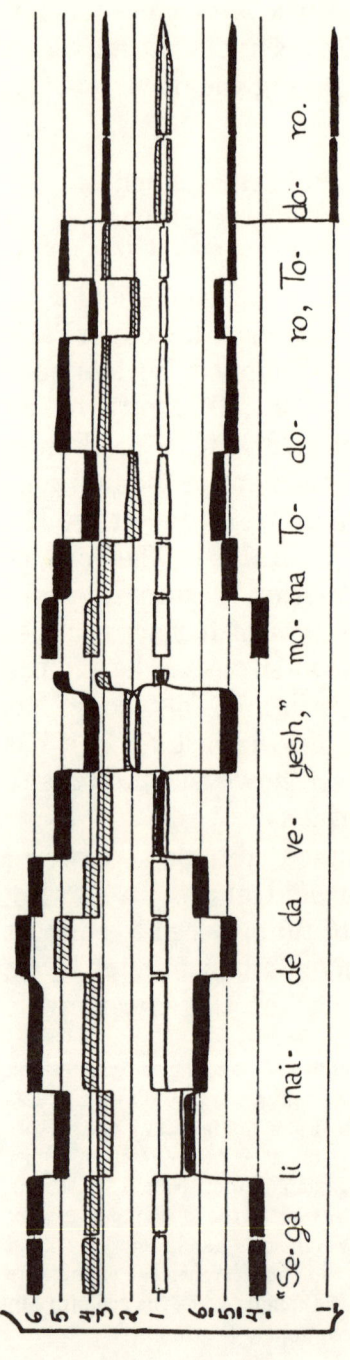

FIGURE 29: TODORO. *The final verse of the third stanza of the folk song Todoro is drawn as sung in 1964 by The Pennywhistlers, an American group, using the arrangement by Philip Koutev, director of the Bulgarian State Ensemble for Folksongs and Folk Dances (private recording; Koutev's group can be heard on Nonesuch H 72011: side 1, band 2). The four different melodies combined in this passage are each shaded differently. The caption for Figure 4 explains the notation.*

Although the second line from the bottom is a drone, the vigorous uniform motion of the other three parts drowns it out in performance and no impression of drone harmonies is created. Rather, the impression is of a series of Western-style harmonies—harmonies completely different from one another—instead of harmonies centered on the same pitch. The lowest-sounding line moves in contrary motion to the top line, an effect characteristic of Western art music but not of traditional Bulgarian singing.

The phrase ends with a change of loudness and timbre also characteristic of performances of Western art music but not found in traditional Bulgarian folk singing, where performers produce a uniform loudness and timbre across all but the extreme ends of their range.

Each stanza of the song is set to the same music, but Koutev's setting gives the first verse of the stanza to a large choir, the second to another large choir, and the third and fourth to a much smaller group of perhaps eight singers, two on a part. Here is the text of the third stanza, with the verses assigned to "I" (first large choir), "II" (second large choir), and "c" (small choir). The English translation is my own.

I: *A TYA MU SE LYUTO SURDI, MOMA TODORO, TODORO,*
      The girl was very angry,   maiden Todoro,   Todoro,

II: *A TYA MU SE LYUTO SURDI, MOMA TODORO, TODORO:*
      the girl was very angry,   maiden Todoro,   Todoro:

c: *"VETRE LE NENAVEINIKO," MOMA TODORO, TODORO,*
      "Miserable, wanton breeze,"   maiden Todoro,   Todoro,

c: *"SEGA LI NAIDE DA VEYESH," MOMA TODORO, TODORO.*
      "you've made me unhappy,"   maiden Todoro,   Todoro.

probably characteristic of the regional style the song represents rather than evidence of an adaptation to Western taste.

Irene Markoff, the American scholar quoted on p. 159, points out that this type of music is heard on Bulgarian radio and television as well as at folk festivals. She adds:

> Such arrangements have become a new art form. The sound could be described as a "collective sound"—one which incorporates the idiomatic components of Bulgaria's regional folkmusic styles. In effect what has happened is the "popularization of folk music through the collectivization of its idiomatic components."
>
> *(Markoff 1976)*

This "collectivization" includes Westernization.*

The same process of discarding dialects in favor of a nationally acceptable sound has been noticed by Pekka Gronow in a recent survey of Russian commercial recordings:

> To the large nationalities of European USSR [,] folk music means either arranged and accultured folk music such as performed by professional "state folk song and dance ensembles" and "academic folk choirs," or a disappearing tradition of remote districts of interest mainly to scholars.
>
> *(Gronow 1975: 93)*

The point of these chapters on harmony is that our Western approach is but one of many, all of them equally worthwhile. Reading about the heterophony of lining out and

---

*Western European art music is widely known and cultivated outside Western Europe and its cultural colonies in the Americas. In the fall of 1976, for example, I heard a concert of this art music played by the Philharmonic Orchestra of Israel, conducted by Zubin Mehta of Bombay, India, and featuring solo pianist Yefim Bronfman, an eighteen-year-old graduate of the State Conservatory in Tashkent, a city in the Russian part of Central Asia. At the Shanghai Conservatory of Music, founded in 1927, some 650 young Chinese study the European masters and only one of seven departments concerns itself with the art music and folk music of China (Zinsser 1981: 152, 154).

the "clashing" counterpoint and biting timbre of Bulgarian song can only suggest this diversity in a small way. Experiencing diverse traditions over an extended period will, I am sure, convince any listener of their worth.

The next chapter concludes this section with a presentation of one of the earliest Western harmonic traditions known, the vocal counterpoint ornamenting services at the Cathedral of Notre Dame in Paris in the 12th century. Changes in our harmonic tradition since that time have not been alterations but enrichments: every subsequent art music has been based on the harmonic principles of this ancient style, except for the experimental music of composers of the present century.

9

Early Western Harmony at Notre Dame

The medieval Roman Catholic choir usually sang Gregorian Chant unaccompanied, individual members singing solo or the group singing in unison. On special occasions, however, while one individual sang his* solo, another might improvise a second melody to accompany the traditional one, as we know from treatises dating as early as the end of the 9th century which discuss the rules to be observed when this was done. At the Cathedral of Notre Dame in Paris, singers of the 12th century developed a large repertoire of such harmonized Chant, improvising upon principles that still dominate Western harmony. These singers and their principles are the subject of the present chapter.

The Singers

A book could cost as much as a house in the 12th century. It was a rare item not easily replaced and sometimes luxuriously bound. Written out by hand on neatly ruled leaves of sheepskin (parchment) or lambskin (vellum), then illustrated with beautifully painted capital letters, a Bible could take more than a year to complete, even though the work was usually done

---

*The choir was entirely male. Women sang Catholic service only in communities of female religious.

by several scribes working at the same time.

The large books used for church services were particularly expensive because their appearance was important and their musical notation required special care. In one case a whole vineyard was given in payment for a copy of just the priest's part in the celebration of the Mass. Most churches, understandably, had but one copy of each of the service books. The choir sang from memory.

It took about two years for a new member of the choir to learn by heart the basic repertoire of unison, unaccompanied Gregorian Chant, for there were five different rituals every weekday and nine on Sunday. Moreover, from day to day and week to week throughout the year the words and music of these rituals changed in keeping with a fixed annual cycle; and outside this cycle stood certain other rituals that also had to be learned: the music for the feast day of the local saint, for the commemoration of the martyrs whose relics lay within the church, for special occasions like the installation of a bishop, and for funerals.

Choir service was not only a demanding profession but an important one. As one medievalist put it, the faithful considered the performance of the daily rituals

> a function of common interest which could not be interrupted or left in abeyance without menacing the security of the people.
>
> *(Luchaire 1957: 105)*

The prayer services, the "Hours," consisted mostly of psalms sung antiphonally. The sacrificial service, the "Mass," included many brief exchanges between the choir and the priest officiating at the high altar. The placement of the choir was dictated by these musical needs, as Figure 30 (p. 166) shows: to facilitate antiphonal singing the members were seated in two groups facing each other, and to assure smooth exchanges with the priest their seats were placed near the high altar. Each half of the choir provided in alternation the readers and solo singers required for a week of services.

Fig. 30

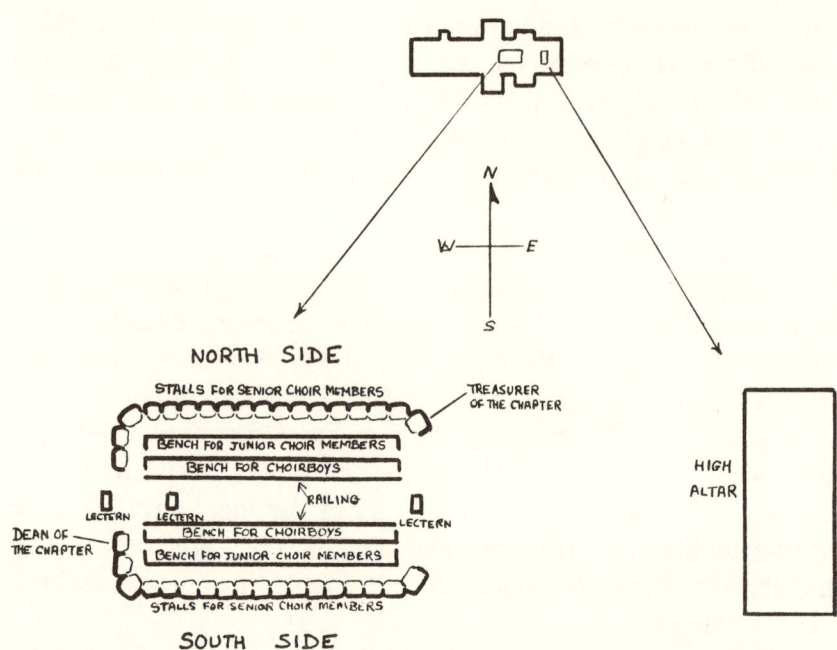

FIGURE 30: THE PLACEMENT OF THE CHOIR. *This drawing shows the placement of the singers in the cathedral at Salisbury, England, which was built between 1220 and 1260 (Harrison 1958: 89).*

The north and south sides of the choir faced each other. Each side had three rows of seats, the ones behind raised above those in front. Senior members sat at the rear in separated wooden stalls; junior members sat on a bench in front of them; the choirboys sat furthest front on the lowest bench.

The facing arrangement, still used today, is a practical result of the fact that much of what the choir sang was antiphonal. Placement of the choir near the altar is also practical, since the choir, as in earlier centuries, has many exchanges with the priest conducting the service.

During most of the year the two halves of the medieval choir alternated by the week in providing readers and solo singers for the services. At Christmas, Easter, and Pentecost they alternated daily.

During the great feasts of Christmas, Easter, and Pentecost the two groups alternated daily rather than weekly. At the Cathedral of Notre Dame, a soloist on such occasions not only sang his part in responsorial songs (in which the melody went back and forth between soloist and full choir) but might join with other soloists to combine the sacred melodic line of the solo part with one, two, and even three other, newly invented solo lines.

Working out a good harmony part to a song is no small achievement. Soloists tended to preserve their more successful harmonizing by writing it down. They also augmented their own repertoires by borrowing successful pieces from the repertoires of other choirs. Some manuscripts from this period have survived. In the art work with which they are often decorated one sometimes finds a drawing showing the soloists, usually not more than three or four,* gathered around a lectern that holds their music (see Figure 31 on p. 170).

Fig. 31

The collection of improvised counterpoint at the Cathedral of Notre Dame was evidently renowned. It dates from approximately 1140-1220 A.D., and the entire repertoire was copied out at least four times for use elsewhere. (The most sizeable of these copies, made around 1250, contains 887 pieces today.)

Around 1275 A.D. an anonymous English theorist undertook to explain the notation preserving this repertoire. Everyone understood the system of clefs and horizontal lines indicating pitch, for these had been introduced by Guido d'Arezzo some two centuries earlier and were used everywhere in Western Europe. But indications of duration in the Notre Dame manuscripts were obscure. No system was yet standard, and this one apparently needed explaining. In the course of his remarks, the Englishman gave us the names of two kinds of counterpoint used at the cathedral, *organum* and *discant*, and

*The small size of surviving manuscripts confirms the picture: only a few singers at a time could get close enough to the pages to sing from the music they contain (the manuscript known as W_2, for example, is only 5⅛ inches wide and 7⅛ inches tall; the musical notation on each page occupies a rectangle measuring only 2⅞ inches by 4¾ inches; a page from W_2 appears on p. 170).

some of the oral history surrounding them:

ET NOTA QUOD MAGISTER LEONINUS,
Now　　　　　　Master　　　　Léonin,
SECUNDUM QUOD DICEBATUR, FUIT
according to　 oral tradition,　　　　was
OPTIMUS ORGANISTA,　　　　QUI FECIT
the best at fashioning *organum*.　He　made
MAGNUM LIBRUM ORGANI　DE
a great　book of *organum* duets　upon the
GRADALI　　　　　ET　ANTIPHONARIO
melodies of the Mass and　the　Hours
PRO DIVINO SERVITIO MULTIPLICANDO;
for　divine　services　　of the whole year;
ET FUIT IN USU USQUE AD TEMPUS
and this book was in use up to the time
PEROTINI MAGNI,　QUI ABBREVIAVIT
of the great Pérotin,　who shortened
EUMDEM ET FECIT　　　　CLAUSULAS
it　　and made [sections called] *clausulas*
SIVE PUNCTA PLURIMA MELIORA,
or　*puncta*,　many　　and better,
QUONIAM OPTIMUS DISCANTOR ERAT...
for　　the best　at making *discant* was he...

(Wooldridge 1901: 154n, my translation)

The consensus among scholars is that the successive careers of Léonin and Pérotin at the Cathedral of Notre Dame correspond roughly to the successive reigns of two French kings: Louis VII (1137-1180) and his son Philippe Auguste (1180-1223). No other documents mention "Leoninus." Five men named "Petrus" held high office in the cathedral at various times during this period, and one of them might possibly be the "Perotinus" referred to. It is more likely, however, that both composers held the lowly position of chorus master, *magister cantus*. The registry books for this minor office up to 1326 have been lost.

Because only solo portions of Gregorian Chant were harmonized as *discant* or *organum*, choirs were able to preserve the responsorial effect of the unharmonized Chant: the alternation of a solo voice and a massive unison sound became the alternation of a small harmonizing group and a massive unison sound. The use of soloists was also practical: each half of the choir provided two or three people skilled at improvising and sight-reading, while the rest had only to sing the unison melodies they already knew by heart.

All these singers were professionals; they may have sung for the Church out of reverence or from a sense of duty, but each singer was paid for his effort on the spot.

> The more assiduous he was, the more he profited. These continual distributions of sous and deniers* to the canons and the chaplains... occurred right in the choir of the church, often in full view of everybody. The canons immediately received the price of an office executed, of an anthem sung. More than that, the canons did not only receive money; they received payments in kind, wine, and even quarters of meat.
>
> *(Luchaire 1957: 111)*

This practice seems strange today, as the same source acknowledged:

> We find it hard to associate religious services with the distribution of money and food; to harmonize the uninterrupted sound of chanting with the clinking of money; to conceive of chapters which

---

*The only coin in France or England at this time was the silver penny, the *denier* (descended from the *denarius* circulated in the Roman occupation). Like the coinage only recently abandoned in Great Britain, 12 *deniers* (pence) = 1 *sou* (shilling), 20 *sous* (shillings) = 1 livre (pound, for which the British symbol is still £). The *sou* and *livre* were not coins but only convenient terms for casting up accounts. One expert reckons the *denier* had 4¢ of silver in it (at 1951 U.S. prices) and a purchasing power four times that (Holmes 1953: 53, 296n55).

are countinghouses and restaurants, where the canon need only appear and sing to be paid and fed.
(Luchaire 1957: 115)

But as he also points out,

these love-feasts were the joy of our fathers. It was sweet to eat and drink in the holy place before the eye of the Lord.
(Luchaire 1957: 116)

The Cathedral

A cathedral has the form of a Latin cross, as you can see in Figure 32 on the following page, the longer hall running from west to east, the shorter (called the "transept") from north to south. East of the transept lies the high altar, and this part of the longer hall is called the "choir"; west of the transept the longer hall is called the "nave."

Fig. 32

FIGURE 31: SOLOISTS HARMONIZING. *Three members of a cathedral choir harmonize Gregorian Chant by reading their parts from the music held above a lectern by the middle singer. This illuminated capital S begins a section devoted to three-voice* discant *in a 13th-century collection of pieces harmonized at services in the Cathedral of Notre Dame in Paris. The page reproduced here is the actual size of the page in the manuscript known as "W_2" (Dittmer 1969: folio 31ʳ). As you can see, the performers' copy shown in the illumination is about the same size.*

The three melodic lines begin at the right of the capital S and move together across the page from left to right, each on its own musical staff of five lines. Only the lowest of the three parts has been provided with words; singers performing the other two parts either applied these words to their own music or simply vocalized. The first two words are "Salvatoris hodie," and above "hodie" you can see pretty clearly that the notes for each voice are vertically aligned with one another. Perfect alignment is not really necessary: the shapes and juxtapositions of the notes in each melody indicate specific rhythmic values which, correctly followed, bring the singers out together at the end of each line.

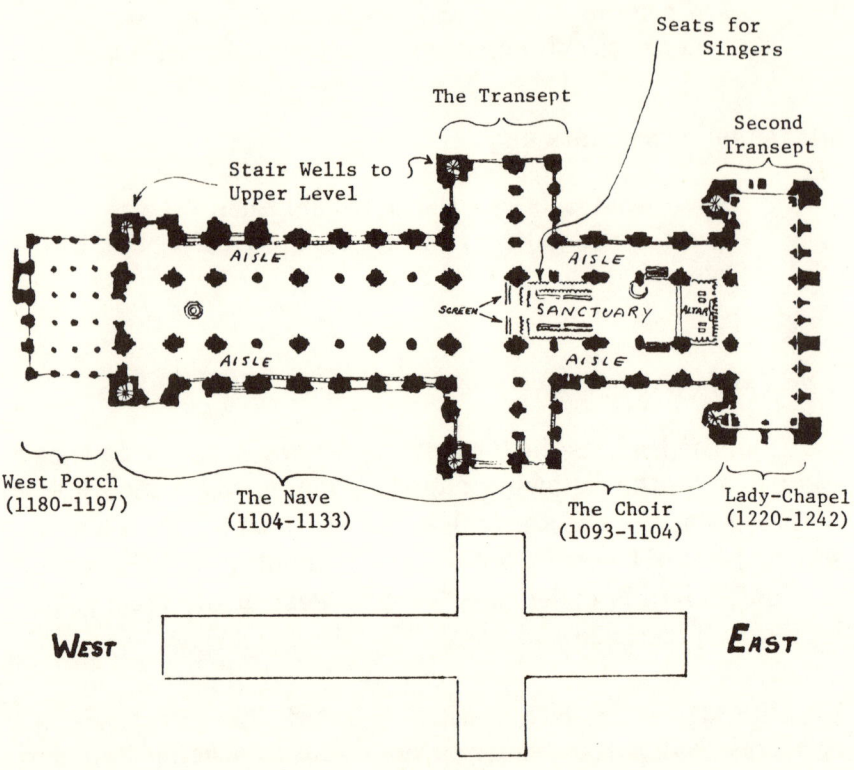

FIGURE 32: THE PLAN OF DURHAM CATHEDRAL. *This building has an interior length of 476 feet, the nave has an interior width of 82 feet, including the aisles, and the interior height of the tower above the choir screens is 210 feet. Such immense buildings took a long time to build—in this case, forty years (Rickman 1862: facing p. 173). At Durham, as at Notre Dame, the builder started with the choir, then built the nave. The large porch at the west end was a later addition, as was the second transept containing the Lady-Chapel. The cruciform plan of the building is especially clear when one disregards the second transept.*

In medieval times stonework, woodwork, or tapestries screened the sanctuary from the view of people in the nave or the aisles of the choir. As in the present-day Eastern Orthodox Church, the sanctuary was in effect a church within a church, and a procession emerging from it or entering it had the dramatic effect of a theatrical entrance or exit.

In the center of the choir lies the sanctuary (sometimes called the "chancel"), the area containing the high altar and the seats for the singers. In the Middle Ages the sanctuary was screened from the eyes of the common people by tapestries (as was probably the case in Notre Dame), by woodwork, or by sculptured stone. This screen is still found in modern churches of the Russian and Greek Orthodox faiths. There were aisles around the sanctuary of the medieval Western European church which set it apart like an island—a church within a church.

In addition to days when a festal outdoor procession was held, climaxing in a dramatic entrance into the cathedral building, there were equally effective moments during the service itself when singers and celebrants would emerge from the seclusion of the sanctuary and move among the common folk in a stately column, their beautiful robes more beautiful by the light of the many candles they carried, their well-trained voices more compelling by their sudden proximity.

The Cathedral of Notre Dame in which services were held until 1182 was a building that no longer exists. It was probably a "basilica," a rectangular hall some 180 feet long by perhaps 70 feet wide, and since the 7th century it had stood where the western half of the present cathedral now stands.

Beyond the eastern end of the old basilica the choir of an immense new cathedral rose during the twenty years from 1163 to 1182. In 1182 the Pope's personal representative consecrated the high altar of the new choir, and services must have been transferred at that time to the new sanctuary. (The rest of the cathedral was not consecrated until 1864.)

A new master builder took over the remaining construction in 1182 or 1183. He first levelled the old basilica, then raised the transept and the nave of the new one. The work was completed in all its essentials by 1208, and the building still stands today. A vessel containing 7.7 million cubic feet of space, it is on the inside 426 feet long, 154 feet wide, and 109 feet high. It has the highest interior attempted up to that time, and to support the high walls of stone against the force of the wind, a new and graceful architectural device was used: the flying buttress (see Figure 33 on p. 176).

Fig. 33

It seems certain that Léonin never heard his music sung in this building. Pérotin, too, may have died before services were held in it. Because their compositions were in use throughout the next century, however, we should consider for a moment the effect of such a vast space on the sound.

To judge from Fritz Winckel's work on this kind of problem (Winckel 1974), a marble box the size of Notre Dame would reverberate each note of the choir some forty-seven seconds. This time is reduced by the coarser stone surfaces actually present, their sculptured details, the added surface of the many free-standing columns, the glazed windows, and the angled vaults, all of which absorb sound energy as well as reflect it. The actual prolongation of sound in Notre Dame—its "reverberation time"—should be around eleven seconds* when objectively measured by instruments (as far as I know, the measurement has never been made). The listener would hear even less reverberation because the subjective impression of sound is soon masked by the general background noise. This means, according to Winckel (1974: 153), a felt reverberation time between three and four seconds.

In pieces sung within the great cathedral, each new moment of music must have ridden upon a sea of sound held over from previous moments. These previous moments not only enriched the new sound but threatened it with confusion, challenging a soloist to decorate the Chant and improvise his

---

*Winckel has calculated that a marble box containing 8,116,240 cubic feet—the volume of the Cathedral of Cologne—should have a reverberation time of approximately fifty seconds; he reports, however, that the actual reverberation time is twelve seconds in the Cathedral of Cologne (Winckel 1974: 150-153). The Cathedral of Notre Dame contains only 7,700,000 cubic feet, or 95% of the volume of the Cathedral of Cologne. Other things being equal (and I do not know that they are), this gives 11.4 as the reverberation time in seconds for the Cathedral of Notre Dame.

counterpoint in a style compatible with lengthy reverberation.* Thus one might include the walls and pillars of Notre Dame as part of the audience ultimately controlling musical composition there.†

Before examining the counterpoint developed in the Cathedral of Notre Dame, let us take a brief look at perhaps the most important aspect of that building: the power and influence of the organization it housed.

The 12th century was the age of great cathedral building in Europe. Just why is not clear, but one factor was surely the economic recovery taking place. French knights had wrested control of the Mediterranean from the Arabs in the 11th century. As a result commerce had been reviving and the population increasing. Businessmen were settling on the lands owned by the Cathedral of Notre Dame and paying rent. Church offerings were increasing, as well as income from fees charged for performing baptisms and marriages and for commemorating deaths. A powerful corporation of men, the cathedral "chapter," administered this growth and loaned money at high interest (the going rate was 43½%). It cleared new land to meet the growing demand for food and for agricultural profit. It not only had its own fields and flocks but controlled hundreds of parish churches, chapels, monasteries, priories, and other religious communities, each contributing to the chapter income.

One researcher estimates the annual income of the Notre

*The decorative alternation of two pitches (see Figure 18 on pp. 92-93, the second phrase in Frame 2 and the middle of the phrase in Frame 4) strike me as admirably suited to lengthy reverberation.

† The Cathedral of St. John the Divine in New York City has a long reverberation time. The American musicologist and organist Stephen Bonta told me that a performance of Bach's *Mass in B Minor* he attended there was a musical disaster due to reverberation. The work of Johann Sebastian Bach (1685-1750) is justly famous for its strong melodic lines, but they are formed upon equally strong, rapidly changing harmonies. The moments of harmonic change are crucial to the effectiveness of Bach's style. They became moments of confusion as the sound of each new harmony battled with the reverberation in the cathedral. Had he been employed to supply all the music for this building, Bach would have been forced to compose differently.

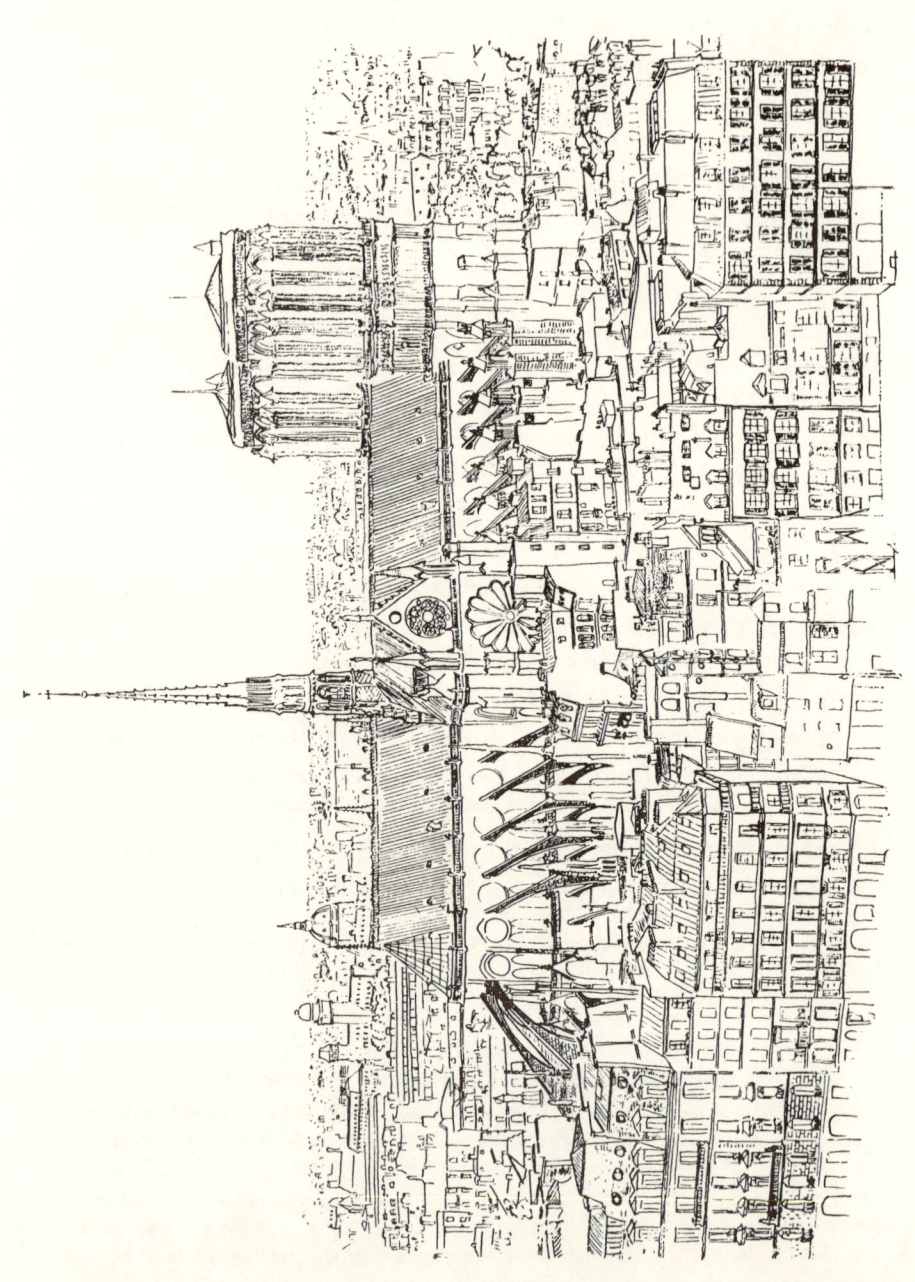

FIGURE 33: THE FLYING BUTTRESSES OF NOTRE DAME. *This drawing from a recent photograph (Jacobs 1968: 92-93) shows the north side of the Cathedral of Notre Dame in Paris. The east end of the building, containing the sanctuary, was dedicated in 1182 and can be seen to the left. The intersection of transept and nave is marked by the spire, which was added in the 19th century. The main entrance at the west end of the building is not visible, but the two large, square towers flanking it can be seen to the right. The spires originally planned for the tops of these towers have never been built.*

Along the north side of the Cathedral is the chapter cloister where the workrooms and apartments supporting the community were located, including the Cathedral school some writers have called "the first true University of Paris" (Temko 1955: 68). The north side is the side shown here.

The flying buttresses are the graceful stone arches pressing in two tiers against the Cathedral walls. Those you see date from the 13th century, but it was for this building that a more modest prototype was apparently invented in the 12th century. The outline of one of these original flying buttresses can still be seen in one of the solid buttressing walls of the building. Later cathedral builders adopted this invention apparently because it relieved the stress imposed on such high stone walls by the pressure of the wind.

Dame chapter at "some eighty thousand Parisian livres" during this period (Temko 1955: 85). In terms of 1975 United States dollars that amount lies somewhere between seven and nine millions. And as the same source points out, the figure does not include the value of the manual labor of "thousands of serfs, whose flesh was as tenaciously held as their souls by the Virgin [that is, by the chapter of Notre Dame]" (Temko 1955: 99).

King Louis VII, whose reign (1137-1180) was the first in the period that concerns us, received his schooling from the chapter of Notre Dame. He strongly supported the cathedral and its bishop. By feudal law he was actually the bishop's vassal and was therefore among the fourteen bearers when, in 1160, Eudes de Sully was carried by litter into Paris to assume his duties as the new bishop. The King's deference to Notre Dame went much further than this, however:

> One night in 1155, finding it too late to return to Paris, Louis VII stopped at the suburb of Créteil, and in accordance with custom lodged there with his retainers at considerable expense to the inhabitants. He had forgotten that the village, although it was less than ten miles from his palace, belonged not to the royal domain but to Notre Dame. When he returned to Paris the next morning and tried to enter the Cathedral, the doors were locked. Bewildered, the sovereign demanded an explanation, and was sharply reprimanded by the canons [the chapter members] for his offense against Mary and her Church. He was ordered to make a public apology, which he did, and then to kneel throughout the day before the closed portals, praying forgiveness. This he did too, like "a very gentle lamb."
>
> *(Temko 1955: 99-100)*

Louis' successor, Philippe Auguste, did not allow the chapter or the Catholic Church in general such authority, but during his reign (1180-1223) the influence of Notre Dame increased in another way. France became a major European power, and the small area Louis had controlled expanded toward the present boundaries of the nation. The importance of the sacred music at the center of the king's domain grew accordingly. What was sung at the Cathedral of Notre Dame came to influence the whole of Western Europe.

Organum

The anonymous Englishman who described the musical traditions of Notre Dame mentioned two kinds of counterpoint, *organum* and *discant*.

To improvise *organum*, one or two soloists would sing the Gregorian Chant very slowly, extending each pitch into a temporary drone just as Bulgarians do today in some of their folksongs (see pp. 144-145 and 156-157). As in modern Bulgaria, the remaining soloist would add a new, faster-moving melody above and around it.* This two-part counterpoint was called *organum duplum, organum purum,* or simply *organum*. Two melodies moving above and around the drone created three-part counterpoint, called *organum triplum*. Three melodies combined with the drone created four-part counterpoint, called *organum quadruplum*.

Because the soloists were paid when they sang these pieces, the fact that they did so is documented by regulations governing how much money should be spent. In 1199, for example, Bishop Eudes de Sully specified that

---

*Bulgarian practice suggests that this faster moving line may have carried decorative effects.

European scholars steeped in art music thought for a long time that the drone in *organum* must have been performed by the choir as a whole, by instruments, or by both. Actually, a single voice can create a musically satisfying drone without the support of an instrument or other voices simply by taking care to pause for breath at points where the musical activity of the other singer, or singers, assures the forward motion of the piece. Indeed, evidence in two of the manuscripts carrying this tradition indicates that the drone part included pauses for breath (Roesner 1979: 175). Cantors in the Eastern Orthodox Church sing psalms today with a drone accompaniment sung by a single voice. Instruments may have been used at Notre Dame to support the soloists performing *organum*, but the music does not require instruments.

SINGULIS CANONICIS PARISIENSIBUS
upon each of the canons of Notre-Dame

VEL CLERICIS MAJORI ALTARI
and upon the clergy attached to the high altar

INSERVIENTIBUS QUI IN NATALI S.
 who, on the Feast of St.

STEPHANI MATUTINIS INTERFUERUNT
Stephen sing Matins:*

6 DENARIOS PARISIENSES [,]
6 Parisian *deniers;*

SINGULIS VERO CLERICIS CHORI
but upon each of the clergy in choir

NON CANONICIS 4 DENARIOS,
who are not canons: 4 *deniers;*

SINGULIS AUTEM PUERIS CHORI 2
however on each of the choirboys: 2

DENARIOS, SINGULIS TAMEN CLERICIS
deniers; nevertheless upon each of the clergy

QUI IN MISSA RESPONSUM VEL ALL[ELUIA]
who, in the Gradual or Alleluia of the Mass,

IN ORGANO TRIPLO SEU QUADRUPLO DE-
sing three- part or four-part *organum:*

CANTABUNT, 6 DENARIOS BENIGNE
 6 *deniers* with our blessing

CONFERIMUS....
we bestow....

(Handschin 1932: 7, my translation)

Although Léonin of Notre Dame did not invent *organum*,

---

*"Matins" derives from the Latin adjective for "of the morning," *matutinus.* This was the first ritual of the Roman Catholic day, held between midnight and sunrise. Payments for Matins were important, for it was difficult to get a presentable choir together at this early hour. The canons, full members of the chapter who received fixed shares of the cathedral income, often left this service to the *pauperi clerici,* the "poor clergy" who did not enjoy fixed incomes and needed the money.

he must have given it much of his attention in the middle of the 12th century, for we have the anonymous Englishman's report that he composed this kind of counterpoint for both the Mass and the Hours of every important feast day of the Church year (see p. 168).

Figure 34 (p. 182) is the beginning of Léonin's setting of the soloist's part of the "Gradual" of the Mass for Christmas Day. The Gradual is a single Psalm verse framed by an antiphon, exactly the same in form as the piece shown on pp. 92-93. The full text of this particular Gradual is given below with the soloist's part underlined. Figure 34 corresponds to just the first two words.

Fig. 34

(Antiphon)

<u>VIDERUNT OMNES</u> FINES TERRAE
Then saw   all the ends of the earth

SALUTARE DEI NOSTRI: IUBILATE DEO
the salvation of our God.   Rejoice   to God,

OMNIS TERRA.
all you lands of earth!

(Psalm)

<u>NOTUM FECIT DOMINUS SALUTARE SUUM:</u>
God has made known   his salvation;

<u>ANTE CONSPECTUM GENTIUM REVELAVIT</u>
    in the sight of the Gentiles   he has revealed

JUSTITIAM SUAM.
his righteousness.

(Antiphon)

VIDERUNT OMNES FINES TERRAE
Then saw   all the ends of the earth

SALUTARE DEI NOSTRI: IUBILATE DEO
the salvation of our God.   Rejoice   to God,

OMNIS TERRA.
all you lands of earth!

(Catholic Church 1959: 409, my translation)

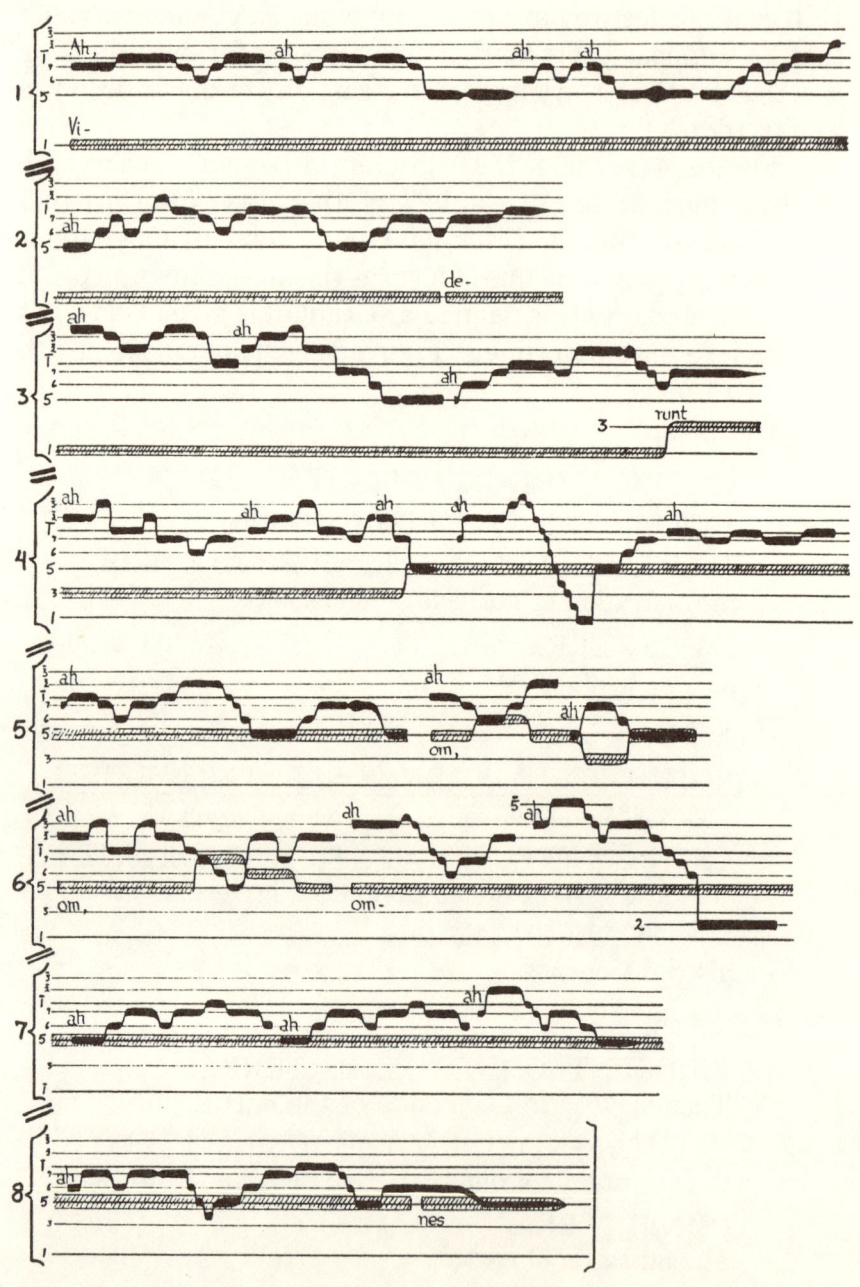

FIGURE 34: *VIDERUNT OMNES. The words sung in this piece are only the first two of a text called the "Gradual" which is designated for use in the Roman Catholic Mass for Christmas Day. Gregorian Chant assigns these first two words to a soloist, and at the Cathedral of Notre Dame in the 12th century one or more additional soloists customarily harmonized such a passage with one or more additional melodic lines on special occasions such as the feast of Christmas. The manuscript known as Wolfenbuttel 677 [W_1] preserves this piece on folios 25^{r}- 25^{v} (transcribed into modern notation in Parrish 1958: 44-45 and in Waite 1954: 67-73). My drawing is from the singing of Otto Johnson and the Chorus of the Danish State Radio (Haydn Society HSE 9100: side 2, band 4). For a general explanation of the notation, see the caption for Figure 4.*

The Gregorian melody is shown as a broad, hatched line. The notes have been extended into drones, as in the Bulgarian women's songs of Chapter 8 (see pp. 144-5 and 156-7). Although a chorus sings this part in the performance I transcribed, the drones could easily have been (and most probably were) sung by a soloist, who took care to breathe when the person performing the other line was not breathing (except in the middle of Frames 5 and 6, where both parts stop together).

The harmonizing melody as sung by baritone Otto Johnson is shown by a solid black line. Such parts were originally improvised; those we find preserved are, presumably, the more successful ones.

A Gregorian melody drawn out into a series of drones and harmonized by one or more faster-moving lines is called organum. *The singers at Notre Dame played dissonance against consonance in organum, stressing the dissonance and letting that disturbing effect drive the music forward to a consonance. Look, for example, at the third phrase of Frame 3: the highest note is one step more than an octave above the level of pitch of the drone, and this is a dissonant harmony; the music then rushes forward to end the phrase with a consonance (a "fifth," explained in a footnote on p. 191).*

Discant, *an older style of harmony in which dissonance is minimized, appears in the second half of Frame 5 and the first half of Frame 6: the two parts move quickly against each other, stressing the consonant harmonies of the fourth, fifth, and unison, while passing over dissonant harmonies quickly.*

From the 12th century on, these two approaches to the interplay of dissonance with consonance have remained basic harmonic principles.

Following the words *"Viderunt omnes"* sung in counterpoint by the soloists, the whole choir in unison would sing the rest of the Antiphon. Then the soloists would introduce the Psalm, once again singing counterpoint, and the choir could follow their counterpoint with unison singing to conclude the section. Finally the choir would sing the whole Antiphon through in unison, and the Gradual would be over.

Discant

The other kind of counterpoint practiced at Notre Dame, *discant*, differed from *organum* because in *discant* the added melody or melodies and the church tune they harmonized all moved at approximately the same speed.

This uniform musical motion, clear and pronounced, was well suited to processing around a church. According to the same anonymous Englishman who gave us the history of the Notre Dame collection, half of the pieces in the collection were for processions. He added that some of the processional music

SOLEBAT ESSE MULTUM IN USU INTER
used   to be very   popular among
MINORES   CANTORES
the lower-ranked singers.
(Wooldridge 1901: xiii, my translation)

Evidently *discant* was not just for soloists. Some of it was memorized by the choir as a whole. *Discant* by this larger group must have been particularly effective in procession, when the voices of a few soloists would have been difficult to hear. According to our anonymous source, *discant* memorized by the "lower-ranked singers" included counterpoint in two, three, and even four parts.

Discant apparently predates *organum*, for it was the earliest type of counterpoint written down in the West. Since before the time of Charlemagne (742-814), poets and musicians had been expanding the Roman Catholic ritual by adding new songs and services and by lengthening old songs with additional words and music. *Discant* was part of this creativity: by adding harmony *discant* expanded an old song without making it longer.

Figure 35 on pp. 189-190 shows *discant* as it appears in an original manuscript, except that there the two melodies have separate musical staffs while here they are shown together on a single staff. The melody of the hymn was composed early in the 11th century and was harmonized some time later by the addition of a second melody, note for note against the first. The hymn is the last of three musical responses that come between the chanted reading of the Epistle and the chanted reading of the Gospel at Mass.*

Fig. 35

The deacon who is to chant the Gospel must first prepare himself. He kneels in prayer at the high altar, then takes the Book of Gospels from its place on the altar and kneels before the priest for a blessing. Finally, accompanied by the First Reader, an incense bearer, and candle bearers, he processes from the altar to the singers' part of the sanctuary. The Gospel reading takes place at a lectern standing between the two halves of the choir (see p. 166).

Our hymn is a *sequentia* or "sequence," one of a great many medieval songs composed to fill with an appropriate text the time taken for the deacon's preparations. The music is partially strophic; in the text below, stanzas with the same music have been given the same number, and the presence of a slight musical difference is shown by adding a diacritical mark (') to the number.

1. VICTIMAE PASCHALI LAUDES
   To the Easter victim   [your] praises

   IMMOLENT CHRISTIANI.
   dedicate,   O Christians.

---

*The Epistle, as the name suggests, is a selection from the letters collected in the New Testament of the Bible which were written by Christ's apostles to newly converted Christians. The Gospel is a selection from one of the four accounts of the life of Jesus found in the New Testament. These accounts are the holiest part of Christian scripture.

2A. AGNUS   REDEMIT   OVES,
The Lamb redeems the sheep;

CHRISTUS INNOCENS PATRI
the sinless Christ to the Father

RECONCILIAVIT PECCATORES.
reconciles sinners.

2B. MORS ET VITA DUELLO
Death and life a battle

CONFLIXERE MIRANDO,
fought quite wonderful;

DUX VITAE MORTUUS REGNAT VIVUS.
the Prince of Life, dead, now reigns alive.

3A. DIC NOBIS MARIA,
Tell us, Mary,

QUID VIDISTI IN VIA?
what saw you on the way?

SEPULCRUM IN QUID VIVENTIS
"The tomb of the Living One

ET GLORIAM VIDI RESURGENTIS.
and the glory, I saw, of His resurrection.

3B. ANGELICOS TESTES,
Angel witnesses,

SUDARIUM ET VESTES.
the towelling, and the garments [I saw].

SURREXIT CHRISTUS, SPES MEA,
Christ has risen, my hope.

PRAECEDET SUOS IN GALILEA.
He goes before His people into Galilee."

2'A. CREDENDUM EST MAGIS SOLI MARIAE VERACI
More to be trusted is Mary, alone and truthful,

QUAM IUDAEORUM TURBAE FALLACI.*
than the Jewish mob's lies.

---

*Anti-Semitic feeling was very strong in Europe at the time these words were composed.

2'B. SCIMUS CHRISTUM SURREXISSE
We know Christ to have arisen
A MORTUIS VERE.
from the dead indeed.
TU NOBIS VICTOR
Upon us,   O Conqueror,
REX   MISERERE.
O King, have mercy.
4. AMEN
Amen.

(Catholic Church 1959: 780; my translation, based on Ruhland 1968: 17)

As in all counterpoint of this period, the two melodies of *Victimae Paschali* share a narrow range and could be performed together at any suitable level of pitch. The modern performance referred to in the caption on the next page uses men's voices; in fact the manuscript preserving this piece was written for the nuns of Las Huelgas, a convent outside the north-central Spanish town of Burgos.

The tradition represented by this music is the tradition of Notre Dame. Medieval Burgos was in close touch with French musical developments, for it lay at the juncture of two heavily travelled pilgrimage routes leading from France to the tomb of the apostle James (Boanerges) in the cathedral at Compostela in Spain's northwest corner. Our example is only one of several pieces of *discant* in early French style found in the Las Huelgas collection.

The performance of this piece, to which I refer in my caption to Figure 35, demonstrates the sweet vocal tone of the Solesmes tradition discussed on p. 79 . The rhythm flows quickly, and the beat is free rather than strict. The manuscript itself tells us nothing about timbre, speed, or the accenting of the beat; it gives only the syllables of text and their pitches. Ritual tradition tells us only that the performance should be

FIGURE 35: *VICTIMAE PASCHALI LAUDES. This piece is a hymn sung at the Mass for Easter Day to accompany the procession of the deacon from the high altar to the lectern where he will read the Gospel. The words and main melody date from the early 11th century. Some time after their composition a second melody was added note for note against the first, forming the kind of harmony known at Notre Dame as* discant.

This piece appears in an early 13th-century manuscript written for the nunnery of Las Huelgas at Burgos in northern Spain. Burgos is on the ancient pilgrims' route to the tomb of the Apostle James at Compostela, in northwestern Spain, and pieces like this are in the tradition carried from Notre Dame and other musical centers in France out along such routes to the various corners of Europe. My drawing of the music is derived from photographs of the manuscript (Ruhland 1968: 11-12) and from a performance of the piece (Telefunken-Decca SAWT 9530-B/9531-B: side 3, band 8).

To show the harmony as clearly as possible I have merged the two five-line musical staffs of the original manuscript, keeping its square note heads and downward tails but leaving the note heads of the second, harmonizing melody empty wherever they do not coincide with the note heads of the basic tune. As you can see, the two melodies are often in unison. Because every line and every space of the five-line staff represent a pitch level in the Western octave series, it should also be easy to observe that the harmony of a fifth (explained in the note on p. 191) is prominent. Many other harmonies are quite brief (Frame 2 is an easy place to see this). The unison, fourth, fifth, and octave were felt to be consonances; all other harmonies were felt to be dissonances. Discant *typically stressed the consonances, setting them off by slipping dissonances between them. (Compare this with the treatment of dissonance in* organum *discussed in the caption on p. 183.)*

The position of the Western octave series is shown at the right end of Frame 1. I have marked pitch level 4 at the right end of every subsequent frame, and you can see that the position of the series never changes. This single number thus gives a key to the pitches represented by the lines and spaces. Medieval singers needed the same information, and in the Las Huelgas manuscript the symbol ♮ *appears at the beginning of each frame to show which line carries pitch level 4. We call such a symbol a "clef," the French word for "key," because it provides the key to reading the pitches correctly.*

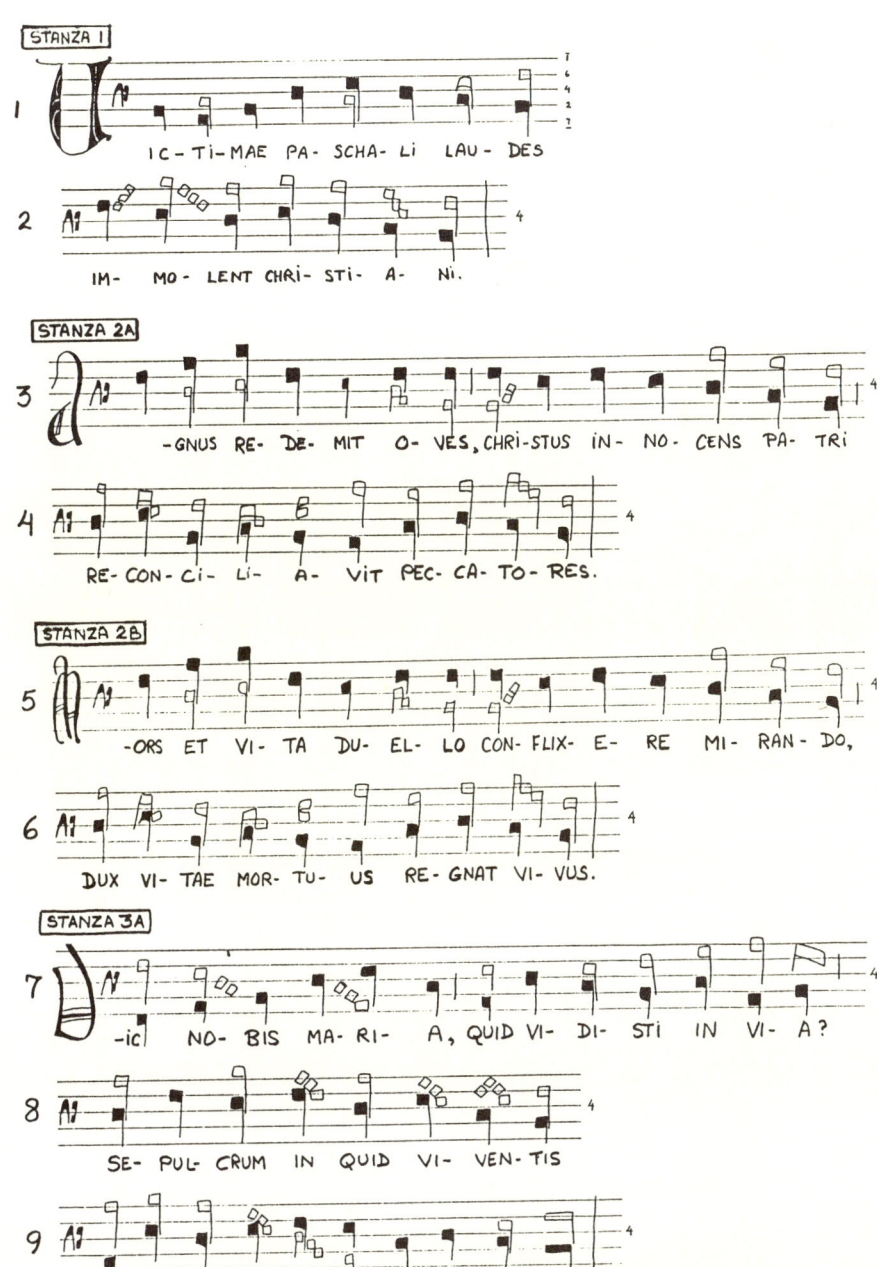

choral. More than this we cannot know for sure. As the leader of the singers who made this recording himself remarks:

> Our manner of performing this music is but one of many possible ways.
>
> *(Ruhland 1968: 11)*

As you can see, harmonies of unisons and fifths* dominate the sound of this counterpoint: they occur more often than any other, and the fifth is the concluding sound of every phrase. This was the harmonic style of 12th-century *discant*: fifths and unisons (or octaves) at every important point in the harmony—at the beginnings of phrases, at the ends of phrases, and at major stresses—and dominating any span of changing harmonies. These intervals were the consonances, the sounds to be sustained with pleasure and heard most frequently in a piece.

All other intervals were apparently dissonant.[†] They appear singly rather than in chains, never at the beginnings or endings of phrases, and rarely at points of stress. Thus *discant* moved from one consonance to another as if they were stepping stones and dissonance a marshy ground between on which one did not place one's full weight.

Discant *versus* Organum

Discant was not replaced by *organum* when *organum* came into fashion at Notre Dame in the 12th century. Léonin and his contemporaries composed in both styles, for many examples of each appear in the oldest layers of the Cathedral's repertoire of harmonized song. Indeed, Léonin's *organum* even incorporates passages of *discant* (see, for example, the end of Frame 5 on p. 182, where "drone" and decorating voices move together in

---

*The terms "unison" and "fifth" belong to a simple system for identifying the amount of separation (technically called an "interval") between pitch levels: one counts the number of levels of the Western octave series contained by the two pitches, including the two pitches themselves. Each space and line in the staffs of Figure 35 represents a pitch level in the Western octave series, so identifying the intervals is easy. In Stanza 1, for example, the second syllable carries the harmony of a third, the last syllable the harmony of a fifth.

† The harmony of a fourth excepted. If you transpose the lower pitch of a fifth up an octave (or the upper pitch down an octave), a fourth results. Thus fifths create fourths (and fourths create fifths) whenever combining melodies are doubled at the octave. Medieval music was often doubled, hence fourths had the same consonant value as fifths.

contrary motion to one another).

Our anonymous English source credits Pérotin with improving on Léonin's work by composing *"clausulas,"* otherwise known as *"puncta."* These were simply expansions of passages where Léonin had speeded up the drone part of his *organum* to achieve a brief feeling of *discant*. Pérotin's *puncta* were for three and four voices, not two. He also created pieces for three and even four voices in which one soloist sang the Chant melody as a series of drones while the others sang in *discant* together against him. Though called *organum*, the technique of these large drone pieces was primarily *discant*.

To mistake the sound of *discant* for that of *organum* would be difficult. When all parts move together, as in *discant*, changes of harmony have rhythmic punch. But when one line moves against a drone, as in *organum*, changes of harmony have no rhythmic punch. The difference is also melodic: in the note-against-note discipline of *discant* there is little room for the rapid, wide-ranging vocal runs of *organum* such as one can see in Frame 4 and Frame 6 on p. 182.

The main difference between *discant* and *organum*, however, is harmonic. Specifically, the two techniques make different use of the same consonance and dissonance. If they were two people, one might say they used the same words to form different kinds of sentences. The harmony of *discant* strides from consonance to consonance, using dissonance briefly to set these stepping stones apart, whereas the harmony of *organum* flows from dissonance—and chains of dissonance—to consonance. The forward energy of *discant* comes from melodic motion, which harmony enriches; the forward energy of *organum* comes from the disturbing power of dissonance as well as from melodic motion.

Look, for example, at the beginning of the *organum* in Figure 34 on p. 182: at first we have a dissonance, a seventh, which then moves to the consonance of an octave. The music, stressing the dissonance by placing it first, plays upon the listener's desire to hear this dissonance replaced by consonance.

In *discant* the harmony of a seventh has the same power to disturb—it is the same "word"—but that power is minimized rather than exploited: the seventh and other dissonances are almost always passed over quickly, unstressed, and a different kind of "sentence" results (see the harmony for the penultimate note of the tune in Frame 4 and Frame 6 on p. 189).

From the 12th century to the 20th Western art music has played dissonance against consonance in these two contrasting ways. Of course many intervals dissonant in the early tradition became consonant later on; but the distinction between dissonance and consonance remained a firm musical principle, and the early techniques for dealing with the distinction were never abandoned.

Instrumental Harmony

Scholars feel that early medieval churchmen considered instrumental sounds improper for official worship (Bowles 1957; Hughes 1974: 253). Gregorian Chant needs no accompaniment, and manuscripts indicate none. Early counterpoint—the *discant* and *organum* we have been discussing—contains melodic lines for which the manuscripts provide no words, and these lines may indeed have been performed in later medieval times by instrumentalists rather than by singers, but it seems unlikely.

Instrumentalists did play in cathedrals and churches on occasions that were not worship services, however. We know, because writers of the time complained about it or enthused over it, depending on their point of view. Such occasions were the grand processions staged by the Church or the secular authorities; church ceremonies other than the celebration of the Mass and the Hours—weddings, for example; religious plays, called "liturgical dramas," which often were tied to specific worship services though not themselves part of the official service; semi-religious folk rituals supported by the Church; and events held in church buildings but not religious at all.

One writer who protested was the 12-century abbot Aelred of Yorkshire, England. His Latin was translated with evident relish some five hundred years later by the Puritan William Prynne, himself protesting against the use of instruments in contemporary worship services of the Church of England (see pp. 109-110). Here is a portion of Aelred's complaint as rendered by Prynne:

> Let me speake now of those who, under the show of religion, doe obpalliate the business of pleasure. . . . Whence hath the Church so many Organs and Musicall Instruments? To what purpose, I pray you, is that terrible blowing of Belloes, expressing rather the crakes of thunder, than the sweetnesse of a voyce? . . . In the meantime, the common people standing by, trembling and astonished, admire the sound of the Organs, the noyse of the Cymballs and Musicall Instruments, the harmony of the Pipes and Cornets.
> *(Davey 1921: 16-17)*

Although music to be played on instruments like these is not identified in the manuscript sources, we can be fairly sure about its harmonic style. Let me discuss first the organ and then other instruments.

The medieval organ was at first not a church instrument. It was for secular entertainment and ceremony among the Romans and retained this role well beyond the time of Charlemagne (d. 814). Only in the 10th century did it begin to be connected with Church functions and only later still, perhaps as early as the 12th century, was it heard during worship services.

Three types of organ existed in 12th-century Europe. The smallest of these a person could carry about and play at the same time. We call it the "portative" organ from the Latin *portatus*, "carried." It hung in front of the body on a shoulder strap, and some models could be rested on the lap. On one side was a keyboard played with two fingers of the right hand, the arm at a right angle to the keys (Sachs 1940: 286). On the other side, or underneath, was a bellows for the left hand. The bellows fed a wind-chest into which the pipes were set in one, two, or three parallel rows (see Figure 36A, overleaf). The pipes gave flutelike tones pitched in the range of the soprano voice.

Fig. 36

Each key of the keyboard sounded one pipe, and the player, to judge from medieval pictures and sculptures, depressed only one key at a time. Some portatives also carried two or three drone pipes (Hickmann 1936: 80-81; Perrot 1971: 272) turned on or off by setting a separate control (Sachs 1940: 287). Evidently the only kind of harmony this instrument created when played by itself was drone harmony.

Some scholars think the portative was strictly for secular entertainment; others grant that it might have been used in church processionals and even taken into the choir stalls of the sanctuary to give the singers their pitch. Its light tone would not have been very helpful in processionals, but in the sanctuary the instrument might have been used at times to give the priest and the singers not only their starting pitch but an unobtrusive drone to keep them from wandering away from the proper pitch frame of the music.

A 12th-century German poem places the portative organ in its more usual context of worldly entertainment, where it was often part of a band:

SI BEGUNDE WOL SINGEN
They started up singing,
SNAELICHEN SPRINGEN,
rapidly dancing,
MIT HERPLIN UNDE MIT GIGEN
with small harps and with fiddles,
MIT ORGENEN UNDE MIT LYREN.
with portatives and rebecs.

(Hickman 1936: 183, my translation)

The largest 12th-century organs were the "great"

organs—fairly modest, fixed installations of thirty pipes or less (Perrot 1971: 280-283). To play a note on a great organ one pulled out a large wooden slide that admitted air to several pipes at once. The pipes were tuned to give not only the main note but also one or two others consonant with the main note: its lower octave or upper fifth, or both, and perhaps even an upper or lower octave of one of these harmony notes. The main note itself was pitched in the range of the tenor voice. Wind to make the pipes speak was supplied by perhaps a dozen pairs of bellows pumped by men standing above them pushing down with their feet or standing below them pushing up with their arms.

The sea of sound produced by pulling out a slide could not

FIGURE 36: SMALL ORGANS. *Until the 10th century, Eastern and Western European organs were secular instruments rather than religious ones. By the 12th century they were established in cathedrals, though probably restricted to functions outside the worship service itself.*

(A): the smallest type of medieval organ, a "portative" (from the Latin portatus, *"carried"), as sketched by Georges Kastner (1852: plate 17, figure 137), probably from a figure sculpted in stone. The player uses one finger of his right hand to play the keyboard (not shown in detail) one key at a time; his left hand raises and depresses a bellows. Frequently these instruments appear with one or two markedly longer pipes at one end of the set; these longer pipes supplied drone notes and could be turned on or off with a special mechanism.*

(B): a medieval mixed band of, from left to right, small kettledrums, cymbals, clarion trumpets, a "positive" organ (from the Latin positus, *"placed," because it could be carried about but had to be placed somewhere to be played), and, hanging from the belt of the second clarion player, a triangle strung with little rings that added a buzzing quality to its sound. The artist, an unknown painter of the late 14-century, shows clearly the operation of this middle-size organ by two men, one pumping the bellows and the other playing the keyboard with two hands, one finger each. Two long drone pipes can be seen sticking up out of the tall end of the organ case. (British Museum Add. Ms. 27695, f. 13.)*

be modified. All pipes connected to one slide spoke together.* The great organ was therefore a harmonic instrument: whenever a single melody was played on it, additional melodic lines moved up and down in rhythmic unison with the main melody but an octave, a fifth, and an octave and a fifth away from it, creating *discant* in parallel motion. The effect could be impressive, as we learn from an English monk of the late 10th century, Wulfstan, who wrote in Latin verse a first-hand account of the great organ at Winchester Cathedral.† Here is a portion of his description as translated into English prose by William Sumner:

> Like thunder the iron tones batter the ear, so that it may receive no sound but that alone. To such an amount does it reverberate, echoing in every direction, that everyone stops with his hands to his gaping ears, being in no wise able to draw near and bear the sound, which so many combinations of pipes produce.
>
> *(Sumner 1962: 36)*

Contemporary sources tell us that organs, evidently playing before or after a service, accompanied hymns and hymnlike pieces. Probably the instrument both supported the voices and alternated with them. The great organ seems especially well suited to processional music. Its slide mechanism naturally prevented organists from playing rapidly, but they could play drones and also melodies moving at a stately speed to the harmony of parallel *discant*.

Smaller, softer organs began to supplant the great organs during the 11th and 12th centuries. These new models were also played from fixed positions but could be moved if necessary from one place to another. We call them "positive" organs from

---

*The first attempt to modify the sound produced by a single slide was a 14th-century device that shut off some of the pipes while allowing the rest to speak. It "stopped" part of the sound, and controls that select which pipes will speak on a modern organ are still called "stops."

† James W. Mc Kinnon (1974) casts strong doubt on the accuracy of his description.

the Latin *positus*, "placed." Instructions for building positive organs have survived from as early as the 10th century.

To sound a positive organ, one or two men worked a pair of bellows by hand or foot at the back of the instrument while the organist, seated in front, depressed the keys of a keyboard with the fingers of both hands (see the bottom of p. 196). The keys worked against a spring, as did the keys of the portative, and the organist could play them much faster than he could work the slides of the great organ, which had to be pulled out and then pushed back in. Some positives had a second keyboard controlling ten or so pipes of bass pitch, and a third controlling a set of high-pitched pipes. The sound of all these pipes was flutelike, even the sound of the bass pipes, because the sounding mechanism was that of a flute: a stream of air directed against a sharp edge in the side of the pipe created turbulence inside and outside the pipe in rapid alternation, thereby causing the air to vibrate inside the pipe itself, which was—like the modern flute—a cylinder.

On a large positive the central keyboard might sound from five to eight pipes for each key, creating *discant* in parallel motion. With both hands free to play and a keyboard free of the cumbersome slide mechanism, the organist may well have played two melodies moving in different directions at the same time, as in the *discant* of Notre Dame. In addition, drone pipes could be sounded by setting a separate mechanism. Finally, by using the different keyboards in various successions and perhaps in combination, the organist could introduce a variety of effects.

We don't know whether in the 12th century the chapter of Notre Dame owned a great organ, a positive organ, or a portative organ, or one or two of each. There was ample room for the larger instruments in the two aisles surrounding the sanctuary of the new choir completed in 1182, or in the single gallery running above the inner of these two aisles. In 1414 an Italian noble reported seeing in Notre Dame "two very large organs, one of which had sixteen bellows . . ." (Sumner 1962: 49 n.3). We are not told where they were placed.

Other kinds of instruments were heard in the churches of medieval Europe, if not as part of the service then as part of events peripheral to it. According to an early 9th-century account of worship at the cathedral at Metz, for example,

> the congregation was gathered in the church, the men standing on the southern side, the women, veiled, on the northern. Into the half-gloom of the church moved the procession of the clergy, bishop, deacons, subdeacons, acolytes, magnificent in white, scarlet, and gold, preceded by lighted candles and swinging censers. As they came, the majestic words of the Psalmist rang out: "Praise ye the Lord. . . . Praise him with the sound of the trumpet:..." And as they sang, cymbals, trumpets, psalterium, organ rang out. Slowly, with great dignity, the procession moved down the left side of the church, and on reaching the altar, the bishop began the Mass.
> *(Bittermann 1929: 405)*

A great many kinds of instruments were available, and undoubtedly a great many kinds were used. Most were pitched in the female vocal range and were used in mixed bands; that is, in ensembles of different-sounding instruments. The concept of a choir or "consort" of instruments, an ensemble of more or less uniform timbre, was not generally accepted until the 15th century (when it was found to express better than the mixed band a new point of view we call "humanism," as I will point out in Chapter 13).

As many as ten players in a band was not unusual. What did they use for music? As the German medievalist Walter Salmen reports,

> composed [that is, written-out] pieces seem to underlie only the smaller part of the musical sounds sung and played prior to the 16th century. . . . thousands of wandering and resident minstrels made music by-and-large without any written

guidance. No picture shows an instrumentalist at a music stand.

(Salmen 1957: 17, my translation)

In other words, they played from memory, improvised, or did a bit of both. The result was most probably heterophony supported with drones.

For drones we have the evidence of instrumental construction: winds were frequently double pipes (Sachs 1940: 282, 287; Marcuse 1975: 651), with the second pipe often with fewer holes than the first or none at all; most stringed instruments had a flat bridge, or just a tailpiece, so the bow usually touched all strings at once* and created a drone (Bachman 1969: passim).

For heterophony we have no evidence, but history and modern examples of improvised music strongly suggest that this kind of harmony was common.

Effective improvisation is the application of a clearly defined style to an overall plan without freezing the details of performance. Musicians of today well versed in bluegrass, jazz, or blues, or in barbershop singing, for that matter, can put a piece together with no rehearsal at all if they know the tune or the plan of the harmony. The plan guiding the medieval band was undoubtedly the tune, since most of the instruments sounded in the same high range.

This reasoning strongly suggests that heterophony was the kind of harmony sounded by the medieval band, just as it is the harmony usually heard today among the melody instruments in bluegrass, jazz, and blues. Heterophony also characterizes modern Muslim instrumental ensembles in North Africa and the Middle East and apparently has done so for centuries; this is suggestive because the connection between Muslim and Christian musical culture was close in the Middle Ages.

From the 8th to the 11th centuries the Muslims controlled

---

*In a few cases the soundbox of the instrument appears narrow enough or sufficiently waisted to let the bow move at an angle to this plane and thus make contact only with an outer string.

all the Mediterranean but its northern shores. Muslim Berbers from North Africa under Arab, Persian, and Syrian leadership invaded Spain at the beginning of the 8th century and held it for eight hundred years. Spanish peasants learned improved methods of agriculture from the Berbers. Christian scholars studied Arabic works on music, history, algebra, theology, astronomy, trigonometry, and medicine, as well as Arabic translations of the Greek philosophers (the translation of Aristotle from Arabic into Latin in the 12th century marked the beginning of modern experimental science). Christian nobles maintained friendships with ruling Berber families in Spain, and intermarriage was common. The retinue of a Berber noblewoman who married a Christian nobleman brought Muslim music into the husband's court. Thus it is not surprising to find the Christian nobility supporting a school for Berber musicians at Jávita (south of Valencia, in eastern Spain) long after the area fell into Christian hands in 1248.

Medieval Christian instruments are themselves the best witnesses to the Muslim presence. The bow, for example, came to Europe from Central Asia, travelling in the hands of Muslim musicians westward from Central Asian courts across North Africa to Spain.* The lute is Muslim, and also the broad, flat zither called a "psalterium" in the account quoted earlier of a procession that opened a 9th-century service in the cathedral at Metz.

Kettledrums are Muslim. The medieval version was about the size of a mixing bowl and was played in pairs (see p. 196 at the bottom, where the Muslim clarion, Europe's herald's trumpet, also appears). Our modern orchestral flute entered Europe from

---

*A handy reference for the Muslim contribution to the instruments of Western Europe is Marcuse (1975). She covers the early bow (pp. 464-467), the lute (p. 416), the flat zither (pp. 209-212), kettledrums (pp. 163-164), the Herald's trumpet (p. 792), and cross flute (p. 565; for the European end-blown model see p. 557). The best summary of European wind instruments in the Middle Ages remains Baines (1957, Chapter IX; 1960). Grove's Dictionaries of Music, Inc., is now putting out a book on instruments culled from its own fine reference work of 1980, *The New Grove Dictionary of Music and Musicians*.

Muslim countries by way of the Balkans (the indigenous European flute was end blown rather than cross blown). Before the Muslims entered Spain, Europeans played cylindrical wind instruments with single, and perhaps double, reeds in the blowing end; these survived as bagpipes in the later Middle Ages, where the Muslim shawm, a conical pipe with a double reed, became the principal member of the reed family in Europe (its descendent is our modern oboe).

Heterophony and drone harmony have continued to the present in several Western traditions. The harmonic techniques of *discant* and *organum* have been supplemented with other ways of playing dissonance against consonance and continue to contribute to an expressive harmonic language. Chapter 13 discusses the beginning of this later development, the intervening chapters being necessary to establish one of its vital elements: the Western approach to rhythm.

Part Three: Rhythm

10

The Nature of Rhythm

The Flow of Time

Because we experience change we imagine that time exists. Our sense of time is our sense of change: we watch the colors of a sunrise gradually pale, we feel our pulses beat, we hear the songs of birds and feel the chill of evening. If there were no change—if by some miracle the light and warmth around us never varied, our inner motions were stilled, and birds no longer sang—there would be no time.

The changes generating our sense of time do not take place at the same rate. When we watch the sweep of the second-hand on a clock we sense time as a steady flow, for example, but when we read a book, examine an intricate drawing, or watch the varied motion of a solo dancer, that sweep of the second-hand is apt to run faster or slower than the time created by the new object of our attention. Thus a movie draws us into its own time flow, and when we leave the theater we check our watches to find out how much "real" time has passed. We cannot judge the passage of clock time by watching a film, nor the passage of film time by watching a clock.

As these examples indicate, change causes us to perceive different kinds of time which are isolated from each other. Even people participating in the same event experience individual flows of time, when the changes constituting the event are not perceived identically by everyone. Thus, among the runners of a race varieties of time may be experienced, and these varieties will be different from those experienced by observers and those experienced by people who watch a clock while the race is going on. The individual can bring different kinds of time together, of course, as when one compares the sense of time generated by viewing a runner with the sense of time generated by viewing the moving hands of a stopwatch. Left to themselves, however, the various kinds of time proceed by themselves, none of them more real or less real than the others.

It is true that we live much of every day by the clock, and the habit has led us to think that time itself flows steadily. In reality, however, there is no such thing as "time itself," only the similar steadiness of certain kinds of change: the motion of stars and clock mechanisms, the oscillation of atoms and molecules. If these changes had a variable character, we would not imagine that time flowed around us in a steady way.

Time is not a thing in itself, then, but a quality of experience, just as gravity is a quality of matter. Bradford Torrey's impression of the seasons in New England makes the point well:

> May is the shortest month of the year. February is at least twice as long.
>
> *(Torrey 1904: 1)*

If different kinds of time are isolates, musical time should be no exception. Certainly Western art music, which moves at characteristically flexible speeds, generates among Western listeners impressions of time isolated from clock time. Do other musical traditions do the same for those who are their carriers? Anecdotal evidence to the contrary is intriguing: in some cases musical time parallels clock time closely enough to suggest that the two are linked.

Consider, for example, the experience of Yuri Arbatsky when he went to the Balkans in the 1930's to study drumming. His musical training was in Western art music, and he apprenticed himself to an Albanian folk musician he identifies only as Mehmed. What Arbatsky reports about this man's sense of musical time is startling:

> I was told to beat with the drumstick on the tupan [an instrument closely resembling our bass drum] at regular intervals. This is usually the simplest of musical performances, if the intervals are short; but it is extremely difficult if the intervals are thirty to forty seconds apart. It was beating of this kind which Mehmed first asked me to do.
>
> Needless to say the first lesson was a complete failure. Yet I was warned for the second lesson. I looked at my watch—unperceived—and succeeded! ... It took me about eight months until I had mastered this exercise which native musicians generally learn in two or three weeks. Moreover, I still looked at my watch during the lessons.
> (Arbatsky 1953: 9-10)

Arbatsky apparently never mastered the exercise. He remained as mystified as we are by Mehmed's ability to create long spans of musical time identical in length when measured with a clock. The fact that native musicians did not have Arbatsky's problem suggests that they grew up in a musical tradition of rigid rather than flexible speeds, where every piece or type of piece proceeds at one speed or contains sections in fixed speeds connected by spans of shifting speed which always shift the same way.

Another possibility is that in Mehmed's musical culture the speed of a piece may vary somewhat from moment to moment but only in such a way that the length of some large span of music always comes out the same in terms of clock time. Such inflexible spans of time seem to govern Javanese orchestral court music, which changes speed frequently. From the study of Javanese music he made in the 1950's Mantle Hood concluded that court musicians seem to have

> a sense of perfect time (in the sense that we speak of perfect pitch among Western musicians), so that

> the overall duration of an orchestral piece is always predictably the same in different performances. This is also true of long repeated sections within a piece.
>
> *(M. Hood 1971: 58)*

Hood has told me that the playing he timed in Java would differ no more than six to eight seconds for a piece a full twenty-five minutes long, and no more than a few tenths of a second for a section of music four minutes long.*

The sense of perfect time that Hood reports may be a form of memory, as he suggests when he likens it to the sense of perfect pitch. People with perfect pitch can recall a sound perfectly regardless of how long it has been since they last heard the sound. All of us can recall a sound perfectly the instant it is replaced by a new sound, as demonstrated by the simple fact that we know it has been replaced. Most of us can even recall a sound perfectly after a brief interruption by another sound. People with perfect pitch have no time limit on this kind of memory † (and may well have no musical ability).

Suppose one remembers a span of time the way one

---

*Richard Wallis, who studied the music of Indonesia a generation after Mantle Hood, offers a different explanation of this remarkable uniformity: that within every section of a piece, whether slow or fast, there is a flow of equidistant decorative notes grouped in twos and multiples of two which maintains a single rate of speed; and that the constant subtotals of time compiled by these groups of decorative notes account for the constant final total of time. As far as I know, his explanation has not yet been checked against recorded examples.

†Everyone I've ever met who has such a memory recalls not just a level of pitch but a quality of sound. A colleague of mine taught himself to remember the pitch level known as "A" (440 vibrations per second) by striking his knee with a tuning fork and then holding the fork to his ear; after a while he would hear the sound of that fork when he struck his knee with his finger, and finally he could hear the fork without striking anything. My wife gained her pitch memory without conscious effort while playing piano as a child. The sounds she remembers are those of a piano, and to help herself hear them she mimes striking the keys of an imaginary piano. As far as I'm aware, scientific studies of perfect pitch have ignored both the quality of the sound remembered and the association of that sound with something else in the subject's memory. In other words, they have tried to study a memory by ignoring the memory. Little progress seems to have been made.

remembers a sound. Then people with perfect time would be those who can recall the length of a span perfectly as measured by the clock, regardless of how long it may have been since they last experienced that span. We all develop this ability in a small way, for we can all count in a steady rhythm for at least a short while, and such counting requires us to make a present span of time equal one that we recall. Western musicians are trained to imagine a span somewhat longer. Thus a drummer places three beats evenly across a span usually filled by four, and a lead guitarist improvises a phrase to fit exactly the gap a singer leaves between one verse of a song and the next.

But these are still relatively short spans. Our musicians do not work with spans as long as those that Mehmed and the Javanese court musicians sense so accurately. Our radio and television performers who do work with such spans—the disc jockey and the game-show host, for example—face a clock. If any of them have a sense of perfect time, the presence of the clock has masked the fact. It may be that perfect time is a gift as widely and randomly distributed among humans as perfect pitch, and that Westerners who have the gift are not recognized for it because our culture makes no use of it.

Rhythm versus Form

Rhythm concerns time felt as a succession of events rather than as a single span. Suzanne Langer, the American philosopher, has expressed as well as anyone the relationship between the two ways of perceiving time:

> The experience of time is anything but simple. It involves more properties than "length," or interval between selected moments; for its passages have also what I can only call, metaphorically, *volume.* Subjectively, a unit of time may be great or small as well as long or short; the slang phrase "a big time" is psychologically more accurate than a "busy," "pleasant," or "exciting" time. It is this volumi-

nousness of the direct experience of passage that makes it... indivisible. But even its volume is not simple; for it is filled with its own characteristic forms, as space is filled with material forms, otherwise it could not be observed and appreciated at all.

(Langer 1953: 112)

Perceiving a span of musical time as a whole—perceiving its volume—we experience mood, a sense that what we are hearing has an overall quality: it is light or ponderous, tense or relaxed, gentle or vigorous, etc. Perceiving the parts of the span—what Langer calls the characteristic forms within its indivisible volume—we experience rhythm and structure. While mood arises from summing the parts, rhythm and structure arise from comparing them. The total effect I have called mood is indivisible because it does not exist when the span is considered part by part. The effects I have called rhythm and structure, on the other hand, depend upon considering the span part by part. When we do so on a small scale—when we compare brief events never far apart from one another in time—our impression is of rhythm. When we do so on a large scale—when we compare events that are of relatively long duration or are considerably separated from one another in time, or both—our impression is of structure, the technical term for which is "form."

Take for example the sound of a steam locomotive racing by. Most of us have heard this sound in the movies, if not in real life. The rapid chugging of the engine and the clacking of the wheels passing over the joints in the track create a series of brief and close events we hear as rhythm. The sound of the whistle, long and loud, stands apart from this rhythm and creates a broad separation between even longer spans of whistle silence. The succession of whistle silence, whistle sound, and whistle silence creates the impression of a three-part form.

We experience rhythm by comparing close events, form by comparing distant ones, and in either case the comparisons, made at the very instant the most recent event occurs, involve not only the passage of time but also our present awareness of how long a span the comparison includes. Thus past and present mingle in our perception of each moment of music, as they do in our perception of all experience; for as Satosi Watanabe has pointed out, past, present, and future exist only in the present:

> What I want constitutes the future, what I have constitutes the present. My conscious will thus splits the present and creates the future. The future is not a later instant; it exists with the present. My will wants the later instant to coincide with the future.
> How do I . . . bring about such a coincidence? The only thing I can do is act on my environment at present in a certain way. But what kind of act should that be? To determine the act, I need a past. The past is not earlier time instants; it is an image of them at present.
>
> *(Watanabe 1972: 160)*

With a few simple changes to give it a specifically musical reference, this passage by Watanabe describes perfectly the way the act of enjoying music is performed: the conscious will splits the sound of the present into present sound and anticipated sound, basing its anticipation upon a present image of past sound.

The Sources of Musical Rhythm

Let me turn now from a general consideration of the nature of time and the effects of serial comparison to a more detailed examination of the conditions generating a feeling of musical rhythm.

In the first place, what is rhythm? I've identified it as the impression we get from making small-scale comparisons among what Langer called the characteristic forms within a span of time. If we cannot make small-scale comparisons of events, we cannot experience the impression of rhythm. It should follow, then, that all perception is rhythmic, for psychologists have found that all perception depends on comparing stimuli rather than on the stimuli themselves (see the summary quoted on p. 33). But we do not seem to feel that our every waking minute is filled with rhythm; therefore the impression of rhythm does *not* arise just from making small-scale comparisons. More must be involved.

It seems to me that the impression of rhythm arises when small-scale comparisons establish that consecutive stimuli are members of a group. To put it another way, a rapid sound series is not a rhythmic sound series unless the sounds form one or more clusters. Let them form, for example, a group of pitches or a set of effects related by changes in some other quality, and they will generate an impression of rhythm.

In the second place, what is the feeling associated with an impression of rhythm? Here we are at a loss for words. There can be no description of rhythmic feeling valid for everyone, because it arises within a person's mind and takes its character from the character of that mind. But whatever the feeling, it seems to arise as readily from irregular groupings of sound as from regular ones and from both subtle and prominent effects.

The dependence of rhythm upon grouping is but an example of the general truth that unrelated perceptions make no sense. Intelligibility is relatedness, the position of an item in a cluster of items. Intelligibility is absent from completely homogenous perceptions, in which the content is a unity, and from chaos, in which the content has only unrelated parts. We strongly prefer an intelligible environment. Indeed, we invent relationships when the environment fails to provide them. Thus we imagine sounds in utter silence and shapes in an undifferentiated surface, and hear pairs of sounds when the stimulus is only an equidistant series of undifferentiated clicks.* The

---

*Pairs of sounds are for us a natural pattern because we are used to hearing them in almost all the music surrounding us. A mind carrying a different musical

random sounds of a rushing stream become musical phrases because the limited range of qualities and timings they present encourage us to imagine related groupings. For the same reason, fragments of speech become words and whole sentences.

The rhythm of grouped events is not always musical. A series of identical groups of sounds tends to induce trance when we endure it willingly and rage when we suffer it against our will. We do not experience music by becoming stupefied or going out of control, however, but by paying attention to the stimuli. *Musical* rhythm requires a series of sounds not only grouped, therefore, but interesting.

When I defined music as a play of sound at the beginning of this book, I was thinking of this quality of being interesting. I wrote that music moves like the play of firelight, projects like a staged play, and obeys arbitrary rules like a game. These actions are all interesting—that is, all of them avoid identical repetition. When groups of sounds engage our interest by their similarities and differences, we sense musical rhythm. An equidistant ticking becomes rhythmic when heard as pairs of sounds, and musically rhythmic when variation makes the pairs interesting.

Sources of variation are changes in the timbre, pitch, loudness, and harmony of sound and in the timing and duration of both sound and silence. The opening of *The Battle Hymn of the Republic*, drawn on Figure 37 (overleaf), shows a musical rhythm achieved by adding variations of timbre and pitch to the monotonous alternation between a short, soft syllable and a long, loud one. In this example, variations of pitch generate at

Fig. 37

---

tradition from ours would presumably impose a different grouping upon the equidistant, identical clicks. Psychologists seem not yet to have recognized the limited validity of results obtained from subjects drawn from only one cultural background. Ira J. Hirsh, for example, determined that a minimum gap of "between 15 and 20 msec [milliseconds] is required for the listener to report correctly which of ... two sounds preceded the other" by testing "a panel of five listeners" not otherwise identified or described (Hirsh 1959: 759, 760). As discussed toward the end of this chapter, my own experience is that different cultures have developed different degrees of sensitivity in this area.

216

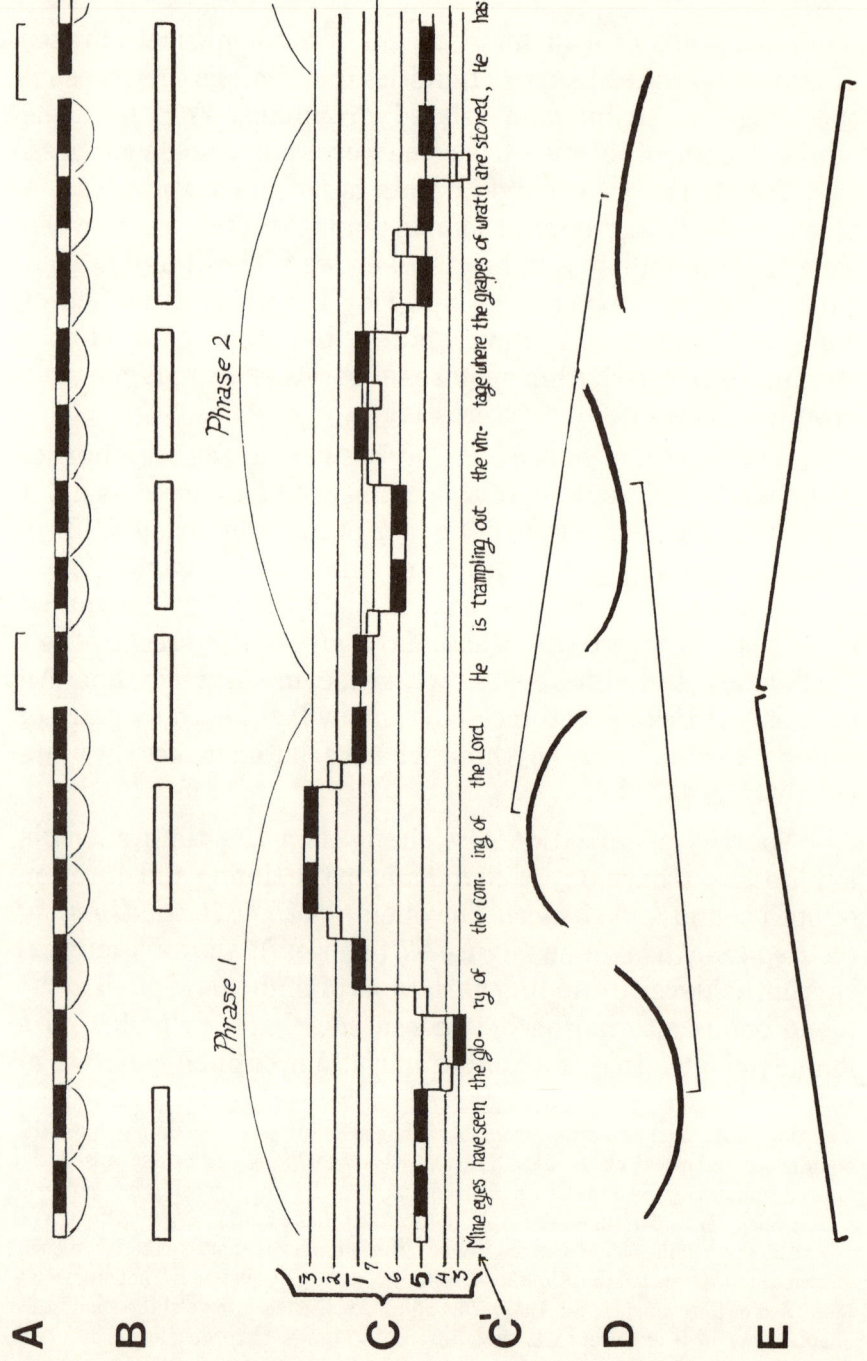

FIGURE 37. *THE BATTLE HYMN OF THE REPUBLIC. The first two phrases of the familiar song are here analyzed into several concurrent series of rhythmic groups to show the complex nature of musical rhythm. Across the center of the figure run the words and tune on a pitch frame containing, for convenient comparison, every pitch level in the Western octave series. For a general explanation of the notation see the caption for Figure 4.*

(A): rhythmic groups formed by contrasts of duration and loudness. Horizontal extension shows relative duration, solid rectangles are loud, and hollow rectangles are soft. Because it is intelligible, this monotonous series generates rhythmic feeling; however, because it is not interesting it does not generate musical rhythm. The two superior brackets call your attention to identical effects that, because of their separation, generate form rather than rhythm.

(B): rhythmic groups formed by repeated pitch. Rectangles show duration; the actual pitches of each group are given in (C) in vertical alignment with these rectangles. Unlike what is shown above in (A), variety in pitch, length, and timing of the groups in (B) renders the series rhythmically interesting, i.e., musical.

(C): all aspects of the tune combined. Horizontal extension indicates duration, loud sounds are solid, soft ones hollow; pitch is shown by placement on the pitch frame, in which levels 5 and $\bar{1}$ have been drawn prominently for visual convenience. All other layers of the figure are vertically aligned with this one.

(C'): vowels and consonants form a nonrhythmic series of timbres. "Lord" rhyming with "stored" generates form.

(D): rhythmic groups formed by melodic shapes. Separation between groups is based on the sense of the words as well as on actual pauses in the sound. The length of these groups makes the rhythm between pairs of them (identified by brackets) slower than rhythms in (A) or (B) above.

(E): rhythmic groups formed by pitch relationships on an even larger scale than those of (D). The effect is a musical rhythm slow enough to generate not a feeling of rhythm but a feeling of form.

least three concurrent series of musically rhythmic groups.*

Musical rhythm is usually discussed as patterns of duration and timing, the other variables I have mentioned being ignored for the sake of simplicity. Before beginning the next section on measured musical rhythm, let me take a moment to define these two qualities.

The duration of an event is how long it lasts, not when it happens. The timing of an event is when it happens, not how long it lasts; more specifically, its timing is the location of its beginning in the rhythmic series. The duration of one event (including the event of silence) determines the timing of the next, of course, and so the two qualities tend to be spoken of interchangeably. They have different effects, however: duration encourages comparison with other durations and acquires a relative importance based on size; timing assigns importance regardless of any quality other than placement in the series. The difference is illustrated in the following couplet on the efficacy of a medical team:

> Willoughby, Coolington, Jones, and Twillingham
> Managed to cure an old man without killing him.

The outstanding weight of "Jones" owes nothing to placement or sound ("man" has equal placement; "Coolington" opens with equal resonance) and everything to size (it has twice the length of any other syllable in the line). The weight of the first syllable of "managed," on the other hand, owes nothing to size or sound and everything to placement, for we treat the first stress in a line of doggerel as an important one.

---

*Concurrent series are the rule rather than the exception in musical rhythm, because usually more than one aspect of the sound varies in a rhythmic way, and more than one set of relationships lays claim to a particular aspect of each sound.

Note: the groups shown on p. 216 are melodic to the extent that they represent pitch relationships, and rhythmic to the extent that they represent time relationships. Clearly, rhythm and melody are not separate aspects of music but overlapping ones. Rhythm, of course, includes many relationships other than those of pitch; and melody includes not only pitch rhythm but also the timeless relationship of each pitch to the pitch frame in which it occurs.

Measured Music and Gait

Much of the world's music has what we call a "free" rhythm—black American hollers, for example, and the songs of the Roman Catholic liturgy. Free rhythm is not uncontrolled rhythm, for musicians always control their music. Free rhythm is rhythm unrestricted in the variety and emphasis of its durational values. Performers time the flow of such music by sensing from moment to moment how much energy and exposure to give each successive event.* A familiar example of free rhythm is the cadenza of Western art music and rock, an unaccompanied solo placed near the end of the music and given over to virtuoso display.

Rhythm that is not free is said to be "measured," meaning it is built with lengths of time measured off into just a few different values. Throughout most of *The Battle Hymn of the Republic*, the syllables of the text use only two durations (see Figure 37). Wagner's *Wedding March* uses five different durations—the opening phrase associated with the words "Here comes the bride!" has four of them—but this variety is not nearly enough to dispel the impression of a severely restricted choice of durations.

Measured rhythm's few durations produce groups varying little in length or internal pattern. In *Todoro*, the Bulgarian folk song shown as Figure 38 on p. 221, for example, these groups have only two different lengths and offer only three different patterns. The groups in Western measured song are mainly of a single length. In the text below I have used virgules (/) to mark off the particular length that dominates the opening of *The Battle Hymn of the Republic:*

Fig. 38

Mine eyes / have seen / the glo- / ry of / . . .

---

*One reason musicians prefer working with a live audience is that the audience enhances this evaluation process, which always goes on no matter what kind of rhythm is involved. In some subtle way performers are able to feel the impact on the audience of what they have just done and to decide what they will do next accordingly.

Changes in the single length dominating a Western song are characteristically slight and brief. In *The Battle Hymn of the Republic*, for example, such changes occur at the ends of phrases, as shown below: the dominant length increases a little (see the underlined words) and then decreases (see the overlined word).

the com-/ ing of / <u>the Lord,</u>/ He / has loosed / . . .

Different durational patterns and group lengths create different qualities of motion. In general, a piece of music in measured rhythm avoids such variety and generates instead a

FIGURE 38. TODORO. *This pictorial notation of the Bulgarian folk song* Todoro *shows the melody for the first two lines of text as arranged by Philip Koutev and performed on tape by the Pennywhistlers (see p. 159). The sound is commercially available on Nonesuch H 72011: side 1, band 2, where it is conducted by Koutev. For a general explanation of pictorial notation see the caption for Figure 4. For a discussion of state-supported folk music in Bulgaria, see p. 155f.*

Durational values throughout this melody are shown as horizontal extensions of the thick melodic line. In terms of the shortest of these extensions the durational values are 1, 2, 3, and 4. You can count these for yourself because light vertical lines have been provided which divide the horizontal progress of the music into durations of the value of 1.

The groups formed by the four durational values have only two lengths: 3 and 4. Grouping is shown by thin, curved lines placed over the thick melodic line. Within the shorter of the two groups the durational pattern is always a unity (see for example the musical setting of the third syllable in Frame 3). Within the longer of the two groups the durational pattern can also be a unity (see for example the musical setting of the fourth syllable in every frame), but in addition we find the durational patterns 2 plus 2 and 3 plus 1 (for the first of these see the opening of any frame; for the second, see the ending of Frames 1, 3, and 4). Other possible combinations of durations within the two established group lengths are avoided.

The several restrictions in the variety of durations used have the effect of stabilizing the musical motion. Stable motion is characteristic of measured rhythm all over the world. This particular motion, though stable in the sense of consistent, strikes Westerners as unsteady

consistent movement. I call the motion of durational patterns and group lengths, whether varied or not, the "gait" of the music, borrowing from everyday speech a word for the quality of motion in a walk or a run. The consistent movement of Western gaits is formed by groups of equal length. The consistent movement of many non-Western gaits is formed by groups of unequal length, as in the example shown in Figure 38. Westerners find such gaits hard to follow because their own

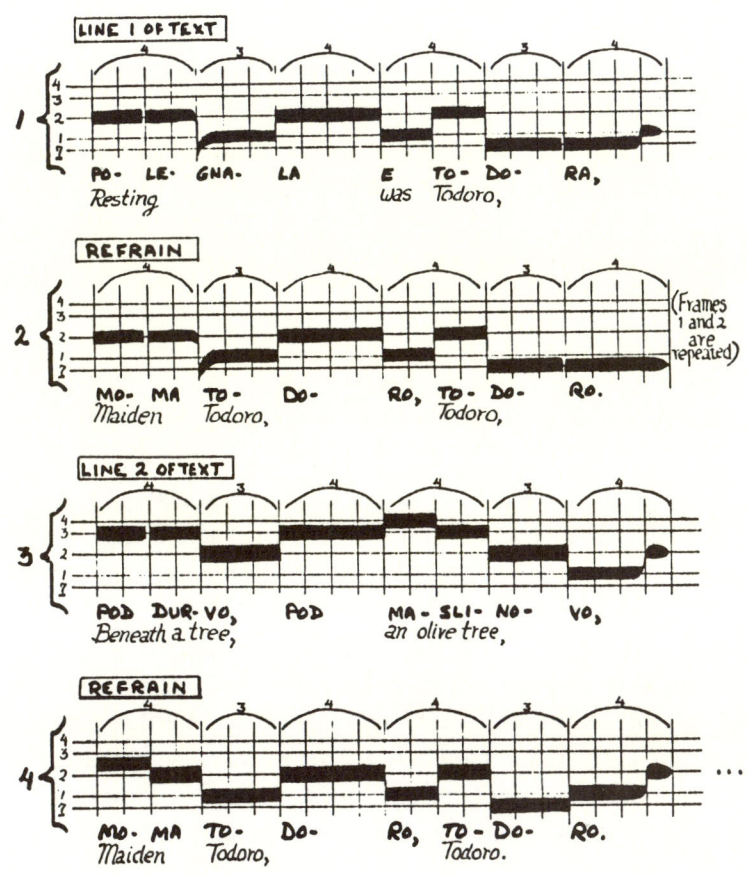

because it shifts back and forth between a group four units long and one three units long. Westerners are used to hearing motion dominated by a single group length.

music does not prepare them for the experience.

Whether its groups are of equal or unequal length, however, gait is a powerful force in measured music, as you can judge by comparing the rhythmic effect of *Dixie* ("Oh, I wish I was in the land of cotton...") with that of *The Battle Hymn of the Republic*: the steps to either march are the same, but the rhythm in each case seems different because the gait is different.*

In short, measured rhythm is rhythm restricted in three ways: the number of different durations presented is few, these durations form groups of only slightly and occasionally varied length, and within each length they arrange themselves in only a few different patterns. So much restriction indicates that the result—a consistent musical motion—must be a goal worth the sacrifice. We will find in the next chapter, however, that consistent musical motion is not always a goal in some Native American song.

Meter

The groups forming the gait of measured music tend to cluster into larger groups we call "measures." When more than one gait is present at the same time, more than one series of measures results. Such simultaneous series are rare in Western music but common in certain other cultures. When they occur, one series will guide the timing of others.

Certain sound effects are used to outline a measure. They are not of the same kind in every musical tradition. In some they are soft, in others loud; in some they involve changes of pitch or harmony, in others they do not; in some they have a particular timbre, in others their timbre varies. When measures occur in simultaneous series, certain sounds will be reserved for signalling the outline of the guiding measures.

---

*Indeed, as we can hear in a fiddler's introductory strokes at a country dance and in the close of a piece of bluegrass music, measured rhythm can make sense as gait alone without the broader organization of the groups into larger groups such as we hear in marches, where the groups form pairs and pairs of pairs.

We call the outline of a measure its "meter" (spelled "metre" by the English and derived from the Latin for a standard of measure, *"metrum"*). We call the sound effects signalling this outline "metrical accents" whether or not they actually have an emphatic sound.* The people of every culture know the language of their metrical accents as well as they know their patterns of speech. Metrical accents of a different kind are as hard for them to understand as foreign speech, especially when hidden in a music sounding much like their own. The main accent of a Western meter is low in pitch and often loud. For this reason Westerners have often misunderstood the rhythm of Native American song, discussed in Chapter 11, and the rhythm of West African drumming, discussed in Chapter 12, because in these cultures the qualities of low pitch and loudness do not identify main metrical accents.

Metrical accents can be equally or unequally spaced, and the musical difference between the two types of spacing is profound. Equally spaced accents form meters through differences in the quality of their sounds; I call such meters "equidistant." Unequally spaced accents form meters through the pattern of their timing, to which differences in sound quality may be added; I call such meters "asymmetrical," because unequally spaced accents never present a symmetrical pattern.

To project an equidistant meter, a piece of music must channel many of its effects toward supporting a particular pattern of sound qualities. The pattern itself must be presented, of course, which means that the metrical accents must have certain kinds of sound; but more than this, sounds blurring the metrical ones must be avoided, and the metrical ones must not be used at other places. To project an asymmetrical meter, on the other hand, a single sound quality properly timed will suffice. The music is free to use all but this one sound at any time for any purpose. This difference between equidistant and

*It is hard to separate the idea of accent from the idea of emphasis, and important to realize that metrical accents are indeed often without emphasis. A more appropriate term than "accent" is needed, but none has yet gained general acceptance.

Fig. 39 asymmetrical meters is illustrated in **Figure 39** opposite.

One might expect a tradition of equidistant meters, burdened as it is by the restrictions I have mentioned, to produce music less rich in content than a tradition of asymmetrical meters. This does not necessarily happen. For example, Western music with its equidistant meters has a rich harmonic language and a minimal rhythmic one, whereas West African music with its asymmetrical meters has a rich rhythmic language and a minimal harmonic one. It seems that the very support equidistant meters require leads to favoring unified rhythms over conflicting ones, which in turn leads to distinguishing unified moments from each other through differences in harmony. On the other hand, the rhythmic freedom made possible by asymmetrical meters leads to favoring conflicting rhythms over unified ones, which in turn discourages the

FIGURE 39: EQUIDISTANT AND ASYMMETRICAL METERS. *The four boxes in this drawing contain four different meters; that is, four different timing patterns formed by the distribution of certain sounds we call metrical accents. Short vertical lines mark off the passage of time into equal intervals within each box. Thick verticals stand for metrical accents.*

An equidistant distribution of metrical accents characterizes the upper and lower boxes on the left. The upper one contains a meter of three accents, the lower a meter of four accents, as you can tell from your own knowledge of the songs quoted there. Without the words to indicate that the grouping of the equidistant accents is different in each case, the difference would not exist. The words remind you of musical qualities that distinguish the accents from one another. Without such differences in quality a series of equidistant accents would not form groups, and the upper and lower series shown here would be identical.

An asymmetrical distribution of metrical accents characterizes the upper and lower boxes on the right, creating in each case a timing pattern that repeats. The pattern of three accents in the upper box and four accents in the lower box emerges clearly without reference to differences in the quality of the sound of the accents.

Music employing equidistant metrical accents must commit a large portion of its sound to defining their grouping. For this purpose

development of harmonies as unified blocks of sound.

Once a meter has been established it becomes a guiding concept, an imagined pattern not always present in the actual sound. Nor must a meter be heard several times before it can assume this role. If understood at once, it becomes at once a guiding concept whether simple and repetitive or irregular. Thus the unchanging meter of a traditional country dance and the changing meter of a modern orchestral work like Carl Orff's *Carmina Burana* are both, once we know them well, concepts against which we judge the very first moment of actual sound.

As this line of argument suggests, the fundamental requirement for performing music is mental, not physical. Musicians need technique, of course, but technique is useless if they cannot imagine what is to come and judge what is taking place. Imagining involves anticipating actual sound with a

	EQUIDISTANT WESTERN METERS	ASYMMETRICAL NON-WESTERN METERS
3 ACCENTS	||||||||||||| "My coun- try, 'tis of thee, sweet..."	||||||||||||||| (Triputala, South India)
4 ACCENTS	|||||||||||||| "Ca- li- for- nia, here I come..."	|||||||||||||||| (Adowa, West Africa)

a rich variety of harmonies has developed in Western music together with a preference for simple rhythms sounded one at a time. Music employing asymmetrical metrical accents, on the other hand, may use many kinds of rhythm at the same time just so long as the meter itself is given some distinctive sound. On this basis a rich variety of rhythmic combinations has developed in West African ensemble drumming, and contrasting harmonies are used hardly at all.

Fig. 40   concept of that sound and its place in the scheme of the music; judging involves comparing actual sound with what has been imagined. Figure 40 calls your attention to evidence that over a

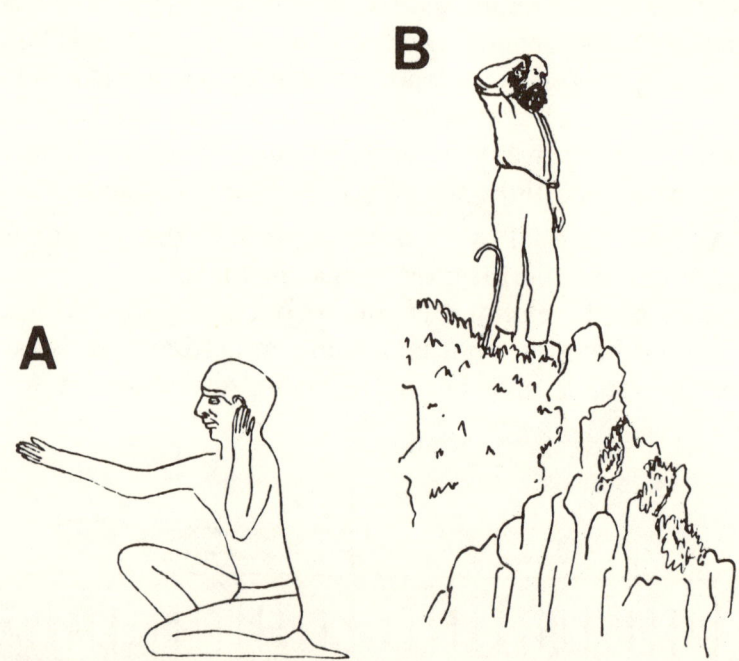

FIGURE 40: MENTAL MUSIC. *Thought is more basic to musical performance than is physical technique: one must have an idea of what is to come in order to turn a succession of sounds into a flow of sounds, and a standard in mind against which to judge what is happening to the sound every moment. Common sense suggests that this must always have been true in human history, and the evidence shown here tends to confirm common sense.*

(A): drawn from the photograph of a sculptured relief in an Egyptian tomb of the Twelfth Dynasty (c. 2000-1800 B.C.). A singer puts his left hand to his left ear to listen to himself (Sachs 1943: plate 2-B facing p. 65).

(B): drawn from a photograph of a Swiss mountaineer of this century standing on a rocky height and cupping his right ear with his right hand to listen to himself yodel (Stapelberg 1958: column 74).

span of forty centuries people have been using their minds to guide their music making. As I point out in Chapter 16, to protect this mental control successful performers do not allow themselves to experience the emotion their audience feels.

From time to time in Western measured music, intentional conflict between concept and sound creates a moment of counterpoint between imagination and experience. The examples on the next two pages are from measured poetry because the rhythms of language are readily conveyed on the printed page and do not require the reader to have a highly developed sense of pitch and timing. Figure 41 overleaf is taken from the classical Roman poet Virgil; Figure 42 on p. 231 from the Elizabethan poet Shakespeare. Fig. 41
Fig 42

The songs of an Anglo-American tradition often include changes of gait—compare, for example, the beginning of *Three Blind Mice* with its middle ("They all ran after the farmer's wife ..."). But the popular favorites of this tradition, the songs still known to middle-aged members of the middle class, rarely include a change of meter. Sometimes, however, they include sounded accents in conflict with the accents of the metrical concept. We will call this effect "syncopation." Examples of it occur in *California, Here I Come!* on the words "I" and "come," and also in *There's No Business like Show Business* on the first syllable of the word "business." But even syncopation is rare in the Anglo-American tradition; it flourishes mostly in the music one can trace to an African background.

Many aspects of a musical tradition can change over the years. A performer extracts the concepts of proper musical behavior from a long series of experiences, but these do not necessarily force stability upon every aspect of a tradition. For example, the emergence of rock music in the mid 1950's brought an alteration in vocal style so drastic that many formerly successful vocalists could no longer find work. There was no change in meter, however. Rock did introduce new harmonic relationships, new instrumental sounds, new and powerful realism in its lyrics, and even a new gait; but its meter of four

228

	1	2	3	4	5	6
	‿	‿ ‿	‿	‿ ‿	‿ ‿	— —

(Line 1) AR- MA VI- RUM- QUE CA- NŌ TRŌ- IAE QUĪ PRĪ- MUS AB Ō- RĪS
          Arms and the man do I sing that first from Troy sailed a- way to

(Line 2) Ī- TA- LI- AM FA- TŌ PRO-FU- GUS LA- VĪ- NIA-QUE VĒ- NIT
          I- ta- ly, ex- iled by his fate, and came to the Ro- man

(Line 3) LĪ- TO- RA MUL- TUM IL- LE ET TER- RĪS IAC- TĀ- TUS ET AL- TŌ
          wa- terside. Much he en- dured on land and much on the sea from

(Line 4) VĪ SU- PER- UM, SAE- VAE ME- MO- REM IŪ- NŌ- NIS OB Ī- RAM,
          vio- lence a- bove: the wrath of re- mem- b'ring, ter- ri- ble Ju- no,

(Line 45) TUR- BI- NE COR- RI- PU- IT SCO- PU- LŌ- QUE IN- FIX- IT A- CŪ- TŌ....
          him in a whirl- wind she seized, on a sharp rock-y crag she im- paled him

FIGURE 41: CLASSIC ROMAN POETIC METER. *Our word "meter" (spelled "metre" by the English) descends from the Latin "metrum" (plural "metra"), by which the ancient Romans meant any unit used for measurement. When they measured their words to give them heightened effect, as in this example, the metra* were patterns of long and short syllables.

The figure shows excerpts from a poem the Romans considered their finest epic, The Aeneid, cast in a meter we call "dactylic hexameter." In composing his words, Virgil (Publius Virgilius Maro, 70-19 B.C.) had in mind the pattern of long (—) and short (⌣) durations shown above the body of the text.

The measures of the metrical plan have been marked off above these longs and shorts by curved lines and within the text by verticals running from top to bottom of the example. There are six measures to a line, hence the prefix "hexa-," meaning "six," in the name of the meter. The metrical accent stands at the beginning of each measure in the form of a syllable considered long because of the sonority of its vowel or because the vowel is followed by two or more consonants.

The gait of these measures, one long syllable followed by two short ones, was called "dactylus" ("finger") by the Romans because fingers have three segments, the first of which is the longest. A slight change of gait marks the end of each line: the last measure carries only two syllables, both of them long.

The poet rarely allows complete agreement between the metrical divisions of a line and the divisions of the flow of syllables into words and phrases (but see the opening of Line 45); frequently quality of gait is altered by replacing two short syllables with one long one (I have placed a box around these long syllables); and in every line there is a major division of the sense (marked with a heavy double vertical) which often falls within the measures of the metrical plan rather than between them.

In short, thinking of the metrical plan and the sounding measures of this poetry as two separate rhythmic lines, we can say that they create a counterpoint Virgil's audience must have been aware of and enjoyed. Such counterpoint characterizes the entire work, and he lessens it only for some compelling reason, as when he reinforces the image of the whirlwind with the rushing effect of uninterrupted dactyls in Line 45, shown at the bottom of the figure.

My English translation attempts to preserve many of the rhythmic features discussed above. For the Latin, see Virgilius 1967: I, 240 and 244.

FIGURE 42: ENGLISH POETIC METER. *This figure shows the opening of a sonnet, a brief and tightly structured English poetic form cast in a meter called "iambic pentameter."*

In composing his words, William Shakespeare (1564-1616) had in mind a pattern of five stressed (|) and five unstressed syllables, the metrical accent being created by stress in English poetry as it is by length in Latin poetry (see p. 229). The prefix "penta-" in the name of the meter means "five" and refers to the fact that every line has five metrical accents and five measures.

Each measure of iambic pentameter has a two-syllable gait, the metrical accent falling on the second syllable while the relative length of the syllables remains unregulated. The word "iambic" descends from the Latin "iambus," meaning the gait formed by a short syllable followed by a long one. Greek satiric poets of the 6th and 7th centuries B.C. were the first to use it, and its name in Greek, iambos, *derives from the verb* iapto, *meaning to attack or wound.*

(A): the syllables laid out according to the meter. The literal meaning of individual words is neither destroyed nor blurred by this strict treatment, but the content is trivialized by being subordinated to an endlessly repeating pattern. As in the Roman example on page 228, the poet has joined syllables into words and words into phrases, not to fit the meter exactly but to form a natural rhythm in counterpoint with the concept of the meter.

(B): the words arranged to emphasize content over meter. As Shakespeare intended, the flow of meaningful sound contains metrical accents and patterns other than iambic. Some of the iambic accents indicated in (A) do not exist here; some of the accents here do not exist in (A). To show that a syllable is long I have spaced it apart from what follows. (As you can see from this spacing, the durational values of English are independent of stress values.) Where pauses are substantial, I have drawn the silent stress (|) a performer uses as a point from which to launch the following unstressed syllable.

Certainly performance patterns other than (B) would also effectively emphasize content, but all of them would vary from the basic iambic concept, as mine does, and as Shakespeare intended they should. For the original text see Sonnet 116 in Shakespeare 1979: III, 777-778.

A

(1) Let me not to the mar- riage of true minds

(2) Ad- mit im- ped- i- ments. Love is not love

(3) Which al- ters when it al- ter- a- tion finds,

(4) Or bends with the re- mov- er to re- move:

(5) O no! it is an ev- er- fix- ed mark, . . .

B

Let me not   to the marriage of true minds /

Admit impediments. / Love is not love

Which alters   when it alteration finds, /

Or bends with the remover to remove:

O no! / it is an ever-fixed mark, . . .

equidistant accents—and its use of stress, low pitch, and harmonic change to communicate that meter—characterizes the swing music that rock replaced and can be found in music at least as old as that of the 13th century (see Schering 1931: no. 10). Nowadays changes of harmony seem to be the most important sound effect associated with Western metrical accents. Indeed, the accentual pattern of the meter in our popular music is usually carried by harmonic change and merely confirmed by changes of stress and melodic pitch.

Imprecision

When discussing equidistance and asymmetry I have presented two metrical plans as if they were exact blueprints that produce exact performances. In reality, musical plans and musical performances are not precise. Small differences continually occur, and it is time now to take account of this fact.

The French experimental psychologist Paul Fraisse has pointed out that

> a basic law of perception is to minimize small differences (tendency toward assimilation) and exaggerate appreciable differences (tendency toward contrast). This law applies equally to the perception of spatial structures and temporal structures.
>
> *(Fraisse 1963: 77)*

Different musical cultures apply this law differently. Thus the instrumentalists in a Balinese *gamelan* (orchestra) demonstrate far greater rhythmic agreement in unison passages than their counterparts in a Western symphony orchestra. That is, differences small enough for our musicians to assimilate remain unacceptably large to the Balinese.

West African drummers also have a finer sense of timing than we do. I remember the shock with which I heard a recording of Beethoven's *Symphony No. 1* after two months of hearing the drumming of the Anlo in southeastern Ghana. The record was one of my own. I had listened to it many times before with pleasure. But now I could no longer enjoy the performance of a conductor as fine as Toscanini and players as fine as those of the NBC Symphony Orchestra. The Africans' level of rhythmic performance had sharpened my own perceptions, and for the first time I was painfully disturbed by the numerous small differences in timing among the NBC players. As Paul Fraisse would say, my tendency toward contrast had been increased.

In addition to performing rhythms imprecisely without being aware of doing so, musicians also purposely stretch them here and there. Ingmar Bengtsson has measured Western musical performance electronically (Bengtsson 1961, 1974) to show that we in the West do not perform the "equidistant" patterns of our metrical accents equidistantly. We vary them by chance, or for momentary musical emphasis, or to create a consistent asymmetrical lilt characteristic of a certain tradition, such as the Viennese waltz. Balkan rhythms are often asymmetrical, and Bruno Ravnikar finds that they, too, are stretched and compressed (Ravnikar 1971): he reports that one cannot really describe these rhythms in the accepted way, as composed of spans in the ratio of 2:3; instead, to be precise one can only discuss the approximate ratios of *average* durational values.

In short there are degrees and types of flexibility and imprecision in the performance of all meters. The models discussed earlier in this chapter must be understood in this context.

11

Native American Rhythm

Cross-Cultural Perception

None of us doubts the existence of cultural values and practices different from our own, but we have trouble imagining them. When we think of people eating with their fingers, for example, we imagine messy people because we would consider it messy to eat that way ourselves. In the words of William Thalbitzer, a student of the East Greenland Eskimos:

> We have no other means of comprehending the heterogenous object than forcing it into the mirror of our own soul—and language—and there, by means of analogy endeavouring to understand the foreign soul and the suppositions from which the image emanated.
>
> *(Thalbitzer 1921: 180)*

Thus we hear an equidistant stress pattern as the governing meter of a piece whether it has that role or not (Chapter 10); we hear sliding pitches as decoration whether they are decoration or main notes (Chapter 4); and we reject a strident percussive singing of Gregorian Chant (Chapter 5).

Because our musical opinions and responses are already fully formed, we can understand the music of another people only through experience. The music we enjoy has taught us to enjoy the music we enjoy, and the music we are willing to try can teach us to enjoy the music we are willing to try. After enough exposure to a foreign music we respond to it with less reference to our own tradition and greater acceptance of the new tradition on its own terms.

There remains, however, the problem of language. To ask about music, analyze it, or explain it to others requires words, and words are not universal. They serve specific cultures. As Edith Trager observed in her article summarizing the Kiowa language of south central Oklahoma:

> Each language is like a different filter, through which experience can be observed and analyzed with only an approach to true objectivity.
> *(Trager 1954: 11)*

That is, full understanding of another people's music is blocked by the concepts and patterns of thought, the assumptions about reality we acquire as members of a particular culture and express with a particular set of words and word structures.

For example, the English language has both the word "music" and the word "medicine." Music and medicine are therefore thought of as separate things by speakers of English, who know that hospitals are not conservatories and that music therapy is the use in medicine of something not normally a part of medicine. The Navajos of the American southwest, however, have no general word for music. They speak of singing, of drumming, but not of the category into which both activities fall as a Westerner thinks of them. Moreover, they connect beating a drum with a particular ceremony for curing illness, one of their many curing ceremonies. They believe that feeling queer while the drum is beating for someone else means you should have the ceremony performed for yourself. Therefore, when the American anthropologist David McAllester asked various Navajos what they felt when they heard the sound of a drum, he found he had asked them about their health (McAllester 1954: 4-5). His intention was to ask them about their response to music.

When scholars trained in German universities began to study non-Western music in the 19th century, they dealt with the problem of cross-cultural perception simply and directly: they described other music in terms of their own and called the process *"vergleichende Musikwissenschaft,"* which means "comparative musicology." Their studies benefited and suffered accordingly: what they wrote could be understood by other European scholars but often reflected little of the reality of the musical systems under discussion.*

A current example of comparative thinking is the observation common in American folk studies that fiddlers "sharp the fourth." The meaning is that fiddlers prefer a level of pitch for the fourth note in the Western octave series (see p. 45) which is higher than the level preferred by performers of Western art music. The implication, intended or not, is that fiddlers play incorrectly—that they know the "right" pitch but raise it anyway, or simply don't know any better. As in the days of *vergleichende Musikwissenschaft*, the intention of saying that fiddlers sharp the fourth is to communicate. One could write with equal accuracy that art musicians flat the fourth, but the reference point for people who read such studies has been art music, not folk music, and so the low fourth of art music is the standard.

Many who study the music of another culture nowadays try to reduce the filtering effect of their own point of view by

---

*The problem was unavoidable, given the prevailing view that the scholar should remain in the study contemplating reports forwarded by travellers and explorers. In fairness I should point out that I myself have opted for comparative thinking in using the label "non-Western" throughout this book, and for the same reason that persuaded 19th-century scholars: clarity of communication. "Non-Western" remains for Westerners the most meaningful label for a tradition outside their own. The American scholar Jon Higgins and others rightly object to defining something by what it is not (like calling air "nonwater") and to the demeaning implications of "non-Western," a term associated with the tendency of Western scholars to patronize other cultures. Higgins himself uses the phrase "the music of contemporary cultures" instead of "non-Western music." I do not find this solution entirely satisfactory for my purposes because "contemporary cultures" includes both Western and non-Western in its meaning.

immersing themselves in the music itself, learning to perform it to the best of their ability from carriers of the tradition. As early as the 1930's Percival Kirby championed this approach in studying the music of the native peoples of South Africa. In the 1960's and early 1970's the American scholar Mantle Hood exerted great influence in this direction at U.C.L.A. as the director of graduate studies in ethnomusicology (the modern term for comparative musicology). His students now teach in universities from Hawaii to Connecticut and stress the role of performance in the study of non-Western music. Traditional scholars have tended to resist this eminently sensible approach, but their resistance seems to be fading.*

By learning to perform non-Western music we have done more than increase our understanding. Rightly or wrongly, the West enjoys immense prestige, and our interest in non-Western music has encouraged non-Westerners to research their own traditions and write about them. This promises not only to reduce the filter that blurs our understanding† but to equalize in the Western view the status of Westerner and non-Westerner in at least this small academic area. Such equality will benefit practical scholarship, as the American anthropologist Aidan

---

*Firsthand experience of non-Western performance practice has already produced a massive increase in Western knowledge and understanding of music. For example, the subject of melodic modes (see p. 86) received little more than twelve columns in the best English-language music dictionary of the 1960's (see Winnington-Ingram et al. 1960), and these were entirely concerned with the Western European tradition. Twenty years later the revision of that article (Powers 1980) ran to one hundred forty-seven columns, sixty of them devoted to non-Western practice.

† Cross-cultural misunderstanding cannot be completely eliminated, I realize, and will always operate in both directions. As David McAllester pointed out to me (McAllester 1975), "Indigenous scholars will have their problems with filters, too, writing in English about concepts that don't exist in English to an audience whose culture they don't understand all that well, either." Our gain in understanding will be in many areas, but most of all in understanding ourselves. For in comprehending other points of view we shall finally comprehend our own, demoting it from ultimate truth to the rank of a peculiar opinion formed by a peculiar history.

Southall concluded after ten years of study in Uganda:

> I come more and more to realize that there are profound depths and hitherto undreamed of dimensions to African cultures which we shall never understand unless they are expounded by African scholars.
>
> *(Southall 1975: 3)*

Our bias against foreign cultures is not uniform. The West does not treat as an equal a culture lacking material wealth, whatever its achievement in the art of living. Thus the phrase "Oriental cultures" has a different ring than the phrase "African cultures." The Far East impresses us, but not black Africa. With the Far East we associate silks and porcelains, calligraphy, and the fabulous wealth of imperial courts, things our own society values highly as evidence of achievement. With black Africa we associate half-naked, illiterate slaves, people in a condition our own society despises as evidence of failure. When we fail to understand an aspect of oriental culture we are apt to fault ourselves and murmur admiringly about the mysteries of the oriental mind. When we fail to understand black Africans, we are apt to call them stupid (or childlike, by which we mean the same thing).

Though I may overstate the problem, I speak of Western attitudes that do exist. They bear strongly upon the subject of this chapter, Native American rhythm. Native American cultures do not, as a general rule, stress material wealth. Our disregard for them is frequently expressed in a word that should be struck from cross-cultural study because its only meaning is pejorative. That word is "primitive."

The Concept of Primitive

There exists no such thing as "a primitive people." Whether the expression signifies people resembling early humans or people living without the benefit of "advanced" technology, its meaning is based on fabrication, not fact, and its overtones impede cross-cultural understanding.

The first of the dictionary meanings for primitive is chronological: of the earliest period, original, and hence—in terms of human beings—ancestral. The word, therefore, cannot be applied in this sense to any present-day people, though we often apply it in the corollary sense of resembling our first ancestors. But no model exists to allow us to make this comparison. We really do not know how the first humans looked, thought, or behaved; we are not even agreed on what distinguishes human from nonhuman, though there seems to be a general consensus that it is not a physical difference but some kind of mental and thus invisible attribute.

The fossils discovered so far tell us that our distinctively human features—our teeth, our large cranium relative to our body size, the look of our hands, and the adaptation of our skeleton to walking and running on two legs—appeared gradually and at different times. Almost four million years ago, for example, a young Ethiopian female with teeth more ape-like than human and a brain one third the size of ours walked and ran and used her hands exactly as we do (Johanson and Edey 1981). The generations linking her to ourselves have been divided by specialists into successive types, which they call "species," but the English anthropologist David Pilbeam points out that these species are not separate:

> Their temporal boundaries are set entirely for convenience and are usually drawn at a [point in geological] time where few or no fossils are known; the absence of fossils creates the impression of a gap, which actually, of course, did not exist. As more fossils become known, the gaps get filled in and the "boundaries" between time-successive species blur, eventually disappearing.
> *(Pilbeam 1972: 8)*

In other words, no sudden change in the fossil record announces our arrival. It is therefore impossible to say at present which of the bones we have discovered, if any, represent the earliest true humans.

Nonetheless, most of us have a vague but firm picture of early people: brutish, slouching, hairy killers wrapped in badly fitted* animal skins—eaters of raw meat who survived in caves by eliminating the opposition. The picture has a title, "Neanderthal," and many supporters. Some of them are influenced by the Bible, which denies that humans developed from nonhumans and depicts our early ancestors as thoroughly modern people living and warring in large social groups and enjoying special status above all other living things. Modern, house-dwelling Judeo-Christians holding this view are naturally inclined to picture small bands of cave-dwelling Neanderthals as closer to animals than to modern humans in both form and behavior.

A second source of support for their view comes from the bones of a Neanderthal, a man forty to fifty years old, deformed by age and arthritis, who died some 40,000 years ago in a cave about fifty miles southeast of the city of Limoges in southern France. His remains were misinterpreted by the leading French anthropologist of the early 20th century, Marcellin Boule, and Boule's concept was accepted by his colleagues and welcomed by the popular press. In the 1950's it was put on canvas by the Czech painter Zdenek Burian. Burian's pictures, like the paintings of George Washington by Gilbert Stuart, became so widely known and accepted that cartoonists and film makers need only introduce a resemblance to establish their subject completely.

A wealth of evidence uncovered since Boule published his views in 1913 has replaced the savage stereotype with a more modern looking human: heavy-browed but probably not hairy, a hunter but not a brute, a person who took care of the sick and

---

*An amusing aspect of our ignorance about early humans is our conviction that their technology must have been crude. If we can fashion leather apparel and fur garments well, certainly those early humans who conquered every danger and solved every problem threatening the existence of *homo sapiens* could do as well as we. A striking example from our own times is the fact that the very best boots for arctic wear are still the boots made by hand by Inuit- and Yupik-speaking people.

injured, buried the dead with flowers, and perhaps began the tradition of cave-painting so beautifully represented at sites occupied by slightly later groups. As the American paleoanthropologist Donald Johanson has said of this person:

> One hears talk about putting him in a business suit and turning him loose in the subway. It is true; one could do it and he would never be noticed. He was just a little heavier-boned than people of today, . . . Could he make change at the subway booth and recognize a token? He certainly could. He could do many things more complicated than that. He was doing them over much of Europe, Africa and Asia as long as sixty or a hundred thousand years ago.
> *(Johanson and Edey 1981: 20)*

Other evidence shows that completely modern skeletal remains not only follow in time the remains of Neanderthals but are also contemporary with them (Trinkaus and Howells 1979: 129). This means the Neanderthals were not our direct ancestors but what we might call distant cousins. Eventually, perhaps, they became more closely related, for some evidence seems to suggest that they disappeared from the fossil record as a separate physical type some 40,000 years ago by merging with us through intermarriage.

A second, insidiously powerful meaning of primitive is the idea of being simple or—in terms of human beings—simple-minded. It derives from the chronological meaning by way of a theory of evolution propounded most forcibly by Herbert Spencer, the self-taught English philosopher active in the latter half of the 19th century. In 1857, at the age of thirty-seven and a year before Charles Darwin and Alfred Wallace made public their theory of evolution by natural selection, Spencer outlined a view of progress he promoted with great success throughout the remainder of a very long life (he died in 1903):

> The investigations of Wolff, Goethe, and Von Baer, have established that the series of changes gone through during the development of a seed into a tree, or an ovum into an animal, constitute an advance from homogeneity of structure to heterogeneity of structure. . . . This is the course of evolution followed by all organisms whatever. It is settled beyond dispute that organic progress consists in a change from the homogeneous to the heterogeneous.
>
> Now, we propose in the first place to show, that this law of organic progress is the law of all progress. Whether it be in the development of the Earth, in the development of Life upon its surface, in the development of Society, of Government, of Manufacture, of Commerce, of Language, Literature, Science, Art, this same evolution of the simple into the complex, through a process of continuous differentiation, holds throughout.
>
> *(Spencer 1857: 244-245)*

Later on he developed more fully his suggestion that intellectual development follows the same law of progress:

> We observed [in his *Principles of Biology*, 1864-1867] how along with the complexity of organization there goes an increase in the number, in the range, in the specialty, in the complexity, of the adjustments of inner relations [of an organism] to outer relations. And in tracing up the increase we find ourselves passing without break from the phenomena of bodily life to the phenomena of mental life.
>
> *(Spencer 1896: 294)*

Differences in mental progress could be seen, he held, among different kinds of humans:

> Other things equal, the less evolved types of organisms take shorter times to reach their complete forms than do the more evolved; and this contrast,

> conspicuous between men and most inferior creatures, is perceptible among varieties of men. There is reason for associating this difference with the difference in cerebral development. The greater costliness of the larger brain, which so long delays human maturity as compared with mammalian maturity generally, delays also the maturity of the civilized as compared with that of the savage.
> *(Spencer 1896a: 52)*

Spencer's assertions have never found scientific support* but remain nevertheless solidly entrenched in the minds of most of us and find expression in the word "primitive." The concept of the mindless savage has resisted abundant evidence of its falsehood, be it the impressive survival technology of desert Bushmen in southern Africa, the amazing navigational skills of early Polynesians, or the worldwide distribution of stone configurations clearly linked to astronomical observation and prediction.

Curiously, among Spencer's followers one often finds people who devote a large portion of their lives to a sincere and sympathetic study of societies they consider inferior. The finest written record of Native American song, for example, was made at the beginning of this century by Natalie Curtis, and at the end of her introduction to the collection she wrote:

> If the Indians' Book can help to a recognition of primitive men as men of latent capabilities; if it can help in ever so small a degree to herald the day when adult races wisely shall guide child races, and civilisation nourish the genius of every people, then will this utterance of the North American Indians be not for the race alone, but for all humanity.
> *(Curtis 1923: xxxvii)*

---

*Indeed, the study of prehistoric brain cases and modern small-headed populations now seems to suggest that the most important aspect of human cerebral development—neurological reorganization—may well have predated enlargement of the case itself (Pilbeam 1972: 73-82).

The paucity or simplicity of a culture's technology often leads us to call the culture primitive. We think it primitive to sight the position of the sun or moon by rocks rather than by telescopes, for example, or to dig for roots with a sharp stick rather than a shovel. But any technology is nothing more than a technical method for achieving a practical goal, and many practical goals are achieved better by simple than by complex means. Plowing the shallow soil of the West African Sahel, the arid region south of the Sahara, would tear apart its fragile fabric and allow the wind to blow it away; farmers of the Sahel plant their seeds by punching holes in the ground with a stick. Roofing an East African house with sheets of corrugated iron manufactured in a modern steel mill fails to ward off the heat of the day and the cold of the night; the traditional East African builder solves the problem with a thick roof of thatch.

In short, Spencer's law of progress is a useless impediment to cultural understanding: its bias favors the industrial West and blocks communication with other societies by prejudging and insulting them. Moreover, there exists a powerful alternative theory: cultures do not progress but simply change, developing or abandoning technology as circumstances dictate, responding to their environment and history with artifacts and patterns of behavior favoring survival and exploiting to good advantage the existing resources.* The power of this theory is that it generates fruitful questions about culture and the

---

*Certain tribes on the western and southern shores of the Caribbean, for example, have survived a severe change in their circumstances by abandoning the complex technology of their ancient life:

> Gone are the intensive horticulture, the dense population, the large villages, the class-structured society, the mounds, temples, idols, and priests, . . . even the technological and esthetic refinements evidenced in the early metallurgy, weaving, ceramics, and stone sculpture. . . . [These tribes] carry on small-scale slash-and-burn farming, and many of them now hunt and fish more than they till the soil. They live in small villages, weave simple cloth, and make only plain pots. Their society is unstratified, their religious cults are scarcely remembered, and the principal survival of former days is the shaman.
>
> *(Steward 1948: 2)*

context of culture, instead of simply asserting our own superiority; it focuses attention on the realities of the present and allows achievement to be recognized and studied; and it promotes the rethinking of our distant past. The idea used to be standard, for example, that primate locomotion evolved from swinging in the trees through walking on the knuckles of the hands to standing upright on the hind legs. "Balderdash," says the paleoanthropologist C. Owen Lovejoy, a specialist in primate locomotion:

> The idea that a chimp represents some sort of halfway stage leading to erect walking is idiocy. Knuckle walking is a specialized adaptation to a particular mode of living. It leads nowhere.
> *(Quoted in Johanson and Edey 1981: 310)*

And the broad, skin-hulled boat of the Yupik-speaking people of southwestern Alaska is not a halfway stage between a floating log and a modern longboat, but a specialized adaptation to the problem of transporting large loads over water (the modern longboat is not as good a solution: it weighs much more and holds much less).

Of particular concern for the present chapter is the fact that Spencer's point of view gets in the way of understanding art. He specifically included manufacture, commerce, and art among the areas of life subject to his law of progress, you will recall, and in a modern definition of primitive art by the former director of the Museum of Primitive Art in New York City, Douglas Newton, we hear echoes of Spencer:

> Properly, it is the art of those peoples who have remained until recent times at an early technological level, who have been oriented toward the use of tools but not machines.
> *(Quoted in Kramer 1982: 18)*

Perhaps Newton is one of those who have devoted their lives to a sincere and sympathetic study of something they consider inferior. If not, it is unfortunate that his reference to Spencer's view of humans developing successively higher levels of technology suggests they follow the same path in art.

Most of us find ourselves at one time or another in the paradoxical position of admiring simplicity yet scorning it for being undeveloped. It seems we have never questioned Spencer's unfounded assumption that to have a technically more complex way of life is to advance. Thus a recent New York Times lead editorial bemoaning the destruction of tribal life by land-development projects all over the world manages to admire tribal ways and yet rate them inferior to our own:

> To the unsentimental, the disappearance of primitive cultures may be a matter of small concern. But technologically advanced society should not so quickly hold itself morally superior to societies that live in enviable harmony with their environment. It is not the "primitive" peoples who have polluted the seas and invented nuclear weapons.
> *(New York Times 1980: 24)*

We often see this paradox in the area of music research. Frances Densmore began her career as a classically trained Western musician, devoted the rest of it to Native American song, and apparently never once doubted the superiority of her own level of musical expression. For example, in explaining the use of a sharp pitch level 4 and a flat pitch level 7 in Ojibwa (Chippewa) song, she quoted in translation the following observation of Ferdinand Gotthelf Hand (*Aesthetik der Tonkunst*, 1837) and let its demeaning implication stand without comment:

> Every teacher of [Western] singing admits that children have special difficulty in thinking these intervals. This is not because [such intervals] are not in accordance with nature, but [because they] are the products of acute reflection and are therefore to be found only where the finer development of the intellect renders them possible.
> *(Densmore 1910: 4)*

She was unfailingly courteous to her native informants, quick to acknowledge their help, and respectful of their wishes regarding the privacy of certain materials. The only serious weakness of her pioneer research was her Spencerian point of view.

The Dakota Sun Dance

The peoples we have for a long time called American Indians prefer to be called Native Americans. They do not accept the current view of most anthropologists that they came to this continent on foot from Asia. It is a reasonable view, however.

Only sixty miles of sea separate Alaska from Siberia, and during the winter the water partly freezes over. The crossing, never difficult, was even easier in the last Ice Age. About 60,000 years ago, for reasons not yet fully understood, water from the sea began accumulating on the continents as snow. Huge caps of snow, compressed to ice, spread over much of Siberia and Canada (see Figure 43 on p. 249). The level of the ocean dropped, while the weight of the ice on the continents forced their centers down and their edges up. As you can see in the diagram, this sequence reversed itself and then repeated not once but many times, often causing the shallow sea between Alaska and Siberia to recede enough to leave a broad, ice-free plain of dry land and good forage. Alaska itself stayed mostly ice-free: once or twice a tongue of ice crept out to the southwest past Anchorage, while above the Arctic Circle another tongue of ice formed south of the northern coastline and pushed westward, but that was all. Animals from Siberia found refuge in Alaska from the ice, and hunters from Siberia followed the animals.

On the Porcupine River in westernmost Canada (see Figure 43) archaeologists have found a hide-scraper of bone 27,000 years old. The site lies at the north end of what was then an ice-free corridor connecting the Alaskan refuge with the Mississippi

Fig. 43

valley. Migration down this corridor, through present-day Edmonton and eastern Montana, must have been fairly rapid because there were no natural obstacles and game was probably scarce.

The migration south may have begun much earlier. Near Puebla, in south central Mexico, there is evidence—"sparse but very suggestive" (Irwin-Williams 1968: 40a)—of hunting and butchering going on 35,000 years ago. In California's Mojave Desert stones apparently shaped into tools have been found in soils estimated to have been laid down between 40,000 and 120,000 years ago (Leakey, Simpson, and Clements 1968: 1022).

FIGURE 43: AN AGE OF ICE. *The upper part of this drawing plots the accumulating of ice upon the North American continent during the last seventy thousand years; the lower part shows where the ice accumulated. Both drawings are adapted from Jennings 1978: 4, 7.*

The chronological record at the top contains a horizontal line above which the accumulation represents enough water extracted from the sea to expose the ocean floor between Siberia and Alaska. As you can see, each time this land bridge appeared it lasted thousands of years. People would have lived and hunted there without any sense of being on a temporary "bridge" except, perhaps, for the memories they preserved in oral tradition. And if they were on the bridge, surely they were in Alaska as well. The majority of scientific opinion presently holds that the people who desire to be known as Native Americans originally came to our continent by walking over this land bridge.

The diagonal lines shading the map derive from those on the chronological record above it: widely spaced diagonals shade the area covered by the two great "Wisconsin" advances; narrowly spaced diagonals shade the area covered by lesser advances. As you can see, the lesser advances took place within the area covered by the greater advances. The heart of Alaska remained free of ice the entire time; it must have been a refuge for game and an invitation to Asian hunters. For more than 25,000 years, between the two Wisconsin advances, this refuge was connected to our own midwestern plains by an ice-free corridor passing through present-day Edmonton, Canada. We assume that the native populations of North and South America came down from Alaska through this corridor.

ADVANCE
EARLY WISCONSIN ADVANCE
LATE WISCONSIN ADVANCE
LESSER ADVANCES
RETREAT
70 65 60 55 50 45 40 35 30 25 20 15 10
THOUSANDS OF YEARS BEFORE NOW

SIBERIA
PORCUPINE RIVER SITE
LAND BRIDGE
ALASKA
ARCTIC CIRCLE
ANCHORAGE
EDMONTON
ICE-FREE CORRIDOR
CONTIGUOUS UNITED STATES
MOJAVE DESERT SITE
PUEBLA SITE

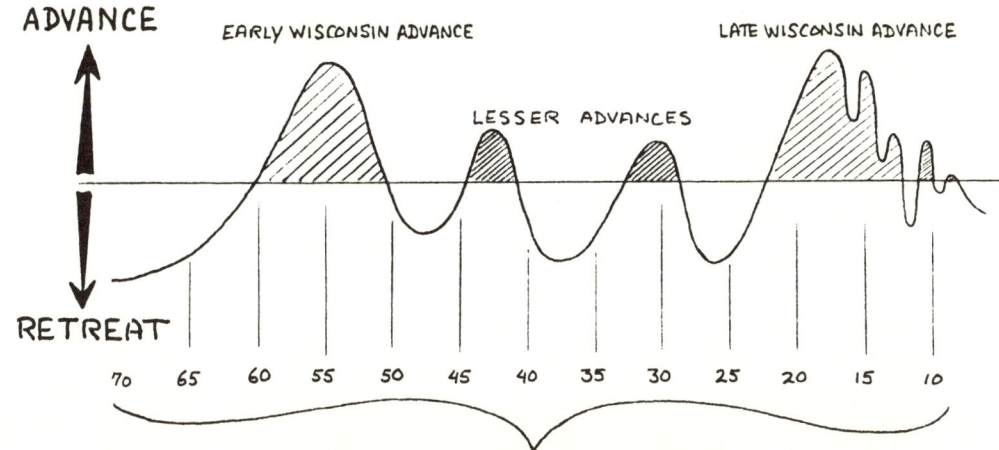

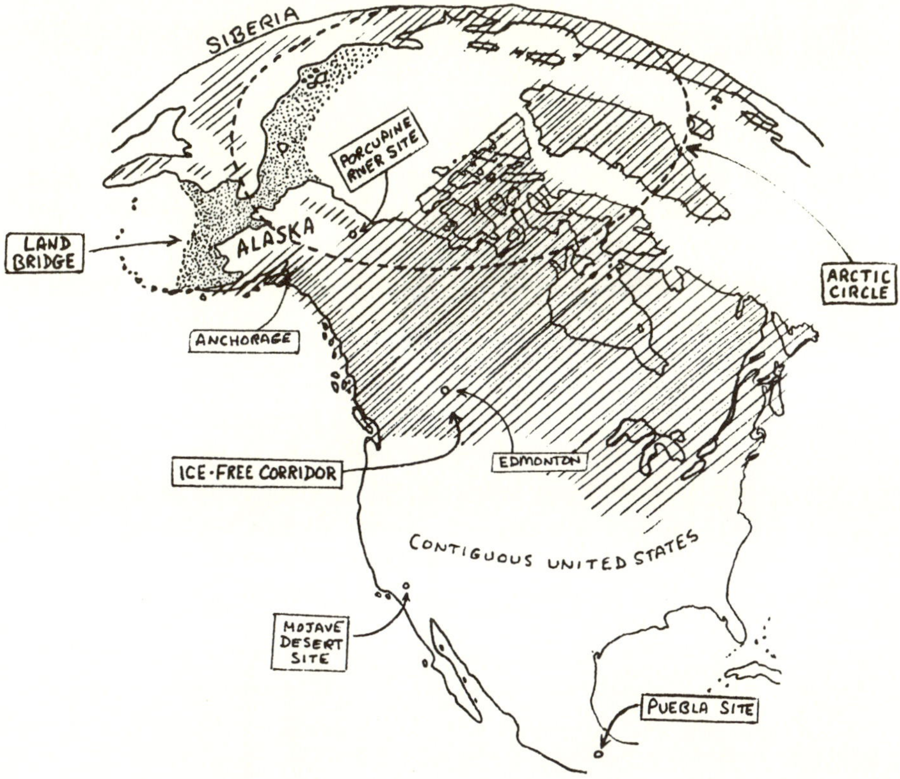

However old the record of human occupation of the New World proves to be, by the time Columbus reached the Caribbean there were probably no more than two and a half million Native Americans in all of North America.* They lived in several radically different environments and had different ways of life. In the arid southwest, for example, they lived in one spot and farmed the land, while along the rainy northwestern coast they wintered in sheltered places but spent the warmer months on the move, fishing or berrying at certain established sites according to the season. On the dry plateau between California and the Rocky Mountains they lived in small and isolated family groups, while in the woodlands of New York several families shared one house, several houses formed a village, many villages belonged to the same tribe, and the tribes held councils together as one nation. Leadership among the hunters and fishers of the arctic was occasional, based entirely on ability and the nature of the activity; among some of the farmers of the southeastern woodlands it was permanent and hereditary.

At present Westerners think of the typical Native American as being like the traditional Dakota of our northern plains: wearing feathered war bonnets, riding horses bareback, and living in tipis. Native Americans themselves have adopted this image as a unifying symbol. Plains tribes like the Dakota developed in what William Brandon has described as a

> land of sweeping vistas [that] lent itself to a restless way of life. Tribes came and went: some split into smaller groups by feuds or simply by a restless desire to go their separate ways; others mingled with strangers to form new tribes. In some respects the land ... was America's aboriginal melting pot.
> *(Brandon 1961:254)*

The restless tribes wandered on foot at first, using dogs for

---

*Excluding the Yupik- and Inuit-speaking people of the Arctic, whom Native Americans consider to be of a different origin than themselves.

pack animals and hunting buffalo at close range with bows and arrows. By 1730, however, the Spanish horse had spread north from New Mexico to Canada while guns, traded in the east for furs, had spread westward to the same area. With a horse and a gun, hunting buffalo was no longer difficult, and more meat could be accumulated and moved than people and dogs had been able to carry in the past. The men of the tribes, the hunters, had spare time and used it to elaborate the art of war.

There had always been fighting on the plains, but now, as Brandon describes it,

> elite soldier societies multiplied, each with special costumes, special grades, special manners, special sacred rites, and special taboos. Wars called for fancy tricks, fancy riding, fancy fighting, . . .
> *(Brandon 1961: 336-337)*

Tahca Ushte, a Dakota medicine man of Winner, South Dakota, recalls that his grandfather was a renowned warrior whose reputation came not from killing but from "counting coup":

> riding up to the enemy, zigzagging among them, touching them with his crooked [coup] stick wrapped in otter fur. . . . That was his way of showing his bravery.
> *(Fire/Lame Deer and Erdoes 1972: 20)*

The Dakota came late to the plains, driven out of their Wisconsin forests and sedentary agricultural life in the 18th century by the guns of the Ojibwa (Chippewa) and in turn driving the Arikara out of the Black Hills of South Dakota. When the whites entered this territory in the middle of the 19th century, the Dakota proved to be fierce warriors; indeed, under Chief Red Cloud they fought the Army of the United States to a standstill.

The Dakota are also dreamers who set great store in visions. A young man would spend four days and nights in a vision pit just large enough for one person to squeeze into.

Huddled there in blackness he might, with luck, feel himself visited by a guiding spirit in the form of an animal who would speak with him and instruct him.

It is because of a vision that a Dakota decides to undergo the ordeal of the Sun Dance, a ritual in which, like Jesus, he gives of his own body, deliberately mutilating it by pulling away from a skewer embedded in the muscles of his chest and attached by a cord to the sacred pole in the center of the dancing ground. Tahca Ushte explains the ceremony as "a prayer and a sacrifice":

> If we offer Wakan Tanka a horse, bags of tobacco, food for the poor, we'd be making him a present of something he already owns. Everything in nature has been created by the Great Spirit, is part of him. It is only our own flesh which is a real sacrifice—a real giving of ourselves. How can we give anything less?
>
> *(Fire/Lame Deer and Erdoes 1972: 198)*

Many devout Christians over the centuries have come to the same conclusion.

Inspired by a vision, the Sun Dance is itself a time for visions. They occur when, exhausted by pain and continual dancing, his mind penetrated by the sun, a man* finally loses consciousness. A vision received at this time is valued above all others.

The Sun Dance is also social. The Dakota consider it not only their oldest and most solemn ceremony, but also their greatest feast, one that brings all the people together. In the past it was a chance for relatives to see each other after a year foraging and hunting in small groups scattered across the northern plains—to exchange news, learn new songs, and reestablish tribal identity. For the young it was a chance to court. Dakota morality, which forbids marriage to a person of the same clan, made it almost impossible for youths to find

---

*The ordeal of the Sun Dance is not undertaken by women.

potential mates during the rest of the year when clan members hunted together.

Figure 44 on the next page shows the opening rhythms of a Sun-Dance song performed in 1939 by several Dakota men for the Western ethnomusicologist Willard Rhodes. The dark vertical wedges stand for equidistant and usually loud drumbeats dominating the sound. To Western ears these drumbeats seem to outline the meter of the song, because in Western music meter is carried by such an equidistant series of sounds—the most important of which are either low in pitch or, like the sounds of the drum, loud, or both.

The voices of the men are almost as loud as the beats of the drum. They sing a series of percussive syllables which almost never coincides with the louder sounds in the series of drumbeats. I show this vocal percussion as a sudden thickening of the melodic line and mark its occurrence with a thin vertical drawn through the pitch frame.

As Westerners we would like these two series of beats to coincide enough to give us the impression of a single meter. They do not do so, and Densmore found a similar discrepancy in 56% of the Dakota and Ojibwa songs for which she was fortunate enough to have the drum accompaniment recorded (Densmore 1918: 39). Moreover, she and other observers have noted that the separateness of voice and drum is not a random effect. As the dance ethnologist Gertrude Kurath wrote in her study of Seneca music in upstate New York,

> [i]n no case is the pattern arbitrary. The flow of the melody and its relationship to the instruments is safeguarded by tradition.
> *(Kurath 1964: 28)*

Here, then, is a distinctly non-Western musical effect: two rhythmic series performed together, yet not together at all in the Western sense of having beats that coincide. Wishing to hear such coincidence, the Westerner tends to imagine the two series as a single one stated by the louder and lower-pitched sound source, the drum, while the voice lags behind from

254

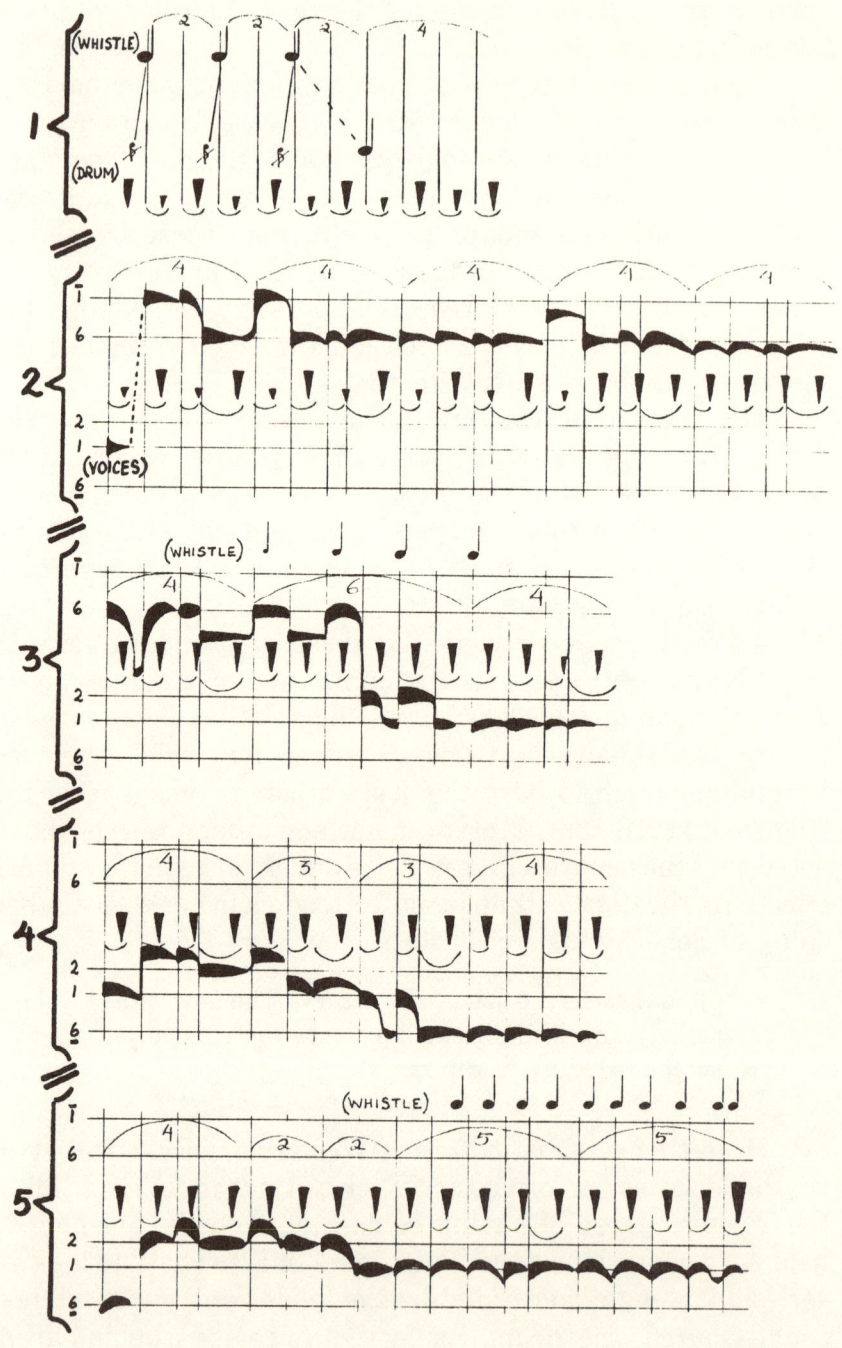

FIGURE 44: A DAKOTA SUN-DANCE SONG. *This pictorial notation shows the timing of whistle, drum, and voices in the first stanza of a Sun-Dance song performed for the American ethnomusicologist Willard Rhodes by John Long Commander, Julian Whistler, and other Dakota men in the summer of 1939 at Wanblee, South Dakota (Library of Congress AAFS-L40: side 1, band 1, first piece). For a general explanation of the notation see the caption for Figure 4.*

Each frame of notation represents one phrase of music.

The timing of the whistle, made from an eagle bone, is shown by the placement of standard musical quarter notes. It is equidistant in Frame 1, not quite equidistant in Frames 3 and 5, and seems to become disassociated from the rhythms of voice and drum in Frame 5. The sound of the whistle is much higher than that of the voices.

The timing of the drum is shown by the placement of vertical wedges drawn larger or smaller as the sound they represent is louder or softer. The timing is equidistant throughout. The drum sounds lower in pitch than the voices, but its symbols have been placed in the middle of the pitch frame to make immediately clear the relationship between their timing and that of the vocal sounds.

The timing of the percussive vocal line is shown by thin verticals drawn through the pitch frame to mark the beginning of each sound. Relative loudness of the sounds is shown by relative thickness of the vocal line. The timing of the voice is generally equidistant and equal to the timing of the drum but offset from it. The singers often advance a single percussive note (move it to the left) out of this equidistant pattern, creating a momentary change of gait. Occasional heterophony among the voices has been ignored.

The gait is a series of paired events, the first a percussive vocal sound (or, in Frame 1, a note of the whistle) and the second a drumbeat. Westerners naturally hear these groups the other way around, with the drumbeat, which is more prominent, first. Our best information, however, indicates that for the Native American the guiding pattern of events is the rhythmic series formed by the voice. Short curves placed beneath the drum part show this grouping, the curves becoming larger whenever the advancing of a vocal pulse creates a group of longer duration.

Measures are formed by the grouping of the gait into larger clusters and have been marked off by curved lines placed above the voice and drum parts (and, in Frame 1, above the whistle part). This larger

beginning to end. This analysis is not valid, however, because "lagging" implies that the parts are meant to coincide but fail to do so. We need a more positive approach reflecting the fundamental truth that a culture does what it means to do. Chance, error, ignorance, or ineptitude may account for a particular instance we observe but not for what is characteristic of a culture.

Differing but parallel rhythmic series hold together in performance because the timing of one guides the timing of all. This is true whether the rhythms are measured or unmeasured, the desired effect precise or imprecise, the sounds coincident or disparate. Even the modern American composer John Cage, exploring the random musical effects of reading one lecture while playing three others on tape machines (see p.32), guided himself by the timing of a pocket watch. Without some central guide, ensembles cannot produce music above the level of a "happening," a mere sampling of the limited chaos of events in everyday life.

What guides the music of the Dakota Sun Dance: the beat of the drum, the motions of the dance, or the rhythm of the voice? Toward the end of her long career in Native American studies Frances Densmore remarked that the melodic stress of the words does not always correspond to their spoken stress and concluded that "the rhythm of the song is the rhythm of the melody in the mind of the singer" (Densmore 1942: 544). She never analyzed the dancing and considered the drumming an accompaniment rather than a guide to the rhythm of the

---

grouping is problematical. Without Native American guidance I have had to rely on the clues of vocal emphasis, melodic symmetry, the advancing of the vocal pulse already described, and pauses. It is impossible to make such judgements free of my own Western bias. Whatever the correct measures prove to be, however, it is certain that they vary in length. The variation in my measuring of the music has been shown by placing within each superior curve a number showing how many groupings of the gait are contained within it.

performance. My colleague William Powers, an anthropologist and student of Native American dance, has made the same point in conversations with me: the rhythm of the drumming and dancing is guided by the vocal line.

Taking the vocal pulse as the guiding rhythm in Figure 44, we see that the drum subdivides it, driving it along just as the strumming of mandolin, guitar, and banjo drives along the deep-sounding pulses of the double bass in bluegrass music. The subdivision does not merely double the speed of the rhythm, as Gertrude Kurath saw in the War Dance of the Seneca. Noting that the dancers' steps always match the beat of the drum, she went on to observe that

> the moderate drum beat and the driving melodic rhythms conflict: the effect on poorer dancers is a heavy thumping, but on good dancers who can carry a double speed, the effect is a virile rebound.
> *(Kurath 1964: 64)*

The difference between Western and Native American rhythmic perception is, among other things, that the Native American does not attach overriding importance to low-pitched, loud sounds, while we invariably do so. The Native American mind can apparently be guided by the timing of a relatively higher-pitched, weaker sound, whereas the Western mind is prevented from responding this way by deeply ingrained habit.

And what of meter? Does the vocal pulse of our example form a hierarchy of groupings? Yes, both gait and measures are present. The gait is a group of two beats, the first in the voice, the second in the drum; the measure is a cluster of these groups varying in length. In Western art music, dance music, and popular songs measures are usually of one length and have an outline, or meter, that repeats over and over. In Native American song measure lengths continually change, producing a continually changing meter.

Westerners tend to think of meter as traditional rather than invented for the occasion, as a pattern selected from a small stock of patterns held in common by all carriers of the tradition. Native Americans, on the other hand, consider the meter of each of their songs as invented for that song, as a unique series rather than a traditional one. Thus the meter of a particular Native American song identifies it just as much as the sequence of its pitches and syllables. This individualizing of meter is strange to Westerners, who expect one song to have the same meter as many others yet retain its identity.

A consistent irregularity of meter is, as I've said, uncommon in our own music. Four hundred years ago, however, it was common in the music of the upper classes, and modern composers have revived the effect. Moreover, it can be heard in our traditional Anglo-American folksongs. Cecil Sharp's pioneering collection of 1917, *English Folksongs from the Southern Appalachians*, contains hundreds of examples* (see Sharp 1932). The reason, I think, is that irregular meters are as natural in music as regular ones, add interest to a performance, and impose on the rote learner no greater burden than regular meters. Thus when my children learned some 16th-century songs by ear at home, they learned the rhythmically changing passages as readily as those in steady rhythm. The process of oral transmission among ourselves and among Native Americans does not discourage meters that change and perhaps even favors them because they enhance the memorable quality of a song.

The Salish Gift Dance

The Salish are a relatively small band of Native Americans living just west of the Rocky Mountains and north of Missoula, Montana, in the western end of the state. "Salish" is their own name for themselves and means "we the people." Whites have always called them Flathead Indians. The Salish do not like

---

*Sometimes he wrote down metrical irregularities by changing the sign for the meter and sometimes by adding a sign extending the duration of a certain note without altering the meter.

this name, perhaps given to them by Lewis and Clark. Passing over the Rockies in 1805, the story goes, the two explorers met the Salish on the other side and mistook them for a people said to live on the Pacific coast. These people were known as Flathead because they bound their infants' heads to alter their shape. Salish heads are normal, and there is no evidence that they ever practiced cosmetic flattening of the skull.

Salish speech relates them to tribes living further west and north, but many other aspects of their culture have apparently been adopted from tribes living further east, on the plains beyond the Rocky Mountains. Today they farm, lumber, and raise stock in and around the fertile valley of the Flathead River.

Like the Dakota of the plains, the Salish value highly the contacts they make with supernatural beings through visions. All their "true and proper" songs come from such contacts and have the power to help them, while "make-up" songs—those an individual composes or learns from someone outside the tribe—have no power and are simply vehicles for socializing.

Songs of the Gift Dance are in this second category and are thought to have been borrowed from plains people around the beginning of the present century. The Gift Dance is a choosing dance for couples. The following description was written of a Gift Dance observed sometime between 1904 and 1909:

> The women form a circle or a three-quarter circle close together, and sometimes join hands. They move round sidewise, following the sun's course, and bringing one foot up to the other with a jerk. The drummers usually stand in the middle of the circle and move around slowly, in the same manner as the dancers do. Occasionally the drummers sit. They and the dancers sing together. In one of these dances which I witnessed four drummers stood back to back, facing the dancers, and turned as the dancers did, so that their faces were nearly always toward the same part of the circle.

The women formed a wide and complete circle on the outside, except at one place, where a gap was left wide enough to allow a person to pass through easily. Many of the dancers joined hands; others put their hands on each other's shoulders or around each other's waists. As soon as the drums started all went round singing. Presently a woman among the spectators took up a man and led him through the opening in the circle to the space inside between the dancers and the drummers. Here they went round together in the same way as the other dancers. Several other women among the spectators did the same, and also some women in the original dance circle left it and took up partners. The couples in the inner circle joined hands or locked arms, and went around in pairs close together. After a time the music stopped and the dancers stood still. Presently it started again, and they continued. This pause was a notification that the next time the music stopped the dance was at an end. At the end of the dance all took their seats except the couples who had formed the inner circle. These now formed in a line. The dance chief advanced toward them and asked each woman in turn what she intended to pay her partner for dancing with her. The chief then called out in a loud voice that so and so would pay such and such an amount to her partner for dancing with her. Most of the payments were small, such as tobacco, fifty cents, a dollar, a handkerchief, etc,; but anything may be given; a blanket, a horse, etc. After a rest the dance started up again and continued in the same way as before, with only this difference, that the men who were chosen as partners in the last dance now returned the compliment to their erstwhile partners by taking them up to dance and giving them presents in return. Most of the men returned a little more than the value they had received from the women. Occasionally this dance is called at the request of any man who says he would like to see the women dance. Then only the women dance. They generally do so in their best style, both in dancing and singing; and at the end of the dance the man may donate perhaps five dollars to the women, the amount being divided equally among them by the dance chief.

(Teit 1930: 388-89)

Figure 45 on p. 263 is part of a Gift-Dance song as Jerome and Agnes Vanderburg, a Salish couple, sang it in the privacy of their home for the American ethnomusicologist Alan P. Merriam. When first adopted the Gift Dance and its songs replaced an earlier and apparently similar social expression called the Round Dance. By the summer of 1950, when this song was recorded, the Gift Dance was being replaced in its turn by the Owl Dance. In thirty years' association with the Salish, Merriam himself never saw a Gift Dance. He remarked in the late 1960's that its songs "are still known and sung occasionally, and general knowledge of the dance is widespread among older informants" (Merriam 1967: 73).

Like our Dakota example, this Salish song presents two simultaneous rhythmic series lacking the kind of mutual reinforcement Westerners prefer. The Dakota, using series with identical timings, simply offset one from the other to create a combined rhythmic effect double the speed of either series

Fig. 45

FIGURE 45: A SALISH GIFT-DANCE SONG. *This notation shows the tune and accompanying drumbeat for part of a Salish Gift-Dance song sung for the American ethnomusicologist Alan Merriam by Jerome and Agnes Vanderburg in the privacy of their Montana home during the summer of 1950 (Folkways FE 4445: side 2, band 7). For a general explanation of the notation see the caption for Figure 4.*

The song contains three almost identical stanzas, each comprising nine phrases of identical length. The illustration runs from Phrase 7 of the second stanza through Phrase 9 of the third, presenting two phrases on each pitch frame. (Continued overleaf.)

The timing of the drum is shown by placement of vertical wedges drawn larger or smaller as the sound they represent is louder or softer. The louder beats on each line are equidistant from one another except where the transition to Stanza 3 causes four of them, starting with the fifth loud beat of Frame 2, to advance as a block (that is, to shift slightly to the left), shortening the time between the fourth and fifth loud beats of the frame and lengthening the time between the eighth and ninth loud beats.

The gait of the drum part consists of two beats, one louder than the other. We don't know whether the drummer thought of the pair as loud followed by soft (trochaic), soft followed by loud (iambic), or sometimes one and sometimes the other. The trochaic grouping that I have shown by short curved lines above the drum wedges fits the entire run of the piece, from the loud opening drumbeat (not shown) to the final downward vocal slur and including the reduction of the drum pattern to a single loud beat in the sixth phrase of Stanza 3. The two durations constituting the trochee have the ratio 3:2, except for the middle of Frame 2 where the beats are equally spaced. The 3:2 ratio is extremely rare in the West, though common in Eastern Europe. The Western mind tends to reconstruct it as the familiar "triplet" effect it most nearly approximates: the lilting gait formed by durations in the ratio 2:1.

The timing of the vocal line is shown by thin verticals drawn through the pitch frame to mark the beginning of each sound, the pulsing of a sustained sound, and the equidistant intervals implied by these effects. The vocal gait is a repeating group of two of these intervals replaced at the beginning of each phrase with a single group of three. The last phrase of each stanza (see the beginning of Frame 2 and the end of Frame 6) and the last phrase of the first half of a stanza (see the end of Frame 4) have a special gait.

Two levels of attractive complexity characterize the fit of the drum to the voice. First, the louder drum beats do not quite coincide with the timing of the vocal line (except for the middle of Frame 2), while the softer drum beats do coincide (except, again, for the middle of Frame 2). Second, two successive groupings of the gait of the drum often sound against three successive groups of two equidistant intervals each in the voice. This broad, two-against-three effect is marked off by the longest of the curved lines placed above and below each pitch frame, as for example, Frame 1.

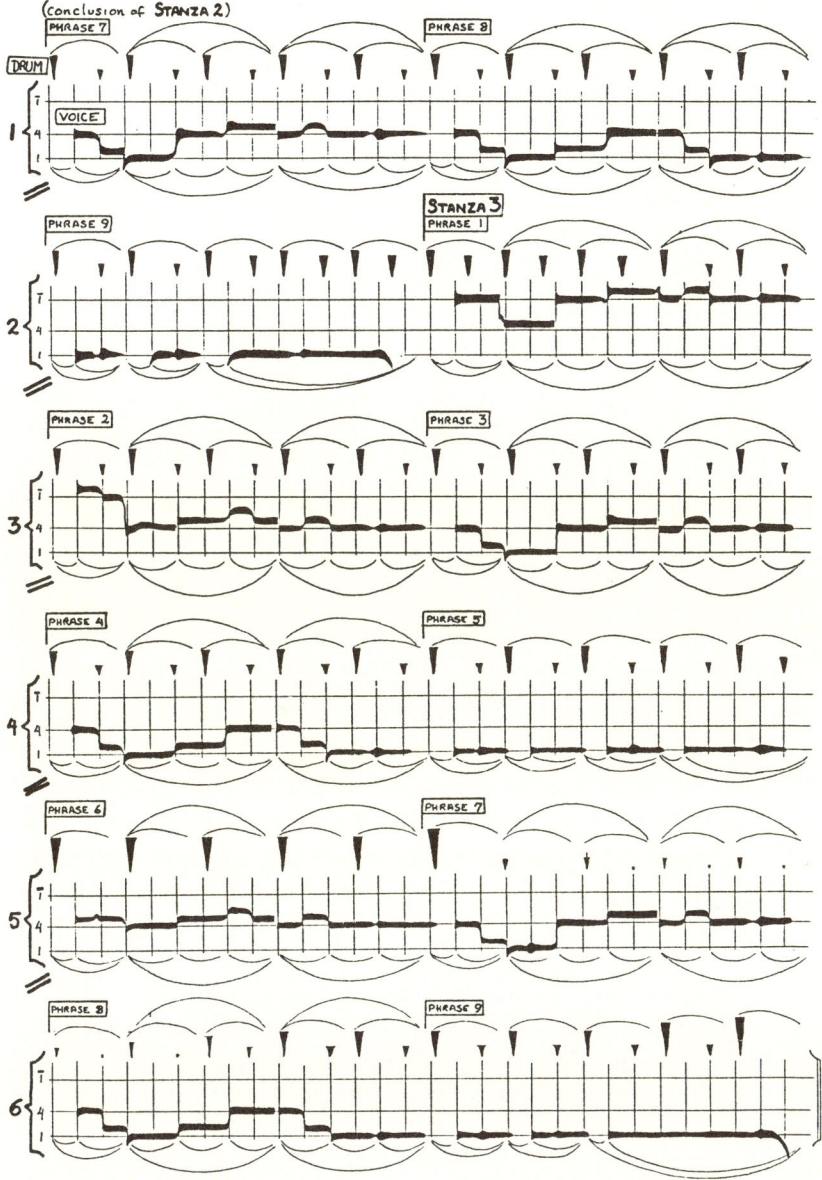

Measures are formed by the vocal phrasing and by the combined grouping just described. They are shown at each point in the notation by the longest curved line appearing above and below the pitch frame. As in the majority of Native American songs, the length of the measure frequently changes.

taken by itself. The Salish, using series with different timings, create not only an offset between them but also what one might call an "interference pattern" that has a rhythm much slower than the speed of either series taken by itself.

Usually Westerners have not perceived the coherence in the disagreement between voice and drum in Native American song. Merriam himself at first called the effect "disjointed" (1951: 374). Later he said the voice and drum were "disassociated" (1953: 6). His surprising final conclusion was

> that coincidence of the two beats [instrumental and vocal] is not an important musical matter for the Flathead and that they tend to be somewhat negligent about it.
>
> *(Merriam 1967: 329)*

The rhythmic consistency of our Salish example can hardly result from negligence. Even inconsistent rhythmic effects, when created by a respected traditional musician like Jerome Vanderburg, must be accepted as a performer's deliberate choice deliberately approved by carriers of the tradition.

Frances Densmore attributed the discrepancy between drum beat and melodic rhythm to lack of intellectual development. Strongly influenced by Spencer's view of evolution (see pp. 241-244), she described Dakota and Ojibwa drumming as a "continuous throbbing" that

> does not require to any extent the action of intellect in its production. It so resembles the unconscious rhythm of life that it may be regarded as actuated by instinct rather than intelligence. In our analysis of song-rhythm we found evidence of *intellect,* and in a consideration of drum-rhythm we find a suggestion of *instinct.* The lack of unity in these two rhythms suggests that the Indian music under analysis belongs to a period of cultural development in which intellect has not assumed full control over instinct. It seems possible that both are acting at the same time, producing what appears to be a

great complexity of rhythms but which is simply the simultaneous occurrence of two manifestations independent of each other.
(Densmore 1920: 67)

Musical differences between cultures are greater than scholars used to think, and it is often misleading to analyze the music of one culture in terms appropriate to another. This chapter has discussed examples of Native American songs showing that aspects of rhythm taken for granted in the West cannot be assumed to operate in Dakota or Salish culture: a coherent rhythmic structure does not require that sounds coincide and is not always outlined by the most prominent beat. The next chapter provides further examples in the rhythms of West African ensemble drumming.

12

West African Rhythm

The Anlo of Anyako

The political map of West Africa was laid out a century ago, not by Africans but by European traders. The boundaries they drew between their spheres of influence had little to do with natural cultural divisions, and when those spheres of influence were taken over by independent native governments in the decades following the Second World War, the old trading boundaries became national borders. As a result, each of the fourteen West African nations is an ethnic mosaic. Ghana, for example, which is not quite the size of Oregon, contains at least twenty different ethnic groups, and the borders of the country have nothing to do with the cultural borders between peoples.

The music of West Africa is even more diverse than the population, for within any one ethnic group there are usually several different musical styles. Because few of these styles have been studied, a complete musical description of a single ethnic group is not yet possible, much less that of a West African nation or of West Africa as a whole. I have therefore limited the following discussion of West African rhythm to the rhythm of one style of music practiced in one particular place: the recreational ensemble drumming performed in a large town in southeastern Ghana called Anyako, a center of traditional culture for a people called the Anlo (pronounced "ahng-law"). Figure 46 opposite shows the location of the Anlo homeland.

Fig. 46

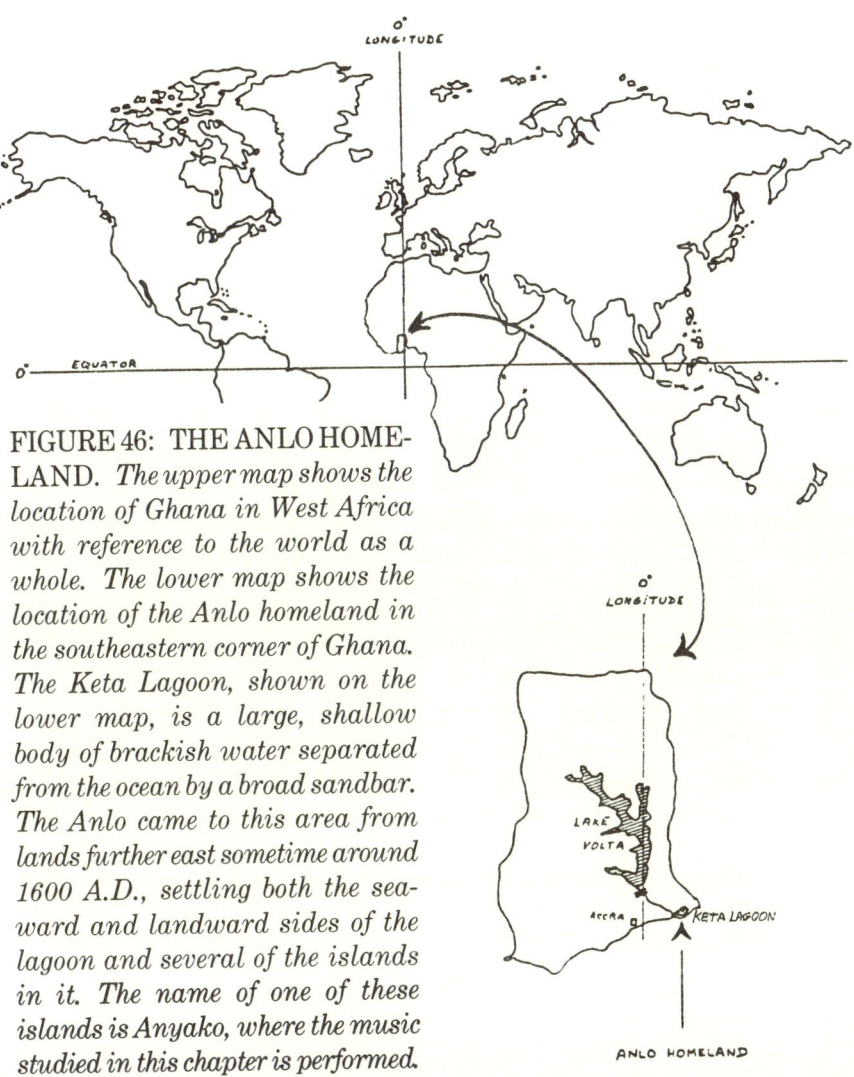

FIGURE 46: THE ANLO HOMELAND. *The upper map shows the location of Ghana in West Africa with reference to the world as a whole. The lower map shows the location of the Anlo homeland in the southeastern corner of Ghana. The Keta Lagoon, shown on the lower map, is a large, shallow body of brackish water separated from the ocean by a broad sandbar. The Anlo came to this area from lands further east sometime around 1600 A.D., settling both the seaward and landward sides of the lagoon and several of the islands in it. The name of one of these islands is Anyako, where the music studied in this chapter is performed.*

More than 5,000 Anlo live in Anyako. It is an island town set in a large body of shallow, brackish water called the Keta Lagoon. In the early days of European contacts the town of Keta, on the seaward edge of the lagoon, was the interface between white and black cultures; Anyako, nine miles away on an island near the landward edge, was the gateway to the interior.

The men of Anyako are weavers, fishermen, or tradesmen; the women often trade or have their own small businesses; some men and women tend small farms on the mainland. For men and women alike music is an amateur activity. Even musicians much in demand do not earn their living in Anyako by performing. Musical occasions are plentiful, but they are not viewed as business opportunities.

Anlo drumming mirrors Anlo social values, which emphasize community over individuality. For example, the town elders have been known to ban or modify a particular drumming if the players, by elaborating too many rhythmic variations, threaten to change the spirit of the music from one of cooperation to one of competition. Furthermore, few drumming situations feature a soloist. The typical performance is a group effort, and it is not unusual to see a highly skilled drummer take one of the simpler instrumental parts in an ensemble.

In keeping with this attitude the Anlo, unlike some other West African peoples, bestow no titles on musicians. They have no "master drummers," for example, for it goes against Anlo values to single out an individual for what is considered to be a group achievement.

The ensemble drumming most often heard in Anyako accompanies dancing to the singing of songs. I shall call it dance drumming. Performances of dance drumming mark religious, political, or social events in the life of the town. Most often they open and close a period of mourning.

Like Westerners, the Anlo celebrate their dead with music. We may think it odd that they include dancing on such occasions, for we ourselves not only lower our voices but also reduce our motions to show respect for the dead; to us, dancing is an unseemly display of energy in such circumstances. But consider how often we dance not merely for entertainment but to acknowledge a social obligation or loyalty to an institution: high society's debutante ball, everybody's high school prom, the fund-raising dance of an Elks Club or firemen's auxiliary—

these are not simply opportunities to relax and kick up our heels but gatherings we attend to celebrate our membership in a certain segment of society. Dance drumming in honor of a dead person provides a similar opportunity: the performing group is the musical club or religious cult with which the dead person was associated, and one attends not just to enjoy the music but to honor that tie.

The Musical Club

A musical club is formed by a youthful peer group with the patronage and protection of one or more older men. Usually the music is one particular style of drumming with its associated songs, but occasionally it may comprise several styles. At the core of the group is a man or woman with the talent to compose new song texts. The words comment on the contemporary scene, usually obliquely. The most famous song composer among the Anlo today, the late Vinoko Akakpo Akpalu, once lost a livelihood because his texts were too timely. He was a canoeman

> who rowed women from Anyako across the vast lagoon to the Keta market. This work prospered at first and many wanted to go with Akpalu for he would sing as he rowed to and fro *[sic]* the market. Soon, Akpalu began consciously or unconsciously to sing about his passengers. If you had nothing much to sell at the market that day or quarrelled on the way, you were most likely sooner or later going to hear your name mentioned in song another day by Akpalu. In short, Akpalu began to comment on people, and not everybody wanted his private life to be made known to the public, so the saying spread, "Who am I to go with Akpalu, or what ware have I to be in Akpalu's canoe [?]" Thus gradually Akpalu found himself without passengers and his canoe job failed.
>
> *(Nayo 1964: 26-27)*

Provided with the two essentials, patronage and a composer, a musical club will organize itself along democratic lines, with elected officers, bylaws, dues, and fines. Usually both men and women belong, and leaders can be of either sex. It is not an exclusive group, as the Anlo scholar, dancer, and drummer Kobla Ladzekpo points out:

> Other headmen and elders have a say in the club's affairs and in the affairs of other clubs. Because Africans live a communal type of life, everybody in the community is looked upon as a member of the clubs. The concept of the clubs is thus very much like that of citizenship.... If your town has two or three dance clubs, you are surely going to take part in the music of at least one of these clubs, and probably more, because you are a child of that town (unless,... you are a Christian and are forbidden by the church to participate in the activities of the clubs, or you are not interested in the art).
>
> *(Ladzekpo 1971: 8)*

When Anlo live outside their homeland they band together for mutual aid because, throughout West Africa, only one's own people have any obligation to help in times of need (such as when money must be raised to ship the body of a relative home for burial). The nucleus of this mutual-aid society is often a dance-drumming club, preferably with its own resident composer. If some members of the club find that they know the same dance-drumming style, they will teach it to the others. If not, the club may send home for teachers.

A dance-drumming club that receives new members from time to time may remain active for several generations; otherwise it lasts no longer than the lives of its female members, for women are the preservers of the song repertoire. Westerners tend to focus their attention on the drumming of a dance-drumming ensemble, but to West Africans the songs are the essence of the music. Women are therefore the core of the club. As one very old drummer told me, describing the end of a club active in Anyako in the 1870's,

> all the women who helped us sing and play—of the society—died, and there remained only the drum[ming]. So they know, the drummers, that they can't play, so everything stopped from there.
> *(Pantaleoni 1972:188)*

After a club becomes inactive, decades may pass during which no one hears its songs and rhythms. Then an old member will die, and at the funeral the music will sound again, perhaps with the help of a dance-drumming club from another town which visits and performs in the forgotten style. Young people, surprised and pleased to hear something new, may decide to form their own club around this style, and the life cycle of the music begins again.

At present Anyako has at least thirty-seven different styles of political, religious, or social dance drumming. One style will differ from another in its rhythms, songs, and often in its instruments, but certain aspects of the music are basic to all Anlo styles. These aspects are: nonequidistant accents in the governing meter; diverging, simultaneous rhythms; a role for high and low levels of sound which is opposite to the role assigned them in Western music; earthward dancing; and low-pitched singing. All but the earthward dancing and low-pitched singing seem to be aspects characteristic of the dance drumming of many West African groups besides the Anlo. The rest of this chapter concerns these more widely distributed aspects because they involve rhythmic principles not familiar to Westerners.

Nonequidistant Governing Accents

A Western concert aims at unified effects: changes of mood, changes of harmony, pauses, sudden louds or softs, the simultaneous and mutually enforcing motion of voices in duet, etc. One hears such togetherness even in the deliberately raucous events staged by some rock groups.

The kind of meter governing this unified style suits it admirably: a group of equidistant but unequally stressed accents we call "beats." Sometimes the beats are dictated by a conductor, but more often they are created entirely by the sound of the music itself. As I discussed in Chapter 10 (p. 223), meter is the pattern of accents outlining a measure. Our equidistant beats cannot outline a measure by their timing alone, for there is nothing in their timing to show where the grouping of the beats begins or ends. Therefore the sound of the music itself must lend a helping hand in contributing changes of quality—differences in stress, harmony, timbre, etc.—to distinguish one beat from another. To give a special sound to a beat, the music must behave in a unified way. (We do not know whether this unified behavior grew out of the practice of using equidistant beats, or the practice of using equidistant beats grew out of such unified behavior, but clearly the two go well together.)

Traditional Anlo dance drumming, on the other hand, aims at a multiplicity of effects, at what one might call energy through simultaneous variety. Several considerably different kinds of musical flow always seem to be going on at the same time; the singing seems barely connected to the galloping rhythms of the drums accompanying it, and even when one listens to the drums themselves, one hears some patterns that do not support others but merely coexist with them.

As you might guess, the kind of meter governing this diversity is different from the kind governing the unified flow of Western music. A governing Anlo meter is formed by a series of nonequidistant, asymmetrical, and uniformly unstressed accents that outline the measure by their timing alone. Figure 47 shows the series most commonly used in Anlo dance drumming. When you tap these accents in a uniform manner with a pencil you hear a repeating pattern. Each repetition corresponds to one statement of the meter—that is, to one measure—and there is no need to reinforce this natural grouping by means of changes in the quality of the sound. In other words, the musical flow of an Anlo piece, unlike that of a Western piece, need not reinforce the governing meter because the governing meter defines itself.

Only one player sounds the governing meter in Anlo dance drumming, usually by striking a wooden stick against a highpitched, clapperless bell of iron. Listening to the bell, the other performers easily keep together regardless of how

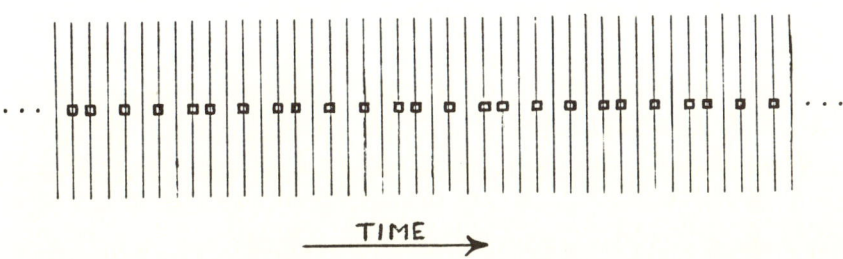

FIGURE 47: A GOVERNING ANLO METER. *This is the most common arrangement of nonequidistant accents used to govern the flow of Anlo dance drumming. Time moves from left to right in the diagram, as shown by the arrow, and is marked off into equidistant moments by the thin verticals. Each small square represents one accent. Tapping the accents with a pencil produces a repeating pattern seven accents long. This repeating pattern is the governing meter, a distinctive outline that drummers and singers can recognize regardless of what other, different patterns might be going on at the same time.*

The governing meter is almost always sounded on an iron bell, and by listening to the bell the performers have no difficulty staying together. Westerners find it hard to follow the bell's asymmetrical pattern because they are used to a governing meter of equidistant beats. For a musician thoroughly familiar with the bell pattern, however, its sounds are as easy to predict as a flow of equidistant beats.

A curious feature of a repeating asymmetrical pattern, from a Westerner's point of view, is that it has no specific point of beginning: any one of its accents will serve equally well as the start of a measure, and each member of the dance-drumming ensemble can think of the pattern as beginning at the point most appropriate for what that member has to perform.

diverse their parts may be simply by maintaining specific individual relationships with the bell's asymmetrical pattern. Their parts are not correct when the drum strokes, dance motions, and songs are merely skillfully performed, but when their performance creates the right rhythmic duets with the sound of the bell.

The principle of controlling the timing of an ensemble by duetting is not restricted to Anlo music, of course. Voice and drum must form a particular and coherent whole in Native American song (see Chapter 11), and in Western ensembles the rhythm of each contributing part must fit correctly with the rhythm of the governing meter. But in Anlo dance drumming the correct fit can be much more different for each contributing part than it can in Western ensemble music, because the flow of Anlo music does not have to be a unified one, as I have pointed out. Indeed, in this music there often arises at one time a wealth of diverging rhythms lacking that common beat the Westerner expects to hear. The next section discusses some specific examples.

Diverging, Simultaneous Rhythms

It is no more difficult to duet with an asymmetrical governing meter than with an equidistant one. In both Anlo and Western ensembles the musicians perform their own rhythms against a governing one they have heard all their lives and can predict effortlessly. The Anlo musician has an advantage, however: an asymmetrical pattern is a time map. That is, against such a pattern the successive features of a duetting part have each of them a recognizably distinct rhythmic character based on timing alone, just as each feature on a map has a distinct placement based on its distance from specific coordinates.

Consider, for example, the rattle part in the recreational Anlo dance drumming called *Atsiagbekor*: it creates an equidistant series of identical sounds, yet in combination with the nonequidistant series of bell strokes it produces composite rhythms that are not identical, as you can see in Figure 48-B on p. 276. The rattle player has a precise feeling for the particular series of composite rhythms the rattles should form with the bell in *Atsiagbekor*, and any other alignment of rattle and bell feels wrong. The same holds true for other alignments of the rattle which occur in other styles of Anlo dance drumming. Two of these are shown in Figure 49 on p. 277.

Fig. 48

Fig. 49

What is true for rattle players is true for all performers in every Anlo dance drumming ensemble: the duet between each part and the bell guides the play of that part. The rhythm of one part may contradict that of another but does not interfere with it because the performers have each their own private focus on the bell. Like Western musicians, they listen to each other and respond to each other's playing, of course; unlike Western musicians, however, they do not depend upon each

FIGURE 48 *(overleaf)*: MAPPING TIME. *As in the previous figure, time moves from left to right and is marked off into equidistant intervals by thin vertical lines.*

(A): the gourd rattle and double bell of iron used in most Anlo dance-drumming ensembles. The gourd is hollowed out through a hole in one end or the other and left empty. Around its smooth, hard surface a net is woven with the same knots the Anlo use in making their fishing nets. The net is usually strung with Moslem prayer beads of wood, as here, or with short pieces of bamboo. The prayer beads have no religious significance for the Anlo but are cheap and readily available in the markets of Accra. Glass beads and shells have been used in the past but are not as durable. The player adjusts the tension of the net with a finger of the hand holding the rattle, and this adjustment controls the quality of the sound.

Good bells are cold-forged from raw iron; less satisfactory ones are cut from the metal gutters used to conduct rainwater from roofs to storage tanks. The striker is a wooden stick. One beats the upper cone to sound the governing meter but both upper and lower cones to sound the rhythmic decoration of songs sung during interludes in the drumming. The upper cone can be damped with the fingers, the lower one by pressing its open end against the thigh. (Continued overleaf.)

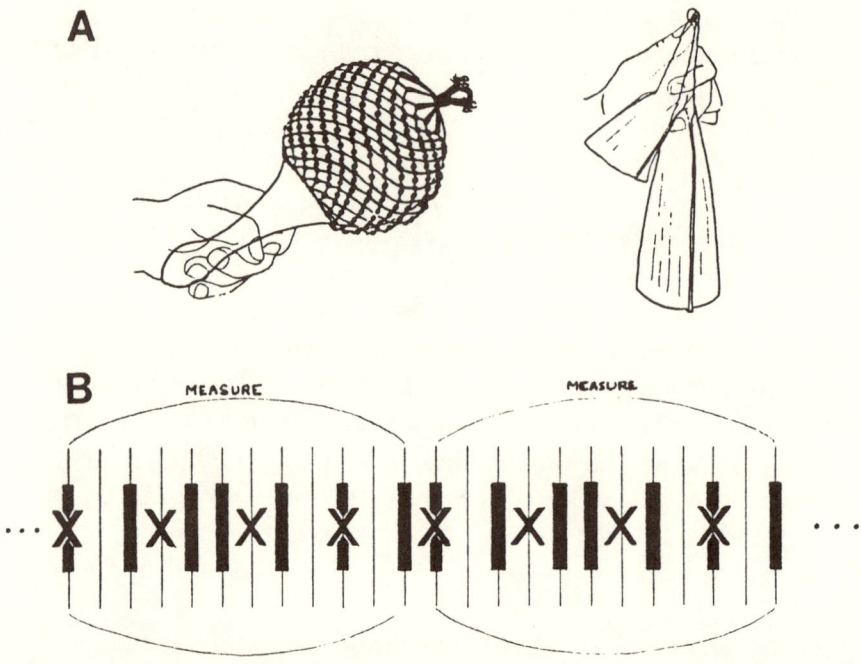

(B): the play of the rattle against the play of the bell in the Anlo dance drumming called Atsiagbekor. *An X marks the strokes of the rattle, while the hollow squares marking the strokes of the bell in Figure 47 have been changed to tall, solid rectangles so they can be easily combined with the X wherever the two coincide. Curved phrase lines set above and below these symbols show the extent of each statement of the bell pattern, which is the equivalent of one measure of music. The point chosen for the beginning of the measure is arbitrary.*

The four rattle strokes are equidistant, as you can see, yet within each measure of the governing bell each stroke has a unique rhythmic context. The rattle player achieves the correct equidistant pattern not by dividing the span of the bell pattern into four equal parts but by placing each stroke of the rattle at a point in time that will generate the right rhythmic duet with the bell. By themselves the rattle strokes are undifferentiated. Against the bell each of them has its own special rhythmic flavor, and this flavor—the rhythm of the duet—is the true rhythm of the rattle. Thus the asymmetrical bell pattern is a kind of time map fixing precisely the proper location for any event.

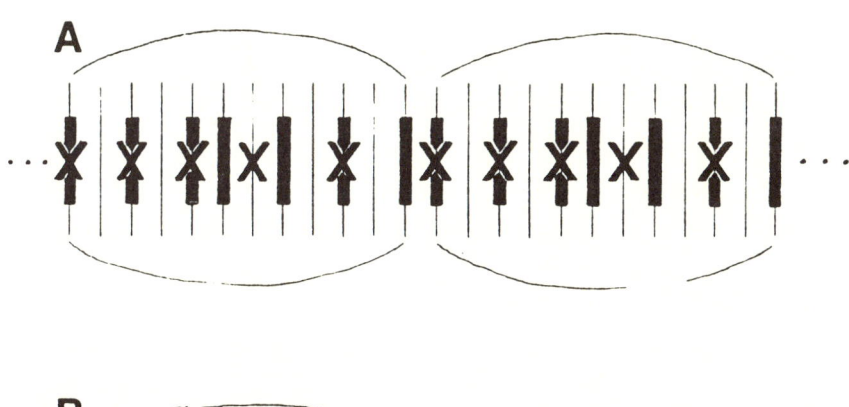

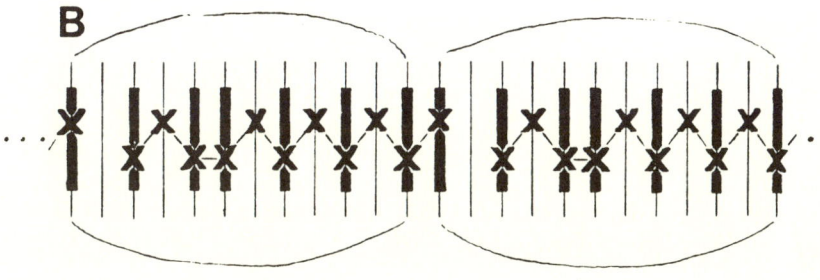

FIGURE 49: OTHER RATTLE DUETS. *As before, time moves from left to right; thin verticals indicate equidistant moments; curved phrase lines gather the repeating bell pattern into the same measures shown in Figure 48-B, for the sake of comparison; X stands for a stroke of the rattle; and a tall, solid vertical stands for a stroke of the bell.*

(A): the distinctive duet between rattle and bell used in the Anlo dance drumming known as Takada. *It might be worth your while to master this duet, tapping the bell part with one hand and the rattle part with the other, for when you have it right you will experience a* **characteristic aspect of Anlo composite rhythms:** *an ebb-and-flow effect resulting from a regular alternation between relaxed and intense rhythmic activity.*

(B): the duet between rattle and bell characteristic of several styles of Anlo dance drumming including Afã, Ahiavivu, *and* Atsiã. *X in the higher position represents an upward stroke of the rattle against the palm of the hand; in the lower position it represents a downward stroke against the thigh.*

other for confirmation of a common beat. They are free, in the memorable phrase of Percival Kirby of South Africa, to create a "deliberate opposition of simple, powerful rhythms" (Jones 1934: 1n). Figure 50 opposite illustrates the relationships in such an ensemble.

Anlo drums can produce language as well as rhythms, and the deliberate opposition of their patterns sometimes amounts to verbal exchange, as in my next example. Talking drums are possible because the Anlo speak a "tone language"—a language in which the meaning of a syllable is determined by its relative pitch and rhythm as well as by its vowel sound and its use of consonants. English uses pitch to clarify meaning. We can say "hello" in many ways that express different attitudes and relationships but, in the context of meeting someone, the word is always some kind of greeting. Among the Anlo, a certain sequence of consonants and vowels can have completely different meanings according to how it is pitched. Thus the low-to-high sequence "màmá" means "division," but the middle-to-high sequence "mamá" means "grandmother"; the three high syllables "núnyálá" mean "wise man," but if the first two of these are raised a bit above the final high syllable—"nűnyắlá"—the word means "washman" (Clements 1972: 26).

Three main drum tones and several modifications suffice to imitate the four levels of pitch used in spoken Anlo. Drummers are careful to approximate the rhythms of speech and, for addditional clarity, may restrict themselves to a small and highly stylized vocabulary, as do the drummers of Central Africa studied by John Carrington (1949). Repetition and context further define the message, but even so it is not every Anlo who can understand the talking drums.

The drum talk to be discussed here comes from the recreational Anlo dance drumming called *Atsiagbekor*. This was once a wartime music and features a platoon of men moving in precise unison to specific signals from the deep voice of the leading drum. Their motions mime the actions of combat and celebrate victory in battle. Behind them a group of women

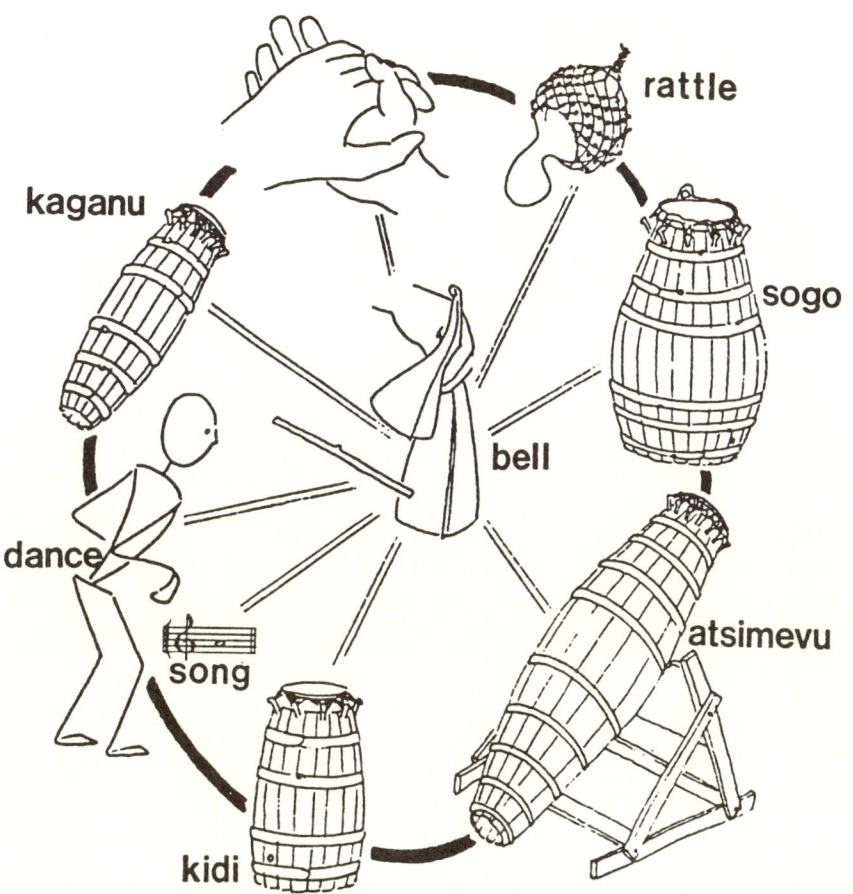

FIGURE 50: ANLO ENSEMBLE RELATIONSHIPS. *The radial arrangement shown here represents the two main features of Anlo ensemble organization: the separate relationship of each part to the play of the bell, and the coordination of all the parts to form a whole. As you can tell from the clapping hands and the dancing figure, no attempt has been made to draw the various elements of the music to the same scale.*

Anlo drums, by the way, used to be made from logs. The homeland is not heavily forested, however, and the more economical barrel construction was readily adopted when introduced early in this century.

move from side to side within a small space, singing. Occasionally one or two men will dance their way forward to the sound of the leading drum and perform a figure by themselves; occasionally the women will come out from behind the men and, in response to a special pattern on the leading drum, dance rapidly across the front of the platoon. The heart of the dance, however, is male, aggressive, and concerted.

A small, broad-headed drum with an open bottom hangs from the side of the leading drum. With a voice pitched in the middle range of the ensemble it chatters enthusiastically about warfare, saying such things as:

KÒMÀ DÓ GBÈ DZÍ, GBÈ DZÍ!
"I'll die in battle, in battle!"

These words are not spoken to the performers or the onlookers but to a slightly larger, deeper-sounding drum hanging beside it. This lower voice responds to such chattering by saying over and over:

KÒ   KÒ   TÓ,   TÓ,   TÓ!
"Just you stop, stop, stop!"

Elders exercise unquestioned authority in traditional Anlo society as the repositories of knowledge and sound judgement. The two drums I have quoted play the parts of brash youth and wise old age contemplating the prospect of war. At the same time, they provide another example of simple, powerful rhythms in opposition, as you can see opposite in Figure 51. An example of greater opposition is given in Figure 52 on p. 282.

The Function of Layers of Sound

The high-pitched instruments of the Anlo dance-drumming ensemble have the least varied parts and interlock to form a rolling gait that generates a steady, equidistant pulse in the top layer of sound. Westerners naturally assume this pulse arises from a single, equidistant meter guiding the whole ensemble, as

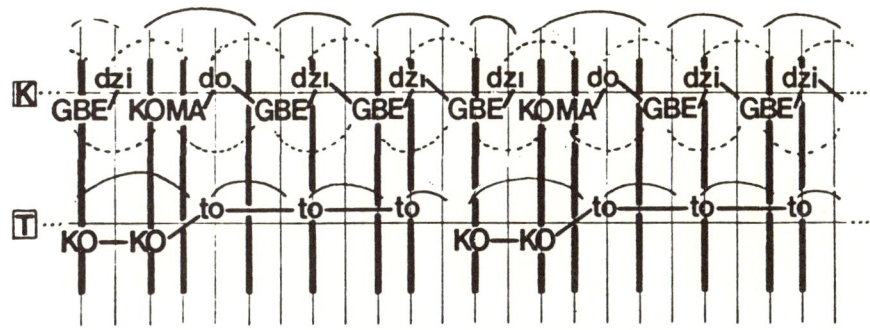

FIGURE 51: RHYTHMS THAT TALK. *The Anlo dance drumming called* Atsiagbekor *includes drum rhythms that can be heard as speech by carriers of the tradition. The drum strokes in this particular example are shown by the syllables of spoken Anlo they convey, the louder ones printed in capitals, the softer ones in lower case. Within each drum part strokes of higher pitch are placed higher on the page than strokes of lower pitch. Time, as before, moves from left to right, with thin verticals standing for equidistant moments and thick verticals for strokes of the governing bell.*

(K): the part played on kroboto, *a very short drum with an open bottom and a wide head sounding in the middle range of the ensemble. "Kòmà dó gbè dzí!" means "I'll die in battle!"*

To the listener, the low-pitched sounds are far more prominent than the high-pitched ones, while to the drummer the high-pitched sounds may seem more prominent because they take more energy to perform. Thus if we were to insist on analyzing this rhythm as the elaboration of a simple group of equidistant beats, those beats could be found in either the low, loud sounds or the high, soft sounds, depending upon our point of view. Dotted curved lines below and above the kroboto *part show the gait created by each of these alternatives. A third possible gait, shown by solid curved lines above the* kroboto *part, is the one I prefer: a simple, powerful, asymmetrical series.*

(T): the part played on totodzi, *a short drum with an open bottom like* kroboto *but with a broader head sounding at the bottom of the range of the ensemble. "Kò kò tó!" means "Just you stop!" and is played against every one of* kroboto's *phrases. It represents the sage voice of a male elder, the authority figure in Anlo culture.*

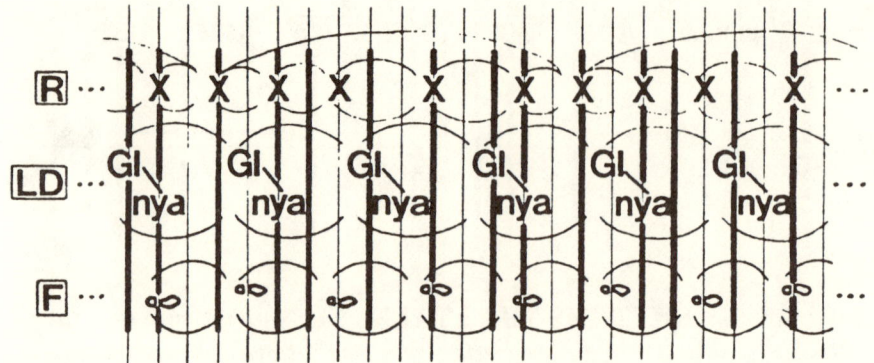

FIGURE 52: OPPOSING RHYTHMS. *This excerpt from the Anlo recreational dance drumming called* **Taka̲da** *shows with particular clarity a feature characteristic of many West African ensembles: what the late Percival Kirby of South Africa called the "deliberate opposition of simple, powerful rhythms" (Jones 1934: 1n). The progress of time and the governing bell pattern are shown as in the preceding examples.*

(R): the rhythm of the rattles, shown by X's. The rattles are typically shaken from side to side rather than up and down. The short curved lines show the gait; the long curved lines gather the asymmetrical gait into phrases.

(LD): the rhythm of the leading drum, shown by the syllables with which the drummers themselves refer to this pattern. These syllables are used here as vocables rather than as spoken language by the player. Capital letters indicate a louder sound than lower case letters and, in this case, a more energetic stroke by the drummer. The curved lines show the gait, which opposes the gait of the other two parts, as you can see.

(F): footprints showing the rhythm of the dancers' feet. This rhythm opposes the gait of the leading drum more strongly than it opposes the gait of the rattles but, like the other two parts, it can be performed easily and accurately if the performer feels it primarily as a simple duet with the governing bell and only in a secondary way as a part in conflict with other parts.

it would if the music were Western. But they have trouble finding the beat of this meter where they expect to hear it, down among the lower-sounding instruments, for there the parts are more varied. Indeed, at the very bottom of the ensemble one usually hears the voice of the lead drum which, like the high voice of the lead guitar in our own rock ensembles, decorates the steadier rhythms of the other instruments with accents and patterns often opposing them.

In short, from the Westerner's point of view the layers of sound in Anlo dance drumming function upside down: the most interesting, varied play is down below where we would expect to hear a steady, dependable beat, while the least interesting, least varied play—the fundamental gait and the all-important guiding pattern of the bell—lies high up where we would expect to hear the most rhythmically free sounds. A lovely illustration of this arrangement can be heard in the interlude music, called *hatsiãtsiã*, with which the Anlo separate periods of vigorous dancing during a dance-drumming session. Figure 53 (overleaf) shows this music. Dancers walk with a gentle swaying motion to rhythms lightly played on several iron bells. Once again, instruments of high pitch carry the fixed rhythmic patterns while those of lower pitch supply variety.

Fig. 53

In 1967 a colony of Anlo living in Accra, the capital city of Ghana (see the lower map on p. 267), formed a mutual aid group, the Dzelukopfe ("dzeh-lu-kawp-fweh") Society, named after the hometown of many members. The core of the society was a dance-drumming club whose composer was a friend of mine, Kofi Kpeglo Ladzekpo of Anyako. The *hatsiãtsiã* bell music shown in Figure 53 was performed for me in June, 1971, as the club sang Kpeglo's songs.

There are actually two main kinds of song in Anlo dance drumming, short and long. The short songs, sung during the dancing part of the performance, need not be composed especially for the club performing them. Long songs, on the other hand, are the exclusive property of the club performing them. They may be heard during the dancing but have their

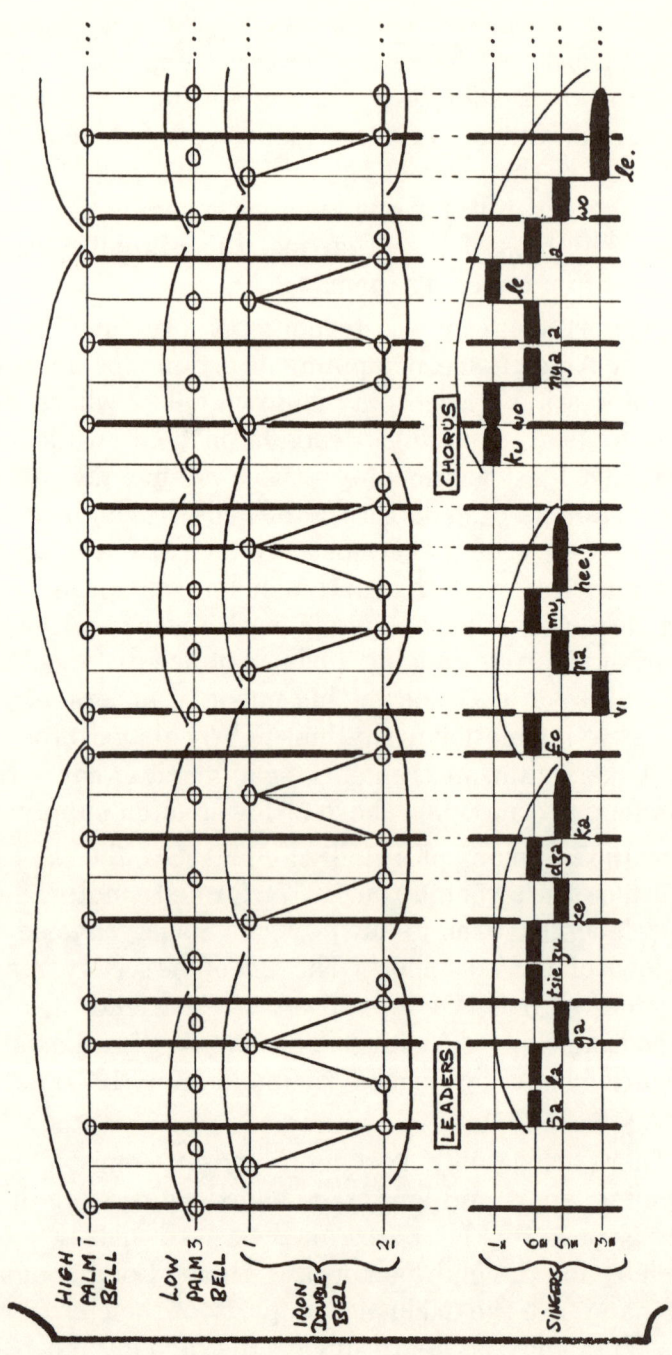

FIGURE 53: THE ROLE OF PITCH RANGES. *This drawing shows a portion of a song by Kofi Kpeglo Ladzekpo performed in June of 1971 by the dance-drumming club of an Anlo mutual-aid society in Accra. The progress of time and the governing bell are shown as in the preceding examples. For an explanation of the numeral pitch notation see the caption for Figure 4.*

Bell sounds, shown as open circles, occupy the upper two octaves of the ensemble's range. The two palm bells are made of iron in the shape of large, open pods. One person plays each of them, holding it in the palm of the hand and striking it with an iron nail. The higher-sounding palm bell outlines the governing meter. The lower-sounding palm bell decorates this meter by filling the first half of it with four equidistant strokes and the second half with three, often adding a few additional strokes without varying this basic pattern. Sometimes one hears an ensemble in which the higher of the two palm bells has the decoration and the lower has the governing meter, but in either case the resulting duet has a distinctive, repeating character.

A single iron double bell decorates the palm-bell duet with various patterns, one of which is shown here. This is in keeping with the principle discussed in the text: the lower the pitch of an instrument the more varied its part. This principle is the opposite of the one used in Western ensembles, where a fixed beat in the bottom range supports rhythmic variety above.

The singers' voices, which occupy the lowest range of all, create the greatest variety, as you can see by comparing the vocal phrasing to the phrasing of the bells.

special place in the interludes, when the drums are silent and the audience can give the singing its full attention. On this part of the club's performance its reputation depends. Drummers rarely rehearse; singers frequently do. The women of the club preserve the long-song repertoire, to which the identity of the club itself is linked. Thus, as I mentioned earlier, if the women die without passing these songs on to a new generation, the club dies.

Songs can be powerful weapons among the Anlo. With a gift for words a composer can easily enhance a person's reputation and just as easily cause it serious damage. Once in a while a dispute among the Anlo will grow to such proportions that a song contest will be arranged to settle it. Each side is championed by a gifted composer, and the encounter is a bitter one. Usually the songs composed for the contest will be banned afterward together with all mention of the dispute.

The Compatibility of Western and West African Rhythm

This discussion should not end without noting an important area of agreement between the Anlo rhythmic system and our own: the use of equidistant meters in both. The Anlo do not use them as we do to govern the flow of the ensemble but rather to form individual contributing rhythms. Note, for example, the decorative double-bell part shown on p. 284, and the parts for the leading drum and the dancers' feet shown on p. 282. An even more striking use of equidistant rhythm occurs when the Anlo fit our four-square Protestant hymns into the same asymmetrical bell pattern governing the timing of these two figures. (They place the beats of the hymn where they place the steps of the dancers in the example on p. 282.)

By all rights traditional Anlo rhythm and European hymns, however compatible, should never have come together. From their first contacts with the Anlo in 1853 the German missionaries from Bremen vigorously opposed native dancing. Their attitude, according to Anlo elders educated in their schools, stemmed from their refusal to distinguish between native social affairs and native cult worship, both of which feature dance drumming. Well into this century any pupil at the missionary schools who had even watched a dance-drumming performance was whipped. When British missionaries replaced the Germans after the first World War, this stern attitude continued. As a result, many Anlo Christians of middle age or older know little or nothing about their own traditional music because they had to abandon it to get an education.

But times have changed. The public school at Anyako now celebrates special events with dance drumming. A native Christian church has arisen, The Apostles Revelation Society, in which festivals and even services are celebrated with traditional music. And on occasion in one place or another one hears a European hymn with its four-square rhythms set into the asymmetrical pattern of the bell as smoothly as if the two traditions belonged together.

The non-Western aspects of Anlo equidistant rhythms are first the fact that they do not exert primary control over the timing of the ensemble and second their sound: the duet between such a rhythm and the bell's governing asymmetry generates a composite rhythm that seems to expand and contract, moving from a period of relatively intense activity to one of relatively sparse activity and back again in a regular manner, as shown overleaf in Figure 54. An enjoyment of this composite rhythmic effect probably explains to some extent the survival of asymmetrical bell patterns in Caribbean music of African origin even in ensembles where the bell does not have a governing role.

Fig. 54

Many writers have pointed out that black music of the Western hemisphere is at least partly rooted in West African traditions, and I will examine the connection in Chaper 16. It makes sense, however, to conclude the present chapter with a brief discussion of the musical basis for this connection.

Western and West African musical traditions are, as it happens, fairly compatible not only in rhythm, which I have been discussing, but in melody and harmony as well. Thus when West African slaves came into direct and prolonged contact with Western musical values on the plantations of the Caribbean and southern United States, those more musically gifted were able to adapt to these values and secure for themselves some slight degree of preferment and privilege as musicians serving their masters' need for entertainment.

As far as rhythm goes, the change was easily effected by promoting equidistant metrical accents from their secondary position in West African ensemble music to the primary position required in our Western tradition. The asymmetrical, high-pitched pattern holding the West African ensemble together was not discarded, as I have already pointed out; it was simply demoted from a governing role to a decorative one, as

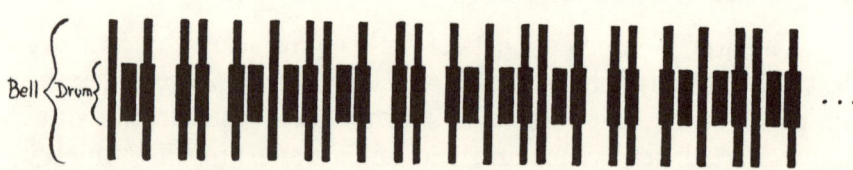

FIGURE 54: COMPOSITE RHYTHM. *This diagram combines the asymmetrical bell pattern seen in previous figures with an equidistant rhythm often sounded on the drum* kaganu *(shown on p. 279), the drum of highest pitch in the Anlo ensemble. The short, thick verticals represent drum strokes; the longer, thinner ones represent strokes on the bell. Time moves steadily from left to right, as before.*

The visual effect of the diagram mirrors the acoustical effect of the duet: the composite rhythm fluctuates back and forth in a regular manner between relatively sparse and relatively dense activity, giving the absolutely identical repetitions of the short kaganu *pattern a broader repeating pattern created by this fluctuation. This broader rhythm of the* kaganu *part is the sound that controls the player's timing.*

blacks accommodated to a Western beat anchored in the bass notes of the music. To this day most black American music and musicians remain noticeably more free of the restraints of this anchor—that is, less insistent on rhythmic unity—than their white American counterparts.

13

The Rhythm of Renaissance Harmony

The Renaissance

The recorded history of Western Europe falls into three broad periods: ancient, medieval, and modern. The first of these lasted a thousand years and was dominated from its midpoint on by the armies of Rome. It was brought to a close in the 5th century A.D. by the more vigorous armies of northern and eastern Europe. The second period lasted another thousand years and was dominated from its midpoint on by the wealth and intellectual force of the Roman Catholic Church. It was brought to a close in the 15th century by the development of superior wealth and intellectual force in secular society. The close of this second period and the beginning of the third concern us here. In music this transition took place roughly between 1450 and 1600, a period in which the harmonies of today's popular music received their basic form and rhythmic importance.

We call this century and a half the Renaissance (pronounced "reh-neh-*saunce*" in America and "ruh-*nay*-sense" in England). The people, events, and ideas of the Renaissance still resonate among us, not only in our classrooms but in our political assemblies and daily commerce. For example, we are as willing as the Spanish and Portuguese monarchies of five hundred years ago to pour vast amounts of money into exploring the unknown; we seek individual wealth as vigorously as the people of that time; we continue to value individual creative talent as they valued the talent of Michelangelo and Shakespeare; and we tolerate in theory if not always in practice those who, like John Hus and Martin Luther, promote their own religious vision. We have broken with the medieval view of a closed society with a fixed hierarchy of roles, of life as a preordained flow of events, and of knowledge as a book already written. The following sweeping and belligerent words of the British historian John Symonds, written to characterize the spirit of the Renaissance, characterize the spirit of our own age equally well as

> the endeavor of man to reconstitute himself as a free being, not as the thrall of ... despotism.
> *(Symonds 1911: 83b)*

The Renaissance ideal of a free human being found strong support in the ancient literature of the Greeks and Romans. Europeans of the 15th century turned to this literature with a passion that

> made young men leave their loves and pleasures, grave men quit their counting-houses, churchmen desert their missals, to crowd the lecture-rooms of philologers and rhetoricians.
> *(Symonds 1911: 86a)*

We call the Renaissance concern for individual expression "humanism." The ancient texts supported humanism in their celebration of human reason and human feeling. The ancient authors could no longer be read in their original context, of course, because the times had necessarily changed. Much of the meaning of the texts was undoubtedly lost for that reason, yet people of the Renaissance felt they were giving this literature a rebirth. The French word for rebirth, *renaissance*, has become our name for those exciting times.

The Sound of the New Humanism

Musicians of the Renaissance did not at first try to revive ancient music. Had they tried they could not have done so, for the few scraps of it we have today were not known to them. What they did find in the ancient texts were eulogies and condemnations of the power of music to arouse feeling. They sought this power, and to get it they used the tools of their own time.

These tools included an impressive technique of counterpoint and harmony inherited from the service-music of the medieval Roman Catholic Church (see Chapter 9). With this technique Renaissance musicians created a sound more sensual than that of the Middle Ages—a sound that fitted the new humanism because it made a more immediate appeal to human emotions.

What did they change? They added the rich effect of choral counterpoint to the medieval tradition of solo counterpoint. They enlarged the range of their harmony by combining in one sound every voice from bass to soprano. They substituted the thicker sound of triads for the hollow medieval consonances of unison, fifth, fourth, and octave. To the contrasting instrumental sounds of a mixed band they added the possibility of a consort, a choir of like-sounding instruments built in several sizes to cover the new, wide range of their harmonies. And when setting a text they tried to evoke the meaning of the words.

In the course of all these changes the traditional technique of composing also changed, and Western European music became in essence the modern system we use today.

From Solo to Choral Harmony

The first change to occur was the move from solo to choral harmony. Throughout the Middle Ages counterpoint had been for soloists, as was the case in the music of Notre Dame we studied in Chapter 9. Ordinarily, massed instruments and voices performed in unison or heterophony (but see the discussion of *discant* on p. 184). During the Renaissance, counterpoint for worldly entertainment remained the work of soloists; but as early as the 1420's, sections of counterpoint were sung by a chorus in certain Italian churches. We know this because the idea of putting more than one singer on each part was so new that the specific instruction "chorus" had to be written in the music at those points where it applied.

In the second half of the same century, the manuscripts that the singers used in church changed in size. Instead of choir books that one singer could hold comfortably in his hands (see page 170) we find choir books with pages as much as a foot and a half across and two feet from top to bottom. These books contain not *more* music than the smaller ones, but music written larger. Clearly such manuscripts were designed to be set upon a lectern in front of many singers rather than held by one or two.

How many singers were in these early choruses? Not the number we find performing in today's choral concerts. The most important chapels—those attached to the main courts of the time—might have as many as twenty or twenty-five adult singers; cathedrals and small courts, ten or so. The Pope's private chapel had nine adult singers in 1436, but this number increased to twenty-four during the second half of the century. As late as the middle of the next century the cathedral in Milan had only twelve adult singers, and this seems to be more like the usual number, though even that figure may be a bit high.

To this total we must add the choirboys, if the chapel belonged to a church. They usually numbered from four to eight and sang in unison the highest of the choral parts. They weren't paid, as the adult singers were, but received instead a rudimentary education in music and Latin plus free room and board. An added benefit was the prospect of graduating to paid work as scribes or adult singers and composers. It was to alleviate the tedious process of training such choirboys by rote that the dual system of syllables and music notation we use today (see pp. 39-40) was invented.

Enlarging the Range of a Harmony

The shift from solo to choral counterpoint in the music of the church was only one result of the delight the Renaissance took in sound for the sake of sound. Another result was the spreading-out of the harmony.

Medieval counterpoint had involved two or three melodic lines sharing a narrow range. A medieval piece had been composed so it could be easily lowered or raised in pitch to suit a particular performing group: women or boys might sing on one occasion what men sang on another, or what mixed groups sang using the middle of the overall available range.

In the course of the 15th century composers began to combine in one piece the different ranges of these voices. By 1500 it was standard practice to combine soprano, alto, tenor, and bass in one harmony. The increased richness of the sound must have struck the ears of that day as forcefully as the increased volume of our own rock music strikes the ears of those who grew up to gentler sounds.

Except in convents, the church choir was a male preserve. Therefore sacred harmony of the Renaissance, though composed for soprano, alto, tenor, and bass, was sung entirely by men. The soprano part was taken by choirboys or adult males specializing in this range by using a beautifully developed falsetto voice.* Other adult males specialized in the alto range, using either the falsetto ("male alto") voice or a voice between falsetto and tenor known today as "contratenor" or "countertenor."

Good adult male voices for every range were eagerly sought by wealthy nobles and wealthy churches, and a lively commercial traffic in singers developed. Agents of church and state kept a lookout for the best voices, and singers went where the money was. Records were kept, since money was involved.

---

*"Falsetto" describes that high, flutelike tone that any male can produce. It has been out of fashion for many generations and has only recently returned to favor through the singing of Rock groups like Crosby, Stills & Nash, and the Bee Gees.

For example we have a letter of June 6, 1448, received by the head of the Medici family in Florence, Italy, from his bank manager in the wealthy trading center of Bruges, in what is now Belgium.

> Respected Sir, and with all honor to my superiors, etc.
>
> I wrote you a few lines from Antwerp through Pitratto the singer, telling you how we could not engage that Mattis, the tenorista [tenor], but that [Pitratto] had found another whom he says he didn't like less. And because he [also] came across a good soprano, of whom he says the chapel has need and [whom] you would be pleased to have, he agreed to bring him. And I, hoping to content you and give you pleasure, . . . agreed to give him the money for his expenses; and as I told you, I paid him in all XIV *liri di grossi* which I charged to the account of our [main office] at Florence. At the rate of 51 and ½ *grossi*, these are 65 and ¼ Venetian ducats that you must make good to them. And Pitratto has taken the responsibility in case you should not be pleased with the soprano. And then only 10 or 12 ducats will be lost on the food and drink en route of which Fruosino says he would be happy to pay half, and I have taken responsibility for the rest. The said [Pitratto] must render you all the horses there. . . .
>
> (D'Accone 1961: 315)

The Polyphony of Josquin des Pres

Undoubtedly it was an agent like Pitratto who brought to the cathedral choir of Milan in 1459 a young man named Josquin des Pres (c. 1440-1521). Like many other professional singers then serving the churches of northern Italy, Josquin, a bass, had been trained in what was at that time the music center of Western Europe—the area around Bruges known as Flanders, lying today partly in Belgium and partly in northeasten France.

The princes of northern Italy had been sending to Flanders for their musical talent for over a decade, looking not just for good singers but for creative ones who could supply their choirs with music. As at Notre Dame in the 12th century, the art of composition was one with the art of singing, and the only difference between improvisation and composition was the small matter of whether or not a musical invention was written down for future use. Josquin turned out to be both a good singer and a gifted composer. He stayed on in Italy forty years, becoming known as the greatest composer of his time. For generations afterwards he was remembered as a great master, and even five hundred years later we can see why. His was the ultimate gift: the ability to fashion an endlessly interesting experience.

His compositions may *not* interest you at first hearing, however, unless you have sung his kind of music. Its appeal is not to the passive listener but to the active and experienced ensemble singer, one used to hearing within a web of vocal sound the expressive curves of each contributing melodic line. We of the 20th century hear all around us a music made up of a single, prominent tune, a rhythmic bass, and a harmonious mass of supporting sound. Josquin's music weaves together at one time many tunes of equal interest. We call such balanced counterpoint "polyphony," from the Greek *polyphones*, "having many voices." Our ears are not ready for polyphony unless, as I've suggested, we have sung such music ourselves and have become used to following inner threads of melody.

Audiences of the 15th century were better prepared. Most of the art music of their day was polyphonic, and the interplay of lines was the main thing they listened for. Harmony was appreciated, but had not yet become the powerful force it is in music today. That development was the work of men[*] who followed Josquin.

---

[*]Renaissance artists often portrayed musical performance, and their work shows that women not only danced and sang but also played instruments. I have pointed out that composing and performing were not considered separate activities as they are today, and it seems to me that since many women performed instrumental and vocal music, they undoubtedly also composed it—chamber music

Josquin's polyphony appears on the next page in Figure 55, Fig. 55
which shows a portion of his *Missa Pange Lingua,* one of many
settings he made of the words of the Roman Catholic Mass. The
passage comes from the Creed, a section of the Mass stating
what Catholics believe about God, Christ, and the Holy
Ghost. These particular words tell of a mystery central to the
Christian faith: that God caused himself to be born as a human
being. The telling is marked dramatically by the congregation.
At the beginning of the Creed they stand. Then, at the start of
the quoted passage, they suddenly kneel.

Josquin's music also marks the words, as you can see: the
voices move in rhythmic unison from syllable to syllable, giving
to each its own block of harmonious sound and the clearest
possible presentation. Elsewhere in his *Missa Pange Lingua*
the presentation is not so clear, the syllables and their harmonic
support being somewhat scattered by a degree of rhythmic
independence among the voices.

The difference is one of texture. Texture in music is the
impression created by the way the components of the music
work together, just as the texture of a cloth is the impression
created by the assemblage of its threads. If an example
emphasizes the forward flow of equally interesting melodies,
we say the texture is "contrapuntal." Such an example can also
be "thick" or "sparse," depending on the number of different
contributing lines and how their juxtaposition strikes us. If, on
the other hand, the example emphasizes successive blocks of
sound, we say the texture is "chordal," a "chord" being a
harmony sounded as a single beat.

The harmonies of Josquin's contrapuntal texture are the
same as those of his chordal texture. I have chosen a chordal
passage for my example because its harmonies can be sorted
out clearly. In contrapuntal passages the vocal lines contribute
to each harmony at separate times, making the progression
from one harmony to another less immediately clear.

---

for the home, for example, and sacred pieces for women's religious groups. Of their
work we know nothing, however. Until recently music history has been researched
and written almost as if women did not exist.

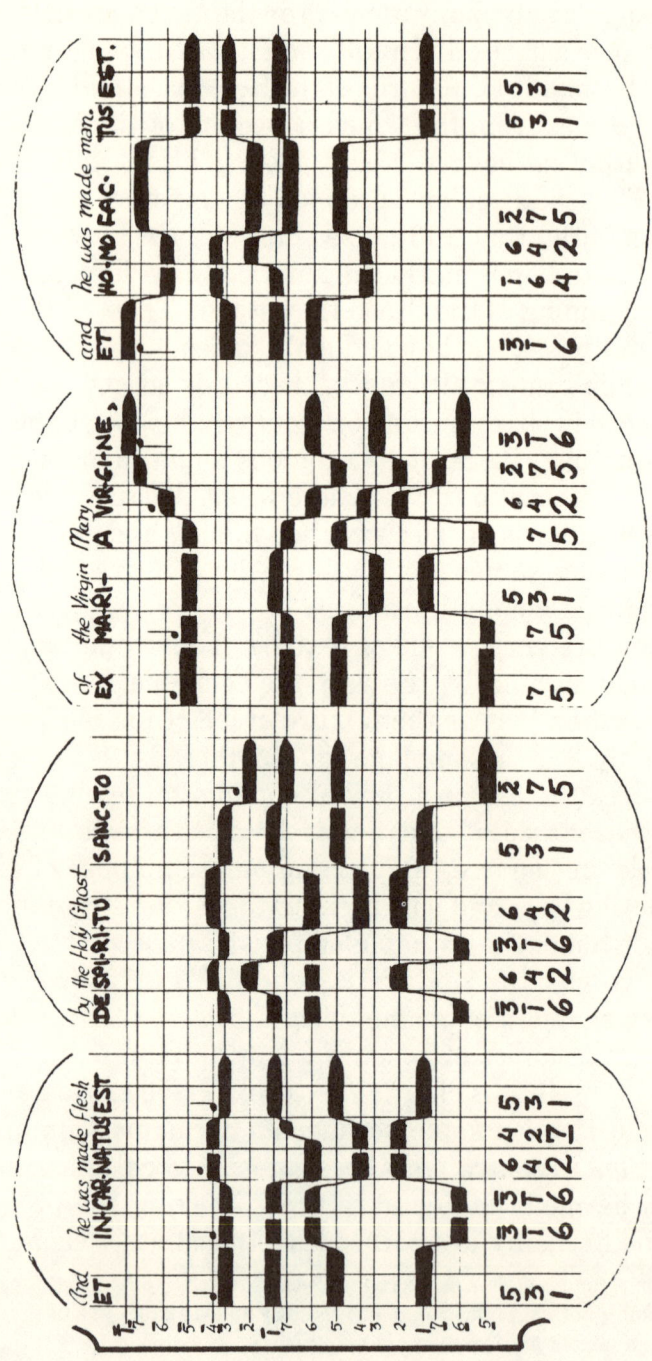

FIGURE 55: ET INCARNATUS EST. *This pictorial notation shows four phrases from the Missa Pange Lingua composed by Josquin des Pres for the Cathedral of Milan around 1500 as they are sung by the Philippe Caillard Ensemble (Musical Heritage MHS 617: side 1, band 3). For a general explanation of the notation see the caption for Figure 4. The vertical lines mark equidistant moments in time.*

Four distinct and often contrasting melodic lines move in rhythmic unison, creating by their combination successive harmonies that have the force of beats. We call such blocks of sound "chords." In all but three cases above, the pitches (or their octave equivalents) form a harmony of three notes a third apart in the Western octave series. This harmonic relationship is known as a "triad." Although triads were not new to musicians of the Renaissance, they became in that period the dominant harmonic effect. They have remained dominant in Western music ever since.

Despite its chordal effect this passage is essentially contrapuntal in design, an interplay of equally interesting melodies which happens to produce—by intent, to be sure, but not by primary intent—a beautiful series of harmonies. Observe, for example, that no melody sounds more tuneful or less tuneful than any other, although the highest vocal line actually uses the first ten pitches of a beautiful tune, the Gregorian hymn Pange Lingua Gloriosi (Catholic Church 1959: 957), marked here by the addition of standard musical notes above or below the appropriate points in the line. It was common practice in Josquin's time to make more or less direct use of a precomposed melody but to spread the quality of tunefulness equally among the parts.

The humanistic interest of Renaissance musicians in the quality of a sound and the meaning of a text is well illustrated by the opening of the fourth and final phrase of this example. Josquin repeats the triad with which he ended the third phrase but gives it a new, high voicing. Singers' voices have a different timbre in different parts of their range, and he undoubtedly made this dramatic upward shift in order to emphasize with a change of timbre the beginning of the most important of the four phrases of text.

Triads and Harmonic Destinations

Renaissance harmonies are distinguished from the harmonies of earlier Western music by the pervasiveness of the triad, the combination of three pitch levels a third apart from each other. Triads are not absent from earlier music but are rare, at least at moments of prominence. We can only conclude that to earlier ears they must have sounded dissonant, the harmonies of unison, fourth, fifth, and octave being preferred (see p. 191).

The audiences served by Josquin and his contemporaries clearly favored triads. As you can see in the summary at the bottom of Figure 55, almost every harmony sounded in the example is a triad. The interval of a third, dissonant in the Middle Ages,* now fills what would otherwise be a series of fifths. A master of polyphony like Josquin was able to compose persuasive melodies for his vocal lines and at the same time form them into a persuasive progression of triadic harmonies.

During the 16th century triadic progression became a rhythmic force, a massive motion from one harmony to the next whether the texture was contrapuntal or chordal. The motive power was the listeners' recognition of harmonic destinations.

A harmonic destination is like a melodic one: a sound the music establishes as a goal. We feel a melody is going somewhere when we recognize that the sound is moving toward or away from a certain level of pitch. Similarly, we feel the harmony of a musical passage is going somewhere when we recognize that the sound is moving toward or away from a certain harmony.

These harmonic destinations are not all of equal importance. Secondary ones are no more than brief islands of clear and stable sound among transitional, blurred harmonic effects. They function like clear but isolated words that give us the gist of an otherwise indistinct utterance. Primary harmonic destinations are more than clear and stable sounds; the music returns

---

*Except in Britain, where its consonance was either a peculiarity of the islands or a relic of an earlier, wider, and unreported practice.

to them again and again, creating by emphasis a few harmonies to which all other harmonies relate. They function like the words and ideas a speaker uses over and over as the theme of a discourse.

The harmonic practices of the 16th century, its triads and primary harmonic destinations, are those we use today. Thus a Renaissance lady of rank such as Italy's Lucrezia Borgia (1480-1519), a knowledgeable patroness of music, art, and letters, would have recognized as familiar friends the harmonies of our hymns, our country-and-western ballads, our Sousa marches, our swing, rock, and bluegrass. The meaning of the words, the timbre of the instruments, and the social context of the performances might be strange, but the triads themselves and their relationship to one another would not.

If triads were the favored kind of harmony in chordal and contrapuntal music at the beginning of the 16th century, they soon became more than that, taking on a governing role in composition: from being the result of melodic flow they rose to become its cause. Whereas men of Josquin's generation and earlier created a melodic flow that generated triads, the composers who followed them created a triadic flow and filled it with melodies.

One aspect of this development was that melodies tended more and more to outline triads. An extreme example appears in Figure 56-A (p. 302) as designed by the late-Renaissance composer Michael Praetorius (1571-1621), and as you can see in Figure 56-B, this melody generates a single triad when sung in overlapping succession by several voices. The melody is like a trumpet call, and the harmonic effect might be explained simply as the incidental and unavoidable result of trying to imitate an instrumental fanfare. But at several other points in the piece, as indicated in Figure 56-C, the sound of a single triad is equally sustained, and at these points there is no attempt to imitate an instrumental fanfare. One has to conclude that the composer's basic idea was to design these melodies to fit within a desired harmony.

Fig. 56

A

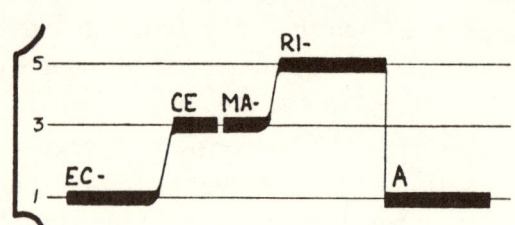

B

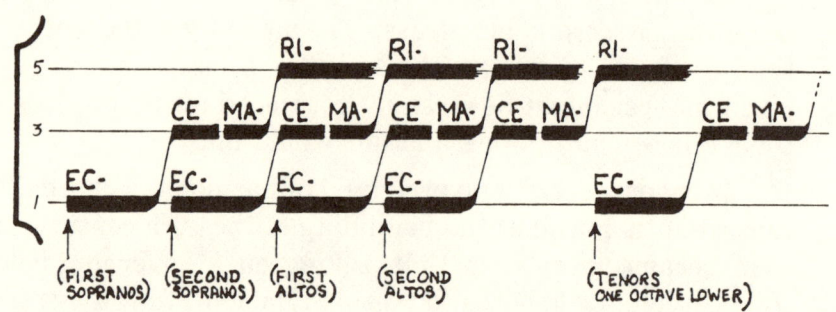

(FIRST SOPRANOS) (SECOND SOPRANOS) (FIRST ALTOS) (SECOND ALTOS) (TENORS ONE OCTAVE LOWER)

C

<u>ECCE MARIA</u> GENUIT NOBIS
See! Mary has born for us

                         SALVATOREM.
                         a savior.

                         QUEM JOHANNES   VIDENS
                         When John the Baptist saw him

<u>EXCLAMAVIT</u>   DICENS
he exclaimed, saying:

                         ECCE AGNUS   DEI,
                         "See, the lamb of God!
                         ECCE AGNUS   DEI
                         See, the lamb of God

<u>QUI TOLLIT</u> PECCATA MUNDI.
who bears the sins of the world!"
<u>ALLELUIA,</u>
Alleluia,
<u>ALLELUIA,</u>
alleluia,

                         ALLELUIA!
                         alleluia!

FIGURE 56: *ECCE MARIA. This is from a polyphonic piece Michael Praetorius composed around 1600 (Westminster XWN 18809: side 1, band 5). For an explanation of the pictorial notation see the caption for Figure 4.*

(A): the opening melodic idea of the piece. It outlines a triad, as you can see, and shows that by this time Renaissance composers first designed their work harmonically and then invented melodic lines to fit the design while creating a contrapuntal effect. This particular melody also captures the meaning of the text ("Look here!") by imitating the shape of a trumpet fanfare.

(B): the opening polyphony, showing how the successive entries of the five vocal lines fit together to sustain the sound of a single triad. By the end of the Renaissance, four-part polyphony had yielded to the thicker texture of five-part polyphony. The technique of imitation—giving a more or less identical melodic idea to one vocal line after another—was characteristic of middle- and late-Renaissance polyphony. It was the natural result of trying to enhance the meaning of certain words by giving them a certain melodic shape.

(C): the full text of the piece in Latin together with its translation. Words given a contrapuntal texture appear at the left, those given a chordal texture appear at the right, and the text as a whole is read from left to right and from top to bottom. The ends of lines are the ends of phrases. Underlining indicates words set contrapuntally to melodies that sustain the harmony of a single triad. Only the first of these melodies imitates a fanfare. The passage comes from the Catholic evening service of Vespers for January 1, the Feast of the Circumcision.

Praetorius was a Lutheran from northern Germany, not a Catholic. But Martin Luther, leader of the beginning of the Protestant Reformation in the first quarter of the 16th century, never objected to using the language, vestments, trained choirs, and much of the ritual developed by Rome. For many years these things were part of the Lutheran service. Ecce Maria *offers a text appropriate to the Christmas season in general and was probably sung by both Protestant and Catholic choirs.*

In addition to such melodic planning, Renaissance composers seem to have begun to favor starting a composition by planning a succession of triads. During the course of the 16th

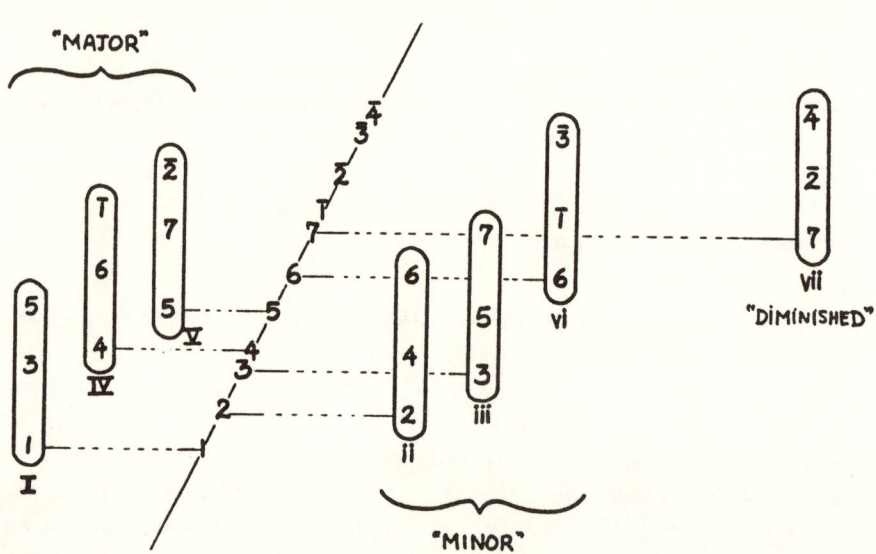

FIGURE 57: TRIADS. *This diagram lays out in numeral notation the seven triads that Renaissance musicians derived from the Western octave series. For an explanation of the notation and the series see pp. 45-46.*

The Western octave series appears on a line slanted from the lower left to the upper right of the diagram. Each pitch level of the series provides the foundation for a triad, a harmony of three pitches a third apart. Each triad is shown as a short, rounded column placed beside the series and in horizontal alignment with it.

The intervals between the pitch levels of the series are not uniform: five are large and two are small. Therefore the thirds formed by these pitch levels are also not uniform: three are large and four are small. Triads to the left of the slanted series line have a large lower third and a small upper third, giving them a different sound from the first three triads to the right of the line, which have a small lower third and a large upper third. We label the two kinds of sound according to the size of the lower third: it is large or "major" on the left, small or "minor" on the right. At the far right is a triad with two minor thirds

century their triadic plans became dominated more and more by what we might call the shift of a fifth: the progression from a triad built upon one level of pitch to another built upon a level a fifth higher or lower in the Western octave series. We hear the shift of a fifth when we sing "Amen" to the accompaniment of a piano or organ at the end of a hymn, and shifts of a fifth accompany the familiar melodic tag "Shave and a haircut, two bits." Of the five triadic shifts occurring in the harmonic plan of most blues, four are shifts of a fifth; every shift in the harmony for *Happy Birthday* is of this type, as are twenty-two of the twenty six in *My Country 'Tis of Thee*.

The shift of a fifth reached its present dominant position in our music during the 16th century. The passage quoted from Josquin's *Missa Pange Lingua* (on p. 298) dates from around 1500 and contains twenty-one triadic shifts, only eleven of them shifts of a fifth. The piece by Michael Praetorius from which I quoted (on p. 302) dates from around 1600, and eight out of every ten triadic shifts it contains are shifts of a fifth.

Figure 57 opposite shows the seven triads available in the Western octave series and the three different qualities of harmony they create. Much of the variety of combination offered by these triads was overlooked by composers of the 17th, 18th, and 19th centuries in their enthusiasm for exploring

Fig. 57

---

and a sound different from any of the other triads: we call it "diminished." The symbol for a triad is the name of its foundation pitch expressed as a Roman numeral in upper case if the triad is major and in lower case if the triad is minor or diminished.

*As you can see, the highest and lowest pitch levels of a triad form a fifth, a harmony medieval listeners considered consonant (except for the diminished fifth between 7 and 4). Triads seem to have derived from fifths, at least in art music. They sound thicker than fifths, and medieval church musicians treated them as dissonances. The Renaissance found that very thickness attractive and accepted triads as consonances, avoiding only the diminished sound (notice how briefly the diminished triad appears in the last syllable of "*incarnatus*" in Figure 55 on p. 298).*

shifts of a fifth. The harmonic system they elaborated is called "tonal," whereas the older system that places equal emphasis upon other kinds of shifts is called "modal" (because Renaissance theorists sought to discuss it in terms of the melodic modes of the Roman Catholic Church).

Why the change? We don't know. The medieval tradition was for listeners to tie their moment-to-moment expectations to the progress of the melodies. The only thing they expected of harmony, in addition to consistency, was that it be consonant or, if dissonant, that it resolve into consonance. The succession of harmonies at the ends of phrases came to follow a standard plan in the Middle Ages, the downward shift of a second, but between these phrase endings the order of the consonances was not standardized.

For Josquin's listeners the harmonic moves between phrase endings remained highly varied while the ending triads came to be dominated by the shift of a fifth. After his time the variety of the harmony in the span between endings grew less and less: although the number of available harmonic moves stayed the same, the number of times they were used decreased dramatically in favor of shifts of a fifth.

Evidently 16th-century listeners were developing a taste for harmonic expectation. More appealing than the simple pleasure of hearing one triad succeed another was the pleasure of anticipating that a particular shift was going to come. Composers satisfied the demand for harmonic destinations by greater and greater use of the particular shift already firmly established at the ends of phrases. Thus the shift of a fifth came to pervade their music.

Metrical Harmony and Opera

Music governed by an equidistant meter, as I pointed out on p. 272, has to channel many of its effects to support that meter because, taken by themselves, equidistant moments in time possess nothing to distinguish one from another. Among these supporting effects, changes of harmony, especially chordal changes, have become very important. Chords not only mark a moment in time in a precise and massive way, they also create metrical groups when varied or repeated in an equidistant pattern.

Thus the tonal harmony that began in the Renaissance became eventually a source of metrical rhythm, as illustrated overleaf in Figure 58. Meanwhile, the bass line of Renaissance polyphony grew more and more important. Why it did so is not hard to guess. Low-pitched sounds have prime importance as metrical cues in Western music (see p. 223) and presumably have always had. Western minds therefore feel the rhythmic force of a harmonic progression most strongly when it involves a change of pitch in the lowest voice. While the shift of a fifth was permeating the flow of Renaissance harmony, giving listeners a greater sense of harmonic destination, the movement of the lowest voice became not just a part of that shift but its driving force.*

Fig. 58

By 1600 the power of the lowest voice was so firmly established that composers of art music were in a position to abandon all pretense of writing for a blend of equally important voices. That they did so was due to nonmusical pressures building up in the world of secular entertainment. The poetic taste of early 16th-century Italy had favored decorous pastoral description and polished, controlled expression as in Figure 59-A on p. 310, but these began to yield in the middle of the century to more dramatic material such as the emotional monologue you see in Figure 59-B on p. 311. A web of equally interesting, simultaneous melodic lines admirably suited the sustained moods created by the early texts but not the frequent shifts of mood created by the later ones, for dramatic outbursts require

Fig. 59

---

*There is considerable evidence that the importance of the lowest voice was established first outside the polyphonic tradition of church music, in the harmonic plans developed for dance music and for the improvised singing of popular poems. Indeed, such plans were known by their bass lines, which had names like *La Folia*, *La Moderna*, and *La Romanesca*. (The song *Greensleeves* is based on *La Romanesca*.)

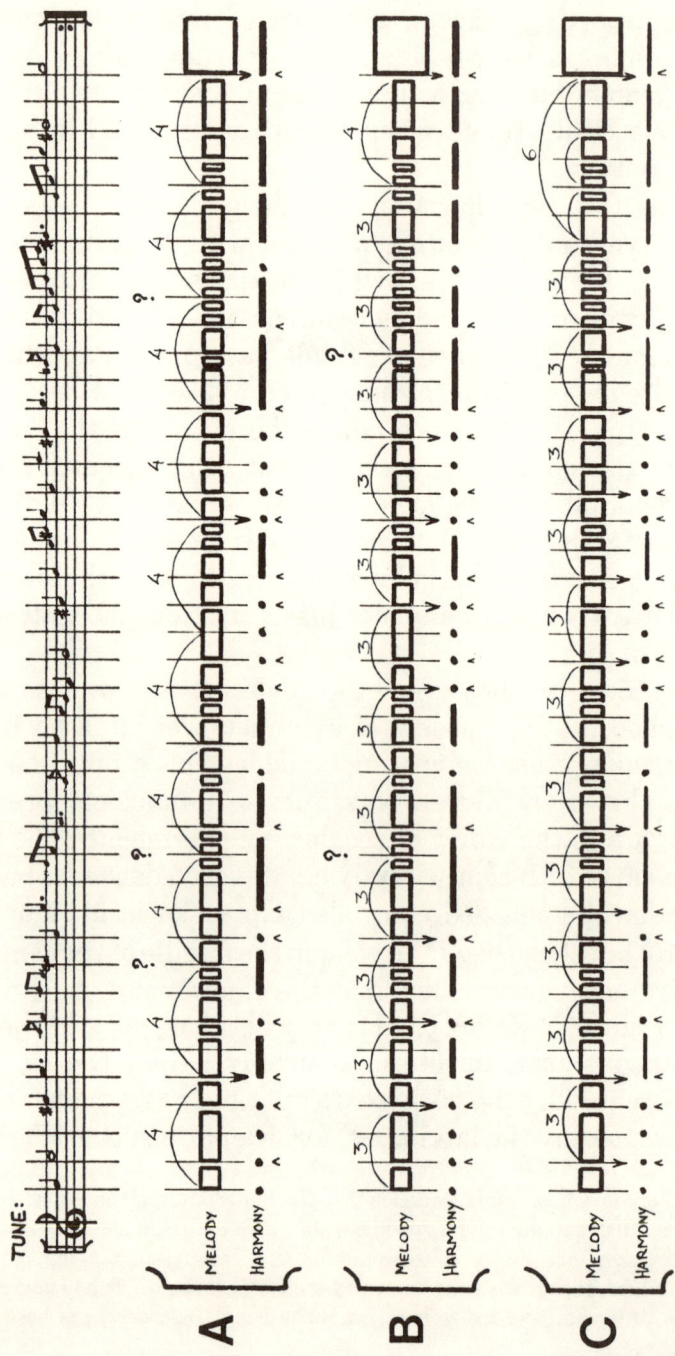

FIGURE 58: METRICAL HARMONY. *These diagrams show how changes of harmony were used at the end of the Renaissance to help create the meter of a piece of measured music. The music for each diagram is the same: the first half of an instrumental refrain composed by Claudio Monteverdi in 1607 for the first act of his opera* L'Orfeo *(Monteverdi 1923: 14-15). Only the durational aspect of the melodic and harmonic rhythms is analyzed, with time marked off into equal intervals from left to right by thin vertical lines. Curved lines above the melody indicate measures. Upward-pointing accents below the harmony show which changes are shifts of a fifth (see p. 305 for a discussion of this shift).*

(A): the weak relationship of harmony to melody when the melody is interpreted in a meter of four equidistant accents. Although this interpretation is entirely believable when the melody is heard by itself, it is not reinforced by the changes of harmony: they fail to mark the beginning of a measure at three places (indicated by question marks above the diagram); and the strongest changes—shifts of a fifth—coincide with the beginning of a measure only four times (indicated by downward arrows placed between melody and harmony) out of a possible ten.

(B): the somewhat stronger relationship of harmony to melody when the melody is interpreted in a meter of three equidistant accents with a closing measure of four equidistant accents. Although this interpretation is entirely believable when the melody is heard by itself, it is not reinforced enough by the changes of harmony: they fail to mark the beginning of a measure at two places; shifts of a fifth coincide with the beginning of a measure only eight times out of a possible thirteen; and although a consistent reinforcement of this meter does begin at the seventh measure it comes too late, for the listener has already accepted the meter discussed below, which receives consistent reinforcement from the beginning.

(C): the strong relationship of harmony to melody when the melody is interpreted in a meter of three equidistant accents, beginning with the third accent, and is terminated with a measure of six equidistant accents. When the melody is heard by itself, this interpretation is entirely believable. It is consistently reinforced throughout by the changes of harmony: they mark the beginning of every measure; shifts of a fifth coincide with these beginnings ten times out of a possible thirteen; and the coordination of harmonic and melodic rhythm is firmly established at the outset.

A

VOI VE N'ANDAT'AL CIELO, OCCHI BEAT' E SANTI,
You travel heavenward, eyes blessed and holy,

CO'L VOSTRO CHIARO LUM' E CON MIEI CANTI,
with your bright light and with my songs,

ET IO CHE SON DI GELO,
while I who am cold,

SENZ' UN CONFORTO SOLO,
without a single comfort,

VORREI LEVARMI A VOLO
would like to raise myself in flight

MA STRUGGENDO MI TORN'IN DOGLIE'N PIANTI.
but, melting with desire, end in sorrow and tears.

COSÌ FACESS'AMORE,
Would you had loved,

OCCHI SERENI VOI,
you eyes serene,

CH'ALL'HOR VEDRESTI PÒI
for then you had seen

QUEL CHE DEE'HAVER UN BEN PIETOSO CORE.
what a compassionate heart should have.

E SE'L VOSTRO VEDER VOI NON POTETE
But if you cannot understand your own heart

GUARDAT' IL MIO CH'IN VOI CHIUSO TENETE.
then look at mine you hold imprisoned within you.

FIGURE 59: A SHIFT IN POETIC TASTE. *The two stanzas shown here come from opposite ends of the 16th century and illustrate a change in the message composers of art songs sought to convey. Rejected love is the subject in both cases, in both the rejected lover speaks in the first person, and in both the object addressed is not the beloved but an organ of the body personified. Notice, however, the differences.*

(A): a stanza of unknown authorship set in four-voiced polyphony by Jacques Arcadelt (c. 1505-1568) and published in Venice in 1539 for the entertainment of members of the upper classes, who sang the parts themselves in their homes. No doubt these people loved with as much passion as we do today, but the matter was expressed poetically with a reserved tone and decorous images. Text and translation (adapted) are from Davison and Apel 1949: no. 130.

music flexible enough to support the irregular rhythms and varied moods of declamation.

These developments in harmony and literary taste created a new texture in art music, shown in Figure 60 on p. 313. You see a series of bass notes providing the foundation for triadic chords while a vocal line moves above the bass, at times agreeing with the chords and at times playing against them. We call this texture "thoroughbass style" because the bass line is

Fig. 60

B

IO PUR RESPÍRO IN COSÌ GRAN DOLORE,
Do I still breathe in such anguish,

E TU PUR VIVI, O DISPIETATO CORE!
and you still live, o pitiless heart?

AHI CHE NON VI E PIÙ SPENE
Ah, that there is no longer hope

DI RIVEDER IL NOSTRO AMATO BENE!
of seeing once again our well-beloved!

DEH MORTE, DANNE AITA:
Oh death, give us help:

UCCIDI QUESTA VITA;
kill this life!

PIETOSA NE FERISCI E UN COLPO SOLO
in pity strike us, and let a single blow

A LA VITA DIA FIN ET AL GRAN DUOLO.
put an end to life and to great sorrow!

(B): a stanza of unknown authorship set in five-voiced polyphony by Carlo Gesualdo (c. 1561-1613), a wealthy prince who published the work himself at his estate outside Naples in 1611. In this admittedly extreme example the reserved tone has yielded to emotional outbursts, and the decorous images have vanished. More important, however, is the dramatic quality of the words: the poet speaks like an actor on a stage. The search for a musical texture appropriate for dramatic declamation led composers to abandon equal-voice polyphony at the end of the Renaissance in favor of a single melody or duet supported by chords and a bass line. Text and translation (adapted) are from Davison and Apel 1949: no. 161.

heard throughout the music and "through" used to be spelled "thorough." The chords could be sounded by a single player using an appropriate instrument such as an organ, harpsichord, or lute, and changing the rhythm of the harmony to support whatever rhythmic nuances the text called for and the singer chose. Such flexibility is beyond the limits of contrapuntal polyphony, where the melodies of several musicians have to fit together and therefore require relatively rigid timing.

Thoroughbass style made possible a new musical entertainment: opera. The example in Figure 60, a vocal line with instrumental bass, comes from the first opera ever performed, *Euridice* by Jacopo Peri (1561-1633), composed at Florence for the wedding of Maria de' Medici, a daughter of the ruling family, to King Henry IV of France in October of 1600.

FIGURE 60: THOROUGHBASS STYLE. *This pictorial notation shows the beginning of Orfeo's lament for his dead wife Euridice. It is from the first Western European opera,* Euridice, *composed by Jacopo Peri in 1600 for performance at the marriage of Maria de' Medici of Florence to King Henry IV of France. For a general explanation of pictorial notation see the caption for Figure 4.*

Using standard notation Peri wrote down only his vocal melody and his bass line—the parts represented here as solid black horizontals—and placed occasional symbols under the bass line to clarify precisely what harmonies he had in mind. From just this much information an instrumentalist could tell what harmonies to play and when to play them. The chording instrument most likely to be used was a harpsichord, lute, or harp. Peri himself does not tell us, because it was not yet the fashion for composers to specify instrumental timbres; although the quality of musical sound was as important then as now, it was the responsibility of those who arranged for a performance.

The broad, hatched horizontals represent the pitch levels of the harmonies called for by Peri's notation as it has been reported by Nino Pirrotta (1968: 68). Below the bass line, I have summarized each harmony in numeral notation, as I did in Figure 55. A sharp (#) following one of these numerals means the pitch indicated by the numeral should be raised.

An opera is a play couched entirely in music. Plays were a well-known medium of expression in the streets, courts, and religious houses of 16th-century Italy. Their staging was often elaborate, involving, for example, the use of the revolving stage, which Leonardo da Vinci had invented at least as early as 1490. Plays had often included solo songs, choruses, and dances, but never a musical accompaniment lasting from beginning to end, because until the end of the 16th century the necessary musical flexibility was not available. The new texture solved this problem.

In northern Italy, where thoroughbass style developed, money was power, and the rich celebrated their authority by sponsoring theatrical events of all kinds, especially on the occasion of a wedding. When Maria de' Medici married, her

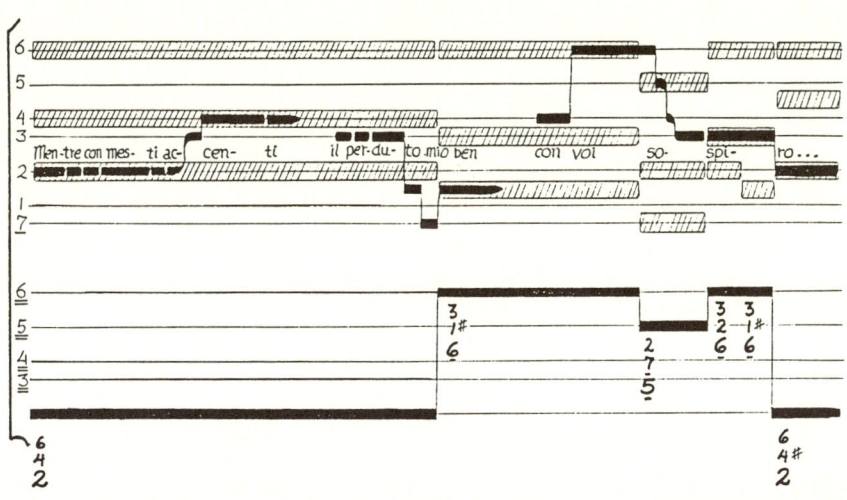

One may play any of the pitch levels of Peri's harmonies at any suitable octave. Here I have gathered them as closely as possible in the same range as the voice to show that they sometimes disagree with the sung pitches. Such dissonance enlivens the music and emphasizes the emotional content of the words. Note, for example, the dissonant treatment of all but the last syllable in the phrase "il perduto mio ben (my lost beloved)."

father, Grand Duke Ferdinando I, marked the event with a five-hour opera staged in a hall three quarters the length of a football field and half as wide. This hall could hold an audience of over three thousand, and behind the scenes more than a thousand men were used just to run the stage machinery. Peri's *Euridice* was staged on the same occasion in a much smaller hall by a noble of lesser rank, Jacopo Corsi. Although both presentations were couched entirely in music, the smaller work happened to be performed a few days before the larger one and thus it became the first Western opera.

The components of Peri's music for *Euridice* were not new. Chordal thinking was well advanced by his time, as I've shown, and even using a bass melody by itself to stand for a series of chords was commonplace.* Solo declamatory singing was also an old idea—the Roman Catholic Church had been using a flexible melodic style for recitation since before the Middle Ages. Indeed, some of those attending the first performance of *Euridice* complained (Palisca 1963: 351) "that the music was tedious, that it seemed like the chanting of the Passion" heard every Easter when the biblical account of Christ's crucifixion was sung in Roman Catholic services.

Music and theater had always had a close association, but in the last quarter of the 16th century the atmosphere of conspicuous consumption dominating the arts of northern Italy stimulated many ideas for bringing these two old companions together in new ways. Peri's vocal melody may have seemed too much like Catholic chant, but the overall effect of his music

---

*I mentioned in the note on p. 307 that dances and improvised songs used such bass lines. So did church musicians. Religious polyphony was published during the 16th century in the form of partbooks—that is, in a set of books each of which held all the music for just one "part" or vocal line. There was no book in which all the parts were brought together. For organists to accompany the singers, a bass line was written out consisting of the lowest sounds to be heard in the piece from moment to moment, whether they were the notes sung by the basses or the notes of some higher part. From this continuous bass (it paused only when all voices paused) the organist could construct appropriate supporting harmonies. Such bass lines appeared in print in the last decade of the 16th century (Arnold 1965: 6).

was novel: the projection of dramatic narration and dialogue in a flexible texture of bass line, vocal line, and supporting chords. His idea received at once the attention it deserved: several of his contempories claimed credit for it, and a general interest in his opera prompted its publication not just once but twice.

The old polyphony did not die out. Composers continued to use it in church music, instrumental ensembles, and pieces for solo keyboard, or for creating music with a thick texture and a fixed mood, music such as the massive choruses with which the acts of an opera usually ended. You often hear the old polyphony in modern works, as a matter of fact. The technique is a permanent addition to the Western tradition.

The appearance of thoroughbass style marks for historians of music the beginning of a new phase of the modern period called "Baroque." They apply this term to developments from 1600 to 1720. While the old polyphony never died, it became of secondary importance compared to thoroughbass music. And while instruments of mellow voice lingered on because they were well suited to the balanced sound of the old polyphony, they became of secondary importance compared to instruments of shriller timbre, which were better suited to perform a prominent tune or duet against a supporting bass. Thus the soft-sounding viol yielded to the louder violin, and the bore of the Renaissance recorder, a vertical flute, was altered to make the piercing upper part of its range more playable.

The new sound proved attractive and appropriate not only in opera but in all kinds of art music, from dances and light songs to serious works. The style spread quickly throughout Western Europe. As an old and conservative London musician lamented in 1676,

> ... our Great Care was, to have All the Parts Equally Heard; ... This Caution made the Musick Lovely, and very Contentive.
> But now the Modes and Fashions have cry'd These Things down, and set up a Great Idol in their

> Room; observe with what a Wonderful Swiftness They now run over their Brave New Ayres; and with what High-Prized Noise, ... which is rather fit to make a Mans Ears Glow, and fill his Brains full of Frisks, &c. than to Season, and Sober his Mind, or Elevate his Affection to Goodness.
>
> *(Mace 1958: 236)*

We still prefer our "brave new ayres" to any other kind of music. The entire repertoire of rock, for example, uses Baroque texture. Country-and-western music, which now commands the full musical attention of a majority of our AM radio stations, falls short of fully developed Baroque texture only to the extent its bass notes fail to form a melody. We remain addicted, as audiences of the Baroque were addicted, to the combination of a prominent tune, a supporting bass, and a solid stream of rhythmic harmonies. The bulk of our musical expression today is essentially the same as our forebears enjoyed almost four hundred years ago.

Part Four: Form

14

The Nature of Form

To create art is to manipulate space and time, the basic dimensions of life. Art is therefore not far removed from the experience of life itself. A thin line, perhaps only an imaginary one, separates sculpture from the objects and enclosures of everyday life, mime and dance from everyday motion, acting from everyday social intercourse, and literature from our everyday use of language.

The traditional artist creates a work of art by extracting an aspect of life from its surroundings and giving it sufficiently rich and self-contained content to make it complete in itself. One sees a brooch, for example, so finely worked that it serves its owner better as an object to be admired than as a clasp;* one sees everyday motions, enlarged and refined, speak a language of their own in ballet; one hears common words put together with uncommon effectiveness on the stage.

---

*The fact that many works of art are also tools tends to obscure their aesthetic worth. Art galleries in New York City only recently began exhibiting ceramics, for example, and it will surely be a long time before they include axe handles and dental equipment in their displays. But tools often have a content sufficiently rich and self-contained to qualify as art. They rarely do so because it is the custom to apply questionable criteria such as uselessness—the vague idea that an object cannot be accepted as art if we all know that its primary purpose is to accomplish some physical task. Such thinking trivializes art, demoting it from an aesthetic experience to a sign of social status by telling us that one should possess art not because one needs it but because one can afford it.

To isolate a facet of life and turn it into a rich and self-sufficient experience is difficult, for without supporting context an action or impression loses much of its coherence. Some artists solve this problem at its source: they refuse to isolate a work of art from its natural context. They mount sculptures and paintings incorporating everyday materials untransformed; they stage "happenings" that consist of the actions and exchanges of life itself; they make music with as little formal structure as possible and welcome the chance intrusion of other sounds. On the other hand, some artists create a more isolated art. Their more traditional approach forces them to build self-sufficiency into their work by strengthening its form: that is, by increasing the cohesiveness of the parts and by extending the whole.

The Cohesiveness of the Parts

Any event or spatial effect has a natural cohesiveness simply because it occupies an undivided time and place in the life of the perceiver and displays a restricted content. Take the view along a beach, for example. In a single span of time we see a single scene, and the contents of that scene are restricted: we would never imagine that they constitute a page of print or an automobile engine because their variety is limited. The same argument applies to what we hear. Sounds have the same degree of natural cohesiveness. We hear the sounds of a neighborhood as we stand in a single place through a single span of time. The sounds may occur randomly, but they have a group identity due not only to this unity of time and place but also to their limited variety. Thus a person can often distinguish one neighborhood from another by sound alone. To give a strictly musical example, any village band will sound to residents of the village like their village band regardless of what pieces are played.

Fig. 61   Figure 61 (opposite) has nice pictures: one can imagine coming upon them in a museum of modern art and mistaking them for products of conscious human effort. Each of them "makes a statement," as people in the art world are fond of saying; in other words, they have cohesiveness. They are not the direct result of human artistry, however. They were generated by computers programmed to display a certain kind of mark in random distribution. Their cohesiveness results from our viewing each of them at a single moment in time, recognizing that each fills a single space, and sensing that each contains a severely limited variety of shapes and colors.

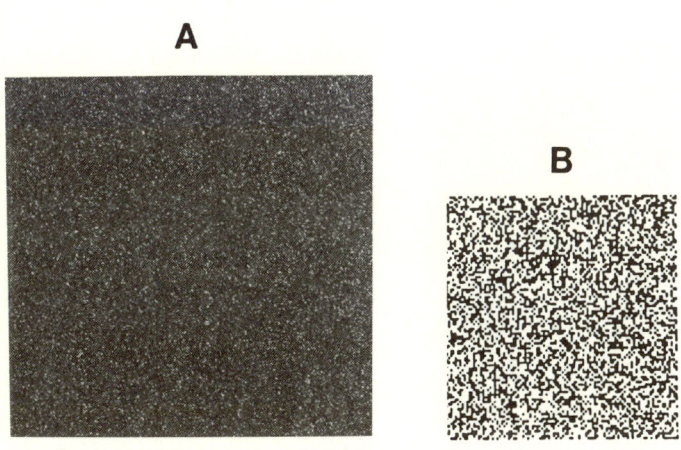

FIGURE 61: NATURAL COHESIVENESS: *These two pictures demonstrate the natural cohesiveness of randomly distributed marks restricted to a single space, a single span of attention, and a small range of variation in size, shape, and color.*

(A): a computer-generated random distribution of marks varying in size but free of clustering. The astronomer Edward J. Groth and his colleagues used this picture in a series allowing visual evaluation of various mathematical models for the clustering of galaxies in the universe (Groth et al. 1977: 96).

(B): a computer-generated random distribution of marks of unvaried size allowed to cluster and thus to form larger marks of varied size and shape. Bela Julesz of the Bell Laboratories used such pictures to investigate the role of the brain in constructing impressions of depth from visual stimuli (Julesz 1971: 21).

The natural cohesiveness of a work is increased by the interest the work arouses. Patterns—that is, the larger forms created by relationships among groups of items—arouse interest. In the computer pictures of Figure 61 patterns exercise only a weak influence, being in A practically non-existent and in B so abundant and diverse that they cancel each other out. Figure 62 provides, below and opposite, examples of simpler, stronger patterning; as you can see, such relationships generate interest that in turn generates additional cohesiveness.

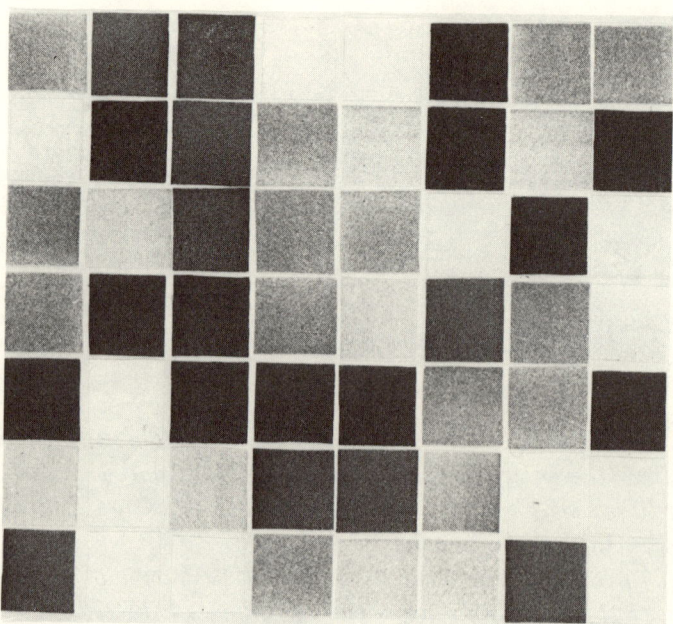

FIGURE 62: THE COHESIVE EFFECT OF PATTERNS. *These two pictures show that the added interest provided by patterns can increase a work's natural cohesiveness.*

(A): tiling on a washroom floor in Stetson University College of Law in Gulfport, Florida. Five degrees of shading have been used to represent the five shades of warm brown in the original flooring. The mind perceives identities and differences among the pieces, compares

The concepts discussed above apply to music as well as art. The natural cohesiveness of time, place, and restricted content lend unity, for example, to the work of a musician of India improvising upon a single instrument and using the materials of a single mode. But to command the attention of an audience for an hour or more, as described in the next chapter, the musician increases the impression of unity by generating patterns. On a small scale they create musical rhythm; on a larger scale, musical form.

B

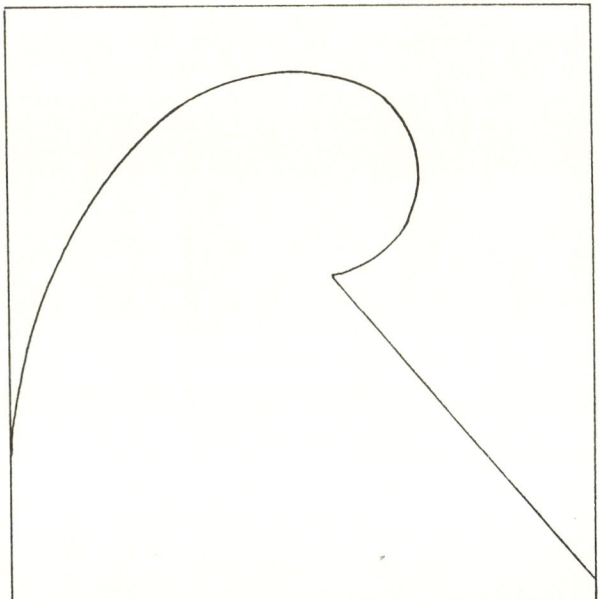

locations and distances, and thereby senses larger relationships (patterns). The effect of patterning is stronger here than in Figure 61-B on p. 321 because the mix here is simpler.

(B): my own drawing. The space within the square is more powerfully unified when divided by the line I have introduced than when left blank: the line arouses our interest by generating shapes we can compare, and comparing them brings them together.

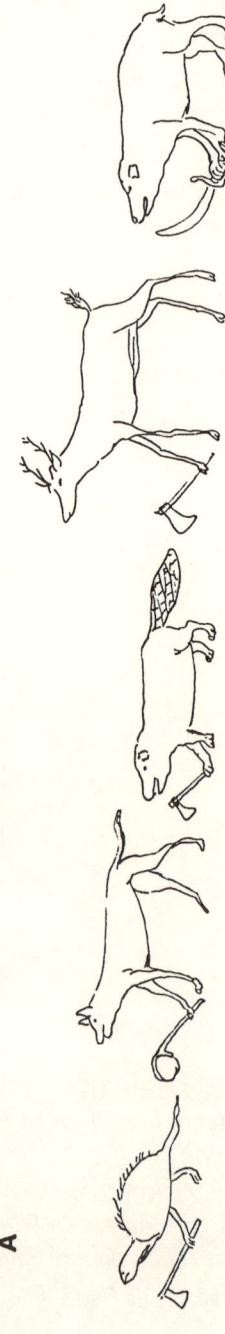
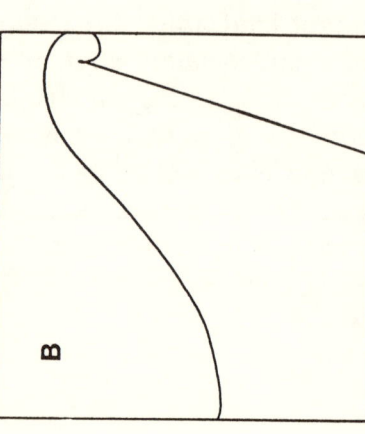

FIGURE 63: THE EXPANSIVE EFFECT OF PATTERNS.
These two drawings show that patterns can increase the breadth of a work by extending its content beyond what one can perceive.

(A): a series of armed animals, each representing one of the matriarchal clans of the Seneca people of New York State, as recorded by a Jesuit missionary in 1666 (Billard 1974: 116-117). As arranged here, the five figures seem to be part of a longer procession; thus the picture extends beyond itself.

(B): my own drawing, in which the obvious incompleteness of the enclosed figure suggests that it ought to be extended past the right edge of the frame.

The Extension of the Whole

Patterns can expand the breadth of a work as well as add cohesiveness to it. They expand it by implying a further set of impressions as yet unperceived. On the opposite page a simple succession of different items of a single type (Figure 63-A) leads the observer to expect additional different items of the same type. By presenting a single item incomplete Figure 63-B encourages the observer to imagine extending the picture to complete it. Both situations occur in music, the one as we listen to successive verses of a hymn, for example, and the other when a more or less predictable flow of sound stops or changes direction unexpectedly.

Fig. 63

Repeating patterns have the same effect as the non-repeating patterns discussed above: they enhance a work's natural cohesiveness and, by encouraging the observer to anticipate further material, they expand the breadth of the experience. Figure 64 below shows the expansive effect of repeating patterns and its musical analog should be clear: just as one can imagine what tiles will appear when the figure is extended upward and to the right, so one can anticipate what sounds the snare drums of a marching band will play when their pattern is extended for another cycle.

Fig. 64

A musical form is a large pattern, an impression of broad

FIGURE 64: THE EXPANSIVE EFFECT OF REPETITION. *The tiles in this picture create light and dark groups resembling the capital letter T. They form a repeating pattern giving one the impression of viewing one part of the whole. Thus present experience expands beyond the confines of the picture in whatever direction one perceives the pattern to be moving.*

relationships among groups of sounds. We receive the impression by comparing now with then—the present moment of sound with moments gone by—on a large scale. The comparison not only enhances the cohesiveness of the musical experience but enlarges it, implying further experiences that will complete or extend what has already happened. This implication is particularly strong when the form of the whole is known in advance. There are four basic relationships that generate musical form.

The Strophic Relationship

The simplest musical form is strophic, a repetition of the same material over and over. Representing the repeated material with a capital letter A we can diagram strophic relationships as follows:

$$A \ A \ A \ A \ A \ \ldots$$

The indication is not entirely accurate, however, because strophic music is never a series of exact repetitions. Thus each stanza of a hymn carries different words; a fiddler varies the melody of a country dance while playing it over and over to accompany the dancers; and repetition in the patterns of high-pitched West African ensemble instruments is relieved by variation in the patterns of lower-pitched instruments accompanying them. Therefore the letter series above is accurate only as a general representation of strophic form; marks indicating variations should be added to make the series an accurate representation of a particular case,* as for example in the following:

$$A \ A' \ A \ A'' \ A' \ \ldots$$

---

*In practice the use of such marks depends on the circumstances of the analysis. One does not need them to make the point that a certain popular song is strophic, for example, whereas even the most general outline of a set of variations requires them.

The Serial Relationship

When the successive portions of a different piece are different rather than variants of the same material, we say they have a serial relationship, diagrammed as a series of different letters:

$$A \quad B \quad C \quad D \quad E \quad ...$$

This series does not describe the form accurately, however, because each new portion, though different, always shares some features with what has gone before. Such a piece is like a soap opera in which new circumstances follow old while the main characters stay the same. The "main characters" in the piece of music are style and timbre: all the portions have the general style of the musical tradition in which they were composed, and they are all performed by sound sources proper to that tradition—a certain voice, the instruments of a particular ensemble, or whatever the case might be. To some degree other features, such as meter, harmonic coloring, or even melody, may also be shared. In short, serial form would be more accurately represented if a common sign standing for these common features were added to the letter series above, thus:

$$A^x \quad B^x \quad C^x \quad D^x \quad E^x \quad ...$$

Such a sign is usually not added; the elements of continuity in a serial relationship are understood rather than stated.

The serial extension of music is sometimes given a "tighter" form—that is, later portions are more closely bound to earlier ones—by the insertion of a refrain, thus:

$$A \quad B \quad C \quad r \quad D \quad E \quad r \quad F \quad ...$$

An occasional and brief refrain does not interfere with the main impression of serial relationship among the successive portions. When, however, the refrain equals or surpasses the other portions in importance, one's impression is of a rondo rather than a serial relationship.

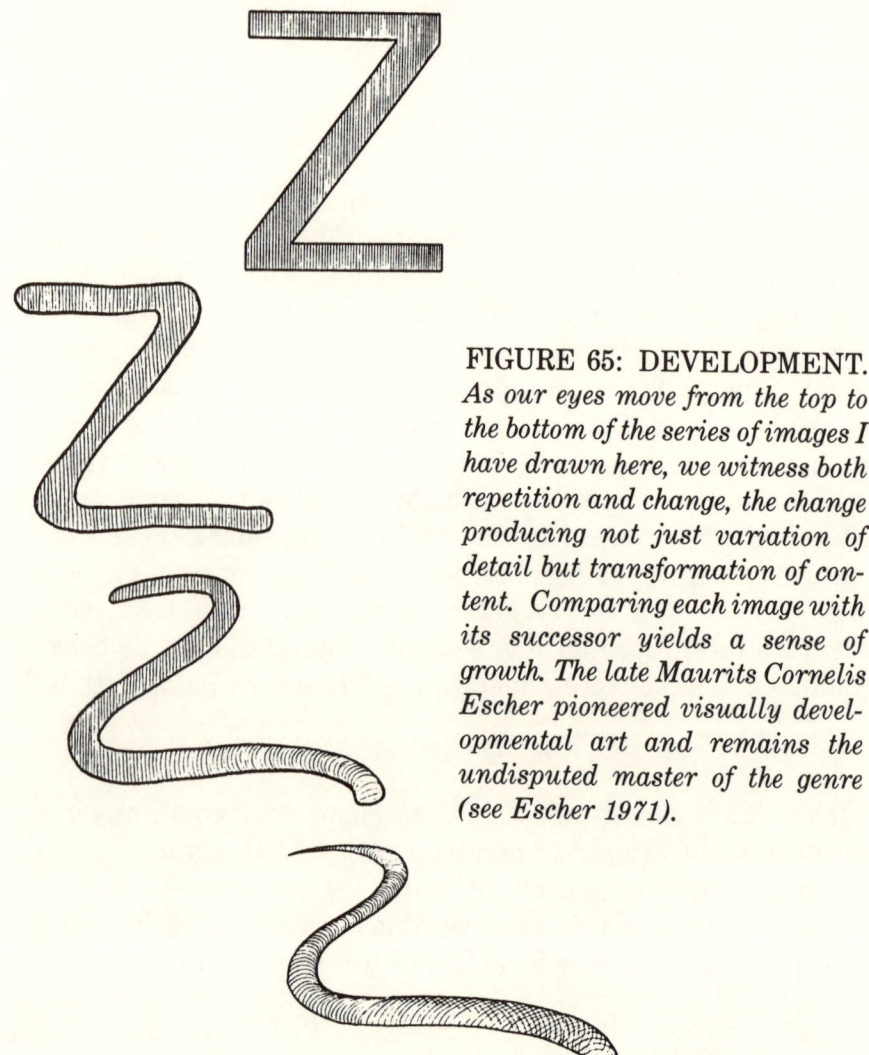

FIGURE 65: DEVELOPMENT. *As our eyes move from the top to the bottom of the series of images I have drawn here, we witness both repetition and change, the change producing not just variation of detail but transformation of content. Comparing each image with its successor yields a sense of growth. The late Maurits Cornelis Escher pioneered visually developmental art and remains the undisputed master of the genre (see Escher 1971).*

The Rondo Relationship

Music in rondo form represents new material in alternation with material heard earlier. Stated as a general case the formal outline of a rondo relationship is:

A B A C A D A E . . .

The outline need not be so long. For example, 18th-century operatic *arias* are typically solo songs in two contrasting sections, the first of which is repeated at the end to give the soloist a chance to improvise some virtuoso decorations. The letter series outlining this relationship is:

A B A′

Longer rondo forms are sometimes tightened up by letting the final portions mirror the opening ones:

A B A C A B A

Sometimes the refrain may even cease to occupy a separate section of the music after its initial presentation and instead appear from time to time as part of the flow of sound in what is basically a serial form:

$$A \quad B \xrightarrow{(A)} C \xrightarrow{(A)(A)} D \xrightarrow{(A)} E \xrightarrow{(A)(A)(A)} \ldots$$

The Developmental Relationship

The fourth and final kind of formal relationship is developmental, in which the members of a series are outgrowths of each other or of a single member. More than variation is involved, as you can see opposite (Figure 65), because differences between members are more than superficial: that is, the basic outline and content also change. The difference between variation and development becomes clear if one looks at the photographs in a

Fig. 65

(1) Where have all the flow-ers gone,
    5   6   5   4   3   2   1
                                 ..

(2) Long time pass-ing?
    1̱   2̄   7-6 5
    ...   ..

(3) Where have all the flow-ers gone,
    5   6   5   4   3   2   1
                                 ..

(4) Long time a-go?
    4   4   3   2
    ..   ....

(5) Where have all the flow-ers gone?
    5   6   5   4   3   2   1
                                 ..

(6) Young girls picked them, ev-'ry one.
    1̄   1̄   2̄   1̄   7   6   5
                                 ...

(7) When will they ev-er learn?
    6   4   2   1   3   5
                             ...

(8) When will they ev-er learn?
    6   4   3   2   1   1
                    ...   .

FIGURE 66: SIMULTANEOUS MUSICAL FORMS. *The eight lines of text represent the eight phrases constituting the first stanza of the song* Where Have All the Flowers Gone? *by Pete Seeger (Fall River Music, Inc.: piano-vocal arrangement, sheet music), which was widely sung in the 1960's. For a general explanation of numeral notation see pp. 45-46.*

Every stanza has the same tune and so the form of the music, considered on the broadest time scale, is strophic. But the tune itself, and therefore the music of each separate stanza, is a rondo (the refrain occurs at line 1, line 3, and line 5). Moreover, within each stanza we find the second half cast in serial form and, within the second half, a suggestion of strophic variation in the last two lines.

As for development, compare lines 2 and 6—sing them, that is, giving every numeral one count (except where two or more dots beneath a numeral tell you to give it two or more counts). You may feel the similarity of lines 2 and 6 strongly enough to call them simply variants of one another. To me, the greater activity of line 6 and its four strong beats seem to create a new melodic contour in which I hear only a faint echo of line 2. The close relationship revealed by comparing the two sets of numerals surprises me. My impression in performance is that the content of line 2 is not repeated in line 6 but is transformed.

THE NATURE OF FORM

family album: pictures of an adult in various poses and costumes taken during the period of a month or so illustrate variation; pictures of the same person from infancy to maturity illustrate development. The following chapter discusses development as a technique used in the classic music of India.

The musical relationships I have outlined usually occur in combination with one another. Thus a classical symphony generates serial form by presenting the listener with a succession of four contrasting pieces, called "movements," but at the same time generates other forms within each movement: one will be a rondo, perhaps, and another a set of variations and therefore strophic, and so forth. Within each section of these smaller forms, moreover, still other forms may be used: the refrain of the rondo may, itself, have a serial form, and one member of that series may be strophic. Figure 66 on the opposite page illustrates the presence of several formal relationships at the same time in a single song.

Fig. 66

15

Developmental Form in the Art Music of India

"High" Cultures

Westerners began discussing non-Western music centuries ago, when their governments started building colonial empires and sending out educated men to take charge of the work. These leaders listened to the music of other cultures with the expectations of the art-music audience to which they belonged at home; and as representatives of a superior, aggressive force, they listened with the arrogance of colonials. In 1557, for example, the Calvinist minister Jean de Léry heard a chorus of five or six hundred "savage men" near what is now Rio de Janeiro and wrote:

> [G]iven that they do not know what the art of music is, those who have not heard them would never believe that they could sing so well.
> *(Harrison 1973: 22)*

By the middle of the 20th century Western attitudes had changed little. Leading ethnomusicologists like the late Curt Sachs no longer denied the musical artistry of non-Westerners but, on the other hand, would not grant that it was fully developed. He and most of his colleagues and students continued to uphold the core of de Léry's colonialism by insisting on an evolutionist interpretation of culture: that it evolves over the ages along a single path, "rising" from crude and simple beginnings to the pinnacle of refinement and complexity found in Western art music. The natural corollary of this view is that the musical progress of "lesser" cultures is best judged by Western art musicians, for they stand furthest along the way that all must follow.

The surprising tenacity of Western arrogance in musical matters has been due in no small part to the balance of power in the world. From the Renaissance to the 1950's Western Europeans were able to impose economic and often political control upon every people they encountered; other cultures did indeed seem like lesser cultures when measured by the authority they wielded.* Today, however, that balance of power is changing, and Western intellectual assumptions are changing along with it. Most scholars now view non-Western music not as a primitive form of Western music but as something different which can enrich their musical understanding.†

The court music of India has interested ethnomusicologists for a long time. To those of the old school it belonged to a select group of traditions offering peculiar respectability because they were patronized by the wealthy, like Western art music, and were accompanied, like Western art music, by a complex body of theory developed by intellectuals within the tradition. The court music of the Middle East, China, and Japan belonged

---

*It is interesting to note that when Western Europeans did not wield authority over another people—when they lived among them as traders or missionaries, as in India in the 18th century—they did not look down on the cultural expression of their hosts.

†Other musics do sometimes contribute to our understanding of earlier Western art-music practice. For example, the way soloists sing the Psalms in a Greek orthodox service goes far to explain how the harmonies of Léonin and Pérotin were probably performed in 12th-century Paris (see pp. 179, 179n). For a second example, drone harmony played on bagless pipes without pausing for breath can be observed in folk performances today all around the rim of the Mediterranean and on through the Middle East to India (see p. 149 for a brief explanation of the technique), which lends strong support to the hints already found in instrumental construction (see p. 201) that medieval tunes were accompanied by drone harmony long before the bag was added to the bagpipe in the 12th century.

to this group and, along with that of India, was commonly referred to by evolutionists as "high" musical culture. The term "high" implied that these traditions were just a pace or two behind Western art music: they were highly developed but had not yet come to use harmony, counterpoint, or notation the way we did.

In the court music of India, for example, Western theorists looking for scales, a favorite Western concept, could find them in abundance. Indian theorists had even divided the octave into twenty-two intervals, ten more than the West uses, in an attempt to account for the melodic variety. For rhythm, too, there was a well-ordered intellectual framework more elaborate than anything the West had developed. Indian harmony, however, consisted of drones and heterophony and seemed to ethnomusicologists of the old school more like accidental effects than deliberate artistry; and they saw that Indian written notation, though ancient and more schematic than our own, was seldom used and had less authority than aural tradition. Thus these Westerners concluded that the West enjoyed a superior music that had moved "beyond" drones to a rich variety of chords and "beyond" aural tradition to musical literacy.

Music as Religion

Many of today's scholars are attracted to Indian music because it offers appealing sound and technical challenge. They do not concern themselves with the relative standing of a culture but submit to the training and standards of an Indian teacher for the insight such discipline might force upon them. Theirs is not a colonial attitude.*

Some of these scholars have been drawn as well to the mystical elements of Indian music, to the view of life it embodies. This aspect has also appealed to people more interested in

---

*Some of the early scholars also advocated learning by participating. Noteworthy among them was the late Percival Kirby of South Africa who said this was "the only way, in my opinion, for a European observer to learn and understand . . ." (Kirby 1968: vii)

states of consciousness than in musical perception. But when Professor Elise Barnett of the City College of New York brought the Indian instrumentalist Rāvi Shankar* to her campus in the fall of 1967, he made the Indian point of view perfectly clear:

> Most of my [American] admirers are young people and I don't want to hurt them. But I am hurt by the association of drugs with our music. Our music is very pure. It is religion, the quickest way to reach God. I don't like someone to sit glassy-eyed at my concert, listening through a haze of his own world. All I ask is a few hours of sobriety and clear-headedness.
> *(Lester 1967: D-21, column 7)*

Every lover of Western music, from jazz buff to opera fan, would second this plea for attentive listening, and some might accept the mention of religion as a valid analogy.

But Shankar was not making an analogy. Traditionally, the music he plays is not *like* a religious expression; it *is* a religious expression, recognized as such by both musicians and society. Thus among the students of the North Indian musician Amjad Ali Khan of New Delhi (see the map on page 337), there were in the early 1970's "two young men ... sent by their native village to master the art of music and thus help their community to worship God in a fitting way" (Higgins 1972: 58). In South India† the traditional view was that

---

*In writing Sanskrit or Sanskrit-derived words with Roman letters one usually places the long sign, a horizontal stroke, over certain vowels not to stress them but to change their sound. Thus "a" has the sound of the vowel in "cut," but "ā" has the sound of the vowel in "balm"; "i" is pronounced as in the word "bit," but "ī" as in the word "elite"; "u" is pronounced as in the word "bull," but "ū" as in the word "rule." The letter "o" always has the sound it carries in the word "go" and may or may not carry the long sign, depending on who writes it.

†North and South India have somewhat different musical traditions. New ideas, styles, and instruments entered India in the North; in the South the older musical ways have tended to be preserved.

> only the musician who had recognized the worthlessness of worldly things, and who knew right from wrong, and who was faithful to tradition could effectively make music. Support for such music came from Hindu communities as a matter of religious duty and honour and within the context of traditional religious practice and obligation.
>
> *(Ries 1969: 28)*

Chanting and hymn singing have been a part of Hindu religious ritual since the early Vedic period on the subcontinent, probably around 1500 B.C. But nonritual Hindu religious music is also very old, going back at least as far as the beginning of *bhakti* in the 7th century A.D. This form of Hindu worship, stressing personal salvation, is still widely practiced. In it the individual seeks union with God many ways, such as meditating, chanting, singing, or repeating the name of God over and over.

Early saintly members of the *bhakti* movement include Purandara Dasa (1484-1564), considered the father of the South Indian classical style. He sang for the Hindu court at Vijayanagar (located not far above the horizontal line marking 10° north in Figure 67 opposite). When the kingdom of Vijayanagar fell to Moslem invaders from North India in 1565, many Hindus migrated south some 400 miles to the protection of the Hindu court at Thanjavur, a city on the delta flats of the Cauvery River just north of the tip of Sri Lanka (Ceylon). There the courtly tradition of Vijayanagar and the religious tradition of *bhakti* were combined with the musical practice of the southeast itself, where musical notation had been carved into rocks as early as the 7th century A.D. Today's South Indian classical repertoire consists mainly of the works of three musicians born about the same time in a town just east of Thanjavur: Syāmā Sāstrī (1763-1827), Tyāgarāja (1767-1817), and Muttuswāmi Dīkshitar (1775-1835).

The demands of politics and religious devotion rarely coincide. Under the patronage of a princely court the South Indian musician was caught between the royal demand for

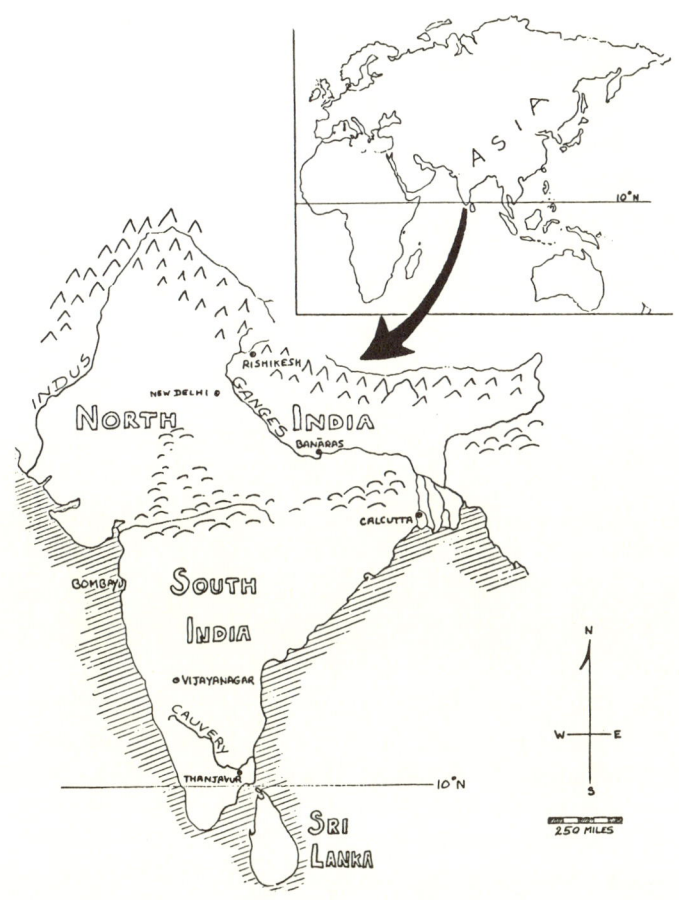

FIGURE 67: A SIMPLIFIED MAP OF INDIA: *The upper figure shows the location of the Indian subcontinent in Asia. The lower figure shows the main features of the area, omitting political boundaries.*

The most prominent feature of North India is a vast plain stretching from the Indus River to the mouth of the Ganges River, bordered on the north by the highest mountains in the world, the Himalayas, and on the south by lesser ranges rising to the high, triangular plateau that is South India.

The distinction between North and South India is cultural, like that between our own North and South: new peoples, new ideas, new musical instruments seem always to have entered the country through the North, while the South has remained the repository of older traditions.

praise and entertainment and society's demand that musicians use their gifts to serve God. Western musicians do not have this particular problem. Although we control our worship music firmly, we don't expect our musicians to be saints or even to tend in a saintly direction. South Indians do, or at least did until quite recently. Tyāgarāja set an example, refusing the patronage of the court at Thanjavur and supporting himself by singing for alms. Even today lucrative work such as supplying the music for India's huge film industry still carries with it a certain stigma.*

The Forces of Change

India freed itself from British domination during the first half of this century, pressing for more and more autonomy in the legislative process and using its strategic importance in World War II to bargain for independence. Independence was achieved in 1947, and in the period between 1947 and 1949 the various princely states were merged with the rest of the country and their courts dissolved. Thus the musicians who had served those courts had to win a new audience for themselves.

The court-music audience had been a small and well-informed gathering of aristocrats willing to grant whatever amount of time the performers might need for their presentation and ready to give them dependable financial support. The sound of the music was quiet, the effects subtle, understood by all as an expression of devotion to God and, in that context only, as entertainment. The courts patronizing classical music were never many, and the number of performers active at any one period was small.

In the second half of the 20th century the princely court has

---

*The pressure of public opinion has not imposed religious constraints on musicians of the North as severely as on those of the South. Thus Ram Sahay (1798-?1844) established himself as the greatest drummer of his age with seven days of spectacular display at the coronation of a prince in the holy city of Banaras (Benares) and accepted from the prince two necklaces of emerald, two of diamond, 400,000 rupees, four elephants, jewelry of gold, and bolts of silk cloth (Roach 1972: 31).

been replaced by concert societies, film studios, record companies, and All India Radio. These institutions are willing to pay for music in the prestigious classical style, but performances must hold the attention of a large and busy audience. An observer reported in 1976 that

> twenty years ago one could hear the great singer Ariakudi Ramanuja Ayyengar, accompanied on the violin* by Papa Venkataramiah, singing continuous free-rhythmic improvisation . . . for one-and-a-half hours, and this within a concert of seven hours' duration. Today concerts average only two-and-a-half to three hours, and the performer must try to accommodate his audience by singing as great a variety of items as possible.
> *(Higgins 1976: 22)*

Under the demands of a new audience the quality of musical performance has also changed. A former director of All India Radio has characterized this change from the performer's point of view:

> In a room, one talks, converses. On the platform one lectures. The informality, the intimacy, the personal direct quality of civilized conversation gives way . . .
> *(Menon 1957: 72)*

Novel instrumental combinations have been introduced, and some of the larger traditional instruments are being modified to survive better the rigors of the concert circuit. The microphone, now a standard part of the concert scene, will undoubtedly influence musical style more and more.

---

*The Western instrument, introduced when the British ruled India, proved to be a perfect vehicle for the classical melodic style. The Indian musician plays it while seated cross-legged, the peg box braced against the instep of the right foot and the tail piece braced against the chest. The positions of the fingering and bowing hands are as Westerners know them. In North India the violin is a solo instrument; in South India it is mainly an ensemble instrument.

The livelihood of musicians has become insecure. They have been forced to exchange the dependable support of a leisured class for the uncertain possibility of winning favor at the box office; in addition, many more of them are competing for that favor than ever circulated in aristocratic circles, because the new audience is so much larger than that of the courts. This job insecurity has affected the training of musicians. Formerly the music student was an apprentice:

> The *gurukula* ("preceptor-family") system of musical education traditionally called for at least ten years of full-time commitment to the study of music, during which the student tried to absorb the musical knowledge of his teacher. Even today, a music student who wishes to become a professional performer often lives with his teacher, helping him with household chores and in return absorbing his style and technique to the point of saturation. Sometimes the teacher accepts his student virtually as a son, and allows him to share meals and participate in other activities which would normally be restricted to members of the immediate family. During these years the student not only learns music in the same general style as his teacher, but tends also to assimilate the smallest mannerisms. The *gurukula* system is applicable not only to music, but to other fields of the arts, trades, and religion as well.
>
> *(Viswanathan 1977: 14-15)*

Today music students cannot afford to devote themselves solely to their master. The uncertainties of the music market persuade many to add to their studies the academic training necessary for a second profession. For example, T. Viswanathan, the professional flutist quoted above, also holds a Master of Arts degree in economics. Many students do not follow the *gurukula* system at all but learn their music in colleges and conservatories.

Thus far I have called the classical music of India "court music," not to suggest that it was strictly confined to the princely courts in the country—you will recall that Tyāgarāja himself sang in public for alms—but because it developed the leisurely style and resistance to change characteristic of those courts. But nowadays, as pointed out earlier, we find the leisurely style severely compressed and novelty and variety welcomed as sources of competitive advantage. Indian classical music is being forced to become popular music of a sort resembling our own art music, which the British scholar David Johnson has correctly described as evolving

> continuously and ruthlessly; one period hardly reaches maturity before it is undermined and superceded by the next. It changes beyond recognition in the space of two centuries, and considerably even during one person's lifetime, so that the pieces which any individual is taught in youth are likely to be outmoded by the time he dies. Only a very few works... survive to be heard by later generations.
> *(Johnson 1972: 87)*

I shall refer to the classical music of modern India as art music.

Rāga Ālāpana

Our first example illustrates an aspect of Indian art music well served by the *gurukula* system of prolonged apprenticeship: *rāga ālāpana*.

The general meaning of *rāga* is "that which is pleasing to the ear." The specific meaning is "melodic type"—that is, a restricted set of melodic behaviors (the Western equivalent, discussed on pp. 86-89, is "mode"). One *rāga* can generate an infinity of different tunes because the melodic restrictions are not upon the tunes' outlines but their details—such as allowed levels of pitch, characteristic melodic turns and phrase shapes, use of decoration, and placement of emphasis. Medieval Western singers, apprenticed for years to the aural tradition of European churches, were able to elaborate hundreds of songs from a few established behavioral sets (one of these sets is given a brief analysis on pp. 88-89). Modern folk singers learn and create the same way:

> Composers are not born with a knowledge of the possibilities of their tradition. Unless a composer be a mimic and a shuffler, he must, in order to innovate inside his tradition, have taken inside himself the instructions that tell him how to combine the elements without determining the final product. The blues singer is not born with a knowledge of blues style, though he may have been blessed with the capacity to acquire it. . . . [B]y listening to blues performance by others, . . . he has derived instructions which enable him to create new songs, within a tradition that encourages singers to do so.
> *(Titon 1977: 57)*

No one knows how many *rāgas* there are. According to eminent authorities in Bombay

> the number known to have been used is in the thousands, and there are performers who can reproduce hundreds of them. The popularity of certain *ragas*, however, tends to bring the effective number to a much lower figure, and many performers get along with not more than about fifty *ragas*.
> *(Boatwright 1960: 5)*

The origin of most *rāgas* is unknown. Details forming a *rāga* just seem to be bits and pieces of melodic behavior which have always travelled together. But occasionally one hears of a modern *rāga* invented by the performer himself, and no doubt most traditional *rāgas* were invented at some time in the past by Indian musicians or by Persian or Central Asian musicians serving the Muslim leaders who successfully invaded India at various times from the 11th century onwards.

Ālāpana means a rhythmically free melody that is improvised. One cannot learn improvisation in a college or lecture hall or conservatory practice room because the key ingredient is imagination, not rational organization or technical skill. But through the *gurukula* system or its equivalent a student has a chance to develop imagination. Immersed in the musical flow of the *rāgas* over a period of many years, the Indian apprentice absorbs the elements of each of them in their proper context, accumulating by osmosis* the basic stuff of imagination: experience.

Of course every member of society who can hear accumulates some of this experience. Patterns of appropriate melodic behavior are broadcast at large within a culture just like manners, modes of dress, and other aspects of group life. Thus when it comes time for the musician to perform for nonmusicians, the occasion is one of mutual understanding.† It should come as no surprise, then, to read that

> [s]ystematic training in the form of improvisation known as rāga ālāpana is traditionally inconceivable. . . . Older musicians, when questioned about how they were taught ālāpana, invariably reply: "I was never taught ālāpana, it just came

---

*My children seem to have acquired language much the same way, learning whole patterns of timing and inflection before the individuality and role of each word was understood. A linguist tries to comprehend a foreign phrase by understanding its components; a child learns its meaning by observing the results of the phrase when spoken as a unit. While the child eventually can produce correct sentences never heard before, the linguist is limited to mimicking existing constructions. Computers will be able to translate from one language into another only when their programs include not only the component words but the behavioral sets of each.

† I consider it a scandal in modern Western art music that so many fine composers have received for decades the financial support of universities and arts organizations while creating musical material so revolutionary and uncompromising that the general listener has not been able to assimilate it into the patterns of musical behavior appropriate to the culture. A concert of modern art music is not an occasion for mutual understanding, except within a very small circle, and has not been for almost seventy years. Had these same composers faced the general art-music public without institutional protection, their innovations would have been more gradual, and they would long ago, by a natural process, have led the art-music world out of its continuing preoccupation with 19th-century masters.

when I attempted it." Any South Indian music student, even a beginner, is capable of singing ālāpana to some extent, almost instinctively.

(Viswanathan 1977: 15)

To put the two terms together, *rāga ālāpana* is rhythmically free melody improvised to suit a particular melodic type. It may be played on an instrument or sung to vocables. Two performances of *ālāpana* in the same *rāga* by the same musician will not be the same. Certain phrases will surely recur—those that have become characteristic of the *rāga* over the years, for example—and if both performances function as introductions to the same precomposed song, anticipation of the song may inject further similarities. But otherwise the performance will sound different each time because the traditional fragments of the *rāga*—the "melodic bundle," as Bonnie C. Wade has aptly called them (Wade 1979: 170)—will have a unique presentation.

The example of *rāga ālāpana* analyzed for developmental form in Figure 68 was performed in the context of *bhakti*, an

FIGURE 68: DEVELOPMENT IN *RĀGA ĀLĀPANA*. *The first two phrases of a devotional song are given here in numerical notation together with a sample of melodic development derived from each by Swami Vidyananda on a plucked string instrument called the vīnā (they can be seen in Figure 69 on p. 347). For the numeral notation see pp. 45-46. The distance between numerals is a rough indication of duration, their relative size a rough indication of relative loudness. Horizontal lines indicate sustained tone; a slanted line or a bend in a horizontal line indicates a slide.*

Song Phrase 1 includes in its latter half a sequence of pitches the instrumentalist alters to produce what at first sounds like an entirely new idea. As you can see, however, this "new" idea really comprises the old idea in a new rhythm with only slight changes in the pitch sequence. The formal relationship between the two ideas is neither repetition, varied repetition, nor contrast; "growth" seems like the most appropriate term, the technical word for which is "development."

Song Phrase 2 provides with its first five pitches the basis for an extended melodic passage by the instrumentalist in which you can see

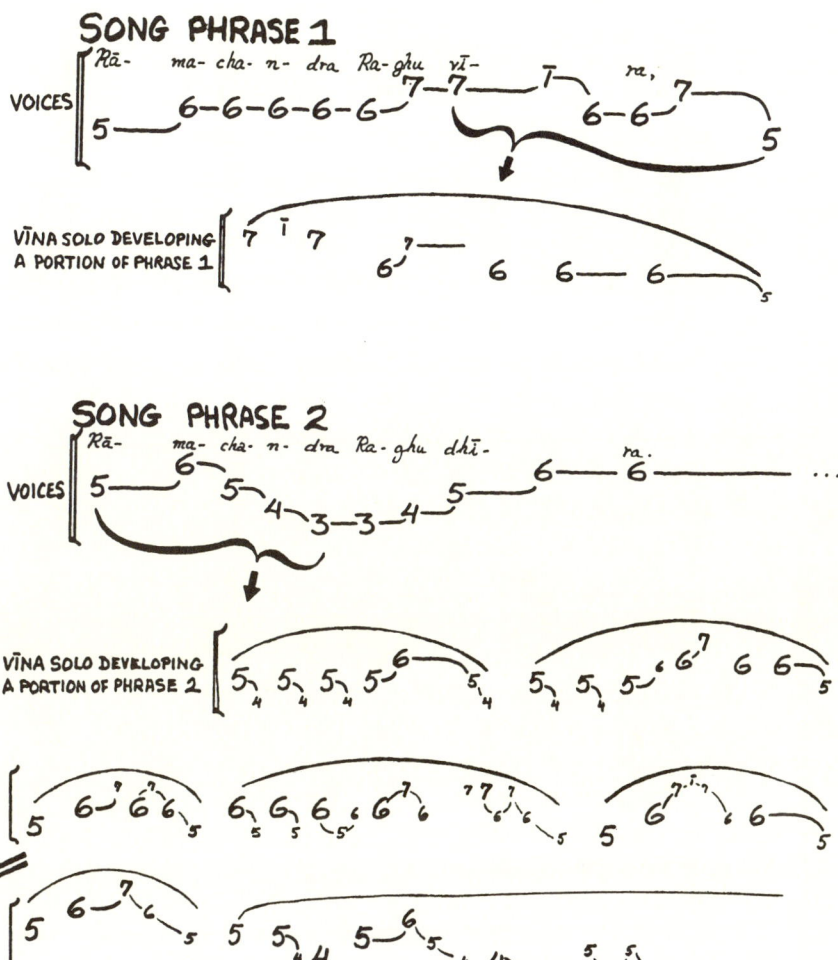

both the growth of new phrases and a tendency to explore the sonority of a single level of pitch through repetition. This exploring tendency is a major characteristic of rāga ālāpana and gives such music an appealingly tentative cast.

ancient form of worship discussed earlier (see p. 336). The music is from an instrumental meditation concluding the singing of a devotional song by disciples of the late H. H. Sri Swami Sivananda at Rishikesh in the Himalaya foothills (see map, p. 337). The object of their devotion is Lord Rāma, a figure more mythological than historical, whom Indians worship as one of the forms of the god Vishnu. Well over 2,000 years ago the poet Valmīki cast the story of Rāma into Sanskrit verse, and the chanting of perhaps a hundred generations of wandering musicians has made this poem a national epic, the Rāmayana, known all over India and Southeast Asia. Indian households quote it more often than most Western households do the Bible, valuing it—as we value the Bible—less for its history than for its moral teaching.

FIGURE 69: THE *SARASVATĪ VĪNĀ*. *This South Indian classical instrument is essentially a hollow wooden tube enlarged at one end to form a bowl with a flat cover and strung along one side with seven metal strings. This particular tube has a second, supplementary bowl fixed to its underside and wrapped in cloth. The musician shown here is Swami Vidyānanda of the Yoga Vedānta Forest Academy at Rishikesh in North India (from the album cover for Folkways recording FR 8903).*

The four large pegs at the upper end of the instrument tighten or loosen the four melody strings to tune them. Fine adjustments of the tuning are made by moving the bead on the other end of each string so that it wedges itself more or less against the flat top of the bowl, causing the string to rise more or less from the flat top and thus to change its tension and pitch. The three remaining pegs control the tuning of the three drone strings, which are strung close together and off to one side of the melody strings.

Two deeply scalloped walls of stiff wax run parallel to each other under the melody strings and extend from the nearest of the melody-string pegs to the beginning of the bowl. Each scalloped peak on one wall is connected to a peak on the other wall by a heavy brass rod, which acts like the metal fret on a guitar: the player can press a string down against it and stop the vibration of the string above that point while letting it continue below. Stopping is usually done with two fingers

The instrumental meditation, drawing on the melodies of the devotional song, is played by Swami Vidyananda on the chief instrument of South Indian classical music, the *Sarasvatī vīnā* (see Figure 69 below). The *vīnā*, a stick or tube strung on one side with metal strings, is an ancient instrument found in one form or another all over the subcontinent. The South Indian form is tubular, with the range of a male vocalist—from low bass to high tenor, and has special bridges that add a buzzing timbre to the sound of the strings (see Figure 70 overleaf).

Fig. 69

Fig. 70

Tāla

Rāga ālāpana is in free rhythm, but much of India's classical music is metered. It, too, undergoes continual change

pressing down together for extra strength. To make the pitch slide, the string can be vigorously depressed in the space between the scalloped walls or pulled to the side.

Both drone and melody strings buzz because they pass over a broad metal bridge curved gently in the direction of the strings. This effect is explained on the next page.

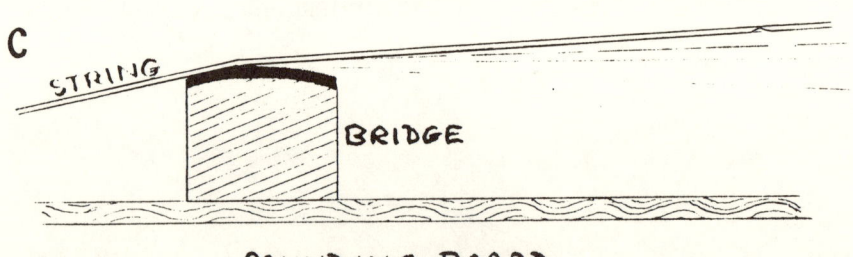

FIGURE 70: THE BUZZING BRIDGE. *A bridge serves three purposes on a stringed instrument: it keeps the strings off the sounding board, provides a terminus for the vibrating length of the string, and transfers those vibrations to the sounding board. The part of the bridge in contact with the string is always of a hard material, shown here as a black band; the sounding board is almost always a thin sheet of wood. The three views here are from the side.*

(A): the narrow Western bridge, which stops the vibration of the string at a point.

(B): a flat bridge, which also stops the vibration of the string at a point if the flat part is tilted as shown.

(C): the broad, curved bridge used on many Indian instruments. Because the hard surface of the bridge extends into the region of the string's vibration, the string beats against it and produces a buzzing

through improvised variation and development, but within the unchanging framework of some particular *tāla*, a traditional pattern of counts repeated over and over. Whether silent or sounded, the *tāla* cycles in the mind of each participant (including the audience) and imposes a strict timing on the moment-to-moment flow of the melody.

This metered melody is anchored in the *rāga* that has been chosen and, more specifically, in a tune either newly composed or received from the aural tradition of the work of an earlier composer.* The tune itself may be in several sections, each the basis for a section of the performance and each designed to give its section a content appropriate to the particular type of piece. Thus if a group of musicians say they will perform the *kriti* "Bruhi Mukundeti" by Sadasiva Brahmendra, which is the *rāga* "*Kuranji*" and in the *tāla* known as *Ādi* it means they will add their improvisations to a song in this *tāla* and *rāga* which

---

*India does not lack notational systems, but the Indian musical mind values creative change above artful reproduction. The worth of gifted Indian performers lies in their creative capacity even more than in their technical proficiency. They are understandably reluctant either to publish the details of their improvisations or to promote a concept of music as the mere reproducing of someone else's ideas. What notation there is scarcely conveys the actual music of a performance and certainly does not approach it as closely as our own written records approach classical Western music.

In her thorough introduction to India's classical music Bonnie Wade (1979: 26) suggests that a parallel to the notational problems of Indian music occurs in our own popular music: we can buy the published and copyrighted notation of a popular Western song, but it will not really be what we hear in the performance. In addition to the richer music of the back-up band, "a popular song is likely to be rendered very differently when performed by two different singers. The tempo may be changed, notes added or omitted, the rhythm almost totally altered. Yet both singers start with basically the same melody."

---

sound. This quality may be dramatically increased by wedging a thread of wool between the string and the bridge on the beating side. William Skelton of Colgate University, who studied the **Sarasvatī vīnā** *in India, once remarked that Western musicians pay good money to have any buzz removed from their instruments, while Indian musicians pay good money to have it put in.*

Brahmendra composed in the musical form known as a *kriti*. (A *kriti* comprises a series of sections, one of which recurs intermittently, in whole or in part, creating what we would call a rondo.) The musicians will improvise not only decorations but entire melodic phrases inserted into the precomposed tune, perhaps an initial *ālāpana*, and at the end one or more whole sections of original melody.

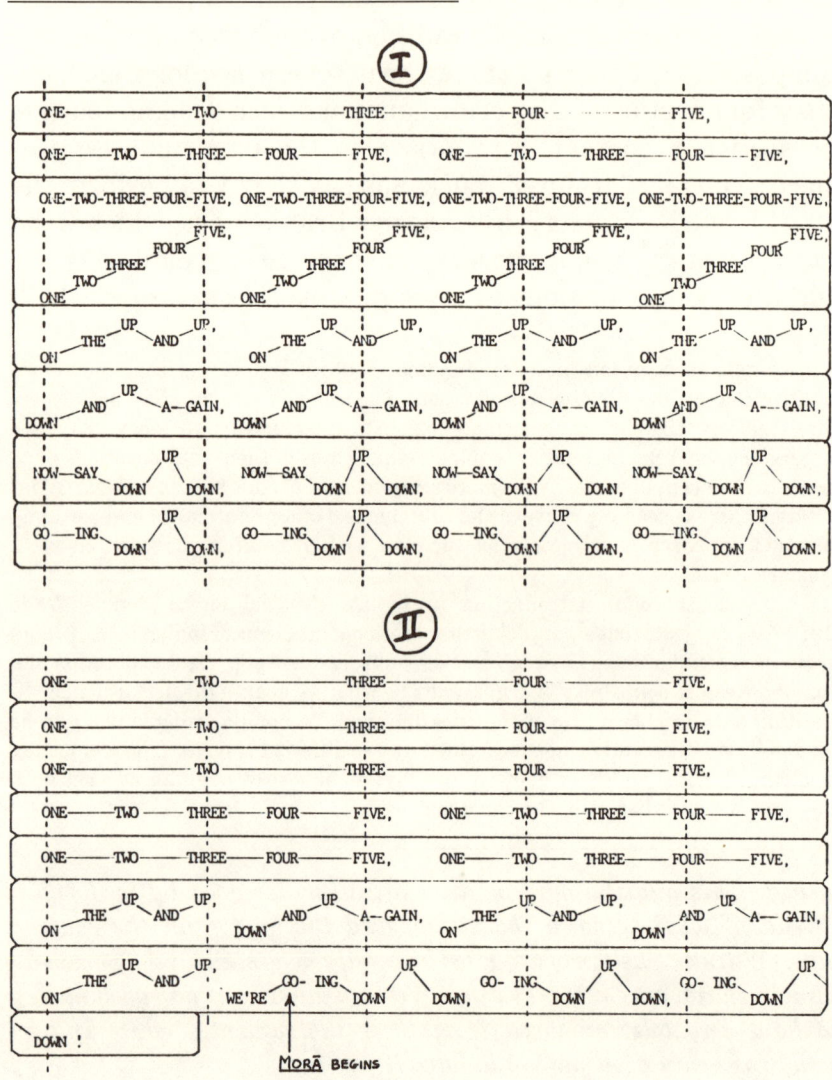

I use the phrase "a group of musicians" because the classical music of India is usually presented not by one person but by a small ensemble. *Ālāpana*, for example, usually involves at least two players, one for melody and one for drone.* Metered music introduces a third player, usually a drummer, with a separate, percussive part. His rhythms (drummers are always men) sometimes underline the governing meter but sometimes do not, for he is always free to run against it for a while, as illustrated oposite. The governing meter

*Recent research suggests that the drone was not always important in India's classical music; that it did not become a full-fledged member of the classic ensemble sound until the 17th century (Wade 1979: 49).

FIGURE 71: *TĀLA* VERSUS RHYTHM. *In each of the eight layers of Chart I a rhythm of five equidistant beats is set against the five equidistant counts of a South Indian governing meter, or* tāla, *known as Khanda Cāpu. Each beat is represented by a word, each count by a vertical dotted line. Starting with the top layer, speak the words while clapping the counts, keeping the speed of the counts uniform as you speak the words of the next lower layer and then the next, on down to the bottom of the chart. A layer that proves difficult should be practiced.*

In the five lowest layers of Chart I, each group of five equidistant beats is inflected: that is, the five words are meant to be sounded at various levels of pitch rather than all at the same level. When you can speak the words of these layers against the tāla *correctly, using just a normally pitched voice, try using exaggerated inflection: a relatively high word should have a high pitch, a relatively low word a low one.*

Finally, try to feel the rhythm of the five equidistant beats as a cluster moving independently of the tāla *but coordinating with it. To do this you will need to increase your speed until the grammatical unity of each group of five words asserts itself regardless of where the clap falls within it.*

Chart II presents the rhythms and tāla *of Chart I as they are played by Ramabhadran and Sivaraman of South India at the beginning of side 2 of World-Pacific recording WP 1437. Perform each layer just once and go on to the next without pausing. A* morā *is an ending pattern differing in length from the* tāla *and begun, as marked here, at a point that will cause a threefold repetition to terminate exactly on the most important beat of the* tāla, *the first.*

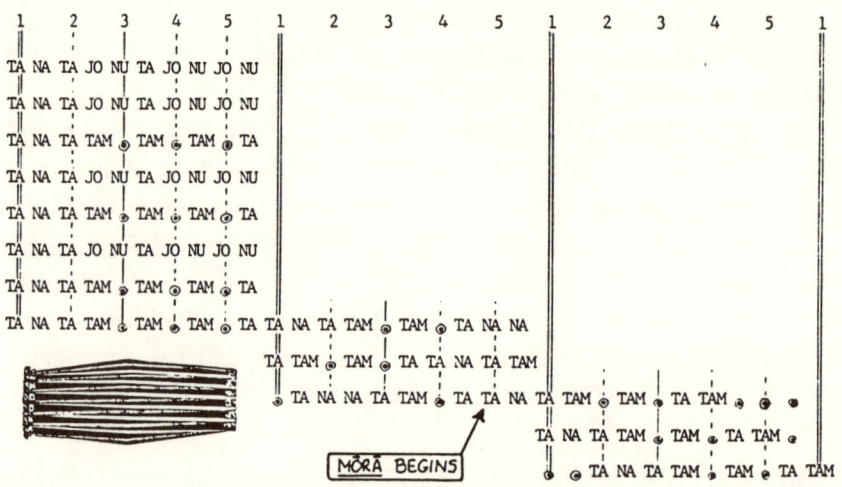

FIGURE 72: RHYTHMIC DEVELOPMENT. *This chart outlines a passage for South India's two-headed classical drum,* mrdanga, *shown in side view from the point of view of the player. The larger, deeper-sounding head is on the left. The smaller, higher-sounding head on the right is tuned to the main pitch level of the* rāga. *Each head has three layers of skin, layers one and three cut away at their centers to form a broad rim around layer two. Slips of straw keep the layers slightly apart. The exposed outer surface of the central layer is weighted to produce a clearly pitched tone (see the footnote opposite).*

The example, adapted from Wade 1979: 144, shows a series of syllables and circled periods representing strokes on the drum and rests between them. Read the syllables aloud from left to right starting at the upper left-hand corner and allowing an equal amount of time to each syllable and each circled period. The framework of vertical lines represents a repeating tāla *of five equally spaced counts. The weaker counts appear as broken lines, the main count (*sam, *pronounced "sum"), as a double line. Accompany with a clap every syllable and every circled period lying on a vertical line. Give the double vertical,* sam, *an especially loud clap.*

The syllable pattern shortens in the central section of the example, diverging from the tāla *pattern as it does so. In the third section it broadens with a* morā *(explained at the bottom of p. 351). This broadening impresses me as development: the basic material seems to have grown into something new.*

itself, the *tāla*, remains unchanged, cycling in the heads of the musicians and their audience and usually visible somewhere in the group as a quiet choreography of slaps, taps, waves, claps, and touchings of thumb to fingertips. When both drummer and melodist run against the *tāla*, it becomes a separate, contrapuntal part. Thus at a concert of Indian art music the audience may find itself actively marking a *tāla* that is pitted against the rhythm of what the audience hears. The result is exciting, as you will find if you master the brief examples given in Figure 71. They are not easy for a Westerner to perform because they deny the basic principle of Western ensemble rhythm, which is mutual reinforcement. Indian rhythms, like those of West Africa discussed in Chapter 12, are governed by meters basically independent of the moment-to-moment effect of the musical flow.

Fig. 71

Development takes place in measured as well as in rhythmically free Indian music, and in purely rhythmic relationships as well as in melodic ones.* Figure 72 opposite shows development in which a basic pattern is so varied that it grows into something new.

Fig. 72

*Indian drumming, like West African drumming, is both melodic and percussive: rhythmic patterns are created by pitch relationships as well as by differences in timbre, loudness, and duration. A stretched membrane does not normally produce a clearly pitched tone when struck, because the partials—the various specific vibration rates of which the tone is composed—are not multiples of a single vibration rate as they are in the case of a vibrating string (see p. 100). Without the aid of scientific theory drummers in several different places in the world discovered long ago that weighting the center of a drumhead turns the most prominent of its partials into multiples of a single rate of vibration and thus produces a more clearly pitched tone. Most Indian drumheads carry at or near their centers a black spot made of flour paste and metallic oxide, a mixture that lasts for a long time; some carry a temporary load of flour paste alone, applied just before playing the instrument. Among every set of drumheads played together one will be carefully tuned to the main pitch level of the octave series called for by the *rāga* of the music.

16

Emotion and Form in American Spiritual Singing

"Real Feeling"

The young people at my college often praise a popular singer for "putting real feeling into a song." However, what they take as evidence of real feeling—body stance, facial expression, vocal effects—are items of stylized behavior. An artist's real feelings lie beneath the surface in the form of energy undifferentiated*; what appears to be feeling is the calculated and controlled use of this energy.

Performers themselves are well aware of this. Thus a free-lance writer who had interviewed the English actor Derek Jacobi about his title role in a television production of *Hamlet* reported that

> by the time the BBC shooting was ready to begin [Jacobi said], "I had an emotional graph in my mind. I knew where the climaxes came emotionally in my head." And he could call upon them at will, despite the fact that the 3½-hour play was shot out of sequence over a period of eight days.
> *(Wasserman 1980: 144)*

---

*This is the current textbook view of emotion (see Pribram 1980: 253-254) widely held since the time of William James (see Wm. James 1890: II, 472-474) and only recently challenged seriously by indications that each emotion may, after all, have its own identity beneath the surface as well as in overt display (Goleman 1984).

Real feeling wells up uncontrolled; the artist's stylized behavior is a highly controlled effect.

How could it be otherwise? A performance, to be successful, must appeal to some established tradition; therefore communication must flow in channels of established behavior. When behavior shifts from established patterns, the reference to tradition dissolves; the performance becomes entirely personal. The audience, for its part, loses the sense of participating in the predictables and unpredictables of a tradition and grows confused, angered, or simply disinterested. The key to the success of a performer is therefore controlled symbolic behavior—the effective projection of the appropriate feeling rather than an out-pouring of inner emotion.

My grandfather was acquainted with the American actor Joseph Jefferson. One night, after seeing Jefferson act the title role of the play that was making him famous, *Rip Van Winkle*, my grandfather asked him why the sleeping scene hadn't seemed to come off just right. The reason, Jefferson explained, was that he had *really* fallen asleep that time. Even for such a passive effect the performer cannot simply *be* but must consciously project symbolic behavior.

We all do this to some extent in daily life because, like the performer, we need to communicate and therefore rely on established behavior patterns. Dustin Hoffman made this point when interviewed about his work as an actor:

> My job is to do you, and the only way that's possible is if I've got you inside me. I've got to find out what you're doing. Nobody simply is, except infants. Once we get self-conscious, we act—all the way to the grave. So, an actor shows you how people act.
> (Schwartz 1979: 40-D, column 2)

Unlike the performer, the audience is free to give itself over to real emotion. But in feeling real emotion it does not discriminate between its own state and that of the performer. When listeners imagine that a singer expresses real feelings, the feelings they perceive are actually their own, stimulated by the singer's symbolic behavior.

When performers perform they also listen. In other words, they are members of their own audience and can be moved like any of their audience by their own performance. This involvement is a pitfall, for as the American psychologist Kate Hevner has explained, the aesthetic experience of any observer is disrupted when the observer's feelings are aroused:

> The art object [e.g., a song being sung] always has a moving effect. It appeals, as William James would say, to the bodily sounding board. . . . [A] suggestion, conscious or unconscious, which finds its answer in a muscular or visceral response will serve to emotionalize the whole experience. Even the bodily symptoms derived from a totally different source may lend their effects to a neutral stimulus, making it seem for a time a beautiful thing, as when the effects of certain drugs enhance all sensation and perception for a short period of time, giving all experience an aesthetic quality. . . . [I]n the aesthetic experience the attention is always, one hundred per cent of it, on the art object. The bodily sensations must be in the background. When they become so prominent that the attention shifts to them, then the attitude is necessarily personal. One is thinking of his own self, his physical being, the art object is forgotten and the aesthetic attitude has disappeared.
>
> (Hevner 1937: 256-257)

In other words, successful artists rely on stylized behavior because personal emotion interferes with their control of the material. While the audience is free to fall in and out of the aesthetic attitude, the performer is not.

Hevner's physiological theory of emotions assumes what no one has been able to prove: that bodily effects *always* accompany emotion. A second approach, the psychological theory of emotions, assumes that emotions are mental and arise from the blocking of a response. The musical theorist Leonard Meyer has summarized it thus:

> An object or situation which evokes no tendency, to which the organism is indifferent, can only result in a non-emotional state of mind.
>
> But even when a tendency is aroused, emotion may not result. If, for example, a habitual smoker wants a cigarette and, reaching into his pocket, finds one, there will be no affective [that is, emotional] response.... If, however, the man finds no cigarette in his pocket, discovers that there are none in the house, and then remembers that the stores are closed and he cannot purchase any, he will very likely begin to respond in an emotional way.
>
> *(Meyer 1956: 13-14)*

Similarly, Meyer argues, if the habitual music listener gets involved with a new piece of music that proceeds entirely as expected, no emotion will result from the experience of the sound itself,* whereas if expectations are blocked, emotion *will* result.

Music that entertains us surprises expectation. Involved listeners, creating the sound in their heads as the physical signals reach them through the air, find their expected response patterns blocked by an unexpected sequence or an unexpected delay in expected sounds. This blocking lends their mental activity an emotional tone according to Meyer. Strangely enough, I might add, when the music is heard again, the same emotional tone prevails and even increases; listeners apparently

---

*But from the *associations* of a sound considerable emotion may be derived. The French horn, for example, is an instrument directly descended from the hunting horn of the Germanic people. Its sound is strongly associated with the woods. Many Germans feel strongly about the forest: *im Wald* ("in the woods") is where life is beautiful, peaceful and noble; where one can live honestly and simply. The huntsman and the forester are hero-types in German films and stories. Thus a few solo notes on the horn conjure up for many Germans a world of values and sensory experience, remembered or merely imagined, all of it with an emotional component.

repeat or even heighten their original expectations and thereby re-experience or even augment the emotional reward of the music. The importance of expectation in this theory explains from yet another standpoint why a musician has to perform more or less predictably and therefore must channel personal emotions into stylized behavior.

The Emotional Content of Music

I have referred to emotions in the plural, but the singular is more accurate. Research seems to show that emotion is not of various kinds but of one kind. Circumstances classify it as love, hate, fear, joy, etc. In the careful words of the psychologist C. Landis, as reported by Meyer,

> when an organism is in a situation which results in a disturbed or wrought-up condition, then the situation plus the reaction gives us the name or word which characterizes the whole as a specific emotion. The reaction itself is not sufficient to differentiate the emotion, . . .
> *(Meyer 1956: 19)*

Music has the power to become part of the situation that stimulates emotion and can thereby specify for us what that emotion is. As every movie-goer knows, music can establish a situation more quickly and surely than speech or visual cues. It lets us know, for example, whether a walk in the moonlight is to be taken as romantic or scary. Outside the movies a whole industry has grown up which sells appropriate musical stimulation to businesses that want to tell us how we feel in various daily situations. People buy the service to help them run offices, department stores, restaurants, supermarkets, etc. Because they seem to find it worth paying for, one imagines that in fact it works.

Music does not stimulate emotion directly. Between what we hear and what we feel lies cultural training. We have been taught to associate certain kinds of music with situations of specific character.* The bowed strings that generate in us a feeling of sentimental warmth will not produce this feeling in people from a different culture unless their training has been the same. Sound has arbitrary rather than inherent content. To put it another way, human feelings are probably much the same in all societies but differ widely in their symbols.

The relationship between the intensity of a feeling and the intensity of its outward expression also varies with the culture. As the British anthropologist John Blacking has reminded us,

> we cannot say that the Kwakiutl [of our northwest coast] are more emotional than the Hopi [of Arizona] because their style of dancing looks more ecstatic to our eyes. In some cultures, or in certain types of music and dancing within a culture, emotions may be deliberately internalized, but they are not necessarily less intense.
> *(Blacking 1973: 33)*

Westerners at concerts of elite Western music internalize their emotion, by and large; those attending jazz concerts are noticeably more outgoing. In examining the impact of emotion on musical form, therefore, this chapter will not be concerned with the *amount* of emotion involved in any particular case because the amount cannot be determined.

Of Ecstasy and Constraint

To make music is to blend ecstasy and constraint. Sounding for the sake of sounding is an act joyful and beyond reason, whereas weaving that sound into a larger whole is a rational process requiring some degree of constraint, however spontaneous the effect may seem.

Each music strikes a balance between ecstasy and

---

*Similarly, cultural training determines how we inflect our speech: Americans turn an utterance into a statement by lowering the pitch of its ending; among the Anlo of southeastern Ghana this is how one turns an utterance into a question.

constraint—between unreasoned and reasoned sound, spontaneous expression and formal expression. In some pieces the formal aspect of the expression is so simple and uniform as to melt into the background of one's impressions, leaving the attention focused fully on the power of the utterance; in other pieces fervor is suppressed in favor of formal relationships; in still others the expression lies between these extremes, or combines the two without sacrificing either.

Whatever the emphasis on spontaneous and formal expression may be, it always reflects values held by carriers of the tradition. Consider for example a performance sacrificing neither ecstasy nor constraint: the singing of a hymn by white worshippers at the Old Pond Primitive Baptist Church in Pond Creek, Pike County, in eastern Kentucky.*

Fig. 73   A visiting male soloist sings without accompaniment the stanzas shown opposite in Figure 73, using the high, unwavering, hard-edged tenor voice characteristic of religious and secular singing in the area. This tune is strophic, repeating with each stanza, and he sings it without variation, making no attempt to give any portion a special rhythmic or melodic effect. This straightforward delivery creates a highly formal impression: a sure and steady flow of energy entirely in the service of a strictly measured poetic and melodic structure.

The congregation, on the other hand, performs without measure or constraint, sobbing, laughing, groaning, and crying out as the force of the words becomes overpowering. Beginning before the end of the first stanza, this chaotic accompaniment steadily grows in loudness until it almost drowns out the soloist. Although an observer from the art-music tradition might well be appalled at what seems like the interference of an unruly audience, there can be no doubt that soloist and congregation are in musical symbiosis: each makes whole the

---

*This can be heard on Library of Congress recording *LBC-1: Religious Music* (1976), side 1, band 4.

Though troubles assails and dangers affright,
Though friends should all fail and foes all unite,
Yet there's one thing secures us, what ever betide:
The scripture secures us, the Lord will provide.

The birds without barns or storehouse are fed.
From them let us learn to trust for our bread.
His saints what is fitting shall not be denied,
So long as 'tis written: the Lord will provide.

His call we obey like Abraham of old,
Not knowing our way, but faith makes us bold;
For though we are strangers, we have a good guide
And trust: in all dangers the Lord will provide.

When Satan appears to stop up our path
And tempts us with fears we're all bound to heed,
He cannot take from us, though oft he has tried,
This heart-cheering promise: the Lord will provide.

He tells us we're weak, our hope is in vain,
The good that we seek we never shall obtain;
But when such suggestions our spirits have tried,
This answers all questions: the Lord will provide.

FIGURE 73: A HARD-SHELL BAPTIST HYMN. *These five stanzas are taken from the singing of Lenville Ball at the Old Pond Primitive Baptist Church at Pond Creek in Pike County, Kentucky (Library of Congress LBC-1: side 1, band 4). The author is John Newton (1725-1807), an ordained minister of the Church of England, who published these words in his 1779 collection,* Olney Hymns. *The Calvinist belief in a pre-destined elect (the "saints" referred to in the second stanza) was held by most English-speaking Protestants prior to the 19th century, and Newton's text is still found in the hymn books of Methodists, Presbyterians, Baptists, and Lutherans. The Calvinist view was abandoned by most Protestants in the 19th century. Baptists who refused to go along with this change came to be known as Hard-Shells.*

musical expression of the other, one supplying the formal structure, one the ecstatic content.

The impact of the text and the open expression of strong feeling are both explained by Primitive Baptist beliefs. All Baptists agree that only a person old enough to form a considered opinion should be admitted into the Christian faith through baptism, the symbolic washing away of one's past life, but on many other points there is no general agreement. Among these is whether Christ's crucifixion remitted the sins of everyone or of only a select few. Primitive Baptists preserve the 16th-century teaching of John Calvin that God decided before Adam drew his first breath just which members of all future generations would be admitted to heaven. Most English-speaking Protestant groups held this belief before the 19th century and then adopted the more generous view that salvation is open to all. The Primitive Baptists kept the old faith, however, insisting, for example, that missionary work is pointless because God has already made His selection. Their stubborn refusal to change their views has earned them the name "Hard-Shell Baptists" and has subjected them to isolation and continual pressure to change. In the light of this background the assuring words of the hymn can be seen to have special significance for members of this congregation.

Why strong feeling should be so openly, individually, and chaotically expressed is explained by the Primitive Baptist belief that God relates to people as individuals, not as groups. Seeking the comfort and assurance of worshipping together, Primitive Baptists naturally sacrifice some individuality but encourage unrehearsed and uncoordinated expression. Other Protestants do not carry individualism this far, favoring instead planned sermons, responsive readings, and unified hymn singing, or even performances by rehearsed choirs and paid instrumentalists and vocalists. Protestants loyal to the Church of England express their worship largely through specialists, verbal as well as musical.

Constrained Congregational Song

The measured, unified singing we hear at concerts and in most churches today was not characteristic of Protestant congregations in this country before the 18th century and did not gain a foothold in our rural churches until the second half of the 19th century. It replaced lining out, the slow and powerful congregational singing style discussed in Chapter 7.

The change began in urban areas of England sometime around 1700 and quickly spread to the coastal settlements of the American colonies: ministers sought to turn their flocks from singing by ear to sightreading musical notation, and from the old, freely timed heterophony to a measured unison (and, if possible, a measured counterpoint). They called the new style "regular singing," "singing by note," or "singing by rule." It represented, in the terms proposed in the previous section, a change in balance between ecstasy and constraint and therefore a change in the values of the participants. It subordinated the act of individual worship to the unity of the overall effect, thereby emphasizing one-to-one communication with the Almighty less and a mediated relationship more.

In the winter of 1710-1711 the Anglican church attended by the wealthy coastal planter William Byrd of Westover, Virginia, made the transition to regular singing without a struggle, and by 1724 the eleven Congregational churches of Boston were won over. The change is understandable if one remembers that urban English fashion exerted a powerful influence on the American coast at this time. Moreover, many of the people in these congregations were less than wholly committed to individual worship and probably saw in the change no conflict with their basic values.

But the reform—for so its proponents thought of it—was not welcomed everywhere. As late as 1774 members of "the old Presbyterian Society" of New York City were still lining out. John Adams called the Society's singing "all the drawling, quavering, Discord in the World" (Adams 1961: 104). Presbyterians in Philadelphia did not begin the shift to singing by rule until the late 1780's (Benson 1962: 192). In 1779 a committee of the First Congregational Church of Sturbridge, Massachusetts —only sixty miles west of Boston—reported open conflict over the change. Proponents of the reform had apparently failed to sway the congregation by democratic discussion and had resorted to surprise attack, interrupting the song leader ("quethiser") as he sang the opening notes of the first melodic phrase to start the lining-out process. The committee summed up the facts as follows:

> With respect to the matters of uneasiness in the minds of some Relative to the proceedings of the Singers in some respects Since the late Endeavours of Learning to Sing by Rule in our Congregation [:] in the first place the Singers Ariseing to Set the Psalm or Strike the Tune when the Quethiser or Quethisers, who were orderly Introduced [i.e., properly appointed] to do that Duty[,] being present[,] [were] attempting to do their Duty[,] were Interrupted[;] & this of the Singers was not as wee Suppose don on a Sudden by Surprise, but by before Determination: further[,] their proceeding to Sing without reading by line, no previous notice being given to thos whose Duty it was to read, & haveing no vote of the Church passed to Sing without Reading.
>
> *(Quoted in Macdougall 1940: 125)*

Wherever singing by rule established itself, the singers began to concertize. That is, in addition to supplying music in the new style for the services of their church they also sang in public occasions that were not services. A sermon usually accompanied this new entertainment, which was called a "singing lecture." The earliest report of such an occasion comes from New England:

> On Thursday last in the afternoon, a Lecture was held at the New Brick Church [in Boston], by the

> Society for Promoting Regular Singing in the worship of God. The Rev. Thomas Walter of Roxbury preach'd an excellent Sermon on that Occasion, *The Sweet Psalmist of Israel.* The Singing was perform'd in Three Parts (according to Rule) [that is, in a counterpoint of three melodic lines sung from musical notation] by about Ninety Persons skill'd in that Science, to the great Satisfaction of a Numerous Assembly there Present.
> (New England Courant *of March 5, 1722, as quoted in Chase 1966: 27)*

Reverend Walter, a good singer himself, probably trained the chorus for this performance. The choral tradition begun by reformers like him has continued unbroken to the present day. Those early regular singers were the direct ancestors of our school, college, and civic choruses.

The Singing School

The reform movement succeeded because it offered the attractive combination of edifying "scientific" instruction in music, social recreation, and business opportunity. The instruction, though designed to improve Christian worship, was given for the most part neither in church nor by churchmen. It had an effect on church services, of course, but became essentially a worldly recreation. An anecdote of New England life recorded by a 19th-century historian captures this point of view:

> By the desire of his wife, Martha..., he finished off in the upper story of the L part [of their home] a hall, with seats all around the sides, so that she could invite her fellow church members and neighbors to hold religious services there, and make them comfortable in summer and winter. It was also used for purposes not religious. Several terms of singing school, and occasional balls and square dances were held there.
> *(Mrs. A. H. Worthen as quoted in Winslow 1972: 110)*

The singing school was what modern educators would call an institute rather than an institution: a course of instruction rather than an academy. The master, often an itinerant, would offer the course as a private enterprise, teaching for a fee mutually agreed upon and selling his* pupils the song book they would need, in many cases one he had compiled and published himself as a business venture. A course, usually offered in the winter, might run less than a month or as long as three or four months, depending on the wishes of the contracting parties. It would end with a concert open to the public such as the one Caleb Jackson, a nineteen-year-old Massachusetts farm boy, reported in his diary:

> Dec. 31, 1805. Very cold. I made 5 shoes and Samuel 4 and we went to Singing School in the evening. There were about 20 of us to sing and 14 or 15 spectators from Old Rowley & Byefield.
> *(Quoted in Buechner 1964: 5)*

Singing schools were popular among young people because they offered a chance to socialize. Fourteen-year-old Elizabeth Fuller of Massachusetts did not join the school in the winter of 1790-1791 but went occasionally for other reasons:

> Jan. 21, 1791. I am writing grammar today. Pleasant weather. Nathan Perry put our horse into their sleigh and carried me to the singing school and back

---

*The 18th-century itinerant singing masters were all men. Richard Steele mentions them in England as early as 1711 (Spectator 1803: II, 134), where by 1724 they had roused the ire of a bishop by their tendency to replace the meager number of tunes a congregation knew for lining out—sometimes no more than two!—with many new songs. He warned his clergy, "But when I recommend the bringing your people, whether old or young, to a decent and orderly way of singing, I do by no means recommend to you or them the inviting or encouraging those idle instructors who of late years have gone about the several countries to teach tunes uncommon and out of the way (which very often are as ridiculous as they are new, and the consequence of which is that the greatest part of the congregation being unaccustomed to them are silenced and do not join in this exercise at all)..." (Curwen 1880: 4)

again. I had a fine ride and a fine evening; they sung a great many tunes. I sang with them.
(Quoted in Buechner 1964: 5)

By the time Caleb and Elizabeth were in singing school, regular singing had spread from Maine to South Carolina (perhaps even to Georgia) and from the coastal plains to the far side of the Appalachians. At least four generations of students had preceded them, and as early as the 1760's some of these students, immersed in the sound and fluent in the notation* of a fairly well-defined musical style, began having musical thoughts of their own in this idiom and writing pieces for their schoolmates to perform. As a result, the singing-school repertoire grew from approximately seventy-four songs during the first half of the century (all of them imported from England†) to thousands of songs by the end of it, most of them American and a good number by Americans not yet in their twenties.

This outpouring of music paralleled a similar creative surge in religious poetry and may have been stimulated by it. Until the 18th century many Protestant congregations sang only

---

*The work of the singing school was to decipher musical notes. The system studied was the one we use today. It involves two different codes, one for rhythm and one for pitch. The rhythmic code uses the shape of the note to symbolize duration and is readily mastered by simple practice drills. The pitch code is more difficult: it uses the position of the note to indicate how high or low the note should sound. Five equally spaced horizontal lines create a ladder called a "staff," and a note placed high on the staff sounds higher than a note placed low on the staff. The apparent simplicity of this system is deceptive because, as you know, the pitch levels of the Western octave series are not equally spaced (see pp. 48-49). To sing them from notation one must be able to tell just where the inequalities lie on the staff. The equidistant lines and spaces of the staff cannot provide this critical information without the addition of a secondary code to show that certain distances are not to be read as equal. Thus people who can sing the Western octave series perfectly well by ear cannot sing it from notation unless they have memorized this secondary code showing them where the series has been placed on the staff.

†In one of the earliest music books printed for the singing-school movement, however, the 5th edition (1726) of John Tufts' *Introduction to the Singing of Psalm Tunes*, there is a setting of the words of Psalm 100 which may be entirely by Tufts himself (Lowens 1964: 53-55). This would make Tufts, a native of Massachusetts, the first published American composer.

biblical texts in their worship services if, indeed, they sang at all. They were the so-called "Dissenters"—the Puritans (later called Congregationalists), Presbyterians, and Baptists—people alienated not only from Rome but from the rituals and music of the Church of England, the main British Protestant denomination. Dissenters recognized no higher religious authority than the Bible and the conscience of the individual. Having cut their ties with traditional forms of worship, they were understandably reluctant to stray from the only written guidelines they had. Some found no biblical authority for singing aloud at services; those who were willing to sing sang only scriptural texts.

But as early as 1673 the Baptist minister Benjamin Keach had persuaded a majority of his flock in the London dock area of Southwark that the Bible actually required the congregation "to sing God's praises according to the best light they have received" (McGlothlin 1911: 297). They began to let in the light of newly composed texts, but only at the end of the communion service and, eventually, at the end of regular Sunday service so that those who disagreed could leave without missing the service itself. In 1691 Keach published some three hundred of his own hymns, calling his collection *Spiritual Melody* (Cates 1948: 6, n7). His son Elias brought the movement to America around 1690, and the views of father and son were adopted by various American Baptist groups from 1712 on.

A flood of hymns poured out from the people during the 18th century, their texts ranging from doggerel to richly expressive verse, their authors from the completely illiterate to the highly educated. The best remembered and most influential of all these poets was one of the earliest, Isaac Watts, Congregational minister of the Mark Lane Independent Chapel in London from 1702 until 1712. His verses are still found in the hymnals of every Protestant denomination in America, and in rural southern congregations he is known as "Old Doc Watts."

"Fuging" Tunes

The reformers, in replacing the individualistic disarray of lining out with the sound of many voices unified in both pitch and rhythm, were reasserting a musical value held in common by Protestants and Catholics a hundred years earlier: the primacy of formal expression over ecstatic expression in the music of the worship service. Protestants had supported this primacy in the 16th century, at the very start of the Reformation, by transforming the unrhymed and rhythmically free language of Psalms and other biblical songs into rhymed and strictly metered verses suited to the kinds of tunes people sang in everyday life (see pp. 111-112). During the 17th century this preference for formal structure had weakened. Now, in the 18th-century singing-school movement, it was reestablished.

The earliest singing-school pieces were strophic, the music for the first stanza repeating with each subsequent stanza. Soon, however, anthems in serial form were added, less to fill the needs of church services than to provide variety in what had become a form of both public and private entertainment in America.

> For this music was much more than a church song sung only of a Sunday morning in church—it was a music of the out-of-doors, of the kitchen hearth, of the blacksmith's forge, and even of the tavern.
> *(Lowens 1964: 280)*

As anyone knows who has enjoyed singing in a chorus or playing in an instrumental group, it can be highly rewarding emotionally to submit to formal musical constraint—to confine one's personal expression to sounds obeying strict rules of pitch and time. The feeling experienced under such circumstances can be just as powerful as, for example, that which lies behind our uninhibited cheering when a spectacular play puts the team we support in the lead. The only difference may be in direction: the force of a person's cheering moves outward, whereas the force of a person's disciplined musical sound fitting perfectly into a well-timed overall effect moves inward.

Greater constraint was imposed on regular singing by the double discipline of the so-called "fuging" (pronounced "fewging") tunes imported from England in the 1760's and then extensively imitated here.* The voices in a fuging tune did more than move together in massive, unified rhythms as they did in strophic hymns and serial anthems: they moved separately as well, the singers of each part forming their own disciplined unity in opposition to the singers of the other parts. One group would introduce a phrase; a second group would then break in on it with the same phrase at a different pitch, while the first group went on to sing different material; a third group would then break in on the second, and so forth. One American composer, William Billings of Boston (1746-1800), expressed his enthusiasm for fuging tunes by describing their effect on an audience:

> Their minds are surprizingly agitated, and extremely fluctuated; sometimes declaring in favour of one part, and sometimes another.—Now the solemn bass demands their attention, now the manly tenor, now the lofty counter [alto], now the volatile treble, now here, now there, now here again.—O inchanting! O esctatic! Push on, push on ye sons of harmony,...
> (Billings, 1961: xxviii (28) n.)

One of the earliest and most enduring of the fuging tunes sung in America was the English composer Joseph Stephenson's *Milford*, shown in Figure 74 on pp. 371-372. The Christmas text indicates that the piece was for recreation rather than for worship, because Protestant churches in America did not begin holding Christmas services until the middle of the 19th century.

---

*"Fuging" was a term derived from "fugue," the name for a piece or section of a piece in Western art music characterized by the kind of counterpoint described further on in this paragraph. The popularity of "fuging" tunes is shown by the fact that nine out of every ten singing-school books published in America between 1760 and 1810 contained this kind of music, usually to the extent of one-fourth of their contents (Buechner 1964: 13a). The modern spelling of "fuging" is "fuguing."

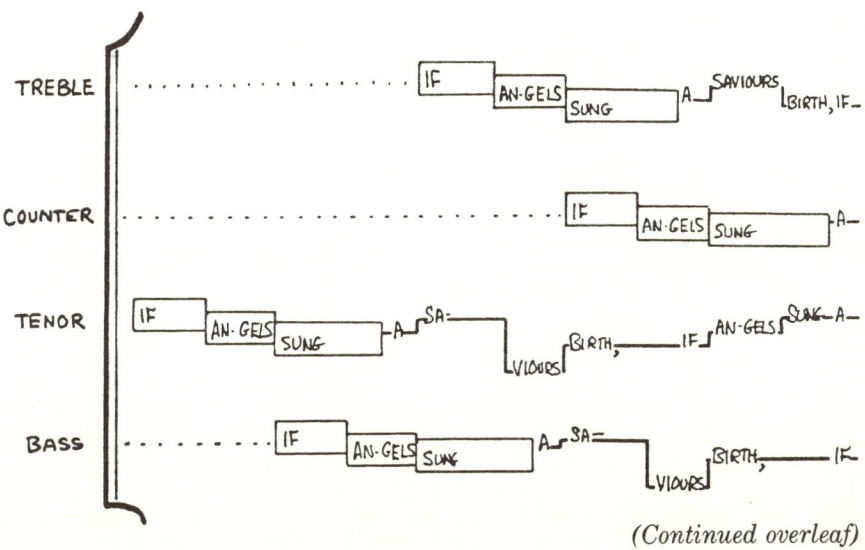

(Continued overleaf)

FIGURE 74: A "FUGING" TUNE. *Joseph Stephenson, an English singing-school master, composed this piece around 1750 (Sacred Harp 1966: 273; Library of Congress AAFS-L11: side 2, band 8). It was soon an American favorite. Syllables stand for sung pitches and are connected by heavy lines to form melodies. The relative height of each syllable within a melody is a rough indication of its relative pitch. Time moves from left to right, and the four melodies—labelled "Treble," "Counter," "Tenor," and "Bass"—are sung together. For clarity's sake they are laid out as if each occupied a separate layer of sound. Actually they overlap in range because all four parts are for men's voices, with women doubling them at the octave.*

In this music vocal expression is constrained in two ways. First, the singers must keep divergence to a minimum within each part so that the parts fit together with the greatest clarity of harmony and rhythm. Where this harmony and rhythm create a massive, unified effect I have drawn light vertical lines connecting the four parts. As you can see, several passages lack these verticals. In such passages the independent motion of the parts is emphasized by "fuging": each part enters separately, singing the same words to approximately the same tune and creating a texture we call "imitative counterpoint." This texture imposes a second constraint on vocal expression, for keeping the parts together when they are moving independently requires even greater control than keeping them together when they are moving in massive unison. Imitative counterpoint was developed in the Renaissance (we saw a brief example in Chapter 13 on p. 302) and elaborated in subsequent periods.

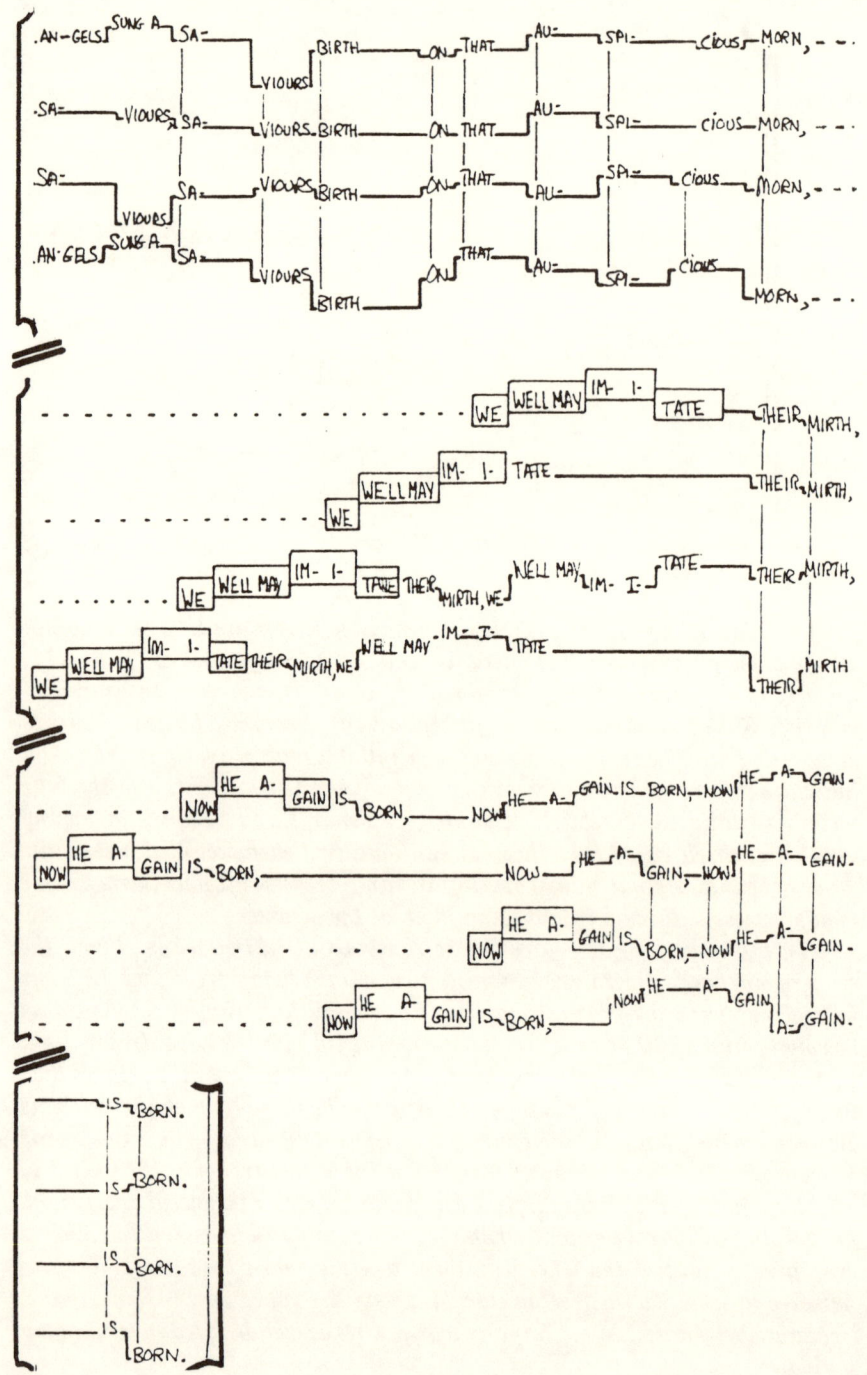

Ecstatic Revival Song

While people along the eastern seaboard were developing more elaborate form and more constrained musical expression in the singing schools, a large and different audience sought just the opposite in revival meetings that began on the far side of the Appalachians in the 1790's and spread rapidly from there into the older settled areas of the country. The following paragraphs briefly summarize the background of this development.

A revival—that is, a group effort to establish or renew God's personal support of the individual—is based on a belief in God and a feeling of personal inadequacy. The revival leader works on these attitudes, exhorting believers to confess their sins and sinners to believe in the power of God to save them. Overwhelming emotion often accompanies this inner struggle.

Solomon Stoddard pioneered this technique among Puritan congregations of the Connecticut valley in the first decades of the 18th century, advising his fellow preachers that

> we are not sent into the Pulpit to shew our Wit and Eloquence, but to set the Consciences of Men on fire; not to nourish the vain humours of People, but to lance and wound the Consciences of Men.
> *(Quoted in Schafer 1963: 334)*

In 1718, when those words were published, the prevailing view among Puritans was that a minister should guide his flock in the proper interpretation of their basic text, the Bible, through a learned and well-reasoned sermon upon some part of it. Stoddard's rather different approach is illustrated in a sermon he published in 1719:

> Every natural man is over-run with the leprosy of sin from head to foot; has not one speck of goodness in him; all his faculties are corrupted utterly.... His whole Soul is like a dead carcass, like a heap of

> carrion, lothsom and noisom, and God may justly abhor him; . . .
>
> *(Quoted in Schafer 1963: 336)*

The power behind this passage was the terror of damnation. Those whom God abhorred were doomed to Hell, and among most Protestants Hell was a far more frightening concept then than now. The closest modern equivalent is perhaps the thought of being eaten away by cancer or the thought of nuclear holocaust. Stoddard had but to convince his listeners of their unworthiness to scare them out of their wits. As he coolly reminded his colleagues in 1724:

> reason will govern men in other things; but it is fear that must make them diligently to seek Salvation.
>
> *(Quoted in Schafer 1963: 341)*

Stoddard's revival was taken up by other gifted leaders whose fire and eloquence sparked an explosion of religious feeling from Maine to Georgia. Jonathan Parsons, describing the effect of his* own preaching in 1741 at Lyme, Connecticut, reports a scene typical of the decade from 1734 to 1744 when the revival reached a peak of intensity:

> Great numbers cried out aloud in the anguish of their souls. Several stout men fell as though a cannon had been discharged and a ball had made its way through their hearts. Some young women were thrown into hysteric fits.
>
> *(Quoted in Walker 1916: 258-259)*

To meet the emotional needs of this revival, which we call The Great Awakening, more and more churches turned from their traditional, metrical Psalm texts to the more pertinent

---

*Early revivalists were all men, probably because their technique required extremely aggressive behavior society did not allow women to display. Women have certainly been capable of providing religious leadership and spiritual guidance, witness Anne Hutchinson in Boston (1634-1638), Ann Lee in upstate New York (1774-1784), and Sarah Pierpont, mentor of Jonathan Edwards in the Connecticut valley (1734-1758).

words and tone of newly composed hymns. In some churches, mostly urban ones, this change accompanied a shift from lining out to regular singing; up country, lining out tended to persist. The Great Awakening was spiritual and verbal but not yet musical among rural folk, who found that the old way of singing, with its slow but powerfully surging melody and its heterophonic harmony (consult page 120), was still an excellent outlet for an individual's fervent emotion as expressed in the new hymn texts.

The Great Awakening ran from approximately 1720 to 1770 in the North and from perhaps 1740 to 1790 in the South. Then, in the last decade of the century, a powerful and uncompromising Presbyterian leader named James McGready carried the old revival preaching from its last stronghold in Virginia to North Carolina and then westward over the Appalachians to Kentucky. There, in the summers of 1798 and 1799, he offered communion services at various small wilderness churches, drumming humiliation and terror into frontier families who faced the rest of the year in isolation and danger. The response was immediate and fervent, the crowds so great that services had to be moved outdoors. As one historian suggests, these people

> needed iron in their souls to stay alive, and the iron did not let them unbend. But in religious life, they were willing to suspend the rules. Then starved feelings feasted to the full on terror and glory, in public, and without shame.
>
> *(Weisberger 1958: 29)*

For a four-day service at Gaspar River in the summer of 1800 people came from as far away as a hundred miles, bringing tents and provisions and camping on the spot. Such an extended outdoor revival came to be known as a "camp meeting," and ministers of different faiths often joined forces to handle the crowds. At Gaspar River, Baptists worked with Methodists and Presbyterians to bring the worshippers to that peak of emotional intensity they believed would bring upon them the saving spirit of God.* As one eyewitness reported:

> The nights were truly awful; . . . the people were differently exercised all over the ground— some exhorting, some shouting, some praying, and some crying for mercy, while others lay as dead on the ground. Some . . . fled to the woods, and their groans could be heard all through the surrounding groves, as the groans of dying men.
> *(Quoted in Weisberger 1958: 25)*

The Camp-Meeting Chorus

Three differences important to the development of revival song distinguished these camp meetings from the services of The Great Awakening: they were complete in themselves, not spread out over the successive Sundays of a year; they were assemblies of strangers, not meetings of an established congregation; and they included many black Americans.†

Those who went to one camp meeting sometimes went to another during the same summer but not with a consistency that would allow their religious leaders to minister to them gradually. Thus each meeting had to accomplish within a few days what in Solomon Stoddard's time had required months

---

*During The Great Awakening the Calvinist view of salvation had prevailed: who was to be saved and who was to be damned had been decided by God before time began, and through an intense religious experience one might find God's assurance that one was of the elect. Under McGready and his successors a different, evangelical view prevailed: the intense religious experience was not an assurance of membership but was itself the act of salvation and could be experienced by anyone with enough faith, God willing. Calvinists held themselves powerless to affect the will of God; Evangelicals believed they could make salvation happen, or at least make it likely to happen.

†White religious services were open to blacks in the 18th century, but there were few black Christians, mainly because owners feared that slaves who became Christian could no longer be treated like farm animals to be worked, sold, bought, or bred as their masters saw fit. Toward the end of the century, however, converting the slaves became a major Protestant effort, and the black presence at white religious gatherings increased dramatically.

and even years: the emotional ground had to be prepared, then feelings roused to a pitch high enough to make the transforming experience of salvation touch, God willing, as many as possible before the meeting ended. Singing, a powerful and efficient way to awaken and heighten the emotions of a group, became a major feature of the camp meeting.

Kentucky's frontier families, drawn from all over the East, were strangers to one another when they gathered for worship at these meetings. Unlike the members of a congregation during The Great Awakening, they had few songs in common. And their leaders, unlike those who guided a congregation, had no time to teach every tune and text they wanted to use. Songs that everyone could sing the first time around were needed.

Sightreading the music was not possible: books of any kind were scarce, and most people at camp meetings were from rural Eastern communities where lining out had never yielded to singing by rule. Moreover, the emotional tone of singing-school songs was constrained, as I have pointed out, providing little direct encouragement for individuals to pour out what was in their hearts. Thus one finds references to lining out at camp meetings but not to singing by rule.

Today's religious segregation of blacks and whites began in the 1820's. Before that time black Americans attended white camp meetings in sizeable numbers and sang with enthusiasm, apparently contributing a distinctly African musical expression they had been able to develop from their diverse ethnic roots while in slavery.* Our camp-meeting witness is John F.

---

*As the black American scholar Portia Maultsby has pointed out, three-quarters of America's black slaves lived on farms and plantations in large groups of from twenty to over a hundred; their compounds were some distance from the master's house, and they were under an impersonal white enforcer. "Away from whites and in the primary environment of their quarters, slaves developed an impressive sense of community life that fostered the establishment of group identification, positive self-concepts, and black solidarity" (Maultsby 1979: 4). Gutman's documentary study (1976) shows that this community, contrary to white opinion, was stable and moral and had a strong sense of continuity. From diverse African backgrounds it was able to forge a common speech, a common code of behavior, and a common music.

Watson, a Methodist layman who was outraged that members of his denomination were singing non-Methodist hymns at these gatherings. His complaint, published in 1819, noted that unofficial hymns and repeating refrains were "most frequently composed and first sung by the illiterate blacks of the society." Such songs constituted, in his opinion,

> a most exceptionable error, which has the tolerance at least of the rulers of our camp meetings. In the blacks' quarter, the colored people get together, and sing for hours together, short scraps of disjointed affirmations, pledges, or prayers, lengthened out with long repetition choruses. These are all sung in the merry chorus-manner of the southern harvest field, or husking-frolic method, of the slave blacks; and also very greatly like the Indian dances. With every word so sung, they have a sinking of one or other leg of the body alternately; producing an audible sound of the feet at every step, and as manifest as the steps of actual negro dancing in Virginia, &c. If some, in the meantime sit, they strike the sounds alternately on each thigh. What in the name of religion can countenance or tolerate such gross perversions of true religion! but the evil is only occasionally condemned, and the example has already visibly affected the religious manners of some whites. From this cause, I have known in some camp meetings, from 50 to 60 people croud [sic] into one tent, after the public devotions had closed, and there continue the whole night, singing tune after tune (though with occasial [sic] episodes of prayer) scarce one of which were in our hymn books. Some of these from their nature, (having very long repetition choruses and short scraps of matter) are actually composed as [they are being] sung, and are indeed almost endless.
>
> *(Watson 1819: 29-31)*

This passage can be interpreted as referring to two different camp-meeting song forms. One is essentially strophic,

EMOTION AND FORM 379

a lengthy chorus endlessly repeated with a change in only one or two words (see for example Figure 75-A on p. 380). The other is essentially a rondo, a succession of "short scraps" of text creating a message that Watson characterized as "disjointed," presumably because each "scrap" was separated from the next by a short refrain (see for example Figure 75-B on p. 381, which happens to lack the "long repetition chorus" Watson tells us was added to give such pieces length). Both forms solved the camp-meeting problem of getting everyone to sing right away: a leader supplied the changing words and the rest sang the repeating ones.

Fig. 75

Eastern singing-school masters were quick to include the new songs in their tune collections.* In pioneering studies of their 19th-century books the late George Pullen Jackson noted that many camp-meeting songs look just like black American spirituals. He assumed that blacks had borrowed from whites, partly because the peak of the camp-meeting movement occurred at the beginning of the 19th century whereas our earliest descriptions of black American spirituals come from just before the Civil War.

The opposite seems to be the case, however: despite lingering doubts in some quarters, it is generally accepted that

*The chorus-and-refrain music of the camp-meeting revival (known as The Second Awakening, The Western Revival, and The Great Revival) appears as early as 1805 in Jeremiah Ingalls' *Christian Harmony* (Exeter, New Hampshire) and perhaps (I have not seen the volume) in Samuel Holyoke's *The Christian Harmonist* of 1804 (Salem, Massachusetts), which uses camp-meeting texts and folk-like tunes (see Lowens 1964: 141-142). Ingalls' songbook has been reprinted in facsimile (Ingalls 1981).

FIGURE 75: CAMP-MEETING SONG FORMS *(overleaf)*. *Four texts show song forms born in the camp meetings of the late 18th and early 19th centuries as the direct result of the singing of black American slaves at those meetings. Because the words and often the music were repetitious, people who had never heard such songs before were able to sing them the first time around. Underlining indicates the portions of each text they would have sung. Once a song was known to them, of course, they would be able to join in even sooner than I have indicated.*

A

> O brothers will you meet me,
> O sisters will you meet me,
> O mourners will you meet me
> On Canaan's happy shore?
>
>   By the grace of God I'll meet you,
>   By the grace of God I'll meet you,
>   By the grace of God I'll meet you
>   Where parting is no more.

O brothers will you meet me,
O brothers will you meet me,
O brothers will you meet me
On Canaan's happy shore?

   By the grace of God I'll meet you,
   By the grace of God I'll meet you,
   By the grace of God I'll meet you
   Where parting is no more.

O sisters will you meet me,
O sisters will you meet me,
O sisters will you meet me
On Canaan's happy shore?

   By the grace of God I'll meet you,
   By the grace of God I'll meet you,
   By the grace of God I'll meet you
   Where parting is no more.

O mourners will you meet me,
O mourners will you meet me,
O mourners will you meet me
On Canaan's happy shore?

   By the grace of God I'll meet you,
   By the grace of God I'll meet you,
   By the grace of God I'll meet you
   Where parting is no more.

[O children will you meet me,
O children will you meet me,
O children will you meet me
On Canaan's happy shore?]

   [By the grace of God I'll meet you,
   By the grace of God I'll meet you,
   By the grace of God I'll meet you
   Where parting is no more.]

(A): the song that Methodist observer John F. Watson described as a "long repetition chorus." The box encloses the text as given in David B. Mintz, Collection of Hymns and Spiritual Songs *(1806), which would have been sung as below the box. The refrain was probably sung to the same tune as the verse, in which case those who never heard the song before would have joined in singing it sooner than I have shown here. My source for the text and the way it was meant to be used is (Jackson 1975: 84-85). Further verses are easily invented and were undoubtedly added at camp meetings. I have invented one and added it, along with its refrain, in brackets at the end of the text.*

B   A { (a) All glory to the Father be,
         (b) O halle, hallelujah,
     A { (a) He sent his son to die for me,
         (b) O halle, hallelujah;
     B { (c) All glory be unto his name,
         (d) Halle, hallelujah,
     C { (e) For he is worthy of the fame,
         (f) O glory, hallelujah.

I long to be in realms above
 O halle, hallelujah,
Where there is naught but praise and love,
 O halle, hallelujah;
I long in Jesus to be wed,
 Halle, hallelujah,
And on his breast recline my head,
 O glory, hallelujah.

Come, come, poor sinners, come away,
 O halle, hallelujah,
Why from your Jesus will you stay?
 O halle, hallelujah;
Come, come, poor sinners, come behold
 Halle, hallelujah,
His face is brighter than the gold,
 O glory, hallelujah.

O come, poor sinners, come and see
 O halle, hallelujah,
Your mangled Saviour on the tree,
 O halle, hallelujah,
He groaned and dy'd for you and me,
 Halle, hallelujah,
That happy, happy we might be,
 O glory, hallelujah.

Farewell, vain world, I bid adieu,
 O halle, hallelujah,
For only Jesus I'll pursue,
 O halle, hallelujah;
My Jesus took me by the hand,
 Halle, hallelujah,
And bro't me to the promis'd land,
 O glory, hallelujah.

(B): the song form Watson described as comprising "short scraps of disjointed affirmations, pledges, or prayers." The New England singing-school teacher Jeremiah Ingalls included this example in his 1805 tune book The Christian Harmony *(see Ingalls 1981: 109-110). As you can see, the verse is broken into "short scraps" by the insertion of a refrain. The third insertion of each stanza was probably identical with the first two in camp-meeting performances but was altered by Ingalls to lessen the repetition. The final insertion in a stanza often differed from the others in keeping with its special status as the concluding phrase. The musical content of each line is labelled with a lower-case letter in parentheses; the musical content of each pair of lines is labelled with an upper-case letter. Although the text has a rondo form, the tune is serial with initial repetition.*

C

A { When I can read my title clear
To mansions in the skies,
I'll bid farewell to every fear
And wipe my weeping eyes.

A { I want to go, I want to go,
I want to go to glory;
There's so many trials here below,
They say there's none in glory.

[Should earth against my soul engage
And hellish darts be hurl'd,
Then I can smile at satan's rage,
And face a frowning world.]

   [I want to go, I want to go,
   I want to go to glory;
   There's so many trials here below,
   They say there's none in glory.]

[Let cares, like a wild deluge, come,
And storms of sorrow fall;
May I but safely reach my home,
My God, my heav'n, my all;]

   [I want to go, I want to go,
   I want to go to glory;
   There's so many trials here below,
   They say there's none in glory.]

[There shall I bathe my weary soul
In seas of heav'nly rest;
And not a wave of trouble roll
Across my peaceful breast.]

   [I want to go, I want to go,
   I want to go to glory;
   There's so many trials here below,
   They say there's none in glory.]

(C): *a song form Watson does not mention. It mixes a standard hymn of the 18th century—in this case by Isaac Watts (see p. 368 and the hymn text in Figure 22 on p. 120)—with one of the standard revival choruses developed in the camp-meeting movement. The Georgia singing-school teacher John G. McCurry included this example in his 1855 tune book* The Social Harp *(see McCurry 1973: 50), and Jackson lists this particular chorus among fifty-seven that appear to have been favorites because each was used with many different hymns (Jackson 1975: 322). The capital letters at the left of the text indicate that verse and chorus were sung to the same tune, a rollicking melody probably belonging to the chorus and adopted for the verse. I have added the three stanzas of verse from my 1819 copy of Watts'* Hymns and Spiritual Songs *(Book 2, number 65). His collection first appeared in London in 1707 and was so well known in the Colonies that probably most of the people at a camp meeting would have been able to sing the verses as well as the chorus once they grasped the tune.*

D

1

```
  ⎧ (a)   Jesus my all to heaven is gone,
A ⎨ (b)   Happy, O happy,
  ⎩ (a)   He whom I fix my hopes upon,
    (c)   Happy in the Lord;
  ⎧ (a)   His track I see and I'll pursue,
A ⎨ (b)   Happy, O happy,
  ⎩ (a)   The narrow way till him I view,
    (c)   Happy in the Lord.

  ⎧ (a)   We'll cross the River of Jordan
A ⎨ (b)   Happy, O happy,
  ⎩ (a)   We'll cross the River of Jordan
    (c)   Happy in the Lord.
```

2

The way the holy prophets went,
Happy, O happy,
The road that leads from banishment,
Happy in the Lord;
The King's highway of holiness,
Happy, O happy,
I'll go, for all his paths are peace,
Happy in the Lord.

We'll cross the River of Jordan
Happy, O happy,
We'll cross the River of Jordan
Happy in the Lord.

3

This is the way I long have sought,
Happy, O happy,
And mourn'd because I found it not,
Happy in the Lord;
My grief a burden long had been,
Happy, O happy,
Because I was not saved from sin,
Happy in the Lord.

We'll cross the River of Jordan
Happy, O happy,
We'll cross the River of Jordan
Happy in the Lord.

4

The more I strove against his power,
Happy, O happy,
I felt its weight and guilt the more,
Happy in the Lord;
Till late I heard my Saviour say,
Happy, O happy,
"Come hither, soul, I AM THE WAY,"
Happy in the Lord.

We'll cross the River of Jordan
Happy, O happy,
We'll cross the River of Jordan
Happy in the Lord.

5

Lo! glad I come, and thou, blest Lamb,
Happy, O happy,
Shalt take me to thee, whose I am,
Happy in the Lord;
Nothing but sin have I to give,
Happy O happy,
Nothing but love shall I receive,
Happy in the Lord.

We'll cross the River of Jordan
Happy, O happy,
We'll cross the River of Jordan
Happy in the Lord.

6

Then will I tell to sinners round,
Happy, O happy,
What a dear Saviour I have found,
Happy in the Lord;
I'll point to thy redeeming blood,
Happy, O happy,
And say, "Behold the Lamb of God!"
Happy in the Lord.

We'll cross the River of Jordan
Happy, O happy,
We'll cross the River of Jordan
Happy in the Lord.

(D): a song form applying the refrain principle of Example B to the chorus as well as to the verse. The "disjointed scraps" of verse are arranged in rhyming pairs, as in Example B, and three of these are on Jackson's list of camp-meeting couplets, each of which was used in many songs (Jackson 1975: 306-319). This example is from McCurry's The Social Harp *of 1885 (McCurry 1973: 21). The tune given there is more repetitive than the words, as you can tell from the letters I have added to the left of the first section of text: lower-case letters in parentheses identify the musical content of each line of words; upper-case letters summarize the musical content of each group of four lines.*

whites borrowed from blacks the basic structure of verse and chorus* common to both spirituals and camp-meeting songs, a structure characteristic of African song and loosely known as call-and-response form.

The Ecstatic Force of Call and Response

"Call and response" means what you might think it means: a solo voice, or a small number of voices, singing a phrase, and other voices responding with the same phrase or an entirely different phrase. This arrangement can produce markedly different formal effects, depending on the length of the call and the length of the response. Figure 76 on the next two pages shows four call-and-response forms used by the Anlo of southeastern Ghana as part of the recreational dance drumming described in Chapter 12. Since the beginning of the 17th century the Anlo have occupied a coastal area midway between the old slaving centers of Cape Coast Fort and Ouidah (Whydah) in West Africa (see Figure 77 on p. 387). Their musical

---

*Religious verse-and-chorus songs were rare among whites during The Great Awakening. Philadelphia Baptists sang one in which each verse generated its own chorus (Downey 1969: 100):

>Here the world and flesh and devil
>We do solemnly renounce;
>Here we vow to cease from evil
>And a life to God announce.
>>Cease from evil,
>>Cease from evil,
>>Cease from evil,
>>And a life to God announce.

Another source of verse-and-chorus form was the interaction of 18th century white hymnody with Native American musical tradition. Missionaries taught Regular Singing, and at least one of their pupils, Samson Occom, became a composer. He included at least two examples of verse-and-chorus form in his popular *A Choice Collection of Hymns* (three editions: 1774, 1785, 1792), which was known to other early publishers of this form such as the white American Joshua Smith (*Divine Hymns*, 1784) and the black American Richard Allen (*A Collection of Hymns*, 1801). See Stevenson 1973: 409-411, 435 n. 143.

relationship to the people on either side of them is close, and this area as a whole furnished almost half the human cargo transported during the 18th century by England, the major supplier of slaves to the American colonies. It is reasonable to suppose that a basic aspect of Anlo music like the call-and-

A

A { (a) Wo yɔ mi, lo!   They have called us, see!
    (b) Wo yɔ mi.   They have called us.
    (c) Yehova nutɔe gado dɔ. Jehova himself has assigned the work.
    (d) Wo yɔ mi.   They have called us.

A { (a) <u>Wo yɔ mi, lo!</u>   <u>They have called us, see!</u>
    (b) <u>Wo yɔ mi.</u>   <u>They have called us.</u>
    (c) <u>Yehova nutɔe gado dɔ.</u> <u>Jehova himself has assigned the work.</u>
    (d) <u>Wo yɔ mi.</u>   <u>They have called us.</u>

B

(a) Mi tso gbee!   Let us bet!
(b) <u>Me wɔ ya!</u>   <u>I'm confused!</u>
(c) Mi tso gbee de dzi!   Let us bet on something!
(b) <u>Me wɔ ya!</u>   <u>I'm confused!</u>
(d) Mi tso gbee!   Let us bet!
(b) <u>Me wɔ ya!</u>   <u>I'm confused!</u>

(Continued overleaf)

FIGURE 76: AFRICAN CALL-AND-RESPONSE SONG FORMS. *These four texts sung by the Anlo of West Africa (see Chapter 12) illustrate different forms possible in songs having call-and-response structure. As on pp. 380-383, underling the words indicates the portions of each text sung by the responding chorus. Underlining of individual letters indicates they are not sounded in the Western way. Lower-case letters in parentheses to the left of the words indicate the musical content of each line; upper-case letters indicate the musical content of groups of lines.*

(A): the equivalent in form of Watson's "long repetition chorus," Figure 75-A. Verse and refrain each supply one stanza of text, the same tune serving both. This song comes from Atsiagbekor processional drumming.

(B): the equivalent of Watson's "disjointed scraps," Figure 75-B. One-line refrains of identical verbal and musical content separate different one-line calls, creating a rondo. This song comes from Atsiagbekor dance drumming.

C

A { (a) Dogbe naye, lo!   [Atsiã music] greets you, lo!
    (b) <u>E wǫ mi wǫ</u>!   <u>Come, let us dance</u>!

A' { (a) Dogbe naye, he!   [Atsiã music] greets you, lo!
    (c) <u>E wǫ mi wǫ, he! aye</u>!   <u>Come, let us dance, hey! indeed</u>!
    (d) <u>E wǫ mi wǫ, he</u>!   <u>Come, let us dance, hey</u>!
    (e) Atsiã yua dogbe naye, lo!   Atsiã music greets you, lo!
    (b) <u>E wǫ mi wǫ</u>!   <u>Come, let us dance</u>!

D

A { (a) Me le yǫge, yǫge, yǫge,   I will call, call, call,
    (b) Gowoe me le yǫge.   Always will I call.
    (c) Aklagba dza nyi, lo!   She has a fine skin, oh!
    (d) Me le yǫge,   I will call,
    (e) Gowoe me le yǫge   Always will I call
    (f) Ne wǫ va 'fe ame.   For her to come to the house.

A { (a) <u>Me le yǫge, yǫge, yǫge</u>,   <u>I will call, call, call</u>,
    (b) <u>Gowoe me le yǫge</u>.   <u>Always will I call</u>.
    (c) <u>Aklagba dza nyi, lo</u>!   <u>She has a fine skin, oh</u>!
    (d) <u>Me le yǫge</u>,   <u>I will call</u>,
    (e) <u>Gowoe me le yǫge</u>   <u>Always will I call</u>
    (f) <u>Ne wǫ va 'fe ame</u>.   <u>For her to come to the house</u>.

B { (g) Me be, ahiavi dzre nuawo dǫ!   I say, "Lover, save things [for me]!"
    (h) <u>Aye</u>!   <u>All right</u>!
    (i) Ahiavi dzra 'batsiawo dǫ!   "Lover, prepare the beds!"
    (j) <u>Aye, aye</u>!   <u>All right, all right</u>!
    (k) 'Hiavi dzre nuawo dǫ!   "Lover, save things!"
    (l) <u>Aye, aye</u>!   <u>All right, all right</u>!
    (m) Dzra 'batsiawo dǫ!   Prepare the beds!
    (h) <u>Aye</u>!   <u>All right</u>!

(C): *a form combining elements of A and B. A disjointed-scraps effect is followed by a response long enough to sound like a stanza of refrain. Some Anlo songs have much longer responses than this one, and the singers of the performing dance club spend hours rehearsing them. This song comes from* Atsiã *dance drumming.*

(D): *forms A and B above combined the opposite way. A stanza of refrain is followed by a disjointed-scraps effect. In performance the first twelve lines of text are sung a second time before going on to the final eight lines, which are also sung twice. This song comes from* Ahiavivu *dance drumming.*

I am indebted to Mr. Kobla Ladzekpo of Los Angeles and Mr. Vincent Kofi Ladzekpo of Accra, Ghana, for the English translations used here.

response form was part of the mix from which black Americans developed their music in the slave quarters to which they were confined in the New World.

Watson found black camp-meeting songs not only heretical but boring, to judge from his published complaint. The music simply repeated and repeated without revealing either a coherent text or a musical structure worth listening to. Of course he was an observer, not a participant; he was listening with what we might call a "concert ear" rather than expressing himself. (A hundred years earlier he would have been a singing-school reformer fighting against lining out.)

For camp-meeting participants the very simplicity and repetitiveness of the songs were their attraction, for these qualities left the singers free to concentrate almost all their

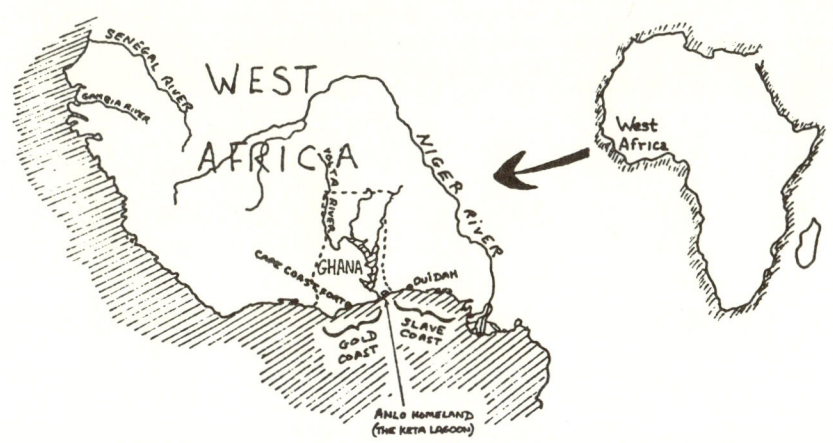

FIGURE 77: THE CENTER OF SLAVING IN WEST AFRICA. *The height of the traffic in black African slaves occurred in the 18th century and was dominated by English merchants. Their main coastal contact with African suppliers was along the coast of present-day Ghana west of the Volta river mouth—a shoreline called "The Gold Coast"—and along the coast somewhat further east—a shoreline called "The Slave Coast." As you can see on this map, the Anlo homeland is located between these two former centers of slave traffic. Today Anlo music is closely related to the music of cultures on either side; presumably this has been true for many centuries.*

attention on the outward thrusting of energy and emotion. We find the same advantage today in some of our popular dance music: what listeners might call the mindlessness of the sound allows dancers to concentrate on the physical experience of dancing. In such music, religious or secular, formal constraint has not been completely abandoned, of course—singer and dancers do conform more or less precisely to the timing of beats and phrases—but the ecstatic element is uppermost and inhibits any tendency to make the form more elaborate.

The ecstatic element in performance becomes most intense when call and response are brief, especially if the response is fixed rather than changing. In such a case the back-and-forth structure revolves in a continuous cycle, drowning any sense of rational dialogue in a mighty, repeating pulse. The call becomes little more than a filling out of this cycle, while the

```
     Power!
        Power!
     Power!
        Power!                Glorify His power!
                                 Power!
     Absolute power!         Glorify His power!
        Power!                   Power!
     Absolute power!
        Power!               Power!
                                Power!
     Power!                  Power!
        Power!                  Power!
     Power!
        Power!               Go-power!
                                Power!
     We need:                Go-power!
        Power!                  Power!
     We need:
        Power!               Power!
                                Power!
     Power!                  Power!
        Power!                  Power!
     Power!
        Power!               Power!
                                Power!
     Praise His power!       Power!
        Power!                  Power!
     Praise His power!
        Power!
```

response becomes less an answer than a rhythmic engine driving the music forward. Figure 78, opposite, is an example. As you would hear if you listened to the recording, continual repetition of an extremely simple form reduces the musical content to mere background sound, emphasizing instead an organically growing power of expression.

Fig. 78

I am not saying that the emotional content of this last example is any greater than that of *Milford* (pp. 371-372) with its more elaborate and constraining form. One expresses emotion in music in the manner established by one's society. Sometimes the manner is outwardly demonstrative, sometimes not, but in neither case does it signify how much emotion is actually felt. Musical form serves a society by providing the appropriate amount of *outward* release for whatever is contained within. The simpler the form, the greater this outward release.

FIGURE 78: CALL AND RESPONSE AS A CYCLING ENGINE. *Bishop J. O. Patterson's Pentecostal Temple and Church of God in Christ, in Memphis, Tennessee, provided this example recorded by Alan Lomax in the latter part of the 1950's (Atlantic 1351: side 1, band 7). The black American congregation sang the responses, which have been underlined; Madam Mattie Wigley sang the calls. A rising or falling accent appears at the end of each call and each response to show a rise or fall in the melody at that point. A rising ending lacks finality, a falling ending creates it; thus the text is phrased in groups of four lines. The performance lasted longer than the quoted text suggests, for the singers always sang each group of four lines twice before going on to new words and usually introduced the same group a second time at some later point in the performance.*

The elements of this structure are brief and the tempo fast. As a result the back-and-forth effect turns into a cycle, a continuous flow in which the response of the congregation becomes a massive beat driving the music forward, while the call becomes a mere interjection. The extremely simple tune allows the attention of performer and listener alike to focus entirely on the outpouring of energy; the ecstasy of sounding is emphasized over the constrained pleasures of musical form.

Coda

17

The Meaning of Music

Meaning

The meaning of something is the reference it makes to something else. Most of what we perceive refers to several things at once. Some of these associations are widely known and accepted throughout our culture, others are more or less unique for each perceiver. Consider, for example, the following headline from a Florida newspaper (St. Petersburg 1978: 8-A):

JUDGE ORDERS MEDICAL PROFILES
OPEN FOR PUBLIC INSPECTION

To a printer the meaning of those words would certainly include, perhaps to the exclusion of other meanings, how the choice of type face, the quality of the inking, and the alignment and spacing of the letters measure up to standards generally accepted in the trade. But to the editor of a rival paper the most important meanings would probably be how these words compare in clarity and forcefulness, in size and placement on the page, with his own heading for the same news item. To the average reader, of course, the meaning would lie in the ideas to which the words themselves refer.

But the words refer to ideas on several different levels of thought at the same time and not necessarily to the same ideas for every reader. On a literal level there is a degree of clarity or ambiguity in the headline varying from one perceiver to the next and resulting from the skill and intent of the editor. It might seem to some that a court has ruled against the privacy of personal health records, an event sure to interest the many elderly people in St. Petersburg. Actually the medical profiles referred to are institutional and professional, not personal: the court allowed the public to check the performance of hospitals and doctors.

On a deeper level the words of the headline ask us how we feel about judges ordering people or institutions about, what we think of doctors and hospitals, and whether we support the right of the public to check up on them. Go yet deeper and the words refer us to our attitudes toward the structure of society and toward the individual's place in it.

Levels of Musical Meaning

Music's audience, like a newspaper's, attaches various meanings to what it perceives. For example, a listener might compare sound quality to memories of similar sound quality, like a printer comparing the inking of a letter to memories of past inkings. We have all experienced musical meaning of this kind if we have ever tried to sing what we have heard sung by a professional and then compared our own sound quality with that of the professional.

Vincent d'Indy, a highly respected composer of the late 19th and early 20th centuries, was an expert on the sounds of modern orchestral instruments. When he attended the first performance of Igor Stravinsky's *Rite of Spring*, given in Paris in 1913, he is said to have risen from his seat in protest at the sound of the very first note, saying "Qu'est-ce que celà?" in a shocked voice—"What is *that*?"—and then striding out of the theater. The sound he heard was that of a solo bassoon, a bass double-reed instrument, playing higher than a bassoon had ever been asked to play before and sounding for all the world like an alto saxophone. D'Indy knew perfectly well what he was hearing, of course; he just could not bear to have the accepted meaning of bassoon sound denied.

Another listener, hearing the bassoon from a different point of view, might have compared the configurations of its melody to memories of similar configurations, like the editor looking at the wording and placement of a headline. Configurational meaning accounts in large part for the meaning of not just melody but harmony and rhythm as well. All of us have become thoroughly acquainted with at least one musical tradition simply by having been exposed to it all our lives, and we refer whatever music we hear to our memory of what we already know. If the two are similar, we enter into the musical flow by anticipating more or less successfully what each new moment of sound will bring; if the two are different enough, we tend to lose interest and call the music, quite accurately, "meaningless."

A musical flow that makes sense by referring us to our memories of the sound of the music we know is called "absolute music"—an experience meaningful in strictly musical terms rather than in terms of something nonmusical such as a dramatic scene or an activity. Much Western art music is absolute music, and many modern examples of it have small success because they fail to refer us to the kinds of musical flow we remember. Some seventy years after the birth of the modern style many professional musicians, as well as concertgoers, still lack sufficient exposure to the new music to accept the way it sounds as the way absolute music ought to sound. Only where this music accompanies nonmusical references—that is, in films, television, and live theater—has it been received without significant resistance.

Music relying for its meaning on nonmusical associations* has no general label; but if these associations follow a logical program or constitute an aesthetic whole—for example, if the

---

*Despite many attempts to discover natural links between musical and nonmusical effects, none has been found. According to one extensive study (Banzet 1955) the correlation is as diverse as the diversity of the people tested.

sound is an attempt to describe a dramatic sequence, a visual impression, or someone's personality—the term "program music" applies (the idea being that the music has been deliberately composed according to a nonmusical outline or program). Many Westerners tend to listen to a piece of music by constructing a nonmusical outline for it whether or not it actually has one. They let the sound accompany something invented by themselves and are quick to make use of any clue the title of a composition might provide. The American composer Aaron Copland gave an interesting example of this process in an interview not long ago (Copland 1981: 96) when he recalled the generous reception given his ballet music, *Appalachian Spring*, which premiered in 1944. People told him that the piece captured perfectly the images and feeling of spring in the Appalachians, but he himself had had in mind only a particular person, the dancer Martha Graham, when he composed it.

Music as Ritual

Beneath the levels of musical meaning already discussed lie powerful associations rarely articulated—emotions, loyalties, ideals—which shape our lives but lie beyond our rational control. I have already mentioned the concepts evoked and feelings produced in some people by the sound of the French horn (see note on p. 357), and no doubt you can supply other examples from your own experience. We tend to overlook the depth within us from which such responses come. Their emotional flavor and the pleasure they bring cause us to disassociate them from the serious affairs of daily life. But these responses proclaim the most serious affair of all: who we are, with whom we identify, and how.

I briefly discussed music as a source of identity in the introduction of this book (see pp. 7-8). Now that the nature of music has been at least partially explored—the kinds of effects driving sound forward and some of the variety they exhibit in human creatures—I would like to suggest that getting in touch with one's identity by means of music is a ritual in the most serious sense of the word.

"Ritual" is generally taken to mean the order of events constituting a religious ceremony, or the ceremony as a whole viewed as a procedure. Everyday usage has extended the word to nonreligious activity one wishes to characterize not merely as recurrent but as cast in a sequence faithfully observed for no compelling reason. Thus we speak not only of "rituals of the church" but of "rituals of the Wednesday afternoon bridge party." Jack Goody has warned (1977: *passim*) that too broad an application renders the word meaningless in anthropological discussions; but I think the application to musical performance is justified because musical performance, like sacred ritual, is not just a fixed procedure but one attempting to influence powerful forces beyond our direct control.

Music certainly depends upon fixed procedures. To recreate a composition or improvise even a single phrase in a coherent style one must conform to certain patterns of behavior and avoid others. There are right notes and wrong notes, right harmonies and wrong harmonies, a pitch frame to observe, and a rhythmic style to maintain, and the proper ordering of these things cannot be disturbed very much without the risk of turning one song into another, one style into another, or an improvised phrase into gibberish. In short, procedure and content are as important and closely regulated in a musical performance as in any religious ritual.

And certainly musical performance seeks to influence forces lying beyond our direct control. They are not the superhuman forces addressed in worship but ones within us: the loyalties and sense of self mentioned earlier. The ability of music to touch our sense of self arises, as I see it, from a fairly simple fact of life: the human organism has no inner eye; it cannot know who or what it is except by observing things outside itself. In the way our friends treat us, the sounds of our usual environment, the smells and textures, colors and climate of our everyday lives, the architecture of our homes, and the shape of our natural surroundings—in all these things we find our identity. When I was with the American army in Japan for a year, the absence of a familiar place setting in the army mess became almost unbearable for me; when a large elm was removed from our street a few years ago, I felt for weeks an almost tangible hole in the air where it had stood. We are tied to our surroundings deeply and subtly because in them we find ourselves.

To the extent that music is a part of our surroundings it is a part of us, and the performance of music with which we identify is a celebration of ourselves. But our sense of self as a unique individual forms only a minor portion of our identity; the major portion consists of our sense of belonging. We are essentially social animals, and above all music celebrates the individual as a member of a group.

The Social Meaning of Music

That music and social structure are related should surprise no one. Music is a social enterprise in itself, a group activity,* an act of communication rather than a monologue, and a product entirely dependent on and judged by the collective taste of society.

The taste of an individual can have no effect on music unless adopted by a group. Unique tastes do occur, or at least tastes unusual in some respect, but "it is a sociological impossibility that such a taste could survive in a social world" (Mueller 1951: 394). When an individual has sufficient social prestige and power, however, like Louis XIV of France (r. 1643-1715), that individual's taste is apt to be adopted by the surrounding group. Our modern symphony orchestra began as a choir of bowed string instruments, with wind and percussion

---

*Solitary music is no exception. Either it recalls a group experience or, as the play of sound observing a certain musical tradition, it asserts the performer's or listener's allegiance to a group.

added on occasion, because Louis favored the sound of bowed strings at his court and the whole of European aristocracy followed suit.

The collective taste of society, influenced from time to time by circumstance, finds expression in every aspect of a musical performance: in the organization of the performers as much as in the sound they make; in their clothing as much as in their choice of instruments; in the social status conferred on them for participating; and in the social status they confer on those for whom they play.

Our modern symphony orchestra is a striking example. The social structure of America is hierarchic, a pyramid of power and achievement, and we find a similar pyramid in the orchestra: at the apex is the conductor, traditionally a man,* in absolute charge and standing over those he controls; the various instrumental groups stationed around him form lesser

---

*In 1977 Judith Somogi became the first woman in this country to be put in charge of an established orchestra, the Utica Symphony Orchestra of Utica, New York. Earlier pioneers like Antonia Brico, Nadia Boulanger, and Sarah Caldwell had to organize their own groups in order to conduct on more than an occasional basis. Now women are beginning to major in conducting in conservatories. About these women Somogi says, "Twenty years ago they didn't think they were capable of it. Now they know they are" (Kupferberg 1978: 5). She tactfully omits suggesting that twenty years ago women were given no reason to hope they would ever be allowed to try.

Women were excluded from conducting positions undoubtedly because men did not want them to have publicly acknowledged authority over men. But a second and more subtle reason was the application to music of a principle well established among the upper classes: the seclusion of women. The English historian David Johnson has identified this principle in the instrumental practice of the 18th century, and no doubt it is much older than that. He writes (Johnson 1972: 23-24) that instruments of that century "can be distinguished as 'professional' or 'amateur,' and amateur ones can be subdivided into 'male' and 'female.'" Professional instruments in amateur concerts were always played by professionals. Amateur instruments were male if solely melodic, female if one could play harmony on them. This division reflected "a society where the men go out to work and meet each other while the women stay put in their own homes—for the 'male' instruments are the sociable ones which fit together into orchestras and chamber ensembles, whereas the 'female' instruments are lone and harmonically self-supporting." Thus at the beginning of the 19th century it was not traditional for women to be in orchestras, not to mention conducting them.

pyramids of their own, chief among them being that of the first violins, whose leader is just below the conductor in the chain of command. The audience, seated in passive respect behind the conductor, forms the least of the pyramids in this structure. Concert uniforms reflect this hierarchy: the audience dresses in what current fashion dictates as moderately formal attire; the players dress more elegantly; the conductor most elegantly of all.

In the 18th century an authoritarian conductor had no place in the symphony orchestra, which at that time played for a relaxed, more or less egalitarian gathering of aristocrats. Of course, someone had to keep time and signal the start and stop of the music, but this was usually the keyboard member of the ensemble (see p. 312), or the leading melodist, or sometimes both of them together.

From the middle of the 18th century to the First World War the power to govern Western society passed from the aristocracy to the middle class. Authority was no longer inherited and unquestioned but had to be proved in competition. Attitudes toward authority became more tense, its symbols more obvious. Reflecting this change, the solo conductor began to take command of the symphony orchestra in the first quarter of the 19th century. Writers were fond of comparing him to an officer leading his troops.*

The authority of the orchestra over the audience became a tangible threat in early 19th-century Vienna. Aristocrats had at best a shaky hold on their positions of privilege after the revolution in France (1789-1799) and the sweeping successes of Napoleon which followed immediately afterward; they therefore ceased attending and supporting symphony concerts, where members of the orchestra—mostly amateur musicians from the upper-middle class—would be above them in the

---

*If you have ever attempted overt individual behavior while listening to symphonic music in a concert hall you have found that the audience, too, is part of those troops and is expected to act in a disciplined way.

hierarchy. When professional musicians took over the playing in the second half of the century, aristocratic patronage resumed because professional musicians were quite clearly a servant class whose place in the social structure of a symphony concert could not be mistaken for the real place of this class in the structure of society itself. (See Weber 1975: 78-79.)

Musical performance does more than reflect social structure, it excuses it. Thus the symphony concert not only symbolizes relationships in a chain of command but also demonstrates that such a chain works to the benefit of all: by submitting to absolute authority one produces an inspiringly beautiful result; individuals lose their autonomy but gain an aesthetic experience and membership in a group; the performers gain the satisfactions of contributing competently, applause, and often some financial reward. Among the Anlo of southeastern Ghana music of a different sort reflects and vindicates a different social structure, illustrating in its own way the same basic principle.

In Anlo society political and social authority is diffuse. The elders elect their chief for life from among the members of the appropriate lineages, but the chief rules *through* the elders and by consensus, not command. Should the occasion warrant, they can remove him, even have him killed, without behaving improperly. Similarly, the dance-drumming ensemble described in Chapter 12 has no conductor. Everyone adheres to the tradition of the particular musical style in a most precise way, and an earnest musical consensus is maintained. The sound of the bell provides the timing, but the *player* of the bell is a person of no authority whatever.

The strongest moral appeals in Anlo society are to the good of the group and to the authority of one's elders. In dance drumming, individual skill is admired but individual ostentation discouraged. There are no titles for drummers of special ability, no honored musical posts to which they can be appointed. Individual display is strictly limited to brief moments of dialogue between drummers, between dancers, and between a dancer and a drummer. The honor due one's elders is reflected in the fact that the commanding voice among the drums, the sound that signals and has the freedom to improvise messages of praise or blame comes from the instrument of deepest pitch. A deep voice is a symbol of age.

In our symphony orchestra, control flows downward from the conductor. In an Anlo dance-drumming ensemble it flows sideways, so to speak: the fit of the parts, with reference to the play of the bell, guides everyone equally. While our symphony affirms the value of hierarchy, Anlo drumming affirms the value of a more communal social structure.

We may object that a concert is a listening experience, not a pledge of allegiance to society; that the proper study of music is the study of sounds, instruments, notations, and composers. But as one psychologist observes,

> when we move away from . . . those sound constructions that we have learned in the West to experience as objects in themselves, we encounter materials other than the customary pitch, rhythm and tone quality that must nevertheless be accepted as musical materials. The capacity of the human physiology to incorporate into musical experience non-tonal associations, physical movement, practical communication, and so forth, is no less a psychological resource for the evolution of musical life than the sensory capacities of the human ear.
> *(Hutchinson 1976: 7-8. ©B. Schott's Soehne, Mainz. All rights reserved. Used by permission of European American Distributors Corporation, sole U.S. agent for B. Schott's Soehne)*

It would be strange indeed if we experienced music without experiencing its context, or if we found no vital connection between the two.

Folk Music versus Popular Music

To some degree the social context of a performance accounts for its musical content as well as for its structure. Thus a need for inducing trance generates repetitive music; for lullabying, gentle music; for group dancing, music in pronounced and measured rhythms, etc. This section considers the effect on musical content of an important aspect of social context usually ignored in the study of music: the degree of intimacy among members of an audience and between audience and performer. These relationships account for a basic difference in content between folk and popular music, categories that scholars do not distinguish clearly at present for lack of understanding.

The audience is responsible for matching musical content to social context, of course, because the audience is the ultimate composer of every musical tradition (see pp. 5-7). If we accept my earlier argument that music celebrates identity (see pp. 7-8), then it becomes doubly clear that the character of the audience is an important part of the context of any performance. In terms of psychological distance an audience may be anything from most intimately related to most distantly related. This range of psychological distance produces a corresponding range of musical style.

The smallest and most intimately related audience has the strongest sense of its own identity—that is, of both its character as a group and the distinctiveness of that character. This audience is fully committed to the music and musicians celebrating its identity and asks nothing more of them than the sound itself. It does not have to be persuaded to listen to this sound, which therefore tends toward an even, unvaried flow of energy devoid of special effects, exhibiting a more or less distinctive timbre, and lacking both the kind of beginning that commands attention and the kind of ending that commands applause. Music with these features I call folk music, defined as music used by the smallest and most intimately related audience to celebrate its distinctive identity. Examples are the holler as a black American sings it alone (see pp. 37-39), the song of a Bulgarian village as two "soulmates" sing it in duet (see p. 155), and a hymn as lined out by the congregation of the Regular Baptist Church of Jeff, Kentucky (see p. 120).

The largest and most distantly related audience has scarcely any sense of itself and therefore no commitment to the music it presently enjoys as its own or to those who provide that music. It can readily be persuaded to shift allegiance to a somewhat different sound, and therefore the music bidding for or capturing that allegiance does so with features designed to persuade uncommitted strangers: it presents an uneven, varied flow of energy, special effects, and a timbre distinctive enough to distinguish the style from that of competitors yet safely within the range of what has already proved successful; its beginnings command attention, its endings command applause. Music with these features I call popular music, defined as music that must compete for the patronage of the most distantly related audience. Examples are the pieces that win approval in the international record market, on the public concert circuit, and at bars and nightclubs serving a mixed and changing audience.

The description above places folk music and popular music at opposite ends of a continuum. Between them are many intermediate styles, including folk music popularized to attract a larger market and popular music adapted to a committed audience.* On such a continuum each item of the Western

---

*An example of the first would be Pete Seeger's singing of an old British ballad for an assembly of high-school students: because the psychological distance between members of the audience and between audience and performer would be fairly large, many deliberately persuasive elements would appear in the musical flow, such as introductory patter, changes of speed, volume, and mood as needed to underline the words of the poem, and of course a well-marked ending. An example of the second would be my wife's singing *Sweet Georgia Brown* to her own accompaniment on our living room piano: over the years that sound has become a celebration of our intimate family circle and has lost some of the persuasive elements of popular music, such as a well-marked beginning, which undoubtedly characterized it when it was competing for public favor.

repertoire takes its place according to circumstances of performance rather than origin, suggesting we ought to include the meaning of performance with such traditional objects of study as chord structure and melodic relationships.

The Meaning of Art Music

Various labels exist for the music with which the elite classes of Western society celebrate their privileged position. Almost all these labels imply superiority of one sort or another. "Art music," the one used in this book, suggests that, by contrast, the traditions of the lower classes are naive or uncouth; "serious music," that their traditions are trivial; "the classics," that their traditions lack outstanding quality. A generation ago it was common to hear a radio program of art music announced as "the good-music hour" and a station specializing in art music advertised as "your good-music station."*

Needless to say, an understanding of music, like an understanding of people, is not promoted by value judgements.† On the other hand, one of the natural places for a celebration of the educated upper class is the schoolroom. Thus, ironically, the labels and attitudes mentioned above draw strong support from music teachers and have done so ever since the American public-school system began in the 1830's. At the university level this support dates back to medieval times. (The first scholarly society devoted to the study of *popular* music was not founded until 1981.)

A decade ago Philip Hart expressed perhaps as well as anyone the characteristic mixture of aesthetic and social

---

*The label "classical music" is largely free of the implications seen here, but using it to refer to all art music would lead to confusion because the phrase already carries a well-defined and limited meaning as the name for European art music of the second half of the 18th century.

†See Brooks 1982 for a fine discussion of this important point.

prejudice found in statements supporting art music:

> [T]he masterpieces of Beethoven, Leonardo, and Shakespeare have an artistic stature immeasurably greater than that of rock music, advertising display, or serial comedy on television. We cannot avoid distinguishing between ubiquitous illustration or entertainment and masterpieces of the rare and unique creative artist. American society, especially, has always tended to place a special value on *quantity* of appeal, in a false application of political and social egalitarianism to an essentially aristocratic activity.
> *(Hart 1973: 482)*

This point of view has been heard so often in one form or another from those we tend to respect—our teachers and others of superior status—that most of us have come to accept it despite the complete absence of supportive reasoning. Thus to many of us it seemed natural that our government, in deciding to fund the arts directly in the early 1960's decided to fund only the elite arts.

Recently, political backing from underprivileged groups has become important in Washington, and the elitist orientation of this funding has had to be modified. As one discomfited observer reported in 1977,

> according to Joan Mondale—President Carter's chief unofficial spokesman on the subject—the arts are defined by the yearning of most Americans for "personal expression." This is warm and democratic, but it does little to distinguish art from basket weaving,* or trained horn players from the brass section of the high school band. As for the National Endowment for the Arts, this important Federal agency is growing increasingly vague about what areas are meant to lie within its

---

*An impossible task, because "in sociology as well as the other social sciences there is little common ground concerning... the nature of art" (d'Azevedo 1973: 4).

mandate. One officer there complained to me recently that of the 12 divisions funded by the N.E.A., only six could properly be called "arts"— the rest include such marginal endeavors as folk arts, handicrafts, inner city community activity, social and ethnic programs and the like.
(Brustein 1977: 11, column 3)

Our discussion of the meaning of music provides the answer to such complaints, for clearly a democratic government has no business promoting the musical identity of the elite while ignoring other groups.*

Although we have been brought up to revere art music as the highest and finest form of Western musical expression, it is, in terms of the identities it celebrates, simply a species of popular music. It seeks to persuade a psychologically distant audience and therefore displays an uneven, varied flow of energy, special effects, a distinctive but more or less safe timbre, and striking beginnings and endings. That these persuasive features have a different sound than in so-called popular music is due less to their "artistic stature" than to their historical roots: our present quasi-egalitarian society descends from a highly stratified one in which the popular music of the upper class developed more or less separately from the popular music of the lower class.

Understanding art music as popular music has two distinct and practical advantages. For one thing, it allows us to tolerate people's arrogant support of art music as a superior form of artistic expression, for we recognize their arrogance as a logical result of celebrating an elite class and appreciate the fact that popular music of any sort must promote itself to survive. More important, we know that such arrogance does not diminish the

---

*Celebration of elite identity is regularly confused with "culture." Thus a note to Exxon stockholders in 1974 reminded them that "with industry's financial help, Wolf Trap, the nation's only park for the performing arts, attracts a cross section of humanity to culture" (Howe 1974). The arts referred to include only ballet, modern dance, art music, and what newspaper critics refer to as "legitimate" theater.

music itself; we are free to enjoy art music as entertainment, to listen to it and perform it according to our various abilities without the paralyzing fear of inadequacy it imposes when worshipped as something sublime.

The worship of art music is still very much with us. It began at the start of the 19th century, promoted by men like Antonin Reicha, teacher of counterpoint at the National Conservatory of Music in Paris. As Reicha wrote:

> To compose a musical masterwork one must have not only a rare gift and a profound knowledge of the art, but a strong spirit as well—one that can hold itself above criticism, endure with a noble courage the opinion of the crowd, and seek no other reward than the feeling of its own superiority. For in every art (but mainly in music, an art of pure creativity), a masterwork of vast conception, unusual effects, and ideas both intimate, sweeping, and sublime can be neither felt nor appreciated by the masses: . . .
> *(quoted in Lazarus 1922: 256, my translation)*

Reicha's voice was but one in a thunderous chorus announcing that the best art was for edification, the creative genius was a seer, and the chance to experience a work of art tested the audience, not the work. Composers of an earlier age—for example Joseph Haydn (1732-1809)—viewed themselves as craftsmen, not geniuses. When someone asked Haydn why he had composed no quintets (music for a quartet of strings with one additional instrument), his answer was simply that no one had ordered any from him (Carse 1940: 7).

Events conspired to reinforce and extend what might have been a temporary fashion in thought: one after another, some gradually and some violently, the absolute monarchies of Europe yielded their power to the middle class. For the elite arts this meant a new audience, large and uneducated—a "mass of anonymous urbanites" as the sociologist John Mueller has called it, drawn

> from office and shop, from banks and colleges, from the professions and public services. Occupied as they were, full time in gaining a livelihood..., they were by no means a leisure class [as the aristocracy they replaced had been], they felt keenly their inadequacies in the arts, and acquired a veritable inferiority complex in their presence. They suffer from this debilitating affliction to this very day. They eagerly emulated the standards of the decaying, but still glamorous, aristocracy by cultivating and supporting the arts, and stood ready to be instructed.
>
> *(Mueller 1951: 290)*

In the long view the history of Western art music has been on its pedestal just a few moments. It deserves our attention, to be sure, but only as one of many rich musical traditions in the world. This book has tried to place our Western tradition in the broader context of a human process found everywhere. My aim has been to suggest that the language of music is as varied as the social groups controlling it; that this varied language follows universal underlying principles of melody, harmony, rhythm, and form; and that, by reinforcing our sense of identity, this seemingly insubstantial art of transient effects provides us with a foundation stone on which to build our sense of permanence.

> from office and shop, from banks and colleges, from the professions and public services. Occupied as they were, full time in gaining a livelihood..., they were by no means a leisure class [as the aristocracy they replaced had been], they felt keenly their inadequacies in the arts, and acquired a veritable inferiority complex in their presence. They suffer from this debilitating affliction to this very day. They eagerly emulated the standards of the decaying, but still glamorous, aristocracy by cultivating and supporting the arts, and stood ready to be instructed.
>
> *(Mueller 1951: 290)*

In the long view the history of Western art music has been on its pedestal just a few moments. It deserves our attention, to be sure, but only as one of many rich musical traditions in the world. This book has tried to place our Western tradition in the broader context of a human process found everywhere. My aim has been to suggest that the language of music is as varied as the social groups controlling it; that this varied language follows universal underlying principles of melody, harmony, rhythm, and form; and that, by reinforcing our sense of identity, this seemingly insubstantial art of transient effects provides us with a foundation stone on which to build our sense of permanence.

Bibliography/Discography

ADAMS, John
    1961   *Diary and Autobiography of John Adams, Volume 2: Diary 1771-1781,* edited by L. H. Butterfield. Cambridge, Mass.: The Belknap Press.

APEL, Willi
    1969   *Harvard Dictionary of Music.* Cambridge, Mass.: The Belknap Press. Second edition, revised and enlarged.

ARBATSKY, Yuri
    1953   *Beating the Tupan in the Central Balkans.* Chicago: The Newberry Library.

ARNOLD, Franck T.
    1965   *The Art of Accompaniment from a Thorough-Bass as Practised in the XVIIth & XVIIIth Centuries,* intro. by Denis Stevens. New York: Dover Publications. Reprint of 1931 edition.

ATLANTIC
    1351   *Southern Folk Heritage Series: Negro Church Music,* recorded and edited by Alan Lomax and Shirley Collins. New York: Atlantic Recording Corporation, 1961. One 12" disc, 33-1/3 rpm; 4 pp. notes inserted.

AVENARY, Hanoch
    1971   "Music," *in* Cecil Roth, editor-in-chief, *Encyclopedia Judaica,* vol. 12, pp. 566-664. New York: Macmillan.

D'AZEVEDO, Warren L.
    1972   "Introduction," *in* Warren L. d'Azevedo, editor, *The Traditional Artist in African Societies,* pp. 1-15. Bloomington, Ind.: Indiana University Press.

BACHMANN, Werner
    1969   *The Origins of Bowing and the Development of Bowed Instruments up to the Thirteenth Century,* translated by Norma Deane. New York: Oxford University Press. Second edition.

BACKUS, John
    1977   The Accoustical Foundations of Music. New York: W. W. Norton. Second edition.

BAILEY, Ben E.
    1978   "The Lined-Hymn Tradition in Black Mississippi Churches," *The Black Perspective in Music,* vol. 6, no. 1 (Spring), pp. 3-17.

BAINES, Anthony
    1957   *Woodwind Instruments and Their History.* New York: W. W. Norton.
    1960   *Bagpipes.* Oxford: University Press. *Pitt Rivers Museum Occasional Papers on Technology [No.] 9.*

BANZET, Micheline
    1955   "Musique et image," *Cahiers d'études de radio-television,* No. 6, pp. 189-193.

BARRAND, Anthony G.
    1983   "The National Tune Index Tackles English-language Folksongs." Paper read July 5 at the Third American Music Conference, University of Keele, England.

BENSON, Louis F.
    1962   *The English Hymn, Its Development and Use in Worship.* Richmond, Va.: John Knox Press. Reprint of first edition, 1915.

BERGEIJK, Willem A. Van, John R. Pierce, and Edward E. David, Jr.
    1960   *Waves and the Ear.* Garden City, N.Y.: Doubleday (Anchor Books).

BERRY, Mary
    1979   "Gregorian Chant: The Restoration of the Chant and Seventy-five Years of Recording," *Early Music,* vol. 7, no. 7 (April), pp. 197, 199, 201-205, 207-209, 211, 213-217.

BIBLE
    [1611]   *The Holy Bible, Containing the Old and New Testaments Translated Out of the Original Tongues . . . Authorized King James Version.* N.Y.: The World Publishing Company, n.d. "Self-pronouncing edition."
    1612   *The Booke of Psalmes, Collected into English Meetre by Thomas Sternhold. Iohn Hopkins and Others: Conferred with the Hebrew, With Apt Notes to Sing Them Withall. . . .* London, The Companie of Stationers. A later edition of *The Whole Booke of Psalmes Collected into Englysh Metre . . .* , 1562.
    1912   *The Bay Psalm Book, Being a Facsimile Reprint of the First Edition, Printed by Stephen Daye at Cambridge, In New England in 1640.* New York: Dodd and Livingston.
    1966   *The Anchor Bible, Vol. 16, Psalms I: 1-50,* translated by Mitchell Dahood, S.J. Garden City, N.Y.: Doubleday.

BILLARD, Jules B.
    1974   *The World of the American Indian,* edited by Jules B. Billard. Washington, D.C.: National Geographic Society.

BILLINGS, William
    1961   *The Continental Harmony,* edited with an introduction by Hans Nathan. Cambridge, Mass.: The Belknap Press [original edition 1794].

BITTERMANN, Helen R.
    1929   "The Organ in the Early Middle Ages," *Speculum,* vol. 4, pp. 390-410.

BLACKING, John
    1972-73   "Folk Music and Dances of Ireland: Review Article," *Irish Folk Music Studies,* vol. 1, pp. 56-59.
    1973   *How Musical Is Man?* Seattle, Wash.: University of Washington Press.

BLADES, James and Jeremy Montagu
    1976   *Early Percussion Instruments from the Middle Ages to the Baroque.* London: Oxford University Press.

BOATWRIGHT, Howard
1960   *Indian Classical Music and the Western Listener.* Bombay, India: Bharatiya Vidya Bharan.

BOWLES, Edmund A.
1957   "Were Musical Instruments Used in the Liturgical Service During the Middle Ages?" *The Galpin Society Journal,* vol. 10, pp. 40-56.

BRANDON, William
1961   *The American Heritage Book of Indians.* N.p.: American Heritage Publishing Company.

BRÖDEL, Max
1946   *Three Unpublished Drawings of The Anatomy of the Human Ear by the Late Max Brödel Assisted by P. D. Malone, Stacy R. Guild, and S. J. Crowe.* Philadelphia: W. B. Saunders Company.

BRONSON, Bertrand H.
1959-72   *The Traditional Tunes of the Child Ballads with Their Texts, According to the Extant Records of Great Britain and America.* Princeton, N.J.: Princeton University Press. Five volumes.
1969   *The Ballad as Song.* Berkeley, Calif.: University of California Press.

BROOKS, William
1982   "On Being Tasteless," *Popular Music,* vol. 2, pp. 9-18.

BRUSTEIN, Robert
1977   "Can the Show Go On?" *The New York Times Magazine* (July 10), pp. 8-9, 11, 54, 56-57, 59.

BUECHNER, Alan C.
1964   "The New England Harmony: A Collection of Early American Choral Music Performed by the Old Sturbridge Singers, Floyd Carson, Singing Master, and Members of the Harvard Wind Ensemble," in Alan C. Buechner, compiler, *FA 2377: The New England Harmony.* New York: Folkways Records. 31 pp. of notes to the recording, inserted.

BYRD, William
1941   *The Secret Diary of William Byrd of Westover 1709-1712,* edited by Louis B. Wright and Marion Tinling. Richmond, Va.: The Dietz Press.

CARRINGTON, John F.
1949   *Talking Drums of Africa.* London: Carey Kingsgate Press.

CARSE, Adam
1940   *The Orchestra in the XVIIIth Century.* Cambridge, England: W. Heffner and Sons.

CATES, Jesse Howard
1948   "American Baptist Hymnody from 1640-1850." Louisville, Ky.: Southern Baptist Theological Seminary. Unpublished master's thesis.

CATHOLIC Church
1934   *Brevarium Romanum ex Decreto Sacrosancti Concilii Tridentini*

Restitutum . . . Pars Hiemalis. Tours, France: Typis Mame.

1959   *The Liber Usualis, With Introduction and Rubrics in English,* edited by the Benedictines of Solesmes. New York: Desclée Company.

CHASE, Gilbert

1966   *America's Music from the Pilgrims to the Present.* New York: McGraw Hill. Second edition, revised.

CLAPTON, Ernest

1934   *Our Prayer Book Psalter, Containing Coverdale's Version from His 1535 Bible and the Prayer Book Version by Coverdale from the Great Bible 1538-41 Printed Side by Side, With an Introduction and Notes on the Sources of Coverdale's Renderings.* London: Society for Promoting Christian Knowledge.

CLEMENTS, George N.

1972   "The Verbal Syntax of Ewe." London: University of London. Unpublished dissertation.

COHALAN, Michael

1981   "Tension in the Cathedral. Gothic Beauty: Was It Form or Function?" *Science 81,* vol. 2, no. 10 (December), pp. 32-37, 39-41.

COHEN, Francis L.

[1964]   "Cantillation," *in* Isidore Singer, editor, *The Jewish Encyclopedia,* vol. 3, pp. 537-549. New York: Ktav Publishing House, Inc.

COHEN, John

1963   *The High Lonesome Sound,* photographed by John Cohen, edited by Patricia Jaffee. New York: Brandon Films. Thirty minutes, black and white, sound, 16 mm.

COLERIDGE, Samuel Taylor

1965   *Biographia Literaria . . . Edited with His Aesthetic Essays by J. Shawcross.* London: Oxford University Press. Two volumes. First published in 1817; first edition edited by Shawcross 1907.

COPLAND, Aaron

1981   "Turning Points: Aaron Copland," interviewed by Katie Leishman, *Quest/81,* vol. 5, no. 5 (June), p. 96.

COURLANDER, Harold

1963   *Negro Folk Music, U.S.A.* New York: Columbia University Press.

CURTIS, Natalie

1923   *The Indians' Book, An Offering by the American Indians of Indian Lore, Musical and Narrative, To Form a Record of the Songs and Legends of Their Race.* New York: Harper and Brothers Publishers. Second edition.

D'ACCONE, Frank A.

1961   "The Singers of San Giovanni in Florence during the 15th Century," *Journal of the American Musicological Society,* vol. 14, no. 3 (Fall), pp. 307-358.

DAVEY, Henry

1911   *History of English Music.* London: J. Curwen and Sons. Second edition.

DAVISON, Archibald T. and Willi Apel
    1949   *Historical Anthology of Music,* [Vol. 1] *Oriental, Medieval and Renaissance Music,* edited by Archibald T. Davison and Willi Apel. Cambridge, Mass.: Harvard University Press. Revised edition.

DAVISSON, Ananias
    1976   *Kentucky Harmony, Or a Choice Collection of Psalm Tunes, Hymns, and Anthems, In Three Parts, Selected by A. Davisson, 1816; Facsimile Edition with Introduction by Irving Lowens.* Minneapolis, Minn.: Augsburg Publishing House.

DENSMORE, Frances
    1910   *Chippewa Music; Smithsonian Institution Bureau of American Ethnology Bulletin 45.* Washington, D.C.: Government Printing Office.
    1918   *Teton Sioux Music; Smithsonian Institution Bureau of American Ethnology Bulletin 61.* Washington, D.C.: Government Printing Office.
    1920   "The Rhythm of Sioux and Chippewa Music," *Art and Archaeology,* vol. 9, no. 2 (February), pp. 59-67.
    1922   *Northern Ute Music; Smithsonian Institution Bureau of American Ethnology Bulletin 75.* Washington, D.C.: Government Printing Office.
    1942   "The Study of Indian Music," *in* C. G. Abbot, Secretary, *Annual Report of the Board of Regents of the Smithsonian Institution . . . for the Year Ended June 30, 1941,* pp. 527-550. Washington, D.C.: U.S. Government Printing Office.

DEUTSCHE GRAMMOPHON GESELLSCHAFT
    ARC 3102   *I. Research Period, Gregorian Chant, Series A: The Office,* performed by the Benedictine monks, Abbey of St. Martin, Beuron, West Germany, directed by Maurus Pfaff, O.S.B. Hamburg: Deutsche Grammophon Gesellschaft, 1957. One 12" disc, 33-⅓ r.p.m.

DITTMER, Luther
    1969   *Facsimile Reproduction of the Manuscript Wolfenbuttel 1099 Helmstadiensis--(1206), W2, With an Introduction by Luther Dittmer.* Brooklyn, N.Y.: Institute of Medieval Music Ltd. "Publications of Medieval Musical Manuscripts No. 2." Second edition.

DIXON, Robert M. W., and John Godrich
    1970   *Recording the Blues.* New York: Stein and Day.

DOUGHTIE, Edward
    1970   *Lyrics from English Airs 1596-1622,* edited by Edward Doughtie. Cambridge, Mass.: Harvard University Press.

DOWNEY, James C.
    1969   *The Music of American Revivalism.* Ann Arbor, Mich.: University Microfilms. Dissertation in Music, Tulane University, 1968, microfilm no. 69-3792.

DU BOIS, William E. B.
    1903   *The Souls of the Black Folk; Essays and Sketches.* Chicago: A. C. McClurge.

ENGEL, Hans
    1968   "Music II: Music and Society," *in* David L. Sills, editor, *International Encyclopedia of the Social Sciences,* vol. 10, pp. 566-575. New York: Macmillan and The Free Press.

EPSTEIN, Dena J.
    1963   "Slave Music in the U.S. before 1860; A Survey of Sources (Part I)," *Notes,* second series, vol. 20, no. 2 (Spring), pp. 195-212.

ESCHER, Maurits Cornelis
    1971   *The World of M. C. Escher,* edited by J. L. Locher. New York: Harry N. Abrams, Inc.

FAGE, J. D.
    1970   "Introduction," *in* J. D. Fage, editor, *Africa Discovers Her Past,* pp. 1-6. London: Oxford University Press.

FARMER, Henry George
    1960   "Moorish Music," *in* Eric Blom, editor, *Grove's Dictionary of Music and Musicians,* vol. 5 (New York: St. Martin's Press), pp. 868-876. Fifth edition.

FEDERAL WRITERS' PROJECT
    1941   "Slave Narratives, A Folk History of Slavery in the United States from Interviews with Former Slaves." Washington, D.C.: Library of Congress. Typescript of interviews conducted 1936-1938, 17 volumes in 33 parts.

FINNEGAN, Ruth
    1970   *Oral Literature in Africa.* London: Clarendon Press.

FIRE, John / Lame Deer and Richard Erdoes
    1972   *Lame Deer, Seeker of Visions.* New York: Simon and Schuster.

FOLKWAYS
    FA 2656   *Music from the South, Field Recordings Taken in Alabama, Louisiana, and Mississippi . . . Volume 7: Elder Songsters, 2,* recorded by Frederick Ramsey, Jr. New York: Folkways Records and Service Corporation, 1956. One 12" disc, 33-⅓ r.p.m.

    FA 2941   *Leadbelly's Last Sessions,* recorded and annotated by Frederick Ramsey, Jr. New York: Folkways Records and Service Corporation, 1953. Two 12" discs, 33-⅓ r.p.m.; recorded in September and October of 1948.

    FA 2952   *Anthology of American Folk Music, Vol. 2: Social Music,* edited by Harry Smith. New York: Folkways Records and Service Corporation, 1952. Two 12" discs, 33-⅓ r.p.m., with booklet.

    FE 4445   *Songs and Dances of the Flathead Indians.* New York: Folkways Records and Service Corporation, 1953. One 12" disc, 33-⅓ r.p.m.

    FH 5458   *Excerpts from Interviews with Dock Boggs, Legendary Banjo Player and Singer,* recorded and edited by Mike Seeger. New York: Folkways Records and Service Corporation, 1965. One 12" disc, 33-⅓ r.p.m.

    FR 8903   *Yoga Music of India, Volume 1, Sung with Veena Accompaniment by Swami Vidyananda.* New York: Folkways Records and Service Corporation, 1964. One 12" disc, 33-⅓ r.p.m.

FRAISSE, Paul
  1963 *The Psychology of Time,* translated by Jennifer Leith. New York: Harper and Row.

GOLEMAN, Daniel
  1984 "Human Emotion under New Scrutiny; Objective Measures Found for Hidden Feelings," *The New York Times* (Tuesday, May 22), section C, pp. 1, 8.

GOODY, Jack
  1977 "Against 'Ritual': Loosely Structured Thoughts on a Loosely Defined Topic," in Sally F. Moore and Barbara G. Myerhoff, editors, *Secular Ritual* (Amsterdam, The Netherlands: Van Gorcum), pp. 25-35.

GORDON, Bonnie B.
  1981 "The Secrets of Notre-Dame," *Science 81,* vol. 2, no. 10 (December), p. 38.

GRONOW, Pekka
  1975 "Ethnic Music and Soviet Record Industry," *Ethnomusicology,* vol. 19, no. 1 (January), pp. 91-99.

GROTH, Edward J., P. James E. Peebles, Michael Deldner, and Raymond M. Soneira
  1977 "The Clustering of Galaxies," *Scientific American,* vol. 237, no. 5 (November), pp. 76-78, 84, 87-90, 95-98.

GUTMAN, Herbert G.
  1976 *The Black Family in Slavery and Freedom, 1750-1925.* New York: Pantheon Books.

HANDSCHIN, Jacques
  1932 "Zur Geschichte von Notre Dame," *Acta Musicologica,* vol. 4, pp. 5-17, 49-55, 104-105.

HARRISON, Frank L.
  1958 *Music in Medieval Britain.* New York: Dover Publications, Inc.
  1973 *Time, Place and Music: An Anthology of Ethnomusicological Observation c. 1550 to c. 1800.* Amsterdam: Fritz Knuf.

HART, Philip
  1973 *Orpheus in the New World: The Symphony Orchestra as an American Cultural Institution.* New York: W. W. Norton.

HAYDN SOCIETY
  HSE 9100 *A Treasury of Early Music: An Anthology of Masterworks of the Middle Ages, the Renaissance, and the Baroque Compiled and Edited with Notes by Carl Parrish, Under the Direction of Mogens Wöldike . . . Record 1: Music of the Middle Ages.* Hartford, Conn.: The Haydn Society, 1964. One 12" disc, 33-1/3 r.p.m.

HEVNER, Kate
  1937 "The Aesthetic Experience: A Psychological Description," *Pyschological Review,* vol. 44, no. 3 (May), pp. 245-263.

HICKMANN, Hans
  1936 *Das Portativ; Ein Beitrag zur Geschichte der Kleinorgel.* Kassel: Bärenreiter.

HIGGINS, Jon B.
    1972   "Film Review," *Asian Music,* vol. 3, no. 2, pp. 58-60.
    1976   "From Prince to Populace: Patronage as a Determinant of Change in South Indian (Karnatak) Music," *Asian Music,* vol. 7, no. 2, pp. 20-26.

HIRSH, Ira J.
    1959   "Auditory Perception of Temporal Order," *Journal of the Acoustical Society of America,* vol. 31, no. 6 (June), pp. 759-767.

HOLMES, Urban T., Jr.
    1953   *Daily Living in the Twelfth Century, Based on the Observations of Alexander Neckham in London and Paris.* Madison, Wis.: University of Wisconsin Press.

HOOD, George
    1970   *A History of Music in New England.* New York: Johnson Reprint Corporation. Original edition Boston, 1846.

HOOD, Mantle
    1971   *The Ethnomusicologist.* New York: McGraw-Hill.

HOWE, R.J.
    1974   [Untitled note in stockholders' brochure]. Houston, Tex.: Exxon Company U.S.A., December. Mr. Howe was Public Relations Manager for the company.

HUCKE, Helmut
    1980   "Toward a New Historical View of Gregorian Chant," *Journal of the American Musicological Society,* vol. 33, no. 3 (Fall), pp. 437-467.

HUGHES, Andrew
    1974   *Medieval Music: The Sixth Liberal Art.* Toronto: University of Toronto Press.

HUTCHINSON, William
    1976   "Psychology and World Music," *Die Welt der Musik / The World of Music / Le monde de la musique* (Berlin), vol. 18, no. 1, pp. 3-8.

IDELSOHN, Abraham Zebi
    1914   *Hebräisch-orientalischer Melodienschatz zum ersten Male gesammelt, erläutert und herausgegeben von A. Z. Idelsohn, I. Band* [volume 1]: *Gesänge der Jemenischen Juden.* Leipzig: Breitkopf & Härtel. English edition titled *Thesaurus of Oriental Hebrew Melodies* (Berlin: B. Hartz, 1923).

INGALLS, Jeremiah
    1981   *The Christian Harmony or Songster's Companion,* with an introduction by David Klocko. New York: Da Capo Press. No. 22 of the series Early American Music, edited by H. Wiley Hitchcock. Contains facsimile of 1805 edition.

IRWIN-WILLIAMS, Cynthia
    1968   "Archaeological Evidence on Early Man in Mexico," *in* C. Irwin-Williams, editor, *Early Man in Western North America; Symposium of the Southwestern Anthropological Association, San Diego, 1968,* pp. 39-41. Portales, N.M.: Eastern New Mexico University, Paleo-Indian Institute. Volume 1, number 4 of *Eastern New Mexico University Contributions in Anthropology* (December).

JACKSON, George Pullen
   1975   *White and Negro Spirituals, Their Life Span and Kinship, Tracing 200 Years of Untrammeled Song Making and Singing among Our Country Folk, with 116 Songs as Sung by Both Races.* New York: Da Capo Press. Reprint of first edition of 1944.

JACOBS, Jay
   1968   *The Horizon Book of Great Cathedrals,* Jay Jacobs, editor in charge. New York: American Heritage Publishing Company, Inc.

JAMES, William
   1890   *The Principles of Psychology.* New York: Henry Holt. Two volumes.

JAMES, Willis L.
   1955   "The Romance of the Negro Folk Cry in America," *Phylon,* vol. 16 (March), pp. 15-30.

JENNINGS, Jesse D., et al.
   1978   *Ancient Native Americans,* edited by Jesse D. Jennings. San Francisco: W. H. Freeman and Company.

JOHANSON, Donald C. and Maitland A. Edey
   1981   *Lucy: The Beginnings of Humankind.* New York: Simon and Schuster.

JOHNSON, David
   1972   *Music and Society in Lowland Scotland.* London: Oxford University Press.

JONES, Arthur M.
   1934   "African Drumming: A Study in the Combination of Rythms in African Music," *Bantu Studies,* vol. 8, no. 2 (March), pp. 1-16.

JULESZ, Bela
   1971   *Foundations of Cyclopean Perception.* Chicago: University of Chicago Press.

KASTNER, Georges
   1852   *Les danses des morts: Dissertations et recherches historiques, philosophiques, littéraires et musicales* . . . Paris: Brandus et Cie.

KATSAROVA-KOUKOUDOVA, Raina
   1954   "Folk Music: Bulgarian," *Grove's Dictionary of Music and Musicians,* vol. 3, pp. 201-211. New York: St. Martin's Press. Fifth edition.

KATSAROVA-KOUKOUDOVA, Raina and Kiril Djenev
   1976   *Bulgarian Folk Dances,* translated by Nevena Geliazkova and Marguerite Alexieva. Pittsburgh, Pa.: Duquesne University Tamburitzans Institute of Folk Arts, and Slavic Publishers. Second printing.

KIRBY, Percival R.
   1968   *The Musical Instruments of the Native Races of South Africa.* Johannesburg, South Africa: Witwatersrand University Press. Second edition (first published 1934).

KOENIG, Martin
   1970   "In the Shadow of the Mountain / Bulgarian Folk Music: Songs and Dances of Pirin-Macedonia Collected in Bulgaria and Produced by Ethel Raim & Mar-

tin Koenig," *in* Nonesuch Records, *H 72038: In the Shadow of the Mountain* . . . , liner. New York: Nonesuch Records. One 12" disc, 33-1/3 r.p.m.

KOENIG, Martin and Ethel Raim
    1984   [Private communication.]

KRAMER, Hilton
    1982   "The High Art of Primitivism," *The New York Times Magazine* (Sunday, January 24), pp. 18, 62.

KREMENLIEV, Boris A.
    1952   *Bulgarian-Macedonian Folk Music.* Berkeley, Calif.: University of California Press.
    1957   "Some Social Aspects of Bulgarian Folksongs," *Journal of American Folklore*, vol. 69, pp. 310-319.

KUPFERBERG, Herbert
    1978   "Women of the Baton—The New Music Masters," *Parade, The Sunday Newspaper Magazine* (May 14), pp. 4-5.

KURATH, Gertrude P.
    1964   *Iroquois Music and Dance: Ceremonial Arts of Two Seneca Longhouses; Smithsonian Institution Bureau of American Ethnology Bulletin 187.* Washington, D.C.: U.S. Government Printing Office.

LADZEKPO, Kobla
    1971   "The Social Mechanics of Good Music," *African Music,* vol. 5, no. 1 (1971), pp. 6-22.

LANGER, Suzanne K.
    1953   *Feeling and Form. A Theory of Art Developed from 'Philosophy in a New Key.'* New York: Charles Scribner's Sons.

LAZARUS, Daniel
    1922   "Un maitre de Berlioz: Anton Reicha," *La revue musicale,* vol. 3, no. 8 (June), pp. 255-261.

LEAKEY, Louis S. B., Ruth De Ette Simpson, and Thomas Clements
    1968   "Archaeological Excavations in the Calico Mountains, California," *Science,* vol. 160, no. 3831 (May 31), pp. 1022-1023.

LEIGH, James W.
    1921   *Other Days.* London: T. Fisher Unwin.

LESTER, Elenore
    1967   "Shankar, Unnerved by the Hippie's Adulation," *The New York Times* (Sunday, October 22), p. D-21.

LIBRARY OF CONGRESS
    AAFS-L8   *Folk Music of the United States: Negro Work Songs and Calls,* edited by Benjamin A. Botkin. Washington, D.C.: Music Division, Library of Congress, 1959. One 12" disc, 33-1/3 r.p.m.
    AAFS-L11   *37th Annual Session of the Alabama Sacred Harp Singing Convention, Birmingham, Ala., August 1942,* recorded by Alan Lomax and George Pullen

Jackson. Washington, D.C.: Library of Congress Music Division, 1959. One 12-inch disc, 33-1/3 r.p.m. Originally issued in 78 r.p.m., 1943.

AAFS-L40   *Music of the American Indian* [Volume 7]: *Sioux,* edited by Willard Rhodes. Washington, D.C.: Library of Congress, Division of Music, Recording Laboratory, 1954. One 12" disc, 33-1/3 r.p.m.

LBC-1   *Religious Music,* edited by Richard K. Spottswood. Washington, D.C.: Library of Congress, Music Division, Recording Laboratory, 1976. One 12" disc, 33-1/3 r.p.m.

LOMAX, Alan
1968   *Folk Song Style and Culture.* Washington, D.C.: American Association for the Advancement of Science.

LOMAX, John A.
1947   *Adventures of a Ballad Hunter.* New York: Macmillan.

LONDON
A 4501   *Gregorian Chant / Chant gregorien,* sung by monks of St. Pierre de Solesmes directed by Dom Joseph Gajard, O.S.B., notes by Dom Gajard translated by Justine B. Ward. London: London Gramophone Corporation, 1959. Five 12" discs, 33-1/3 r.p.m.

LOWENS, Irving
1964   *Music and Musicians in Early America.* New York: W. W. Norton & Company, Inc.

LUCHAIRE, Achille
1957   *Social France at the Time of Philip Augustus,* edited by Louis Halphen, translated by Edward B. Krehbiel. New York: Frederick Ungar. Original edition in French, 1912.

LYRICHORD
LLST 7157   *Music of the Rain Forest Pygmies of the North-East Congo,* recorded and annotated by Colin M. Turnbull. New York: Lyrichord Discs, 196-. One 12" disc, 33-1/3 r.p.m.

MACDOUGALL, Hamilton C.
1940   *Early New England Psalmody, An Historical Appreciation 1620-1820.* Brattleboro, Vt.: Stephen Daye Press.

MAHEU, Richard F.
1976   [Letter received in December.]

MARCUSE, Sibyl
1975   *A Survey of Musical Instruments.* New York: Harper & Row.

MARKOFF, Irene
1976   [Letter dated October 21.]

MARSH, J. B. T.
1880   *The Story of the Jubilee Singers, With Their Songs.* Boston: Houghton, Mifflin. Revised edition.

MAULTSBY, Portia K.
1979   "Black Spirituals: A Manifestation of the Black Aesthetic." Unpublished paper,

delivered at the Conference on Rural Hymnody, Berea College, Berea, Kentucky, April 28.

MCALLESTER, David P.
- 1954 *Enemy Way Music: A Study of Social and Esthetic Values as Seen in Navaho Music.* Cambridge, Mass.: Peabody Museum. Volume 41, number 3 of *Papers of the Peabody Museum of American Archaeology and Ethnology* (Harvard); number 3 of *Reports of the Rimrock Project, Values Series.*
- 1975 [Letter dated November 14.]

MCCURRY, John G.
- 1973 *The Social Harp,* edited by Daniel W. Patterson and John F. Garst. Athens, Ga.: University of Georgia Press. Facsimile of 1855 edition.

MCGLOTHLIN, William J.
- 1911 *Baptist Confessions of Faith.* Philadelphia: American Baptist Publication Society.

MC KINNON, James W.
- 1974 "The Tenth Century Organ at Winchester," *The Organ Yearbook* (Netherlands), vol. 5, pp. 4-19.
- 1979-80 "The Exclusion of Musical Instruments from the Ancient Synagogue," *Proceedings of the Royal Musical Association,* vol. 106, pp. 77-87.

MENÉNDEZ PIDAL, Ramón
- 1924 *Poesía juglaresca y juglares; aspetos de la historia literaria y cultural de España.* Madrid: [Tip. de la "Rev. de archivos"].

MENON, Narayana
- 1957 "The Impact of the West and Western Technology on Indian Music," *Bulletin of the Institute of Traditional Cultures* (Madras), pp. 70-80.

MERRIAM, Alan P.
- 1951 "Flathead Indian Instruments and Their Music," *Musical Quarterly,* vol. 37 (July), pp. 368-375.
- 1953 "Songs and Dances of the Flathead Indians," *in* Alan P. Merriam, compiler, *FE 4445: Songs and Dances of the Flathead Indians.* New York: Folkways Records and Service Corporation. 7 pp. of notes to one 12" disc, 33-⅓ r.p.m.
- 1967 *Ethnomusicology of the Flathead Indians.* Chicago: Aldine Publishing Company. Viking Fund Publications in Anthropology No. 44.

MEYER, Leonard B.
- 1956 *Emotion and Meaning in Music.* Chicago: University of Chicago Press.

MILTON, John
- 1959 "Of Education," *in* Don M. Wolfe, editor, *Complete Prose Works of John Milton, Vol. II: 1643-1648,* pp. 362-415. New Haven: Yale University Press. Essay originally published 1644.

MONTEVERDI, Claudio
- 1923 *L'Orfeo, Favola in Musica,* edited by G. Francisco Malipiero. London: J. & W. Chester, Ltd.

MUELLER, John H.
1951 *The American Symphony Orchestra: A Social History of Musical Taste.* Bloomington, Ind.: Indiana University Press.

MUSICAL HERITAGE
MHS 617 *Choral Music of the Renaissance: Josquin Des Pres,Missa Pange Lingua; Claude Le Jeune, Six Polyphonic Chansons, Psalm 45.* Tinton Falls, N.J.: The Musical Heritage Society, 1965. One 12" disc, 33-⅓ r.p.m., with notes by Philipe Caillard and Bernard Gagnepain translated by Herman Adler.

NAYO, Nicholas Z.
1964 "Akpalu and His Songs: A Study of the Man and His Music." Legon, Ghana: University of Ghana, Institute of African Studies. Unpublished thesis for the Diploma in African Music.

NETTL, Bruno
1973 *Folk and Traditional Music of the Western Continents.* Englewood Cliffs, N.J.: Prentice Hall. Second edition.
1983 *The Study of Ethnomusicology. Twenty-nine Issues and Concepts.* Urbana, Ill.: University of Illinois Press.

NEW WORLD RECORDS
NW 252 *Roots of the Blues,* recorded and edited by Alan Lomax. New York: Recorded Anthology of American Music, Inc., 1977. One 12" disc, 33-⅓ r.p.m.

NEW YORK TIMES
1980 "Twilight of the Primitive," *The New York Times* (Saturday, October 8), p. 24. Anonymous editorial.

NONESUCH
H 72011 *Music of Bulgaria: Soloists, Chorus and Orchestra of the Ensemble of the Bulgarian Republic, Phillipe Koutev, Conductor.* New York: Nonesuch Records, 1970. One 12" disc, 33-⅓ r.p.m., recorded in 1955 in Paris.
H 72034 *A Harvest, A Shepherd, A Bride: Village Music of Bulgaria Collected in Bulgaria and Produced by Ethel Raim and Martin Koenig.* New York: Nonesuch Records, 1970. One 12" disc, 33-⅓ r.p.m., recorded in 1968.
H 72038 *In the Shadow of the Mountain: Bulgarian Folk Music, Songs and Dances of Pirin-Macedonia Collected in Bulgaria . . . by Ethel Raim and Martin Koenig.* New York: Nonesuch Records, 1970. One 12" disc, 33-⅓ r.p.m., recorded in 1968.

OLMSTEAD, Frederick L.
1968 *Journey in the Seaboard Slave States, with Remarks on Their Economy.* New York: Negro Universities Press. Reprint of 1856 edition.

PALISCA, Claude V.
1963 "Musical Asides in the Diplomatic Correspondence of Emilio de' Cavalieri," *The Musical Quarterly,* vol. 49, pp. 339-355.

PANTALEONI, Hewitt
1972 *The Rhythm of Atsiã Dance Drumming among the Aṉlọ (Eʋe) of Anyako.* Oneonta, N.Y.: H. Pantaleoni.

PERROT, Jean
    1971   *The Organ, from Its Invention in the Hellenistic Period, to the End of the Thirteenth Century,* translated by Norma Deane. London: Oxford University Press.

PILBEAM, David
    1972   *The Ascent of Man: An Introduction to Human Evolution.* New York: Macmillan Publishing Company, Inc.

PINES, Maya
    1973   "Two Astonishingly Different Persons Inhabit Our Heads: We Are Left-Brained or Right-Brained," *The New York Times Magazine* (September 9), pp. 32-33, 121-122, 124-127, 132, 136-137.

PIRROTTA, Nino
    1968   "Early Opera and Aria," *in* William W. Austin, editor, *New Looks at Italian Opera: Essays in Honor of Donald J. Grout,* pp. 39-107. Ithaca, N.Y.: Cornell University Press.

POWERS, Harold S.
    1980   "Mode," *in* Stanley Sadie, editor, *The New Grove Dictionary of Music and Musicians,* vol. 12, pp. 376-450. Washington, D.C.: Grove's Dictionaries of Music, Inc.

PREECE, Carol Aiken
    1981   "Elche's Living Mystery," *Américas,* vol. 33, no. 1 (January), pp. 40-44.

PRIBRAM, Karl H.
    1980   "The Biology of Emotions and Other Feelings," *in* Robert Plutchik and Henry Kellerman, editors, *Emotion: Theory, Research, and Experience. Volume 1: Theories of Emotion,* pp. 245-269. New York: Academic Press.

RAIM, Ethel
    1975   "In Search of a Voice: Ethel Raim on Balkan Vocal Style, Interviewed by Abby Newton and Bob Norman," *Sing Out!,* vol. 24, no. 1 (March-April), pp. 8-10.
    1977   [Letter dated February 22.]

RAYNOR, Henry
    1972   *A Social History of Music from the Middle Ages to Beethoven.* New York: Schocken Books.

RCA VICTOR
    LM 6057   *History of Music in Sound, Vol. 1: Ancient and Oriental Music.* New York: RCA Victor, 1957. Two 12" discs, 41 pp. of notes by Egon Wellesz.

READ, Albert
    1976   [Private communication, no date.]

REYNOLDS, William
    1976   *Companion to Baptist Hymnal.* Nashville, Tenn.: Broadman Press.

RICKMAN, Thomas
    1862   *An Attempt to Discriminate the Styles of Architecture in England from the Conquest to the Reformation . . . with Considerable Additions, Chiefly*

Historical, by John Henry Parker. Oxford and London: John Henry and James Parker. Sixth edition.

RIES, Raymond E.
   1969   "The Cultural Setting of South Indian Music," *Asian Music,* vol. 1, no. 2, pp. 22-31.

RITCHIE, Jean
   1980   *Singing Family of the Cumberlands,* illustrated by Maurice Sendak. Port Washington, N.Y.: Geordie Music Publishing. First edition 1955.
   1981   [Letter dated March 24.]

ROACH, David
   1972   "The Banaras Bāj—The Tablā Tradition of a North Indian City," *Asian Music,* vol. 3, no. 2, pp. 29-41.

ROEDERER, Juan G.
   1974   "The Psychophysics of Musical Perception," *Music Educators Journal,* vol. 60, no. 6 (February), pp. 21-30.

ROESNER, Edward
   1979   "The Performance of Parisian Organum," *Early Music,* vol. 7, no. 2 (April), pp. 174-189.

ROTH, Cecil, and Geoffrey Wigoder
   1970   *The New Standard Jewish Encyclopedia,* edited by Cecil Roth and Geoffrey Wigoder, Garden City, N.Y.: Doubleday and Company, Inc.

ROUGNON, Paul
   1925   "Origines de la notation musicale moderne (étude historique)," *in* Albert Lavignac and Lionel de la Laurencie, editors, *Encyclopédie de la musique et dictionnaire du conservatoire, deuxième partie: technique—esthétique—pédagogie* . . . (Paris: Delagrave), pp. 364-404.

RUBIN, Arnold
   1969   "Prizewinners / Laureats," *African Arts / Arts d'Afrique,* vol. 2, no. 2 (Winter), 9-11.

RUHLAND, Konrad
   1968   "Notre-Dame-Epoche und ars antiqua / Notre Dame epoch and ars antiqua," *in* Telefunken-Decca *SAWT 9530-B/9531-B: Ars Antiqua* . . . , insert, pp. 3-20. Hamburg, West Germany: Telefunken-Decca Schallplatten-Gesellschaft.

SACHS, Curt
   1940   *The History of Musical Instruments.* New York: W. W. Norton.
   1943   *The Rise of Music in the Ancient World East and West.* New York: W. W. Norton.
   1960   "Primitive and Medieval Music: A Parallel," *Journal of the American Musicological Society,* vol. 13, pp. 43-49.

SACRED HARP
   1966   *Original Sacred Harp, Denison Revision, 1966 Edition: The Best Collection of Sacred Songs, Hymns, Odes, and Anthems Ever Offered the Singing Public for General Use.* Cullman, Ala.: Sacred Harp Publishing Company.

ST. PETERSBURG TIMES
- 1978 "Judge Orders Medical Profiles Open for Public Inspection," *The St. Petersburg Times* (Florida), (Thursday, April 27), p. 8A.

SALMEN, Walter
- 1957 "Bemerkungen zum Mehrstimmigen Musizieren der Spielleute im Mittelalter," *Revue belge de musicologie,* vol. 11, pp. 17-26.

SAUNDERS, Frederick A.
- 1948 "Physics and Music," *Scientific American,* vol. 179 (July), pp. 32-41.

SCHAFER, Thomas A.
- 1963 "Solomon Stoddard and the Theology of the Revival," *in* Stuart C. Henry, editor, *A Miscellany of American Christianity,* pp. 328-361. Durham, N.C.: Duke University Press.

SCHERING, Arnold
- 1931 *Geschichte der Musik in Beispielen; dreihundertfünfzig Tonsätze aus neun Jahrhunderten.* Leipzig, Germany: Breitkopf and Härtel.

SCHOLES, Percy A.
- 1962 *The Puritans and Music in New England, A Contribution to the Cultural History of Two Nations.* New York: Russell and Russell. Re-issue of 1934 edition.

SCHWARTZ, Tony
- 1979 "Dustin Hoffman vs. Nearly Everybody," *The New York Times* (Sunday, December 16), Section 2, pp. 1, 40.

SEYBOLT, Robert F.
- 1970 *The Private Schools of Colonial Boston 1635-1775.* Westport, Conn.: Greenwood Press. Original edition 1935.

SHAKESPEARE, William
- 1979 *The Complete Illustrated Shakespeare,* edited by Howard Staunton, illustrated by John Gilbert, foreword by Solomon J. Schepps. New York: Park Lane. "Park Lane 1979 edition," three volumes in one.

SHARP, Cecil J.
- 1932 *English Folk Songs from the Southern Appalachians Collected by Cecil J. Sharp, Comprising Two Hundred and Seventy-Four Songs and Ballads with Nine Hundred and Sixty-Eight Tunes, Including Thirty-Nine Tunes Contributed by Olive Dame Campbell,* edited by Maud Karpeles. New York: Oxford University Press. Second edition; two volumes bound as one.

SHELLEY, Mary W. G.
- 1957 *Frankenstein.* New York: Almat Publishing Corporation. Pyramid Books edition, a reprint of edition of 1838.

SMITH, Hallett
- 1946 "English Metrical Psalms in the Sixteenth Century and Their Literary Significance," *Huntington Library Quarterly,* vol. 9, pp. 249-271.

SOUTHALL, Aidan
- 1975 [Letter], *African Studies Newsletter,* vol. 8, no. 3 (June), pp. 3-4.

SOUTHERN, Eileen
    1971   *Readings in Black American Music.* New York: W. W. Norton.

SPENCER, Herbert
    1857   "Progress: Its Law and Cause," *Westminster Review* (April), pp. 244-267.
    1896a   *The Principles of Psychology.* New York: D. Appleton and Company. Third edition.
    1896b   *The Principles of Sociology.* New York: D. Appleton and Company. Third edition.

STAPELBERG, Reinhold
    1958   "Jodeln," *Die Musik in Geischichte und Gegenwart,* vol. 7, columns 73-82. Basel-Kassel: Bärenreiter.

STEVENSON, Robert
    1973   "English Sources for Indian Music Until 1882," *Ethnomusicology,* vol. 17, no. 3 (September), pp. 399-442.

STEWARD, Julian H.
    1948   "The Circum-Caribbean Tribes: An Introduction," in Julian H. Steward, editor, *Handbook of South American Indians; Smithsonian Institution Bureau of American Ethnology Bulletin 143,* vol. 4, pp. 1-41. Washington, D.C.: Government Printing Office.

STEWART, G. W.
    1931   "Problems Suggested by an Uncertainty Principle in Acoustics," *Journal of the Acoustical Society of America,* vol. 2, no. 3 (January), pp. 325-329.

STRUNK, Oliver
    1965   *Source Readings in Music History: Antiquity and the Middle Ages, Selected and Annotated by Oliver Strunk.* New York: W. W. Norton. Translations by Oliver Strunk.

SUMNER, William L.
    1962   *The Organ.* London: MacDonald. Third edition.

SYMONDS, John Addington
    1911   "Renaissance, The," *The Encyclopaedia Britannica, A Dictionary of Arts, Sciences, Literature and General Information,* vol. 23, pp. 83-93. New York: The Encyclopaedia Britannica Company. Eleventh edition.

TANGENT
    TNGM 120   *Scottish Tradition 6, Gaelic Psalms from Lewis, Selection and Commentary by Morag Macleod.* London: Tangent Records for the School of Scottish Studies, University of Edinburgh, 1975. One 12" disc, 33-1/3 r.p.m.

TEIT, James A.
    1930   "The Salishan Tribes of the Western Plateaus," edited by Franz Boas, in H. W. Dorsey, Chief Clerk, *Forty-Fifth Annual Report of the Bureau of American Ethnology . . . 1927-1928,* pp. 23-396. Washington, D.C.: Government Printing Office.

TELEFUNKEN-DECCA
    SAWT 9530-B/9531-B   *Ars Antiqua; Organum-Motette-Conductus; Frühe Mehrstim-*

migkeit; Capella antiqua München, Konrad Ruhland. Hamburg, West Germany: Telefunken-Decca Schallplatten-Gesellschaft, 1968. Two 12" discs, 33-⅓ r.p.m.

TEMKO, Allan
   1955   *Notre-Dame of Paris.* New York: Viking Press.

TEMPERLEY, Nicholas
   1979   *The Music of the English Parish Church.* London: Cambridge University Press. Two volumes.

THALBITZER, William
   1921   *The Ammassalik Eskimo II, No. 3: Language and Folklore.* Copenhagen: I Kommission [for Videnskabelige Undersøgelser i Grønland] Has C. A. Reitzel. Volume 40, pages 113-564 of *Meddelelser om Grønland,* edited by William Thalbitzer.

THUREN, Hjalmar
   1914   "On the Eskimo Music in Greenland," *in* William Thalbitzer, editor, *The Ammassalik Eskimo II; Contributions to the Ethnology of the East Greenland Natives,* pp. 1-45. Copenhagen, Denmark: Kommissionen for Videnskabelige Undersøgelser i Grønland. Originally appeared in *Meddelelser om Grønland,* vol. 40, no. 1 (1911), pp. 1-45.

TITON, Jeff Todd
   1977   "Talking About Music: Analysis, Synthesis, and Song-Producing Models," *Essays in Arts and Sciences* (University of New Haven), vol. 6, no. 2, pp. 53-57.

TRADITION
   TLP 1011   *American Folk Tales and Songs Told by Richard Chase and Sung by Jean Ritchie and Paul Clayton,* recorded by Liam Clancy and George Pickow. New York: Tradition Records, 1956. One 12" disc, 33-⅓ r.p.m.

TRAGER, Edith C.
   1954   "Notes on the Kiowa Language," *in* Willard Rhodes, editor, *Music of the American Indian: Kiowa,* pp. 9-11. Washington, D.C.: Department of Interior, Bureau of Indian Affairs.

TREITLER, Leo
   1982   "The Early History of Music Writing in the West," *Journal of the American Musicological Society,* vol. 35, no. 2 (Summer), pp. 237-279.

TRINKAUS, Erik and William W. Howells
   1979   "The Neanderthals," *Scientific American,* vol. 241, no. 6 (December), pp. 118-119, 122, 125-133.

VANSINA, Jan
   1965   *Oral Tradition: A Study in Historical Methodology,* translated by H. M. Wright. Chicago: Aldine Publishing Company. French original published in 1961.

VERGILIUS, Maro (Publius)
   1967   *Virgil, with an English Translation by H. Rushton Fairclough.* Cambridge, Mass.: Harvard University Press. Revised edition in two volumes.

VISWANATHAN, T.
- 1966-67 "Karnatak Music and Foreign Students," *Souvenir of the Indian Fine Arts Society* (Madras), pp. 103-107.
- 1977 "The Analysis of Rāga Ālāpana in South Indian Music," *Asian Music*, vol. 9, no. 1, pp. 13-71.

WACHSMANN, Klaus
- 1962 "Criteria for Acculturation," in Jan LaRue, editor, *Report of the Eighth Congress* [of the International Musicological Society], *New York, 1961*, vol. 1, pp. 139-149. New York: American Musicological Society for the International Musicological Society.

WADE, Bonnie C.
- 1979 *Music in India: The Classical Traditions.* Englewood Cliffs, N.J.: Prentice-Hall.

WAITE, William G.
- 1954 *The Rhythm of Twelfth-Century Polyphony, Its Theory and Practice.* New Haven: Yale University Press.

WALKER, Williston
- 1916 *A History of the Congregational Churches in the United States.* New York: Charles Scribner's Sons.

WASSERMAN, Debbi
- 1980 "I, Derek Jacobi," *American Way* (American Airlines), vol. 13, no. 10 (October), pp. 140-142, 144-145.

WATANABE, Satosi
- 1972 "Creative Time," in J. T. Fraser, F. C. Haber, and G. H. Müller, editors, *The Study of Time: Proceedings of the First Conference of the International Society for the Study of Time, Oberwolfach (Black Forest), West Germany*, pp. 159-189. New York: Springer Verlag.

WATSON, John F.
- 1819 *Methodist Error or Friendly Christian Advice to Those Methodists Who Indulge in Extravagant Religious Emotions and Bodily Exercises.* Trenton, N.J.: D. & E. Fenton

WATZLAWICK, Paul, Janet H. Beavin, and Don D. Jackson
- 1967 *Pragmatics of Human Communication, A Study of Interactional Patterns, Pathologies, and Paradoxes.* New York: W. W. Norton.

WEAKLAND, Rembert G., O.S.B.
- 1967 "Music, Sacred, History of," in William J. McDonald et al., editors, *New Catholic Encyclopedia*, vol. 10, pp. 105-109. New York: McGraw-Hill Book Company.

WEBER, William
- 1975 *Music and the Middle Class. The Social Structure of Concert Life in London, Paris and Vienna.* New York: Holmes and Meier.

WEINREICH, Gabriel
- 1979 "The Coupled Motions of Piano Strings," *Scientific American*, vol. 240, no. 1 (January), pp. 118-127.

WEISBERGER, Bernard A.
- 1958 *They Gathered at the River.* Boston: Little, Brown and Company.

WERNER, Eric
- 1959 *The Sacred Bridge; The Interdependence of Liturgy and Music in Synagogue and Church during the First Millenium.* New York: Columbia University Press.
- 1960 "The Jewish Contribution to Music," *in* Louis Finkelstein, editor, *The Jews: Their History, Culture, and Religion,* pp. 1288-1321. New York: The Jewish Publication Society of America. Third edition.

WESTMINSTER
- XWN 18809 *Motets for Christmas and Easter,* sung by the Philippe Caillard Vocal Ensemble, conducted by Philippe Caillard. New York: Westminster Records, 1959. One 12" disc, 33-1/3 r.p.m.

WILLOUGHBY, Harold
- 1935 *The Coverdale Psalter and the Quatro-Centennary of the Printed English Bible . . . With a Facsimile Reproduction of the Psalter.* Chicago: The Caxton Club.

WINCKEL, Fritz
- 1974 "Space, Music, and Architecture," *Cultures* (UNESCO), vol. 1, no. 3, pp. 135-203. Subtitle of this issue: *Music in a Changing World.*

WINNINGTON-INGRAM, R. P., Walter H. Frere, and H. K. Andrews
- 1960 "Modes," *in* Eric Blom, editor, *Grove's Dictionary of Music and Musicians,* vol. 5, pp. 797-804. New York: St. Martin's Press. Fifth edition.

WINSLOW, David J.
- 1972 "The Rural Square Dances in the Northeastern United States: A Continuity of Tradition." Philadelphia, Pa.: University of Pennsylvania. Unpublished doctoral dissertation.

WOOLDRIDGE, Harry Ellis
- 1901 *Oxford History of Music, Volume I: The Polyphonic Period, Part I: Method of Musical Art, 330-1330.* Oxford: Clarendon Press.

WORK, John W.
- 1940 *American Negro Songs and Spirituals; A Comprehensive Collection of 230 Folk Songs, Religious and Secular, With a Foreword by John W. Work.* New York: Bonanza Books.

WORLD-PACIFIC
- WP 1437 *Drums of North and South India,* with notes by Harihar Rao and Leonard Stein. Hollywood, Calif.: World Pacific, 195-. One 12" disc, 33-1/3 r.p.m.

ZINSSER, William
- 1981 "A Reporter at Large: Shanghai Blues," *The New Yorker* (September 21), 142, 144, 146, 148, 150, 152, 154, 156, 158, 161-62, 164-65.

Index

Accent, asymmetrical, 272, 288; __, ambiguous rhythm of, fig. 39; __, unambiguous rhythm of, fig. 39; equidistant, 272, 288; iambic, fig. 42; metrical, 223; stress implied, 223n; see Meter.
Adams, John, 363.
Ādi tāla, 252.
Aelred of Yorkshire, 194.
Aeneid, fig. 41.
Aesthetik der Tonkunst, 246.
Afã, fig. 49(B).
African, dance, European opposition to, 286f; __, interlude music of, 283; slaves, 75, 288; see Rhythm, West African.
Ahiavivu, fig. 49(B,C).
Akpalu, Vinoko Akakpo, 269.
Ālāpana, 341f, 347, 350f; see Raga.
Alaskan game refuge, fig. 43.
Allen, Richard, 384n.
All India Radio, 339.
Alma Redemptoris Mater (Hermannus Contractus), 82f, fig. 15.
Alto, male, 294n.
Amazing Grace, fig. 21(C).
America the Beautiful, fig. 21(B).
American music, plural, see Music.
Amjad Ali Khan, 335.
Androva, Vasilka, fig. 28.
Anlo, 232, 266, 270, 384f, 401, figs. 76(C), 77; composite rhythms, fig. 49(A); dance drumming, fig. 47; __, characteristics, 271, fig. 49(C); __, ensembles, figs. 48(A,B), 50; __, recreational, fig. 52; __, styles, fig. 49(B); drum made from log, fig. 50; homeland, fig. 46; migration, fig. 46; mutual aid society, fig. 53; rhythm, 287; see Drumming.
Anthems, in serial form 369.
Anticipation, melodic, 33.
Antiphon/Antiphonal, 94, 95n, 165, 181/184, fig. 18(A,Ps); origin of, 95n.
Anyako, fig. 46.
Appalachian Spring (Copland), 9, 396.
Applause, reward for submission, 401; distinguishes folk from pop, 403f; as harmony, 102.
Arbatsky, Yuri, 208f.
Arcadelt, Jacques, fig. 59.
Arezzo, Guido d', 39f, 86, 74, 167.
Aria, form of, 329.
Arikara tribe, 251.

Aristocracy, European, preference for bowed strings, 399; non-authoritarian conducting among, 400; loss of power, 400; patronage of music interrupted, 400f.
Arrogance and power, Western cultural, 332f.
Art, tools as, 319n; difference from life, 319; nature of, 406n; trivialized, 319n.
Art music, 90, 395, 406f; alienation of modern, 344n; as elite, 405f; of modern India, 247; labels for, 405; new textures of, 1600's, 311; trivialization of, Western, arrogance of, 333; __, circular breathing, 149n; __, rhythm v. Native American, 257; __, voice quality, 146f.
Articulation, harmony of, 101.
Arwhoolie, 41f, 47f, fig. 5.
Asymmetrical series, fig. 51(K,T); see Bell pattern, Gait, Meter.
Atsiã, Atsiagbekor, 274, 278, figs. 49(B), 51, 76(A).
Audible range, see Sound.
Audience, 394, 400, 403f; at bars and nightclubs, 3, 102, 404; committed, 403; control of music, 3, 5f, 7, 9, 158; determines style, 77; dictates, 9; effect on speech melody, 69; enhances performing, 219n; opinion of, importance, 4; psychological distance of 403f, 404n; types of, 403; uncommitted, 403.
Auditory nerve, as second ear, 24.
Auld Lang Syne, fig. 21(B).
Aural tradition, inferior, 334; and vocal style, 86; as valid history, 76, 76n; source of historical style chanting, 71; transmission, 258.
Authoritarian conductor, 399f.
Authority, musical reflection of, 400f.
Ayyengar, Ramanuja, 339.
Bach, Johann Sebastian, 175n.
Bachmann, Werner, 150, 201.
Backus, John, 15, fig. 1.
Bagpipe, medieval, 203; bag, advantages of, 149; bagless, 333n; __, circular breathing, 149; fingering, closed, 146f, fig. 26; fleahole, fig. 27; influence on vocal timbre of Bulgarian, 143f; tuning, 148f.
Bailey, Ben, 137.
Baines, Anthony, 147, 149n, 202n.
Balance, sense of in ear, 18.
Ball, Lenville, fig. 72.
Ballad stanza, fig. 21(B).

Ballet, as elite, 407n.
Bands, medieval, 201; __, guided by tune, 201; __, mixed, 200, 292, fig. 36(B).
Banjo, five-string, drone, 150.
Baptists, 362, 368, 375, fig. 73; beliefs, musical corollaries of, 362; "Hard-Shell", 362, fig. 73; Philadelphia, 384n; Primitive, 362.
Barnett, Elise, 335.
Baroque, 315; shrill timbre of, 315; texture in our popular music, 316.
Barrand, Tony, 128n.
Bars, audience at, 3, 102, 404.
Bartók, Béla, 45.
Basilica, of Notre Dame (preceding Cathedral), 126.
Bass, guitar, see Guitar; line, fig. 59; part in singing-school music, fig. 74; string, fig. 19.
Bassoon sound, meaning of, 394f.
Battle Hymn of the Republic, 215, 220, fig. 37.
Beat, inflected, fig. 71.
Beatles, The, 31.
Beavin, Janet H., 31, 33.
Beethoven, Ludwig van, 26, 31, 232.
Beginning, folk v. pop, 403f; without conductor, 400.
Behavior, stylized, 354f.
Bell, African, 273, 401; asymmetrical patterns, 272, 288, figs. 48(B), 54; construction, fig. 48(A); double, figs. 48(A), 53; duet with governing, fig. 52(I); palm, fig. 53; pattern, fig. 48(B); rhythmic duet with, fig. 48(B); see Hatsiātsiā.
Beluthova, Magda Borisova, fig. 26.
Bengtsson, Ingmar, 233.
Berbers, debt of Europeans to, 201f.
Bergeijk, Willem A. Van, 26.
Berry, Mary, 3.
Beuron, monks of, 86n, fig. 14.
Bhakti, 336, 344.
Bias, cultural, 146.
Bible, 51; Temple ceremony in, 65n; cost in Middle Ages, 164; force of among Dissenters, 368; see Dissenters, Old Testament, Psalms.
Billard, Jules B., fig. 63.
Billings, William, 370.
Bittermann, Helen R., 145.
Black American, holler, 404; lingua franca, 377n; music's African roots, 385/387; spirituals, source, 377f; vocal technique, conscious, 131; see Holler.
Blacking, John, 11, 359.
Blacks, number of in early white congregations, 376n.
Blue note, 43.
Bluegrass, harmonizes with environment, 101; heterophony in, 201; meter absent in, 222n.
Blues, composing, 248; heterophony in, 201.
Boatwright, Howard, 342.

Boggs, Dock, 60n.
Bonar, Horatius, 136.
Bonner, Sidney, 129.
Bonta, Stephen, 175.
Books, choir, medieval, 164f, fig. 31; Renaissance, 293.
Borgia, Lucrezia, 301.
Boris I, king of Bulgaria, 139.
Boulanger, Nadia, 399n.
Boule, Marcellin, 240.
Bow, drone created by, 201; Muslim source of, 202.
Bowles, Edmund A., 193.
Brain, right v. left sides, 76, fig. 13.
Brandon, William, 250f.
Breathing, circular, 149, 149n.
Bremer, Fredrika, 37.
Brico, Antonia, 399n.
Bridge, buzzing of instrumental, fig. 70.
British ballad, 404n.
Brödel, Max, fig. 2
Bronfman, Yefim, 222n.
Bronson, Bertram H., 34, 113n, 126.
Bulgaria/Bulgarian, bagpipe, see Gaida; folk music, haying song, fig. 28; __, wedding song, fig. 26; __, Western adaptation of, 159f, fig. 29; __, influence of Eastern Orthodox style on, 139; __, new national style of, 155f; __, radio influence on, 139f; __, Turkish style absent in, 101; State Ensemble for Folksongs and Folk Dances, fig. 38; pomaks, 139; see *Ne Treperi, Todoro, Vetar Vee.*
Burger court, 3.
Burian, Zdenek, 240.
Burlin, see Curtis, Natalie.
Buttress, flying, fig. 33.
Byrd, William, planter, 117n, 363.
Cage, John, 32.
Caldwell, Sarah, 399n.
Caillard, Philippe, fig. 55.
California Here I Come, 227, fig. 39.
Call-and-Response Form, 384f, figs. 76, 78; defined, 384; ecstatic force of, 388.
Calvin, John, 362.
Calvinist belief, fig. 73.
Camp meeting, 376f; chorus, 376, fig. 75(C); emotional intensity of, 375; immediacy of, 376; integration at, 377; mixed membership of, 377; role of music in, 377; songs, common verse-couplets in, fig. 75 (D); see also Revivals, Song, Song Forms.
Cantors, in Eastern Orthodox Church, 179n.
Cape Coast Fort, 384, fig. 77.
Carmina Burana (Orff), 225.
Carter, President, 406.
Caruso, Enrico, 24.
Cathedral, form of, 171, fig. 32; Chapter, 175; see Notre Dame.

INDEX 433

Catholic Church, compline, figs. 9, 10; English break with, 109; gradual of the Mass, 181, fig. 34; hierarchy of, 362; Hours, fig. 10; musical values of, 369, fig. 56; prayer hours, fig. 10; Sequence of the Mass, 185f, fig. 35; see Antiphon, Chant, Gregorian Chant, Mode, Psalm, Music tradition.
Cauvery River (India), 336, fig. 67.
Chapman, Amy, 129f.
Chapman, Reuben, Governor, 129.
Chance, 32, 188, 233, fig. 61.
Chancel, 173.
Chant/Chanting, defined, 75; Gregorian, 64f, 94, fig. 18(Ps); melodic style, 75, 81, 94; of Gospel, 185; singing of, Roman Catholic, 3; see Jewish, oral tradition, Psalms, Yemenite.
Chanter pipe, Bulgarian, fig. 27(A).
Chapel, pope's private, 293.
Charlemagne, 194.
Chase, Gilbert, 115.
Chippewa (Ojibwe) tribe, 187, 246, 251.
Choice Collection of Hymns, A (Occom), 384.
Choir, average range, fig. 6; books, medieval, 164f, fig. 31; __, Renaissance, 293; boy, Renaissance, 293; __, training, 39f; cathedral area, 171, fig. 32; congregational singing v., 94f, 109f; medieval, 164f; see Concert, Voicing.
Choral groups, early American, 364f.
Chord/Chordal, figs. 55, 59; defined, 297; superior to drone harmony, 334; structure of, 405; texture, fig. 56; thinking, 314; triadic, 301, 311.
Chorus, in 18th-century hymn, 384n; Renaissance, 293.
Chorus Master (magister cantus), 168.
Circular breathing, 149.
Christian Harmonist, The (Holyoke), 379n.
Christian Harmony, The (Ingalls), fig. 75(B).
Christmas, late adoption by Protestants, 370.
Christopher, F., 126.
Chukarinova, Penka Nikolova, fig. 26.
Church of England, 362, fig. 73.
Classes, social, relation to music, 400f, 405, 408.
Classical music, 51; as worship in India, 335f, 338; competitive, India, 340; __, the West, 341; style, pressure to change in India, 339; the classics, 405.
Clef, fig. 35.
Clements, George, 278.
Clements, Thomas, 248.
Closed fingering, of bagpipe, fig. 26; of woodwind, 146.
Cochlea/Cochlear, 18f, 23f, fig. 2.
Cohen, F. L., 69.
Cohen, John, 118, fig. 22.
Cohesiveness, of form, natural, 320f, fig. 61; __, musical, 321, fig. 62; of patterns, 322, fig. 62; of random marks, 321, fig. 61.
Coleridge, Samuel Taylor, 34.
Collection of Hymns, A (Allen), 384n.
Collection of Hymns and Spiritual Songs (Mintz), fig. 75(A).
Cologne, Cathedral of, interior volume, 174n.
Commander, John Long, fig. 44.
Communication, 398; reliance on established patterns, 355.
Comparison, cohesiveness from, fig. 62.
Complaynt of Scotlande, 126.
Compline, figs. 9, 10.
Composers, 402f; first published American, 367n; teenage, 18th-century American, 366f.
Composing, v. improvisation, 51f, 296, fig. 34.
Composite rhythm, see Rhythm.
Composition, 397; by rural white teenagers, 366f; v. improvisation, 51f, 296, fig. 34.
Concert ear, 387.
Concertgoers, 395.
Concerts, choir, 2f, 364f; listening experience, 402; symphony, 401.
Conductors, authoritarian, 400f; control over orchestra, absence of, in African ensemble, 402; women as, 399n.
Congregational singing, song, 82; choir take-over of, 94f; constrained, 363; take-over of choir by, 109f.
Congregationalists, 368.
Consonance, Bulgarian v. Western, 109, 141, 143; defined, 106; medieval, 191f, fig. 35; Renaissance, 292, 306, fig. 57; triads as, fig. 57; see Thirds.
Consort, defined, 200, 292; instrumental, 200.
Constrained musical expression, fig. 74; see Emotions/Emotional.
Constraint, formal musical, 388; see Ecstasy and constraint.
Continuous ("circular") breathing, 149.
Contrapuntal texture, fig. 56.
Contratenor, 294.
Copland, Aaron, 10, 396.
Corsi, Jacopo, 314.
Cotton, John, Rev., 113, 115.
Counter voice, fig. 74.
Counterpoint, compatible with reverberation, 175; defined, 99; harmony in medieval, 191; imitative, figs. 56, 74; improvised, 167; polyphonic (equal-voiced), fig. 55; Renaissance, 293; rhythm against meter, 227, Figs. 41, 42; Indian, 351/353, fig. 71; v. heterophony, 143, fig. 25; vocal, ornamenting church services, 167f; see Discant, Organum.
Countertenor, 294.
Counting coup, 251.
Courlander, Harold, 38f, 52.

434 INDEX

Court music, China, 333; Indian classical style of, 338; of India, 333f, 340f; Japan, 333; Middle East, 333.
Court, princely Indian, 336/338.
Coverdale, Miles, fig. 21(A).
Creed of the Mass, defined, 297.
Cross-cultural perception, 234f.
Cruciform plan of cathedral, fig. 32.
Cultural bias, 234f; uneven, 238.
Culture/Cultural, meaning, 393; change, 2; evolutionist interpretation of, 9, 241f, 334; stability, 2; see also High cultures.
Curtis, Natalie, 243.
D'Accone, Frank A., 295.
Dactylic hexameter, fig. 41.
Dakota tribe, 247, 250f, 259; see Sun Dance.
Damnation, 18th-century fear of, 374.
Dance, music for group, 403; drumming club, 269f; __, Dzelukopfe, 283; __, drumming of, 401; __, Anlo, fig. 47; funeral, 268f; modern, as celebration of elite, 407n; West African, acculturation of, 6f.
Dancer, dialogue between drummer and, 401.
Dark Was the Night (Haweis), 130, fig. 24.
Darwin, Charles, 241.
Davey, Henry, 194.
David, Edward E., Jr., 26.
Davis, Samuel, 128f.
Declamation, music for, 307/311; dramatic, Renaissance, fig. 59.
Decoration, 51f, 86, 91; 127f, 131f, 341f, figs. 22-26, 28; Bulgarian, 146f, 151f; modal, 91, 341, fig. 23; vocal, 146; see Gregorian chant.
Densmore, Frances, 246, 253, 256, 264f.
Denver, John, 9.
Development, figs. 65, 66, 68, 72; v. variations, 329/331, fig. 65; see Form.
Dialogue, music for dramatic, 307.
Diminished triad, fig. 57.
Discant, 167f, 179, 184f, 191f, 193, 198f, 203, figs. 34, 35; early French style, 187; three-voiced, fig. 31; v. organum, 191f.
Dissenters, 368f; force of Bible among, 368, hymn-singing among, 368.
Dissonance, 191f, fig. 57; Bulgarian, 143; defined, 106; in thorougbass music, fig. 60; medieval, v. Renaissance, 292, 306, fig. 35; see Thirds.
Divine Hymns (Smith), 384n.
Dixie, 222.
Drama, liturgical, 193.
Dress, hierarchy of, at concerts, 400.
Drone, 146, 148f, 150f, 155, 159, 179n, 198, 201, 253, fig. 29; continuous ("circular") breathing for, 149; defined, 148; gaida, 148; harmony, 148f, 195, 203, 333n, 334; pipes, Bulgarian, 148; __, organ, 195, 199, figs. 27, 36; solo, fig. 34.

Drum, Anlo, fig. 50; Indian, fig. 72; language, figs. 51, 72; leading, rhythm of, fig. 52(LD); Native American timing of, fig. 44; talking, 204f, fig. 51; vocables, figs. 52(LD), 72.
Drumbeat, 187f, inflected, fig. 71.
Drumhead, weighting for pitch, 353n.
Drummer, dialogue between dancer and, 402; Mai-kalangu, 3; West African, 401, see Timing.
Drumming, African melodic, 353n; Ahiavivu dance, fig. 76(D); Anlo, 266f, 292; Atsiã dance, fig. 76(C), Atsiagbekor processional, fig. 76(A); Balkan, 208f; cross rhythms in, 353, figs. 71, 72; Dakota, 264f; for African dance, 268, 384, 401f; Indian melodic, 353n, Northern Indian, 338n; Ojibwa, 264f; South Indian, figs. 71, 72; syllables for Indian, fig. 72; West African, 353n; __, ensemble, figs. 39, 48(A,B); see Anlo, Dance.
Du Bois, William E. B., 128.
Duet, rattle, fig. 49; rhythmic with bell, fig. 48, fig. 52(F).
Dulcimer, three-string, 150.
Duration v. timing, 218.
Durham, plan of Cathedral of, fig. 32.
Dzelukopfe Society, 283.
Eagle-bone whistle (Dakota), fig. 44.
Ear, as psychological resource, 402n; bony levers of 16, 18, fig. 2; inner, 17f, fig. 2; __, elastic membrane of, 23; __, electric discharge of, 24; __, __, part of brain, 14, 24, fig. 2; mechanical response of, 14f, fig. 2; middle, 17f, fig. 2; second, nerve lines as, 21.
Eardrum, 17, fig. 2.
Eastern Orthodox, ritual music, 139; __, drone in, 112; __, style, 139.
Ecce Maria (Praetorius), fig. 56.
Economic recovery, medieval, 175.
Ecstatic element in music, 388; see Constraint, Ecstasy and constraint.
Ecstasy and constraint in music, 359, fig. 78; balance between, 359f, 363; simultaneous, 360; see also Constraint.
Edey, Maitland A., 241, 245.
Edward, Prince of England, fig. 21(B).
Edwards, Jonathan, 374n.
Egalitarianism in art disapproved, 406.
Elastic membrane of inner ear, 23.
Electronic instrument, timbre produced by, 100.
Elite, art music as, 405f; arts, 406f; music, school support of, 405.
Embellishment of Gregorian Chant, 91; see Decoration.
Emotions/Emotional, calculated, 354f; content of words, fig. 60; expression, Hopi v. Kwakiutl, 359; __, musical, 362f, 369f, 377, 388f; inner, 355; label by circumstance, 358; not separate, 354; psychological theory of,

356f; physiological theory of, 356f; separate, 354n.
Emphasis, implied by "accent," 223n.
Ending, musical, 403f; see Music, start and stop.
Energy, flow, in popular music, 404; __, in folk music, 403f.
Engel, Hans, 6n.
English Folksongs from the Southern Appalachians (Sharp), 258.
Ensembles, see Drumming.
Epistle, 185n.
Epstein, Dena J., 39, 129.
Equidistant accents, 280, 288.
Erdoes, Richard, 251f.
Escher, M. C., fig. 65.
Ethnomusicology/Ethnomusicologists, 237, 332f.
Et Incarnatus Est (Josquin), fig. 55.
Euridice (Peri), 314, fig. 60.
Ewe, 2; see Anlo.
Expression, calculated in acting, 355; constrained, fig. 74; __, v. ecstatic, 359f, 389; ecstatic, force of, 359; force of, 369; historical shifts between formal and ecstatic, 369; see Emotions/Emotional.
Fage, J. D., 76n.
Fanfare, trumpet, fig. 56(A,C)
Farmer, Henry George, 147.
Falsetto, 294n.
Feeling, "real," 354.
Feeling v. expression, 359.
Ferdinando I, Grand Duke of Florence, 314.
Fiddle, 2; drone, 150.
Fiddler, 222n, 236.
Fifth, growth of importance in Renaissance, 304f; harmony of, fig. 35; in familiar songs, 305; interval of a, fig. 57; shift of a, 305f, fig. 58(A,C).
Film industry, stigma of supplying music for Indian, 338; modern music accepted in, 395; studios as patron of music in Indian, 339.
Fingering of bagpipe, closed, 146f, fig. 26.
Finnegan, Ruth, 76n.
Fire, John, 251f.
First World War, music reflects social change preceding, 400f.
Fisk Jubilee Singers, 43n.
Flanders, source of Renaissance musicians, 295.
Flat and sharp, 103f, fig. 20; defined, 103.
Flathead tribe, see Salish.
Fleahole, bagpipe, fig. 27.
Flow of energy, in folk music, 403; in popular music, 404.
Flute, Bolivian, 6; cross-blown, Muslim origin of, 203.
Folk music, alteration by schools, 140; harmony of Bulgarian, 143; harsh vocal style, Bulgarian, 143, 146; __, European, 79; medieval remnants in, 149f, fig. 28; national style of Bulgarian, 140, 155, 158, fig. 29; nature of, 403f; popular music contrasted with, 403f; song cycles, Bulgarian, 142.
Folksong, Bulgarian wedding, fig. 26; __, haying song, fig. 28; __, Westernization of, fig. 29.
Form, 11; computer-generated, 321, fig. 61; developmental, 329f; __, in art music of India, 332f; expanding (extending), 325; generated by computer, 321, fig. 61; musical, 325f; __, natural cohesiveness of, 320, fig. 62; rondo, 327/329, 350, 379, figs. 66, 75(B); serial, 327, figs. 66, 75(B); __, repetition in, 327; v. rhythm, 212; see Development, Strophic.
Formula, speech, 53; tune, 52f, 62f, 81f, 87, 94, figs. 5, 8, 12, 14, 15.
Fourteeners, fig. 21(B).
Fraisse, Paul, 232.
French Horn, nonmusical associations of, 357n.
Fugal effects, 32.
"Fuging" Tunes, 369f, fig. 74; *Milford*, 370f, fig. 74; popularity of, 370n; origin of name, 370n; texture of, 370.
Fuguing, see "Fuging" Tunes.
Gaida, 146f, 147f, figs. 26, 27; player, fig. 27(A); tuning, 148f; see also Bagpipe, Drone.
Gait, 219, 227, 257; asymmetrical, fig. 52(R); defined, 221; Native American, figs. 44, 45.
Gamelan, 2; Balinese, 232.
Ganges River, India, fig. 67.
Gaspar River, Kentucky, 375f.
Gates, J. M., Rev., 134, 143, fig. 25.
Gesualdo, Carlo, fig. 59(B).
Gethsemane (Haweis), 130, fig. 24.
Ghana, 384, figs. 46, 77.
Gift-Dance song, fig. 45; see also Salish.
Gold Coast, Africa, fig. 77.
Goldstein, Jakob, cantor, 79n, figs. 11(A,B), 12.
Good music hour, 405.
Gospel, chanting of the, see Chant.
Governing bell, see Bell.
Governing meter, see Meter.
Grace note, 148.
Gradual of the Mass, 181, fig. 34.
Graham, Martha, 396.
Grammar and tune formula, 70, 72, figs. 11, 12, 14, 15.
Great Awakening, 375f, 384n; dates of, 375.
Great Revival, 379n.
Greek Orthodox service, 333n.
Gregorian Chant, 63, 64f, 81, 87, 164f, 219, 234, figs. 14, 16, 18; decoration in, 86f, 91; hymn, fig. 55; repertoire, 64; reform of, 79n; solo parts harmonized, 167, 169, fig. 31; vocal style, 79f; __, official, 79n.
Gregory I, pope, 64.

Gregory II, pope, 64n.
Gronow, Pekka, 162.
Groth, Edward J., fig. 61.
Grounds and Rules of Musick Explained, The (Walter), 117.
Guéranger, Dom Prosper, 79n.
Guido, d'Arezzo, 39f, 86, 102, 167.
Guitar, 6; electric bass, 7; partials (harmonics), 25; similarity to vīna, fig. 69.
Gurukula system, 340f; improvisation through, 343.
Hall, John, 123.
Hamlet, controlled behavior in acting of, 354.
Hand, Ferdinand Gotthelf, 246.
Handschin, Jacques, 180.
Happy Birthday, shifts of a fifth in, 305.
Hare, Marie, 146.
Harmonica, 23.
Harmony/Harmonic, 395, 397, fig. 74; Bulgarian, 141; changes of, fig. 58(A,C); coordination and melodic rhythm of, fig. 58(C); country-and-western, 301; defined, 71; destinations, 300f; drone, see Drone; expectation, 306; medieval instrumental, 201; medieval organ, 195f; medieval solo vocal, fig. 31; metrical, 232, 307; modal, 306; of a fifth, fig. 35; of environment, 101; of partials, 100; patterns of, 106; plans, Renaissance origin, 307n; progressive Western tolerance for, 107; relationship to melody, fig. 58(A,B); Renaissance, 294, figs. 55, 58; rhythms, 307/311, 316; tonal, 306; triadic, 300f; variety declines, 305f; v. counterpoint, 99; West African, metrical function absent in, fig. 39; Western, metrical function of, fig. 39; __, v. W. African, 224.
Harp, use at end of Renaissance, fig. 60.
Harpsichord, 312, fig. 60.
Harrison, Frank, Ll., 332.
Hatsiātsiā, 283.
Hausa, changes in music of, 4.
Haydn, Joseph, 408.
Headline, meaning of, 395.
Hearing, 14; nonexistent sounds. 22f.
Henry IV of France, 312.
Henry VIII of England, 112, fig. 21.
Herald's trumpet, 203.
Here the World and Flesh. 384n.
Hermann the Crippled, 86, fig. 15.
Hermannus Contractus, 86, fig. 15.
Heterophony, 109, 119, 122f, 150, 201, figs. 22, 44; black American, fig. 25; Bulgarian, 143; defined, 109; in Indian music, 334; in Western art music, 122; reflects philosophy, 119; v. counterpoint, 143, fig. 25.
Hevner, Kate, 356.
Hexameter, fig. 41.
Hickmann, Hans, 195.
Higgins, Jon B., 236n, 339.

High cultures, 332, 407n; meaning of, 334.
High Lonesome Sound, 118, fig. 22.
Himalayas, fig. 67.
Hindu religious ritual, chanting in, 336.
Hirsh, Ira J., 215n.
Hoffman, Dustin, 355.
Holcomb, Roscoe, 146.
Holler, 52, 53, 60f, 82, 127, 219, 404, figs. 8, 15(A); as signal, 37; black American, fig. 8; __, intervention, 36; characteristics, figs. 5, 8; choral, 38; flexible melody of, 39; __, in hymns, 37; names for, 36; origin, 36n; slides, fig. 5; solo, 36, 38; style, 36, 49; __, melodic, 41f; yodel in, fig. 5.
Holmes, Joseph, 38.
Holmes, Urban T., Jr., 169n.
Holyoke, Samuel, 121, 379n.
Honky-tonk piano, 9.
Hood, George, 117, 118.
Hood, Mantle, 209f, 237.
Hopi tribe, emotional expression of, 359.
Hopkins, John, 112.
Hours, Catholic, 66/68, fig. 10.
Hucke, Helmut, 64n.
Hughes, Andrew, 193.
Humanism, 200; defined, 291; in music, fig. 55; sound of, 292.
Hus, John, 291.
Hutchinson, Anne, 374n.
Hymnody, interaction of white with Native American singing, 384n.
Hymns, 37, 301, 325f, 370, 378, 404, fig. 15(A); defined, 123; European, joined to African rhythm, 287; Gregorian *(Pange Lingua),* fig. 55; hamboning of, 378; medieval, fig. 35; see Gregorian Chant, Holler, Sequence.
Hymn singing, early American, 126; among early Dissenters, 368.
Hymn-writing movement, 367.
I Don' Know You (Ledbetter), 60, fig. 8; text 60f.
I Heard the Voice of Jesus (Bonar), 136f, fig. 25.
Iambic pentameter, fig. 42; see Accent, Meter, Rhythm.
Ice Age in North America, fig. 43.
Idelsohn, Abraham Zebi, 71f, 77n, figs. 11, 12.
Identity, music celebrates, 403f; through sound, 7.
Imagination, 25.
Imitation, technique of, figs. 56, 74.
Imprecision, rhythmic, 232.
Impressions, drug-enhanced, 356.
Improvisation, 60n, 164, 167, 201, 344, 397,; 402; Indian, 351n; v. composition, 51, 296, fig. 34.
Inclina Domine, fig. 18.
Independence, India's, 338.
India, map of, fig. 67; North v. South, fig. 67; music of, 334f, 347/349.

Individuality, see Primitive Baptists, beliefs.
Indus River, fig. 67.
Industry, popular music, 12; see Muzak.
Indy, Vincent d', 394.
Ingalls, Jeremiah, 379n.
Innovation, tempered, 9f; extreme example, 9.
Instruments/Instrumental, 402; amateur v. professional in 18th-century, 399n; choice of, 399; electronic, 100; female, 399n; groups, 399; in medieval church, 179n, 193, 200; male, 399n.
Interlude music, West African, 283.
Interval, consonant, 107; defined, 191; see Fifth, Third, Triad.
Introduction to the Singing of Psalms (Tufts), 367n.
Introit, 91, fig. 18.
Inuit people, 240n, 250n.
Irene, Goodnight (Ledbetter), 60n.
Irwin-Williams, Cynthia, 248.
Jackson, Don D., 31, 33.
Jackson, George Pullen, 379, fig. 75(C).
Jacobs, Russell, Elder, 116n.
Jacobi, Derek, control of emotion by, 354.
James, Willis, 37.
Javanese, musicians, 211; orchestral court music, 209.
Jazz, 3, 51, 101, 201, 335, 359.
Jefferson, Joseph, symbolic behavior by, 355.
Jerusalem, sack of, 66.
Jewish, chant, 71; music, ancient, 65, 66n, 71, __, of the Temple, 65n, 66; __, roots of Christian ritual in, 65; prayer hour, fig. 9.
Jews, of Babylon, 66; of Yemen, 71; __, ancient style of, 71; __, history of, 71.
Johanson, Donald, 241, 245.
John XIX, pope, 40n.
John XXII, pope, 94.
Johnson, David, 341, 399n.
Johnson, Otto, fig. 34.
Jones, Arthur M., 278.
Josquin des Pres, 295f, 305f, fig. 55.
Joy to the World, 39f, figs. 6, 7.
Julesz, Bela, fig. 61.
Kaba gaida, see Gaida.
Kaganu drum, fig. 54.
Kastner, Georges, fig. 36.
Katzarova-Koukoudova, Raina, 158, 159.
Keach, Benjamin, 126, 368.
Keach, Elias, 126, 368.
Keta Lagoon, fig. 46.
Kettledrums, 203.
Key change, 51.
Keyboard, black notes, fig. 7; history, fig. 7.
Khanda Cāpu tāla, fig. 71, 72.
Kiowa language, 235.
Kirby, Percival, 237, 334n, fig. 52.
Koenig, Martin, 141, 154, figs. 26, 28.
Koutev, Philip, 159, figs. 26, 38.

Kramer, Hilton, 245.
Kremenliev, Boris, 142, 154.
Kriti, 349f.
Kroboto drum, fig. 57 (K,T).
Kurath, Gertrude, 253f.
Kutev, see Koutev.
Kwakiutl tribe, emotional expression of, 359.
Ladzekpo, Kobla, 270, fig. 76(D).
Ladzekpo, Vincent Kofi Kpeglo, 283, figs. 53, 76(D).
Lame Deer, 251f.
Langer, Suzanne, 211f.
Las Huelgas, 187, fig. 35.
Lauds, fig. 10.
Law, Andrew, 127.
Law of progress, 241f.
Leadbelly (Ledbetter), 53/60, fig. 8.
Leading drum, rhythm of, fig. 52(LD).
Leakey, Louis S. B., 248.
Ledbetter, Huddie, 53/60, fig. 8.
Lee, Ann, 374n.
Left Beaver Old Regular Baptist Church, 116n.
Leigh, James W., 39.
Lent, 87.
Leonardo da Vinci, 313.
Léonin (of Notre Dame, Paris), 168, 174, 181, 191, 333n.
Léry, Jean de, 332.
Lester, Elenore, 335.
Liber Usualis, fig. 16.
Lightfoot, Gordon, 9.
Lining out, 363, 387, 404; black, modern, 128; chanting, 118; defined, 108; functional use, 123n; history,108; modern white, 118; procedure, Gaelic, 116; process, 364; reform of, 117; shift away from, 375; slow, 117f; style, 108; technique, 108.
Listener, music's meaning for, 394.
Lloyd, Ll. S., 106n.
Lomax, Alan, 36n, fig. 78.
Lomax, John, 37f, 60n, fig. 5.
L'Orfeo, fig. 58.
Louis VII of France, 168, 178.
Louis XIV of France, 398.
Lovejoy, C. Owen, 245.
Luchaire, Achille, 169f.
Lullaby, influence of social context on, 403.
Lute, Muslim origin, 202; in thoroughbass, 312; fig. 60.
Luther, Martin, 291.
Lutherans, figs. 56, 73.
Macdougall, Hamilton C., 121, 127.
Mace, Thomas, 315f.
Macleod, Morag, 116.
Mai-kalangu drummer, 44.
Major third, see Triad.
Mapping time, fig. 48.
Marcuse, Sibyl, 201, 202n.
Marian worship, 82f.

Mark Lane Independent Chapel, London, 368.
Markoff, Irene, 162.
Marsh, J. B. T., 43n.
Marshall, Thomas J., fig. 5.
Marx, Josef, 149n.
Mass, 165, fig. 10; Gradual of the, 181, fig. 34; Sequence of the, 185f, fig. 35.
Mass in B Minor (Bach), 175n.
Matins (matutinus), 180n, fig. 10.
Maultsby, Portia, 377n.
Mavrikova, Magda Georgieva, fig. 26.
Mbande, Vinancio, 159n.
McAllester, David, 235, 237n.
McCurry, John G., fig. 75.
McGlothin, William J., 126.
McGready, James, 273.
Mc Kinnon, James W., 66n.
Meaning, 395f; configurational, 395; levels of musical, 394; of bassoon, 394; of headline, 393, 395; of words, 393f; __, to an editor, 393, 395; __, to a printer, 393; __, for a listener, 394; memory and, 394; nature of, 393f.
Meaningless music, 395.
Measures, defined, 222; Native American, fig. 44; in Native American song, fig. 45; poetic, English, fig. 42; __, Latin, fig. 41.
Medici, Maria de', 312, fig. 60.
Meditation, instrumental, Indian, 347.
Mehmed, Albanian folk musician, 209.
Mehta, Zubin, 162n.
Melody/Melodic, 353n; and rhythm, fig. 58; in country-and-western music, 316; behavior, predictable, 31f, 343; chanted v. tuneful, 81; continuity, 31; defined 31, 33, 35, 91; development, fig. 68; direction of, 45; governs text, 113n; harmonic, 301, fig. 58; importance to humans, 77; influenced by text, fig. 56(A); meaning of, 395; mental, 35; passage, 31, 33, 39, 95; precomposed, in new composition, fig. 55; predictability, 31f, 35, 43f, 95; relationships, 405; rhythm, in Native American song, 256f; speech as, 69f; stability, 35; style, 32, 41f; __, v. mode, 94; surprise, 34; uncertainty, 34; white v. black, 41f, figs. 4, 5; see Holler, Improvisation, Tune formula.
Memory, as a source of meaning, 394f.
Menéndez Pidal, R., 202.
Menon, Narayana, 339.
Merriam, Alan P., 261f, fig. 45.
Meter/Meterical, accents, 223; equidistant, 306; equidistant v. asymmetrical, 223f; __, iambic, fig. 42; common, fig. 21(B); cues, 222; dactylic hexameter, fig. 41; __, entymology of, fig. 41; defined, 223; English poetic, fig. 42; flexibility of, 233; governing, fig. 53; __, Anlo, fig. 47; __, asymmetrical, fig. 47; __, Indian, 351/353, fig. 71; __, of equidistant beats, fig. 47; harmony, fig. 58; hexameter dactylic, fig. 41; iambic pentameter, fig. 42; __, entymology of, fig. 42; irregular, 258; Native American, 257; pentameter, iambic, fig. 42; reinforced by harmonic change, fig. 58; Renaissance harmony, fig. 58; rhythm in counterpoint with, figs. 41, 42; __, Indian, 351/353, fig. 71; Roman poetic, fig. 41; stability of Western, 227/232; traditional v. unique, 257f; West African, 353; see Harmony, Sternhold.
Methodists, 375, 378, fig. 73.
Meyer, Leonard, 357.
Michelangelo, 291.
Middle class, European, supplants monarchy, 408.
Milford (Stephenson), ("fuging" tune), 370, 389, fig. 74.
Milton, John, 122.
Mintz, David B., fig. 75(A).
Missa Pange Lingua (Josquin), 297f, 305, fig. 55.
Mocquereau, André, 79n.
Modal harmony, 306.
Mode, 65, 95, figs. 17, 18(Ps); defined, 64f; different from style, 94; Gregorian, 87, fig. 16; __, defined, 86, 94, fig. 16; __, features of, 86; in antiphons, 95; Indian, similar to Western, 341f; melodic, 64f; v. scale, 87/90, figs. 16, 17; v. tune, 87; v. tune formulas, 87; Western, similar to Indian rāgas, 341f.
Modern music, 395.
Modulation, defined, fig. 8.
Monarchy, European, yields to middle class, 408.
Mondale, Joan, 406.
Money, medieval, 169n.
Monologue, nonexistent in music, 398; dramatic, 307.
Monteverdi, Claudio, fig. 58.
Mood, manipulated for audience, 404n.
Morā, fig. 71.
Mrdanga, fig. 72.
Music, absolute, 395; African roots of black American, 385/387; American, plural, 51; ancient Jewish, 65; and the two sides of the brain, 76f, fig. 13; arises from thought, fig. 40; art, see Art music; as religion, 335, 397; as ritual, 397f; as source of identity, 397f; as vindication of social structure, 401; black American v. West African, 288f; books, for medieval church, 164f; __, for Renaissance choir, 293; Bulgarian, see Bulgaria; celebrates identity, 403f; classical, 51, 405n; __, of India, as worship, 335f; __, metered, 347; content of, 27; context, 403; country-and-western ballad, 301, 316; court, see Javanese; declamation in, 307/311; defined, 3; ecstatic element in, 388; effects, variety of, 396; emotion in, see Emotions/

Emotional; __, psychological theory of, 356f; __, physiological theory of, 356; emotional associations with, 357f, 396; emotional content of, 358; expression constrained in, fig. 74; folk, see Folk music; fundamental need, 12f; fundamental to humans, fig. 13; government funding of, 406; hearing, 14; importance of, 11f, fig. 13; innovation in, 9f; intimacy of, 155; listen to, 396; meaning, social, 398; __, levels of, 396; meaningless, 395; measured, 160; mental control of, 165; metered, 351/353; modal, 91; modern, 395; Muslim, relationship to Western, 147f; Native American, see Drum, Gait, Hymnody, Melody, Rhythm, Timing; nature of, 396; natural law v. taste, 106; need for, 11f, fig. 13; new, 395; __, enjoying, 27f; 19th Century, modern preoccupation with, 344n; nonmusical associations of, 357n, 395f; perceiving, 213; popular, 407; __, dance, 388; __, industry, 12; __, persuasive characteristics of, 404n; __, nature of, 403f, 409; __, scholarly study of, 405; __, social context of, 403; "program," 396; reflection of society, 11f; repetitive, 403; rules of, 3; school, 41, 140, fig. 4; "serious," 405; sight-reading, origin of, 39f; social meaning of, 398, 401f; start and stop, 400, 403f; study of, 403; teachers, 405; trivialization of, 12f; understanding of, 405; unwritten basis, 41; see also Art music, Audience, Baroque, Camp Meetings, Jewish.
Musica Disciplina, 154.
Musical, club, West African, 198; consensus, 401; content, American social context of, 403; __, of simple form, 389; corollaries, 362; decoration, 51f, 86, 91, 127f, 131f, 341f, figs. 22-26, 28; __, Bulgarian, 146f, 151f; __, modal, 91, 341, fig. 23; emotion, 389; expression, African, 377; __, constrained, fig. 74; flow, 395; form, 389; imagination, 25; innovation, 9f; materials, 402; meaning, 394; nonmusical, links with, 395n; organization mirrors society, 401f; performance, as ritual, 396f; __, as social expression, 399; staff, 41; style, 401, 403; __, defined, 32; __, Eastern Orthodox, see Bulgaria; tradition, 3, 395, 398n; __, Roman Catholic, 79, figs. 55, 56; see Sound.
Musician, 403; cabaret, 3; court, 152f; economic insecurity, 246; Indian, need of second profession, 247; Javanese court, 209f; 19th-century orchestral amateur, 400; professional, 394f, 401.
Musicology, comparative, 236.
Muslim invaders, of India, 336.
Muttuswami, Dikshitar, 336.
Muzak, 12, 101, 358.
My Country 'Tis of Thee, 49, 108; shifts of a fifth in, 305, fig. 4.
Napoleon, impact on orchestra, 400.
National Endowment for the Arts, 406.
Native Americans, distribution in North America, 250f; migration route, 247f, fig. 43; origin, 247f; visions of (Dakota), 215f; see Arikara, Dakota, Drum, Gait, Hopi, Hymnody, Inuit, Kiowa, Kwakiutl, Melody, Navajo, Ojibwa, Rhythm, Salish, Timing, Yupik.
Navajo tribe, 235.
Nave, 171.
Nayo, Nicholas Z., 269.
Neanderthal, 240f.
Nebuchadnezzar, 65f, 71.
Negro spiritual, see Spirituals.
Ne Treperi, 143f, 151, fig. 26; see Bulgaria.
Nettl, Bruno, 36.
Newton, A. P., 76n.
Newton, Douglas, 245.
Newton, John, fig. 73.
Nightclubs, audience at, 404.
Notation, 402; early Indian, 334, 336; limitation of, 41; misleading, 39; pictorial explained, 41; __, system, fig. 4.
Note, as ritual, 397; origin of symbol, 40; variable pitch of; fig. 19.
Notre Dame, Cathedral of, 173, 292, fig. 33; chapter income, 175/178; reverberation time in, 174; see Organ.
Nour, Amir I. M., 159n.
Octave, 46; Indian, 334; origin of term, fig. 6; see Western octave series.
Ojibwa (Chippewa), 246, 251, 253.
Old Pond Primitive Baptist Church, Kentucky, 360, fig. 73.
Old Testament, Christian musical source in, 72.
Olmsted, Frederick L., 38.
Olney Hymns (Newton), fig. 73.
On Top of Old Smokey, 108, 113n.
Opera, 3, 312f, 315, 335; as conspicuous consumption, 314; defined, 314; first, 314; Western European, fig. 60.
Operetta, 9.
Oral tradition, see Aural tradition.
Orchestra, symphony, 3, 238, 402, 399f; xylophone, of Southern Mozambique, 159n.
Orfeo, L', fig. 58.
Orff, Carl, 225.
Organization, musical, mirrors society, 401f.
Organ, 312; medieval, 194f; great, 195/197f, 199; in Notre Dame, 199; portative, 194, 199, fig. 36(A); positive, 198f, fig. 36(B); small, 194, fig. 36; Winchester Cathedral, organ at, 198.
Organum, 167f, 179, 179n, 180f, 191f, 203, fig. 34; duplum, 179; purum, 179; triplum, 179; quadruplum, 179.
Originality, 51f.
Ouidah (Whydah), 384.

Pange Lingua Gloriosi, Missa (Josquin), fig. 55; Gregorian hymn, fig. 55.
Papa Venkataramiah, 339.
Paris, *Rite of Spring* performed in, 394.
Parsons, Jonathan, 374.
Partch, Harry, 10.
Partials, 100.
Passage (Melodic), 35, 39; essence of melody, 63; see Melody/Melodic.
Patrick, Millar, 138n.
Patronage, royal, for Indian music, 336; for popular music, 404.
Patterns, 322f; asymmetrical, fig. 47; bell, figs. 48(B), 54; repeating, 325.
Patterns, nature of, 322f; figs. 61-64.
Patterson, Bishop J.O., fig. 78.
Pennywhistlers, The, 159.
Pentameter, iambic, fig. 42.
Pentecostal Temple and Church of God in Christ, Memphis, fig. 78.
Pepys, Samuel, 117n.
Perceiver, meaning unique for, 393f.
Perception, cross-cultural, 234f.
Percussion, added to symphony orchestra, 398f.
Performance, circumstances determine style of, 404f; Puritan Psalm style, 113/115f.
Performers, as audience, 356; dress, 400; organization reflects society, 399.
Peri, Jacopo, 314, fig. 60.
Pérotin (of Notre Dame, Paris), 168, 174, 192, 333n.
Perrot, Jean, 195.
Philippe Auguste, 168, 178.
Phrase, predictable aspect of melody, 43.
Piano, 49/51f; false pitch of, 102f; keyboard, fig. 20; tuning, 8f.
Pierce, John R., 26.
Pierpont, Sarah, 374n.
Pilbeam, David, 239, 243n.
Pines, Maya, 76.
Pipes, see Drone, Bagpipe.
Pirrotta, Nino, fig. 60.
Piston, Walter, 102f, fig. 19.
Pitch, 16, 341, 402; and space, fig. 1; as metric cue, 307; decorative alternation of, 175n, fig. 18; fixed, 102, fig. 3(A,B); fluctuation of by black Americans, 131; frame, 35, 43, 62, 95, 218n, 397; __, altered, fig. 8; groups, rhythm of, fig. 37(B); high, fig. 1(A); low, fig. 1(B); level, function in African music, 280/283; __, role of, fig. 53; memory, 210n; origin, 16; perfect, 210; piano, misrepresents, 102f; range, Western, fig. 6; ranges, role of, fig. 53; sliding, 43, 86, 91, 127.
Point of beginning, fig. 47.
Polyphony, 296, 307; defined, 296; equal-voiced, see Counterpoint; four-voice, fig. 55;

religious, 314n; shift to five voices, figs. 56(B), 59(B); survival of, 315; Western, end of equal voicing, fig. 59(B).
Pomaks, 101.
Popular music, characteristics of, 403f; flow of energy in, 404; manipulation of effects in, 404n.
Power, hierarchic, 399f.
Powers, Harold S., 237n.
Praetorius, Michael, 301, fig. 56.
Predestination, 362, 376n, fig. 73.
Predictability, harmonic, 106, 300; melodic, 31, 35, 343.
Preece, Carol Aiken, 79.
Presbyterians, 375, fig. 73; leader, 375.
Price, Mary, 130f, figs. 24, 25.
Prime, fig. 10; suppressed, 68.
Primitive, as brutish, 240; as crude, 240n; as early, 239; as simple-minded, 241; as without technology, 244.
Primitive Baptist, beliefs, musical corollaries of, 362.
Primus Tonus, see Tone 1.
Princely Indian courts, 336, 338.
Prine, Ila B., 38.
Protestants, fig. 73; Christmas, late adoption by, 370; congregational singing style of, 363; early conservatives v. early radicals, 109f; musical value held in common with Catholics, 369; predestination among, 362.
Prynne, William, 194.
Psalm 8, Yemenite tradition, fig. 11.
Psalm 23, fig. 21.
Psalmody, 129; Jewish and Christian, 72; see Psalms.
Psalms, 66, 72, 94, 165, 181; __, Book of, 72, 111; __, Christian musical text, 72; chanted, 94f, fig. 14; Greek Orthodox performance of, 179n, 333n; measured, 111f; slow singing of, 117n; __, Gaelic, 116; __, Jewish, fig. 14; see "Sternhold and Hopkins."
Psalms of David Imitated (Watts), 95n, 129n.
Psalterium (zither), 202.
Public-school, support of elite music in, 405.
Puncta, 40, 192.
"Punctum contra punctum," 99.
Purandara Dasa, 336.
Puritans, 111, 116.
Puritans, during Great Awakening, 373; see also Dissenters.
Pyramid structure of orchestra, 399f.
Quintets, why Hadyn composed none, 408.
Radio, All India, 339; influence on Bulgarian music, 139f.
Rāga, 150n, 341, 349, 353n; ālāpana, 341f, 351, fig. 68; and melody, 341; number of, 342; origin of, 342.
Raim, Ethel, 141, 146n, 155, figs. 26, 28.
Ram Sahay, North Indian drummer, 338n.

Rāma, Lord, 346.
Ramabhadran, South Indian drummer, fig. 71.
Rāmayana, 346.
Ramsey, Frederick, Jr., 60, figs. 8, 24.
Randomness, 31, 32, 188, 321, fig. 61.
Rattle, duet, fig. 49; ___, with bell, fig. 48(B); gourd construction, fig. 48(A); tension of net, fig. 48(A).
Ravi Shankar, 7, 335.
Ravnikar, Bruno, 233.
Read, Albert, 19.
Record/Recording, aluminum disc limitations, 60; companies, Indian, 339; market, as most distant audience, 404; Russian commercial, 118.
Red Cloud, chief, 251.
Reed, mechanics of vibration, 147n.
References, nonmusical in music, 395.
Reformation, Protestant, fig. 56.
Reformers, of singing, 363f.
Refrain, Gregorian, 95.
Regular Baptist Church of Jeff, Kentucky, 404.
Regular singing, accompanied Great Awakening, 375; beginning of, 363f.
Reicha, Antonin, 408.
Renaissance, choir books, 293; chorus, 293; composers, fig. 56; defined, 290; dominant harmonic effect, fig. 55; harmony, 294, 297/300, figs. 55, 58; ideas, 211; imitative counterpoint in, figs. 56, 74; metrical harmony of, fig. 58; shift in poetic taste, fig. 59; triads as consonances, acceptance of, fig. 57.
Réôme, Aurelian de, 154.
Reuchlin, Johannes, 76n.
Revivals, camp-meeting, beginning of, 375; definition of, 373; emotional basis of, 373f; frontier, 375; meetings, 373; outdoor, 375; see also Song, ecstatic revival.
Revivalists, always male, 374n.
Revolution, French influence on orchestra, 400.
Reynolds, William, 127.
Rhodes, Willard, 253, fig. 44.
Rhythm, 395, 403, fig. 74; African, compatible with Western, 286; ambiguity of equidistant accents, fig. 39; as a cycling engine, 388, fig. 78; composite, 275, 287, fig. 54; constraint of ensemble, fig. 74; cross, in Indian drumming, 351, figs. 71, 72; defined, 213f; development, fig. 72; diverging, fig. 72; drum, fig. 72; durational, fig. 37(A); dynamic, fig. 37(A); flexibility of, 233; free, 219; groups, 218; harmonic, 307, 316; iambic, fig. 21(B); imaginary, fig. 45; imprecision of, 232f; Indian, 353; invented, 214; meaning of, 395; measured, 219; ___, defined, 222; ___, for dance, 403; melodic, figs. 37(D,E), 58(C); multiple, fig. 37(C); musical, 213f, 323; Native American, 234, 256f; ___, v. Western, 257; of pitch groups, fig. 37(B); of rattles, fig. 52(R); offset, 261; opposing, fig. 52; parallel, 256; radial, fig. 50; stability of, fig. 38; that talk, fig. 51; two against three, fig. 45; unambiguous asymmetrical accents, fig. 39; v. form, 212; West African, 271f, 353; Western ensemble, 353; ___, biased perception of, fig. 44; ___, dependent on context, fig. 48(C), see Anlo, Melody.
Rhythmic development, Indian, fig. 72; organization, Western v. African, 271f; perception, Western v. Native American, 257, fig. 44; reinforcement, Western principle of, 353.
Riddle, Almeda, 146.
Rip Van Winkle, example of actor's control in, 355.
Rishikesh, North Indian religious retreat at, figs. 67, 69.
Ritchie, James, 123.
Ritchie, Jean, 123/126f, 130, figs. 23, 24.
Rite of Spring (Stravinsky), 394.
Ritual, anthropological meaning of, 397; ceremony, religious, 397; day, Christian, fig. 10; Hindu religious, 336; music as, 397f; song as, 397.
Roach, David, 338n.
Rock, 227/232.
Roederer, Juan G., 16, 27, 34.
Roman Catholics, see Catholics.
Rondo, 329, 350, 379, figs. 66, 75(B).
Roth, Cecil, fig. 8.
Rougnon, Paul, 86n.
Row, Row, Row Your Boat, fig. 21(C).
Rubin, Arnold, 159n.
Ruhland, Konrad, 187/190.
Sachs, Curt, 81n, 150, 195, 201, 332.
Sahay, Ram, 338n.
St. John the Divine, Cathedral of, 175n.
Salisbury Cathedral, placement of choir, fig. 30.
Salish tribe, Gift Dance, 258f; ___, song, 259, fig. 45; locale, 258; Owl Dance, 261; Round Dance, 261.
Salmen, Walter, 200f.
Salvation, Calvinist view of, 376n; evangelical view, 376n; sermon, 373f.
Sanctuary, 173, fig. 32.
Sanskrit, romanization of letters, 335n.
Sarasvatī vīnā, 347, figs. 69, 70.
Saxophone, alto, 394.
Scale, fig. 17; v. mode, 87/90, figs. 16, 17; musical, 90f; Western, 90f, 334, fig. 17.
Scholes, Percy A., 113.
Schoenberg, Arnold, 10.
School music, 41, fig. 4; Bulgaria v. America, 140; for Berber minstrels at Játiva, 202; melodies, characteristics, fig. 4; opposed to heterophony, 122.
Schoolroom, 405.
Screen, Cathedral, 125, fig. 32.

Second Awakening, 379n.
Seeger, Mike, 60n.
Seeger, Pete, 9, 404n, fig. 66.
Segregation, unusual in early white churches, 129.
Self, sense of, 397.
Seneca, 253, fig. 63.
Sequence (sequentia) of the Mass, 185f, fig. 35.
Serial form, 327, figs. 66, 75(B); see Form.
Serious music, 405.
Sermon, early Puritan view of, 373f; Regular Baptist view of, 119/121.
Service, nonrevival, 373.
Sext, fig. 10.
Seybolt, Robert F., 117n.
Shakespeare, 227, 291, fig. 41.
Shanghai Conservatory of Music, 162n.
Shankar, Rāvi, 7, 335.
Shape-note singing, 40.
Sharp and flat, 103f, fig. 20; defined, 75.
Sharp, Cecil, 258.
Shawm, 203.
Shelley, Mary, 52, 65.
Sight reading, congregational, 138; difficulty of, 367n; medieval, 39f.
Simpson, Ruth De Ette, 248.
Singers, buying of, 294f; placement in cathedral, fig. 30.
Singing, by rule 364; declamatory, 314; lecture, 364; responsorial, 167; see also Regular singing, Reformers.
Singing School, 373, 387; as a business, 366; as a social gathering, 366; as entertainment, 369; composers for, 367; conflict over, 363f; concerts, 364; masters, 379; movement, 369; nature of, 365; see also Regular singing, Reformers.
Singsong, 69f.
Sitar, 7.
Sivaraman, South Indian drummer, fig. 71.
Skelton, William, fig. 70.
Slave Coast, The, fig. 77.
Slave compounds, life in American, 377n.
Slavery/Slaving, 75, 288, 377, 385, figs. 75, 77.
Slide/Sliding, 43, 86, 91, 127.
Smith, Halltett, fig. 21(B).
Smith, Joshua, 384n.
Social classes, 400f, 405, 408f.
Social Harp, The (McCurry), fig. 75(C,D).
Society, and music, 398; and headlines, 394; chief and elders of, West African, 401; status of performers in, 399; structure of, American, 399; ___, West African, 401f; taste of, 399; see also Music.
Solesmes-sur-Sarthe, Benedictine Abbey of St. Peter, 79n, 86n, 187; singing of monks of, 91, fig. 18.
Solfège, 40.
Soloists, medieval harmony by, fig. 31.

Somogi, Judith, 399n.
Song, Anlo, 283/286; aria, 329; arises from speech, 69f; as ritual, 397; black at white camp meetings, 378; Bulgarian village, 404; ___, harvest, 154f; call-and-response, 384, figs. 75, 76, 78; forms, camp meeting, 378, 379, fig. 75; ecstatic revival, 373, 376, immediately singable, 376, fig. 75; praise, 4; verse-and-chorus, 384n; Western popular, sketchy notation of, 349n.
Sopranos, male, 294.
Sound, as identity, 7f; audible range of, 15f; lyric tenor, 9; musical, defined, 14; quality of remembering, 394; of environment, support from, 397; source of, 14; speed of, fig. 1; subjective, 14; transmission of, 14f; vibrations, fig. 3; ___, electrical response to, fig. 2; ___, mechanical response to, fig. 2; see Vibration.
Sousa march, 301.
South India/Indian, fig. 67; vīnā, 347, figs. 69, 70(C).
Southall, Aidan, 238.
Southern, Eileen, 37.
Space and pitch, fig. 1.
Special effects in popular music, 404; absence of in folk music, 403.
Speech formula, 53.
Speed, manipulated in popular music, 404n.
Spencer, Herbert, 241f, 245, 264.
Spiritual Melody (Keach), 368.
Spirituals, black, similar to Native American, 378; ___, source of, 377f; ___, unacceptable to whites, 43n; white, 379f.
Sri Swami Sivananda, H. H., 346.
Stancheva, Kremena, fig. 28.
Stanza, repeating singing-school, 369.
Stephenson, Joseph, 370, fig. 74.
"Sternhold and Hopkins," 112, 115.
Sternhold, Thomas, 112, fig. 21(B); ___'s meter, fig. 21(B,C).
Steward, Julian H., 244n.
Stoddard, Solomon, 373f; humiliation technique of, 373.
Stops, 198n.
Stravinsky, Igor, 394.
String, buzzing of, figs. 69, 70.
String instruments, core of symphony, 398f.
Strophic form, 62, 185, 360, 369, 378f, figs. 66, 75; ___, variation of, 326; hymns, 370; relationship, 326.
Strunk, Oliver, 40.
Stuart, Gilbert, 240.
Style, art music, 341, 407; as fixed as ritual, 397; Bulgarian vocal, 61; classical Indian, pressure to change, 339f; coherent, 397; defined, 32; holler, 62f; v. mode, 94; modern, 395; of past, 11; performance circumstances influence, 405; pressure to

condense Indian classical, 339; rhythmic, as fixed as ritual, 397; religious vocal, 86, 108f; ___, from aural tradition, 86; thoroughbass, 311f, 315, fig. 60; ___, in church, 314n; vocal, calling voice v. concert voice, 121; ___, plain v. decorated, fig. 23; ___, technique of Black Americans, 131; see Chanting.
Subramanian, V. V., 150n.
Sully, Eudes de, 178f.
Sumner, William, 198f.
Sun Dance, 252; music of, 256; song, 253, fig. 44.
Supreme Court, slow change in, 4.
Swami Vidyananda, 347, fig. 69.
Sweet Georgia Brown, 404n.
"Sweet Psalmist of Israel, The," (singing lecture), 364f.
Syāmā Sāstrī, 336.
Symbolic behavior, 355f.
Symonds, John, 291.
Symphony orchestra, 3, 331, 399f, 402.
Synagogue, 64; beginning of, 66; prayer hour, fig. 9.
Syncopation, defined, 227.
Tahca Ushte, 251.
Takada, rattle duet, fig. 49; recreational dance drumming, fig. 52.
Tāla, 347/349, 353, figs. 71, 72.
Tambura, Tampura, see Tanbura.
Tanbura, 150n.
Tartt, Ruby Pickins, 129f.
Taste, moulded by individual for society, 398.
Teit, James A., 261.
Television, modern music helped by, 395.
Temko, Allen, 178.
Temperley, Nicholas, 117n.
Temple, destruction of, 65f; music of Jewish, 65n, 66.
Tenor, hard-edged, 360; in "fuging" tune, fig. 74; lyric, 9.
Terce, fig.10.
Texture, Baroque, 316; defined, 297; see Art music, Style, thoroughbass.
Thalbitzer, William, 234.
Thanjavur, 243f, 336, fig. 67.
Theater, modern music helped by, 395.
There's No Business Like Show Business, 227.
Thirds, fig. 57; major. fig. 57; medieval dissonance and consonance, 300; see Triad.
Thoroughbass, dissonance in, fig. 60; notation, fig. 60; see Style.
Three Blind Mice, 227.
Thuren, Hjalmar, 113n.
Timbre, 7f, 11, 35, 43, 51, 86, 100, 404, fig. 3(B); as identity, 7f; Baroque, 315; Bulgarian, 146; electronic production of, 100; essential, 404; importance of, 9; modified by blacks for whites, 43n; not specified by early composers, fig. 60; oboe, fig. 3(C); vocal, piercing, 146; see Bagpipe, Sound quality, Tone quality.
Time, clock, 208; defined, 207; different kinds of, 207f; musical, 208, 212; perfect, 209f.
Timing, Native American, fig. 44; v. duration, 218; West African sense of, 232f; ___, ensemble, 401.
Titon, Jeff Todd, 342.
Todoro, 159, 219, figs. 29, 38.
Tonal harmony, 306.
Tone 1, 87/90, 94, figs. 17, 18; characteristics, fig. 16(A,B,C,D).
Tone quality, see Timbre.
Torrey, Bradford, 208.
Toscanini, Arturo, 233.
Totodzi drum, fig. 51(T).
Tracts, Gregorian, 87, 91.
Traditional aural and vocal style, 86; diversity of, 163; emotional, in music, 360; see Style, vocal.
Trager, Edith, 235.
Transient tones, 24f.
Treble, in "fuging" tune, fig. 74.
Treitler, Leo, 70n.
Tremolo, 150f, fig. 28.
Triad, as consonance, fig. 57; defined, 300; diminished, fig. 57; dominates melody, 301; dominates music, fig. 55; generated by melody, 301; in Western octave series, 305f, fig. 57; rare in Middle Ages, 300; rhythm of, 300; symbols for, fig. 57.
Trill, Gregorian, 91.
Trillo, 151.
Tristropha, 154.
Trumpet fanfare, fig. 56(A,C).
Tufts, John, 367n.
Tune formula, 52f, 62f, 81f, 87, 94, figs. 5, 8, 12, 14, 15; ___,ancient, 53; ___, and grammar, 53, 70; ___, definition, fig. 12; ___, Gregorian, fig. 14; ___, in holler, fig. 5; ___, in melody, 82; ___, in ritual, 70; ___, principles, 53; ___, similarity of Jewish and Catholic, fig. 14; ___, text clarified by, fig. 11(B); ___, text expanded by, fig. 15(B); ___, Yemenite, fig. 12; "fuging," 369, fig. 74; strophic form of, 360; v. mode 87; see "Fuging" tunes, Tone 1.
Tuning fork, fig. 3(A,C).
Tyāgarāja, 338, 341.
Understanding (cross-cultural perception), 234f.
Utica Symphony Orchestra, 399n.
Valmīki, 346.
Vanderburg, Agnes, 261, fig. 45.
Vanderburg, Jerome, 261/264, fig. 45.
Vansina, Jan, 76n.
Variation, v. development, 329/331, fig. 65; in holler, 62; relieves form, 235f; rhythm, musical, due to, 215.

Vedic chanting, 336.
Venkataramiah, Papa, 339.
Vergleichende Musikwissenschaft, 236.
Vespers, fig. 10; service of, fig. 56(C).
Vetar Vee, 154, fig. 28.
Vibration, 14f, 18/19, 22f; complex, 18/19; multiple, 18/19; sound, fig. 3; __, recording of, fig. 3; see Reed.
Vibrato, 131, fig. 24; bagpiper's, 151.
Victimae Pashali Laudes, 185f, fig. 35.
Viderunt Omnes, 181, fig. 34.
Vidyananda, Swami, 347, fig. 69.
Vienna, musical threat in, 400f.
Vijayanagar, 336.
Viṉā, fretting and structure, fig. 69; range and timbre of South Indian, 347, fig. 70; Sarasvati, fig. 68.
Violin, 3, fig. 3(B,C); as Indian instrument, 339n.
Virgil, 227, fig. 41.
Vishnu, 346.
Visions, Dakota, 251f.
Viswanathan, T., 340, 344.
Voice, calling v. concert, 121.
Voice from Galilee, The (Bonar), 136f, fig. 25.
Voicing, choral, fig. 55.
Volume, manipulated in popular music, 404n.
Wachsmann, Klaus, 106n.
Wade, Bonnie C., 344, 349n.
Wakan Tanka, 252.
Wallace, Alfred, 241.
Wallis, Richard, 210.
Walter, Rev. Thomas, 117, 365.
Warren court, 4.
Washington, 406.
Watanabe, Satosi, 213.
Watson, John F., Methodist observer, 377f, 387, fig. 75(A).
Watts, Isaac, 129, 129n, 368, figs. 22, 75(C); known as "Old Doc Watts," 368.
Watzlawick, Paul, 31, 33.
Weakland, Rembert G., 66.
Weinreich, Gabriel, 8n.
Werner, Eric, 71, 76n.
West Africa, 384, fig. 77; ensemble patterns, 326; see also Ahiavivu, Anlo, Atsiá, Atsiabekor, Bell, Black American, Call-and-response, Cape Coast Fort, Conductors, Dancing, Drumhead, Drummer, Drumming, Ghana, Gold Coast, Ladzekpo, Meter, Music, Musical, Oiudah, Organization, Performers, Rhythm, Slave Coast, Slavery, Society, Song, Timing.
Western octave series, 45, 49/51, figs. 6, 7, 57; movable, 49/51; notes, of the, 45; repeats, 46; spacing unequal, 46f, figs, 6, 7.
Western Revival, 379n.
When I Can Read My Title Clear (Watts), 119, fig. 22.
Where Have All the Flowers Gone? fig. 66.
Whistle, Dakota eagle-bone, fig. 44.
Whistler, Julian, fig. 44.
White, George L., 43n.
Whydah (Ouidah), 384, fig. 77.
Wigley, Madam Mattie, fig. 78.
Wigoder, Geoffrey, fig. 9.
Winckel, Fritz, 174.
Winds, added to orchestra, 398f.
Winnington-Ingram, R. P., 237n.
Wisconsin advances, fig. 43.
Wolf Trap, 407n.
Women, as conductors, 399n; in Renaissance music, 296nf; instruments proper to (18th-century), 399n.
Wondrous Love, 126f, 131, fig. 23.
Wooldridge, Harry Ellis, 168, 184.
World's Fair (1939), fig. 13.
Wulfstan, monk, 198.
Yemen Arab Republic, 71.
Yemenite, chanting, 72; __, of Psalm 8, figs. 11, 12.
Yodel, yodeling 33n, 91, 148, 155, figs. 5, 28.
Yoga Vedanta Forest Academy, fig. 69.
Yupik people, 240n, 245, 250.
Zaïre, pygmy song of, 36n.
Zaria, court of the Emir of, 4.
Zinkova, Vesa Atanasova, fig. 26.
Zinsser, William. 162n.
Zither (psalterium), 202.